A Special Issue of
Cognition & Emotion

Autobiographical Memory Specificity and Psychopathology

Edited by

Dirk Hermans
University of Leuven, Belgium

Filip Raes
University of Leuven, Belgium

Pierre Philippot
University of Louvain, Belgium

and

Ismay Kremers
University of Groningen, The Netherlands

LONDON AND NEW YORK

First published 2006 by Psychology Press

Published 2018 by Routledge
2 Park Square, Milton Park, Abingdon, Oxon OX14 4RN
52 Vanderbilt Avenue, New York, NY 10017

First issued in paperback 2018

Routledge is an imprint of the Taylor & Francis Group, an informa business

Copyright © 2006 Taylor & Francis

All rights reserved. No part of this book may be reprinted or reproduced or utilised in any form or by any electronic, mechanical, or other means, now known or hereafter invented, including photocopying and recording, or in any information storage or retrieval system, without permission in writing from the publishers.

Notice:
Product or corporate names may be trademarks or registered trademarks, and are used only for identification and explanation without intent to infringe.

British Library Cataloguing in Publication Data
A catalogue record for this book is available from the British Library

Typeset DP Photosetting, Aylesbury, Bucks

ISSN 0269-9931
ISBN 13: 978-1-138-87323-0 (pbk)
ISBN 13: 978-1-84169-987-5 (hbk)

Contents*

Editorial
Autobiographical memory specificity and psychopathology
Dirk Hermans, Filip Raes, Pierre Philippot, and Ismay Kremers   321

Introduction
Autobiographical memory specificity and psychopathology: The broader context of cognition and emotion research
Filip Raes, Dirk Hermans, Pierre Philippot, and Ismay Kremers   324

Regular articles
Reducing specificity of autobiographical memory in nonclinical participants: The role of rumination and schematic models
Philip J. Barnard, Edward R. Watkins, and Cristina Ramponi   328

Retrieval of autobiographical memories: The mechanisms and consequences of truncated search
J. Mark G. Williams, Stella Chan, Catherine Crane, Thorsten Barnhofer, Jess Eade, and Helen Healy   351

Impact of depressive symptoms, self-esteem and neuroticism on trajectories of overgeneral autobiographical memory over repeated trials
John E. Roberts, Erica L. Carlos, and Todd B. Kashdan   383

Reduced autobiographical memory specificity and affect regulation
Filip Raes, Dirk Hermans, J. Mark G. Williams, and Paul Eelen   402

Retrieval-induced forgetting of autobiographical memory details
Ineke Wessel and Beatrijs J. A. Hauer   430

Autobiographical memory in depressed and nondepressed patients with borderline personality disorder after long-term psychotherapy
Ismay P. Kremers, Philip Spinhoven, A. J. Willem Van der Does, and Richard Van Dyck   448

Facets of autobiographical memory in adolescents with major depressive disorder and never-depressed controls
Willem Kuyken and Rachael Howell   466

---

* This book is also a special issue of the journal *Cognition & Emotion*, and forms issue 3/4 of Volume 20 (2006). The page numbers are taken from the journal and so begin with p. 321.

Effects of age, dysphoria and emotion-focusing on autobiographical
memory specificity in children
*Lyndsey E. Drummond, Barbara Dritschel, Arlene Astell,
Ronan E. O'Carroll, and Tim Dalgleish* 488

Brief reports
Autobiographical memory in dysphoric and non-dysphoric college
students using a computerised version of the AMT
Kathleen Newcomb Rekart, Susan Mineka, and Richard E. Zinbarg 506

Suicide attempts: Patients with and without an affective disorder show
impaired autobiographical memory specificity
*Max M. Leibetseder, Rudolf R. Rohrer, Herbert F. Mackinger,
and Reinhold R. Fartacek* 516

Autobiographical memory specificity in adults reporting repressed,
recovered, or continuous memories of childhood sexual abuse
*Richard J. McNally, Susan A. Clancy, Heidi M. Barrett, Holly A. Parker,
Carel S. Ristuccia, and Carol A. Perlman* 527

Autobiographical memory deficits in schizophrenia
Nikki Wood, Chris R. Brewin, and Hamish J. McLeod 536

Invited paper
Capture and rumination, functional avoidance, and executive control
(CaRFAX): Three processes that underlie overgeneral memory
J. Mark G. Williams 548

Subject Index 569

Editorial

Autobiographical memory specificity and psychopathology

Dirk Hermans and Filip Raes
University of Leuven, Belgium

Pierre Philippot
University of Louvain, Belgium

Ismay Kremers
University of Groningen, The Netherlands

We carry our past with us in a form we call memory. This psychological function is of vital importance to our daily functioning. Its significance becomes obvious when we try to imagine what it would be like to have to live without it. Without memory, we would not learn from past experiences. We would not even be able to recognise our environment and would feel surrounded by a succession of impressions without any perceived continuity. What surrounds us at this very moment would not be linked with our impressions from moments ago, because these would already been "forgotten".

One type of memory that is central to our functioning as an individual is autobiographical memory (e.g., Conway & Pleydell-Pearce, 2000; Nelson & Fivush, 2004). It refers to that aspect of memory that is concerned with the recollection of personally experienced past events. It contributes to an individual's sense of self, to his or her ability to remain oriented in the world, and to pursue goals effectively in the light of past problem solving (Williams, 2004).

Within the broader domain of autobiographical memory research, the ability to retrieve "specific" autobiographical memories has received a lot of attention

---

Correspondence should be addressed to Dirk Hermans, Department of Psychology, K.U. Leuven, Tiensestraat 102, 3000 Leuven, Belgium; e-mail: dirk.hermans@psy.kuleuven.be.

© 2006 Taylor & Francis
DOI:10.1080/02699930500473616

during the last 20 years.[1] After initial observations that suicidal patients are characterised by a more "overgeneral" autobiographical memory (Williams & Broadbent, 1986), it has become increasingly clear that the inability to retrieve specific memories forms a chief characteristic of those who suffer from major depression (e.g., Wessel, Meeren, Peeters, Amtz, & Merckelbach, 2001) or who have been victim of (childhood) abuse (e.g., Hermans et al., 2004). Exactly two decades of research have led to an ever-increasing number of publications—at present more than 150—that focused on autobiographical memory specificity, and that helped to unravel the complex relationship between memory specificity and psychopathology. The picture that is emerging is intriguing from both a scientific and a clinical point of view. The fact that reduced memory specificity is not only a symptom of psychiatric conditions, like depression or posttraumatic stress disorder, but is almost certainly involved in the maintenance of these disorders, has put this topic on the scientific agenda of a steadily growing group of researchers.

This Special Issue grew out of a Special Interest Meeting that took place 7–9 May 2003 at Lignely, Belgium. The meeting was hosted by the four guest co-editors of this Issue, and was made possible by the financial support of the Fund for Scientific Research (Belgium) and was part of the Scientific Research Network "Acquisition and Representation of Evaluative Judgements and Emotions". The Lignely conference was part of an exciting series of similar meetings that was initiated by Professor Mark Williams and that will soon go into its fifth edition, with previous meetings held in Beaumaris (UK, 2000), Cambridge (UK, 2001), Lignely (Belgium, 2003) and Oxford (UK, 2005). Neither the Lignely meeting, nor this Special Issue could have been realised without the constant help and inspiration provided by Mark Williams and Paul Eelen.

After a short opening paper that places the topic of "Autobiographical Memory Specificity" in the broader context of cognition and emotion research, the Special Issue includes 12 outstanding contributions—8 standard articles and 4 brief reports—highlighting various aspects of the field. Mark Williams kindly agreed to write a closing paper that integrates the findings from these separate contributions.

REFERENCES

Conway, M. A., & Pleydell-Pearce, C. W. (2000). The construction of autobiographical memories in the self-memory system. *Psychological Review*, *107*, 261–288.

Hermans, D., Van den Broeck, K., Belis, G., Raes, F., Pieters, G., & Eelen, P. (2004). Trauma and autobiographical memory specificity in depressed inpatients. *Behaviour Research and Therapy*, *42*, 775–789.

---

[1] Specific autobiographical memories refer to memories of events that happened once and are typically shorter than one day (e.g., "*I felt happy when my brother visited me last Friday evening and we watched a DVD together*").

Nelson, K. D., & Fivush, R. (2004). The emergence of autobiographical memory: A social cultural developmental theory. *Psychological Review, 111*, 486–511.

Wessel, I., Meeren, M., Peeters, F., Arntz, A., & Merckelbach, H. (2001). Correlates of autobiographical memory specificity: The role of depression, anxiety and childhood trauma. *Behaviour Research and Therapy, 39*, 409–421.

Williams, J. M. G. (2004). Experimental cognitive psychology and clinical practice: Autobiographical memory as a paradigm case. In J. Yiend (Ed.), *Cognition, emotion and psychopathology*. Cambridge, UK: Cambridge University Press.

Williams, J. M. G., & Broadbent, K. (1986). Autobiographical memories in suicide attempters. *Journal of Abnormal Psychology, 95*, 144–149.

Introduction

Autobiographical memory specificity and psychopathology: The broader context of cognition and emotion research

Filip Raes and Dirk Hermans
University of Leuven, Belgium

Pierre Philippot
University of Louvain, Belgium

Ismay Kremers
University of Groningen, The Netherlands

Scientific discoveries often emerge from serendipitous or accidental findings, while researchers are actually in pursuit of something else (for such examples, see Roberts, 1989). The same goes for the discovery of this issue's central phenomenon of overgeneral memory (OGM). While actually conducting a study on mood-congruent memory in suicidal patients, Williams and Broadbent (1986) were surprised that many of their patients tended to produce memories in the form of overgeneralised summaries of similar events, so-called *overgeneral categoric memories*, rather than the requested specific memories, that is, memories for 1 day singular personal events from one's past. This kind of scientific research, in which unplanned results or unexpected findings lead researchers into new and uncharted directions is also referred to as *discovery research* (Skinner, 1965, as cited in Roane, Fisher, & McDonough, 2003, p. 35). The seminal study by Williams and Broadbent initiated a particular line of research in which the phenomenon of OGM has been further explored. Twenty years of research along this line has now made clear that it has been a discovery path worth pursuing and that the original observation has proven to be far from a red herring. And it should become clear from the papers to follow in this Special

---

Correspondence should be addressed to Filip Raes, Department of Psychology, University of Leuven, Tiensestraat 102, 3000 Leuven, Belgium; e-mail: filip.raes@psy.kuleuven.be

Issue, that the research line on OGM, at its current stage, has outgrown the stage of mere *discovery research* and has progressed to the stage of what Mace calls *programmatic research*, in which specific hypotheses are tested (Mace, 1994, as cited in Roane et al., 2003, p. 35).

Although this Special Issue has a particular focus on autobiographical memory specificity and psychopathology, this domain of research should be viewed against the broader background of cognition and emotion research—a research domain to which the term "broad" appropriately applies. Whereas the study of cognition in relation to *normal emotions* has been around for quite a while (see Power & Dalgleish, 1997), the last two decades have witnessed a growing interest in the study of cognition in general and of information processing in particular in relation to *disturbed emotions* (i.e., emotional disorders). This approach to emotional disorders from an information-processing perspective has been developed across the various stages of information processing, including the encoding of information (e.g., attentional processes), the interpretation of information (e.g., reasoning processes), and the activation or retrieval of information from memory (memory processes). An example is the study of "biased/selective information processing" (e.g., the study of attentional and memory biases in anxiety and mood disorders). Although much of the early research was related to emotional disorders (mood and anxiety disorders), a wide range of psychological disorders is now being studied from an information-processing perspective (e.g., the study of reasoning biases in schizophrenia or selective attention in eating disorder patients).

Given the different types of psychopathology on the one hand, and the various stages of information processing on the other, one could arrange every one of these studies in one of many cells of a matrix with psychological disorders on the vertical axis and information-processing stages on the horizontal axis. If we are to place the study of OGM within such a matrix, it is useful to recall how the phenomenon of OGM was first and unintentionally discovered. As already mentioned, when Williams and Broadbent (1986) first described OGM, they were actually examining whether attempted suicide patients would show mood-congruent recall, a well-described memory bias in the mood-memory research tradition (for reviews, see Blaney, 1986; Matt, Vázquez, & Campbell, 1992). Whereas researchers in this domain had always primarily focused on quantitative aspects (e.g., response latencies, number of memories, etc.), Williams and Broadbent now "discovered" a possibly important qualitative mood-biasing effect on memory retrieval that concerns the type or sort of memories being recalled (i.e., specific vs. overgeneral). So, from that point of view, the literature on OGM is best placed in that cell of the matrix where depression (or mood disorder in general) crosses (selective) memory processing or memory biases. In the years following the seminal study by Williams and Broadbent, however, the study of OGM has considerably broadened its scope, both vertically and horizontally in the above-described matrix. As for the "vertical scope enlargement" of the field, for example, researchers started to examine the phenomenon's generalisability to other mood disorders than just major depression (e.g., seasonal affective disorder and bipolar disorder) as well as to psychiatric disorders other than mood disorders (e.g., anxiety disorders, eating disorders, and schizophrenia). Also, the field soon started to enlarge its scope in a vertical fashion, including the study of the relationship between OGM and other processes than just memory processes, for example, thought processes (e.g., rumination), motivational processes (e.g., cognitive avoidance), and neurocognitive and neuropsychological processes (e.g., executive functioning).

The scope-enlargement of the field of OGM and psychopathology can be logically understood from at least two points of view. First, it forms part of the "normal" development of any new field of scientific endeavour to explore a phenomenon's generalisability as well as its correlates in order to elucidate its key underlying processes (in this case, for example, ruminative thinking processes, executive deficits, and motivational-avoidance processes; see Williams' closing contribution to this Issue for more details). Second, given the nature of OGM as being a *memory* phenomenon (at least in part), it has close connections to other psychological processes or functions. As such, the field was bound to expand its scope to other psychological functions than just memory.

Twenty years of research in this particular field have made it increasingly clear that OGM constitutes a far from trivial epiphenomenon of depressed mood, but rather represents a trait-like feature with a high level of both clinical and theoretical relevance. Therefore, we would like to end this brief introduction by pointing to some of the possible clinical and theoretical implications of this distinctive line of research on OGM (in relation to psychopathology). First, the fact that OGM appears to represent a likely trait- or vulnerability marker for depression and depressive relapse makes it an interesting phenomenon to the further study and elucidation of the mechanisms underlying vulnerability to (chronic) depression. Second, OGM is more of a *process* matter, rather than a *content* matter (e.g., researchers in this field are not so much interested in the content and valence of peoples' autobiographical memories, as well in the form in which memories are recalled, that is, their specificity). As such, this field holds promise for the development of a more process-focused type of clinical assessment, using performance-based measures (in this case the Autobiographical Memory Test, or AMT). Third, given that OGM pertains to an important vulnerability process in depression, the results of this particular research area can be expected to serve important inputs to clinical interventions (e.g., prevention of depressive relapse) in the near future (e.g., Serrano, Latorre, Gatz, & Montanes, 2004). Fourth, as goes for the study of information processing and psychopathology in general, the study of OGM holds promise for the overarching goal of furthering our knowledge on the interaction between cognitive and biological functioning in psychopathology. In this respect, recent developments within the field of research on OGM clearly parallel recent evolutions in the broader field of psychopathology research that is being conducted from an information-processing perspective. These evolutions show that scientists are increasingly using, for example, brain imaging techniques and cortisol measurements and the like, in combination with experimental paradigms from experimental cognitive psychology.

Finally, given the intertwinedness of OGM and mood and other cognitive processes than just memory processes, this particular domain will certainly stimulate further theorising and empirical research in the broader field of cognition and emotion.

REFERENCES

Blaney, P. H. (1986). Affect and memory: A review. *Psychological Bulletin, 99*, 229–246.

Matt, G. E., Vázquez, C., & Campbell, K. W. (1992). Mood congruent recall of affectively toned stimuli: A meta-analytic review. *Clinical Psychology Review, 12*, 227–255.

Power, M., & Dalgleish, T. (1997). *Cognition and emotion: From order to disorder.* Hove, UK: Psychology Press.

Roane, H. S., Fisher, W. W., & McDonough, E. M. (2003). Progressing from programmatic to discovery research: A case example with the overjustification effect. *Journal of Applied Behavior Analysis, 36*, 35–46.

Roberts, R. M. (1989). *Serendipity: Accidental discoveries in science.* New York: Wiley.

Serrano, J. P., Latorre, J. M., Gatz, M., & Montanes, J. (2004). Life review therapy using autobiographical retrieval practice for older adults with depressive symptomatology. *Psychology and Aging, 19*, 272–277.

Williams, J. M. G., & Broadbent, K. (1986). Autobiographical memory in suicide attempters. *Journal of Abnormal Psychology, 95*, 144–149.

Reducing specificity of autobiographical memory in nonclinical participants: The role of rumination and schematic models

Philip J. Barnard
Medical Research Council Cognition and Brain Sciences Unit, Cambridge, UK

Edward R. Watkins
University of Exeter, UK

Cristina Ramponi
Medical Research Council Cognition and Brain Sciences Unit, Cambridge, UK

> Two experiments are reported in which nondysphoric participants, not prone to excessive levels of rumination in everyday life, were asked to retrieve autobiographical memories using the Williams and Broadbent (1986) procedure (AMT). In the first experiment, two variants of a self-related category fluency task were interleaved among sets of autobiographical memory cues. In one variant (blocked) a normal model of analytic rumination was induced by grouping prompts on a single superordinate theme together. In the other (intermixed) prompts from several different themes were grouped together. It was predicted that the blocked variant would reduce the number of specific memories recollected and increase the number of categoric memories relative to the intermixed variant. This prediction was confirmed and provides the first demonstration of a bidirectional causal influence of analytic rumination on the balance between specific and categoric retrievals. A second experiment showed no alteration in this balance when the same fluency manipulation involved animal-related categories rather than self-related ones. The results support a two component model of autobiographical retrieval being driven in part by the extent to which an analytic mode of processing is adopted in the short term and in part by the level of differentiation in self-related schematic models.

Overgeneral autobiographical memory (Williams, 1996) refers to a phenomenon where individuals, when asked to recall specific personal memories, produce categoric summaries of repeated events (e.g., "making mistakes" or "playing

---

Correspondence should be addressed to Philip J. Barnard, MRC Cognition and Brain Sciences Unit, 15 Chaucer Road, Cambridge CB2 2EF, UK; e-mail: philip.barnard@mrc-cbu.cam.ac.uk

golf every week") rather than memories of events that occurred at a particular place and time (e.g. "beating my friend Paul at golf last Saturday"). Overgeneral memory is a clinically important phenomenon. (1) Compared to controls, overgeneral memory is elevated in depression (see Williams, 1996 for a review) and in patients with posttraumatic stress disorder (McNally, Litz, Prassas, Shin, & Weathers, 1994; McNally, Lasko, Macklin, & Pitman, 1995). (2) Overgeneral memory predicts future prognosis, with increased categoric recall associated with poorer long-term outcome in depression (Brittlebank, Scott, Williams, & Ferrier, 1993; Mackinger, Pachinger, Leibetseder, & Fartacek, 2000; Peeters, Wessel, Merckelbach, & Boon-Vermeeren, 2002), seasonal affective disorder (Dalgleish, Spinks, Yiend, Kuyken, 2001) and in posttraumatic stress disorder (Harvey, Watkins, Mansell, & Shafran, 1998). (3) Categoric memory recall is associated with poor social problem solving (Evans, Williams, O'Loughlin, & Howells, 1992; Goddard, Dritschel, & Burton, 1996, 1997; Pollock & Williams, 2001).

Recently, research has begun to investigate the mechanisms that may underpin the relative proportions of specific versus categoric memories retrieved during autobiographical recall. One candidate explanation is the hypothesis that ruminative self-focus increases the contribution of categoric retrievals relative to specific retrievals: "the rumination hypothesis" (Watkins & Teasdale, 2001, 2004; Watkins, Teasdale & Williams, 2000; Williams, 1996). Depressive rumination is defined as "behaviours and thoughts that focus one's attention on one's depressive symptoms and on the implications of those symptoms" (Nolen-Hoeksema, 1991). Phenomenologically, such rumination consists of perseverative thinking on repetitive and narrow themes about self-related material, such as one's symptoms and problems. Such rumination exacerbates dysphoric mood (Nolen-Hoeksema, 1991), and increases the likelihood, severity and duration of syndromal depression (e.g., Just & Alloy, 1997; Kuehner & Weber, 1999; Nolen-Hoeksema, 2000; Spasojevic & Alloy, 2001).

Consistent with the hypothesis that rumination is involved in the maintenance of overgeneral autobiographical memory recall, Watkins, Teasdale, and Williams (2000) found that a brief distraction induction (imagining nonself-related scenes, e.g., "think about a boat crossing the ocean") increased specific memory recall in dysphoric and depressed individuals, whereas a rumination induction (thinking about self and symptoms, e.g., "think about how sad or happy you feel") maintained categoric memory recall. Further support for the hypothesis comes from correlational studies demonstrating that naturally occurring levels of self-reported rumination are positively associated with degree of categoric memory recall in both normal participants (Ramponi, Barnard, & Nimmo-Smith, 2004) and depressed patients (Raes, Hermans, & Eelens, 2003).

Closer analysis of the relationship between rumination and overgeneral memory has suggested that two particular variables may be important in determining the specificity of memory recall: (1) the particular "mode" of processing adopted during ruminative processing of self-related meanings; and (2) the properties of self-representations "in place" at the point of retrieval (for a fuller analysis, see Ramponi et al., 2004). First, recent evidence suggests that there may be a number of distinct modes of processing within rumination, each of which has distinct functional properties (e.g., McFarland & Buehler, 1998; Trapnell & Campbell, 1999; Treynor, Gonzalez, & Nolen-Hoeksema, 2003; Watkins, 2004; Watkins & Baracaia, 2002; Watkins & Moulds, 2005). Specifically, Watkins and Teasdale (2001) compared the effects on categoric memory recall of analytical (ruminative) self-focus, nonanalytical (experiential) self-focus (e.g., "focus on the experience of" self and physical sensations), analytical nonself-focus (e.g., abstract, philosophical items like "think about whether ends justify the means"), and nonanalytical nonself focus (distraction) inductions in individuals with major depression. A double dissociation was found between the effects of self-focus and the effects of analytical thinking: Increased self-focus was associated with increased negative mood but did not influence categoric memory recall; increased analytical thinking was associated with increased categoric memory recall but did not influence negative mood. Watkins and Teasdale (2004) replicated these findings, demonstrating that in depressed patients, experientially focusing attention directly on feelings reduced overgeneral memory, whereas analytical thinking about feelings maintained overgeneral memory. Thus, an abstract, analytical mode of processing, whether self-focused or not, is implicated in the maintenance of categoric memory recall in depressed patients, suggesting that overgeneral memory retrieval may depend on the adoption of this analytical mode of processing at retrieval.

Second, autobiographical memory recall has been associated with the degree of elaboration in self-related representations. Eldridge, Barnard, and Bekerian (1994) found that participants who provided more elaborated and differentiated descriptions of a typical day at work recalled more detailed autobiographical memories of a working day from the previous week, than those with less differentiated representations. Ramponi et al. (2004) found that categoric memory recall in nonclinical participants was significantly predicted by an individual difference variable indexing differentiation in affect-related self-representations, the Level of Emotional Awareness Scale (LEAS; Lane & Schwarz, 1987), in which descriptions of self-related feelings in various interpersonal scenarios can be coded for degree of differentiation. Higher levels of differentiation in affect-related self-representations as indexed by the LEAS were associated with lower levels of categoric memories and higher levels of specific memories. Thus, the empirical evidence to date suggests that a low level of differentiation in self-representation is linked to elevated retrieval of categoric memories, as is rumination in a more analytical mode of processing.

Interestingly, there are theoretical accounts that hypothesise a dynamic mental dialogue between schematic and propositional levels of self-representation in which exchanges can occur in different modes of processing (Interacting Cognitive Subsystems, ICS; Teasdale, 1999; Teasdale & Barnard, 1993). In this theory, self-representations are argued to take the form of schematic models. These are encoded as "implicational" meanings, a more abstract level of representation than propositional meanings. Schematic models capture regularities underlying instances of ideation and integrate them with the direct products of processing visual, auditory, and body state information. They are inherently generic rather than referentially specific propositional meanings and are linked to our experience of affect. So, for example, a generic negative self-representation may interlink attributes of compromised self-agency, repeated instances of unachieved goals, lowered bodily activation with sadness and inaction. These schematic models give rise to the particular propositional representations about the self that underpin rumination.

The ICS theoretical framework further characterises maladaptive rumination as involving the adoption of an analytical, evaluative mode of processing in the context of a relatively unelaborated, undifferentiated, and negative self-representation. In analytical rumination rather more attention is paid to "propositional" representations of the self than to schematic models of the self. When coupled with an undifferentiated schematic model of the self, this mode of processing is hypothesised to contribute to a state of "depressive interlock". In this state, negative models of the self generate cognitive products (e.g., memories, judgements) that contribute to the regeneration of the same negative models, and so on, with the resulting ongoing stream of ruminative thought on closely related themes acting to maintain depression (Teasdale & Barnard, 1993). That is, within the ICS model, the combination of an analytical mode of processing focused on self-related propositional meanings and relatively impoverished schematic models of the self are the setting conditions for perseverative, repetitive rumination. Under these conditions, the processing of schematic models is relatively automatic and the propositions generated are more likely to simply reflect generic or categoric regularities. In consequence, the kinds of schematic connections that would otherwise support the generation, elaboration and enrichment of context specific meanings are underutilised (see also Teasdale, 1999). Following these assumptions of the ICS model, Ramponi et al. (2004) proposed "the schematic model and executive mode" hypothesis, which predicts that the combination of an abstract, analytical mode of processing and a relatively impoverished schematic model active at retrieval play a causal role in determining the balance between specific and categoric contributions within autobiographical memory retrieval. Indeed, the evidence reported by Ramponi et al. (2004) was consistent with both analytical rumination and relatively impoverished self-representations contributing to the specificity of autobiographical recollection. Within the ICS model, the "schematic model and executive mode" hypothesis can be considered a more detailed two component specification of the rumination hypothesis.

Confirmation of the hypothesis that rumination causally influences the balance between categoric retrieval and specific recollections requires the demonstration of a *bidirectional* effect of manipulating rumination, i.e., increasing rumination reduces the specific contribution in autobiographical memory, whilst reducing rumination increases that contribution. To date, experimental studies in depressed patients have only demonstrated that shifting depressed patients away from rumination reduces categoric memory recall, presumably because depressed patients are near ceiling for both rumination and categoric memory recall, making them unresponsive to attempts at increasing rumination. In contrast, a normal healthy sample would be expected to show a pattern of autobiographical memory retrieval characterised by high, near-to-ceiling, levels of specific memories and relatively few categoric responses. Thus, a strong test of the rumination hypothesis would be to induce an analytical mode of rumination in healthy, nondysphoric participants. If the hypothesis is correct, this induction should *reduce* recall of specific memories and increase recall of categoric memories.

Within the ICS account, this analytical mode of rumination can be induced by providing participants with a task in which attention to propositional meanings about the self predominates over attention to schematic meanings about the self. Indeed, Ramponi et al. (2004) have found that measures indexing both this mode of rumination and undifferentiated schematic models are correlated with categoric memory recall: A logical next step is to test the causal direction of these correlations via experimental manipulations.

A recent theoretical analysis (Barnard, 2003, 2004) has advanced the idea that the particular mode in which the processing of self-related meanings occurs may be linked to a general parameter—rates of change associated with different levels of representation. In depressive interlock, the *same* negative self-related schematic models are continually regenerated. This implies a low rate of change in model content but with some higher rate of variation in the specific propositional meanings that are generated, moment to moment, from the particular model in place at that time. By analogy with vision or audition, it was argued that attention is drawn to the things that change in the internal mental landscape rather than the things that are relatively constant in that landscape.

This analysis suggests that it should be possible to induce a form of rumination in normal participants simply by asking them to repeatedly generate self-related information on the same theme. This should *increase* the likelihood of focusing attention on the specific propositional meanings that are generated and *reduce* the likelihood of paying attention to higher level schematic meanings, thereby shifting processing into an analytical mode. With less attention paid to the content of schematic models and their interrelationships, there should be less scope for thematic variation in a stream of thought and, with that, less diverse potential for accessing specific memories. Such "blocked" generation of self-related information on the same theme should induce a normal, but nonvalenced, model of analytical rumination. From both the rumination and "mode and schematic model" accounts, this induction procedure should reduce the number of specific memories recalled for a short duration afterwards. In contrast, if the themes on which participants are asked to generate self-related material vary from instance to instance, participants should pay a normal, or even an increased level of attention to schematic model content, leading to reduced analytical rumination, and sustain or even boost recall of specific memories.

As well as testing the predictions derived from the ICS account, this rate-of-change methodology has several other advantages. (1) It overcomes the practical problem of how to manipulate rumination in nondysphoric participants, since the effectiveness of the standard rumination manipulation in influencing mood and cognition is known to depend on some degree of pre-existing dysphoric mood (Lyubomirsky & Nolen-Hoeksema, 1995; Nolen-Hoeksema, 1991). (2) It ensures that the effects of processing mode can be investigated independently from any confound of inducing negative mood. Most standard manipulations of rumination also exacerbate negative mood, making it hard to disentangle any direct effect of rumination on cognitive processing from an indirect effect of rumination on cognitive processing via increased negative mood (Lyubomirsky & Nolen-Hoeksema, 1995; Nolen-Hoeksema, 1991). It is important to note that this rate-of-change methodology induces a mental state that is phenomenologically similar to rumination on a number of dimensions, i.e., repeated thinking on a narrow self-related theme, with little variability at a schematic level, but does not require negative valence.

The first experiment therefore sought to invoke two different modes of processing self-related meanings (more propositional-more analytic vs. more schematic-less analytic) in a normal healthy sample of nondysphoric individuals by interleaving one of two variants of a self-related category fluency task in between discrete episodes of autobiographical retrieval. We predicted that a high rate of change in self-related themes on the category fluency task would sustain a high level of specificity in autobiographical recall, while a low rate of change in self-related themes would reduce the contribution of specific recollections and increase the contribution of categoric responses.

EXPERIMENT 1

Method

Design

Screened volunteers were randomly allocated to either a category fluency task with prompts blocked together by superordinate theme ("blocked" condition) or to the same category fluency task with prompts intermixed across superordinate theme ("intermixed" condition). The category fluency task was interleaved with an autobiographical memory task. The experiment used a

2 (Condition: blocked, intermixed) × 3 (Block: first block, second block, third block) factorial design.

Participants

The participants were 36 nondysphoric individuals from the volunteer panel of the Cognition and Brain Sciences Unit. Since the purpose of the experiment was to create an experimental analogue task with rumination-like properties, but in a normal healthy sample, any participants with a BDI score ≥ 13 or a rumination score ≥ 51 did not fulfil our selection criteria and were replaced. Table 1 summarises the profiles of the participants for the blocked and intermixed conditions. The two groups were matched for sex distribution, age, BDI scores, and verbal ability as measured by the National Adult Reading Test (NART; Nelson, 1982). Since prior research (Ramponi, et al., 2004) has shown influences on autobiographical recall of both schematic model differentiation as indexed by the LEAS, and rumination, as indexed by the Response Style Questionaire (RSQ) of Nolen-Hoeksema, Morrow, & Fredrickson (1993), the two groups were matched on these indices. There was also no difference between the groups on RSQ distraction.

Materials

Self-related category generation task. Participants were given 30 s to write down as many different examples as they possibly could of a particular event or action, in response to a prompt printed on a response sheet. Participants practised the task by generating as many different examples as possible of the things they typically need to do before taking a trip. In the main task, participants were given a series of 15 category fluency prompts that were derived by substituting three superordinate themes (*working, relaxing at home,* and *socialising outside the home*) within five sentence frames. The frames were: (1) "Generate as many different examples as possible of the feelings you typically have when x-ing"; (2) "Generate as many different examples as possible of the typical consequences or outcomes you have when x-ing"; (3) "Generate as many different examples as possible of the activities you would typically do when x-ing; (4) "Generate as many different examples as possible of what you typically pay attention to when x-ing"; (5) "Generate as many different examples as possible of how you might typically benefit from x-ing".

The self-related category fluency task was presented in three tranches interleaved with administration of the autobiographical memory test: The first tranche preceded the first 6 Autobiographical Memory Test (AMT) cue words, the second tranche was administered in between the first and second sets of 6 AMT cue words, and the last tranche between the second and final sets of 6 AMT cue words.

The only difference between the blocked condition and the intermixed condition was the organisation of the presentation of the full set of category fluency prompts. In the blocked condition each tranche of five category fluency prompts was on a *single* superordinate theme, whereas in the intermixed condition the prompts were drawn randomly from the three superordinate themes, but with different themes occurring no more than twice. Hence, in the blocked condition there is no or little change in self-related theme within a tranche, while there is a higher rate of change in the intermixed condition. The three tranches of blocked or intermixed cues were presented in a Latin square design, with 6 different order formats per condition.

Autobiographical Memory Test (AMT). Participants were given 30 seconds to recall a specific personal memory for each of 6 positive (e.g., happy), 6 negative (e.g., failure), and 6 neutral cues (e.g., bread), using the standard instructions (Williams & Broadbent, 1986), with cue words printed on cards. Participants practised two examples before testing began. Following common practice, the autobiographical memory cue words were always presented in the same fixed order, with each set of six cues being split between 2 positive, 2 negative, and 2 neutral items (Set 1: happy, guilty, grass, devoted, grief, pottery; Set 2: relieved, hopeless, wildlife, hopeful, rejected, ladder; Set 3: proud, failure, bread, amazed, helpless, shallow). Word sets were matched for emotionality and word frequency.

Response latency was recorded and all responses were tape-recorded and transcribed by the experimenter. After all the cue words were shown, the experimenter went through the list of words and reminded the participants of the memory they produced for each cue. For each memory the participant had to say how pleasant the memory of the event was on an 11-point scale where -5 indicated a very unpleasant memory and $+5$ a very pleasant memory. Participants also indicated how long ago the event of the memory took place by referring to a 6-point time scale: 1 = "Less than a week ago", 2 = "less than a month ago ", 3 = "less than three months ago ", 4 = "less than six months ago ", 5 = "less than a year ago ", and 6 = "more than a year ago".

The transcribed responses from the AMT test were scored following criteria previously used by Goddard, Dritschel, and Burton (1996) and Williams and Dritschel (1992). Categoric events were defined as a summary of repeated events. Extended events were defined as events that lasted a period of time longer than a day. Specific events were defined as events that occurred at a particular place and time and that lasted less time than a day. Failure to recall a memory within 30 s was coded as an omission. If the response was simply an association it was classified as such (e.g., "*Happy Days*, the TV series, springs to mind"). The experimenter and an independent rater categorised the memories, with good interrater reliability (agreement on a random sample of approximately 10% of the memories was 98%, $\kappa = .94$).

Mood measures. Since rumination (Nolen-Hoeksema, 1991) and self focus (Watkins & Teasdale, 2001) have both been linked to alterations in mood state, visual analogue scales were also administered at six points interleaved during the procedure to monitor for any differential effect on mood state of the experimental manipulation. Mood was assessed for happiness, sadness and anxiety with participants shown three horizontal lines 10cm long, each subdivided in to ten partitions running from 0 (not at all) to 10 (extremely). Participants responded with a number to indicate their current state on each of the three mood dimensions.

Individual differences measures

Mood state over the last week was assessed using the Beck Depression Inventory (BDI; Beck, Ward, Mendelson, Mock, & Erbaugh, 1961). The BDI is a 21-item self-report measure of depression. The extent to which participants were prone to rumination was assessed using the Response Style Questionnaire (RSQ; Nolen-Hoeksema et al., 1993). The RSQ consists of two subscales, one for rumination and one for distraction (Nolen-Hoeksema et al., 1993). The rumination subscale has 21 items assessing how frequently one thinks about the symptoms of depression when one is sad or depressed on a 4 point scale (e.g., "How often do you think about how sad you feel"). The distraction subscale consists of 12 items assessing how often one manages to distract from symptoms of depression (e.g., How often do you think "I'll concentrate on something other than how I feel"). Differentiation of affect-related schematic models was measured with the Level of Emotional Awareness Scale (LEAS; Lane & Schwarz, 1987). This scale consists of 20 scenarios which describe in 2–4

TABLE 1
The profiles of participants in the blocked and intermixed conditions in Experiment 1

	Blocked (N = 18)		Intermixed (N = 18)			
	Mean	(SD)	Mean	(SD)	t(34)	2-tailed probability
Sex	6 m/12 f		6 m/12 f			
Age	26.44	(7.50)	27.56	(8.54)	−0.415	0.68
BDI	3.33	(2.52)	4.50	(3.47)	−1.15	0.26
NART errors	15.39	(7.64)	14.22	(4.75)	0.55	0.59
LEAS total	78.89	(8.80)	76.89	(8.78)	0.68	0.50
RSQ rumination	37.50	(6.09)	36.17	(8.21)	0.55	0.58
RSQ distraction	29.28	(3.91)	27.44	(4.84)	1.25	0.22

BDI, Beck Depression Inventory; NART, National Adult Reading Test; LEAS, Level of Emotional Awareness Scale; RSQ, Response Style Questionaire.

sentences a situation involving two people, self, and one other (e.g. "Your boss tells you that your work has been unacceptable and needs to be improved. How would you feel? How would your boss feel?"). Participants write a description of what he/she would feel and what the other person would feel in that situation. The responses are scored according to a scheme that distinguishes six levels of emotional awareness (Lane, Quinlan, Schwartz, Walker, & Zeitlin, 1990). These are determined by the qualitative nature of the words used to describe reactions. This scale is directed at capturing the sophistication of emotional descriptions, rather than of events in the world. The experimenter and an independent rater categorised the LEAS, with good interrater reliability (agreement on a random sample of approximately 10% of the responses was 91%, $\kappa = .86$).

Procedure

Participants were tested individually. After a preliminary overview, participants practised the category fluency task, and then practised the AMT. The interleaved blocks of fluency prompts and autobiographical memory cues were then administered. All participants in both conditions went through the following sequence: first visual analogue mood assessment, one tranche of 5 category fluency prompts, second visual analogue mood assessment followed by 6 autobiographical memory cues. This sequence was then repeated twice more, giving three blocks of AMT recall (Block 1, Block 2, Block 3), each in close temporal proximity to mode induction and mood assessment. Both category fluency prompts and autobiographical memory cue words were presented in written form. The relevant instructions *were repeated* before each tranche of five category fluency prompts and before each set of six autobiographical memory cues. Following completion of the experiment, participants were tested on the NART, completed the BDI, RSQ, and LEAS questionnaires. The whole session lasted between 90 min and 120 min.

Results

Autobiographical memory retrieval

Consistent with previous findings with nondysphoric participants (e.g., Ramponi, et al., 2004), specific memories were the predominant response to cues. Table 2 shows the mean numbers of responses in each of the scored categories. In addition to the basic means, this table shows the percentage of the total number of responses, excluding omissions, which were specific. While this percentage score allows for differential rates of omission, application of the empirical logit transformation also reduces any biases from floor and ceiling effects (see Ramponi et al., 2004). Since the overall number of categoric and extended memories is small, theses two categories were summed and the logit ratio of specific to categoric plus extended was computed for each participant's

TABLE 2
Responses on the Autobiographical Memory Test in Experiment 1

	Blocked (N = 18)		Intermixed (N = 18)	
	Mean	(SD)	Mean	(SD)
Specific	14.33	(2.42)	15.83	(1.89)
Categoric	0.39	(0.61)	0.11	(0.32)
Extended	0.89	(1.02)	0.39	(0.70)
Associations	0.28	(0.06)	0.28	(0.06)
Omissions	2.11	(1.93)	1.39	(1.61)
Specific answers (%)	91.51	(7.54)	97.03	(5.32)
Logit ratio sp/(cat+ext)	1.01	(0.37)	1.33	(0.32)

output. This index enables examination of what influences the balance between qualitatively different responses irrespective of the overall levels of accurate retention, association responses, or omission.

Two 2 (Condition: blocked, intermixed) × 3 (Blocks of trials: First block, second block, third block) analyses of variance were conducted on both the percentage and logit ratio measures of the specificity of autobiographical retrieval. Both analyses showed a reliable effect of condition: Percentage measure: $F(1, 34) = 5.76, p < .025$; Logit measure: $F(1, 34) = 5.29, p < .05$. As predicted, the blocked condition, with a constant self-related theme resulted in a lower proportion of specific relative to nonspecific autobiographical memories than the intermixed condition where the self-related themes were varied within a tranche. Further, the effect was maintained across all three blocks of trials. In neither case was there an effect of trial block: Percentage measure: $F(2, 68) = 0.35, p > .1$; Logit measure: $F(2, 68) = 0.46, p > .1$, nor an interaction between condition and trial block: Percentage measure: $F(2, 68) = 0.87, p > .1$; Logit measure $F(2, 68) = 1.59, p > .1$.

Further analyses on the means shown in Table 2 showed that the number of specific memories recalled was higher in the intermixed condition than in the grouped condition, $t(34) = -2.07, p < .025$, one-tailed, and both categoric and extended memories, while small in absolute number, were more frequent in the grouped condition: Categoric $t(34) = 1.71, p < .05$; Extended $t(34) = 1.71, p < .05$, one-tailed tests. The number of associations and omissions did not differ as a function of condition: Associations: $t(34) = 0.0$; Omissions: $t(34) = 1.22$; both $ps > .1$.

To assess whether the valence of the AMT cue word affected recollection, valence was entered into separate ANOVAs on the percentage and logit indices of memory specificity. The analysis of the percentage measure showed no effect of valence, $F(2, 68) = 1.35, p > .1$, and no interaction between valence and condition, $F(2, 68) = 0.81$, $p > .1$ (percentage of specific memories recalled: to positive words, $M = 95.7$, $SD = 8.3$; to negative words, $M = 92.0$, $SD = 12.5$; to neutral words, $M = 95.2$, $SD = 11.2$). For the analysis using the logit index, the effect of valence was marginal, $F(2, 68) = 2.93$ $p = .06$, and again there was no interaction between valence and condition, $F(2, 68) = 0.62$, $p > .1$ (logit index for: positive words $M = 0.95$, $SD = 0.25$; for negative words $M = 0.82$, $SD = 0.32$; for neutral words $M = 0.94$, $SD = 0.28$). Whilst the age of memories actually recalled did not differ as a function of condition: Blocked: $M = 3.65$, $SD = 1.04$; Intermixed $M = 3.14$, $SD = 1.21$; $t(34) = 1.35$, $p > .1$ two-tailed, there was a trend for memories in the intermixed condition to be rated as of lower pleasantness than those in the blocked condition: Intermixed: $M = 0.47$, $SD = 0.56$; Blocked: $M = 0.96$, $SD = 0.96$; $t(34) = 1.88$, $p < .1$, two-tailed. This latter trend is most likely attributable to the slightly lower proportions of specific memories given in response to negative cue words. There was greater headroom for an increase to these cues in the intermixed condition relative to that for the neutral and positive cues.

Category fluency

No predictions were made concerning the total number of examples produced in response to the 15 category fluency prompts in each condition. In fact, rather more examples were generated in the intermixed condition than in the blocked condition: Intermixed: $M = 68.11$, $SD = 8.88$; Blocked: $M = 60.83$, $SD = 14.33$; $t(34) = -1.83$, $p < .1$ two-tailed. In order to establish whether this borderline effect contributed to the main effect of condition, two analyses of covariance were carried out on the percentage and logit ratios indexing relative memory specificity, again with condition and trial block as factors. When the number of examples generated was covaried out, the effect of condition remained significant on both measures: Percentage: $F(1, 33) = 6.33$, $p < .025$; Logit ratio: $F(1, 33) = 5.01$, $p < .05$, and none of the interactions approached significance.

Mood ratings

The data from the analogue scale mood checks were also subjected to separate 2 (Condition) × 6 (Time point in experimental sequence) ANOVAs for the ratings of happiness, sadness and anxiety. For happiness ratings, there was a reliable overall effect of time point in sequence, $F(5, 170) = 3.13$, $p = .01$, no effect of condition, $F(1, 34) = 1.12$, $p > .05$, and no condition by point in sequence interaction, $F(5, 170) = 1.95$, $p > .05$. For sadness ratings, there was also a reliable overall effect of time point in sequence, $F(5, 170) = 3.44$, $p = .01$, no effect of condition, $F(1, 34) = 0.45$, $p > .05$, and no condition by time point in sequence interaction, $F(5, 170) = 1.32$, $p > .05$. Sadness tended to peak just prior to the second set of autobiographical cues. For the anxiety ratings, there was an effect of time point in sequence, $F(5, 170) = 5.86$, $p < .001$, no effect of condition, $F(1, 34) = 0.02$, $p > .05$, and no condition by time point in sequence interaction, $F(5, 170) = 0.82$, $p > .05$. Anxiety tended to systematically decrease over the time course of the experiment. The experimental manipulation thus had no *differential* effects on affective state across the experimental procedure.

Correlational analyses

Since the two groups of participants were not only low in number but also selected to lie in a low range of BDI scores and to exclude those predisposed to high levels of rumination, correlational analyses were restricted to the exploration of the relationship between dependent measures. In order to take out the effect of the experimental manipulation, the numbers of specific memories, omissions, and the examples generated on the self-related category fluency task were all normalised. Normalised performance on the self-related category fluency task showed a trend towards a positive relationship with the normalised numbers of specific memories recalled $r(34) = .29$, $p = .08$, two-tailed, a large negative correlation with omissions, $r(34) = -.47$, $p < .005$, two-tailed, and no relationship with the logit transformed ratio index of specificity in recall, $r(34) = -.10$, $p > .1$, or the percentage of all output that was specific, $r(34) = -.15$, $p > .1$. Thus, independent of the experimental manipulation, those participants who produced more examples on the category generation task made fewer omissions on the AMT task, but generative capability per se was not associated with the relative proportion of specific to nonspecific responses.

Discussion

Consistent with our hypothesis, the two sets of category fluency tasks had differential effects on the balance between the different types of autobiographical memories recalled in close temporal proximity to the fluency task: Compared to intermixing the themes on which self-related material is generated, generating self-related material all blocked on one superordinate theme reduced specific memory retrieval and increased categoric and extended memory. Correcting for any minor but differential contribution of omissions (which did not reliably differ between conditions), the balance of different types of memory in autobiographical recall alters as a function of the category fluency task with significant differences in the percentage and logit ratio indices, even when marginal differences in self-related generativity are covaried out. This finding is consistent with the rumination hypothesis by demonstrating that a manipulation proposed to increase analytical thinking (and, which phenomenologically produces repeated thinking about a narrow self-related theme, i.e., rumination) reduces the proportion of specific memory recall.

The processing mode and schematic model hypothesis implies that analytical processing about self-related material is *necessary* to influence autobiographical memory retrieval. Indeed, many theoretical approaches emphasise a critical role for self-models, for example, a "working model of the self" (Conway & Pleydell-Pearce, 2000), in driving autobiographical recollection. In addition, there is extensive empirical work indicating that, in a number of paradigms investigating the relationship between cognition and emotion, effects tend to occur when the processing of material is self-referenced but not otherwise (for reviews, see Ellis & Moore, 1999; Teasdale & Barnard, 1993). On the other hand, evidence outlined earlier clearly shows that depressed patients sustain categoric responses following analytic rumination irrespective of *whether it is self-focused or not* (Watkins & Teasdale, 2001, 2004). There is also evidence (Watkins et al., 2000) that a brief distraction induction involving imagining nonself-related scenes reduces categoric memory in dysphoric and depressed individuals. Therefore, prior to discussing the wider implications of the current findings on the induction of different modes of processing in nondysphoric participants, it is clearly advisable to establish whether the effect of our manipulation is linked to the self-related content of the fluency task. This is particularly important since there is already some evidence in the literature of a possible link between autobiographical memory performance and a general, nonself referenced test of category fluency (Williams & Dritschel, 1991).

If an alteration in the mode of processing is sufficient, then the finding of Experiment 1 should replicate with a category fluency task in a nonself-related domain. If, as we predict, based on Ramponi et al. (2004) and Conway and Pleydell-Pearce (2000), the effect is linked to the fact that autobiographical memory and the category fluency task both involve self-related model content being generated in close temporal proximity, then a category fluency task grouped around a common theme that is nonself-related should have no effect on memory retrieval (i.e., a high level of specific recollection maintained). The second experiment was carried out to evaluate these alternatives.

EXPERIMENT 2

Method

The design, the procedure and the material were identical to the one adopted in Experiment 1 except that the prompts were non-self-related. For the category fluency task, each superordinate theme was replaced with an analogue theme for animals: thus the theme of "work" was replaced with "foraging to obtain food and drink", the theme of "relaxing at home" with "when animals are at rest in condition of relative safety", and the theme of "socialising outside the home" with "when interacting with other animals or humans". The five sentence frames were similar to Experiment 1, but modified where necessary for the animal domain. Again each frame was applicable to all three themes of animal behaviour (e.g., Generate as many different examples as possible of what animals might need to pay attention to in their environment when they are trying to obtain food or drink /when at rest.../ when interacting with other....). Prompts were again organised either with a single theme in a tranche of five fluency prompts ("blocked") or with the themes intermixed within a tranche of five prompts ("intermixed").

Participants

Since the prediction is that the effect obtained in Experiment 1 will not occur with a nonself-related manipulation, a power analysis was conducted based on the percentage and logit indices empirically observed in Experiment 1. This analysis showed that a sample size of 24 in each group would yield a power of 86% for detecting a difference at the .05 level on the percentage measure and 94% power on the logit ratio measure. The total number of participants was therefore increased to 48 nondysphoric individuals from the volunteer panel of the Cognition and Brain Sciences Unit. As with Experiment 1, participants with a BDI $\geq$ than 13, or a RSQ $\geq$ than 51, were replaced. Participants were randomly assigned to either the blocked or intermixed fluency conditions. Table 3 summarises the profiles of the participants in these two groups. As with the previous experiment, the groups were matched for sex distribution, age, BDI, RSQ, LEAS, and verbal ability as measured by the National Adult Reading Test (NART; Nelson, 1982).

Results

Two 2 (Condition) × 3 (Trial blocks) ANOVAs were carried out on the percentage and logit ratio measures. In neither analysis were there any effects of condition or block and no interaction between them: Percentage measure: condition $F(1, 46) = 1.59$, $p > .1$, trial block, $F(2, 92) = 1.99$, $p > .1$; interaction

TABLE 3
The profiles of participants in the blocked and intermixed conditions in Experiment 2

	Blocked (N = 24)		Intermixed (N = 24)		t(46)	2-tailed probability
	Mean	(SD)	Mean	(SD)		
Sex	7 m/17 f		9 m/15 f			
Age	28.29	(8.37)	25.54	(7.56)	1.19	0.24
BDI	3.58	(3.62)	3.56	(2.93)	0.02	0.98
NART errors	15.25	(5.87)	13.29	(4.63)	1.28	0.21
LEAS total	76.54	(8.99)	76.67	(9.18)	−0.05	0.96
RSQ Rumination	35.88	(8.44)	36.25	(8.92)	−0.15	0.88
RSQ distraction	28.13	(5.56)	29.50	(5.17)	−0.89	0.38

Note: For abbreviations see Table 1.

TABLE 4
Responses on the Autographical Memory Test in Experiment 2

	Blocked (N = 24)		Intermixed (N = 24)	
	Mean	(SD)	Mean	(SD)
Specific	15.25	(1.78)	15.63	(1.66)
Categoric	0.13	(0.34)	0.04	(0.20)
Extended	0.71	(1.08)	0.42	(0.50)
Associations	0.25	(0.68)	0.17	(0.48)
Omissions	1.67	(1.24)	1.67	(1.40)
Specific answers (%)	94.85	(8.15)	97.05	(3.30)
Logit ratio sp/(cat+ext)	1.24	(0.40)	1.29	(0.27)

between condition and trial block, $F(2, 92) = 0.54$, $p > .1$; Logit measure: condition $F(1, 46) = 1.38$, $p > .1$, trial block, $F(2, 92) = 1.08$, $p > .1$, interaction between condition and trial block, $F(2, 92) = 0.84$, $p > .1$.

The means for all the memory measures are shown in Table 4. None of the differences between conditions on these measures approached significance, $t(46)$ all < 1.25, all $ps > .1$. There was also no difference in the age of memories retrieved: Intermixed: $M = 3.24$, $SD = 1.11$; Blocked $M = 3.30$, $SD = 1.05$, $t(46) = 0.19$, $p > .1$, nor on the rated pleasantness of those memories: Intermixed: $M = 0.72$, $SD = 0.59$; Blocked: $M = 0.60$, SD 0.63, $t(46) = -0.68$, $p > .1$. For the animal fluency task, the overall numbers of examples generated are in a comparable range to that obtained on the self-related fluency task of Experiment 1, but in this instance the difference between the numbers produced in the intermixed and blocked conditions did not approach significance: Intermixed: $M = 64.46$, $SD = 14.92$; Blocked: $M = 61.33$, $SD = 12.92$; $t(46) = -0.78$, $p > .1$.

The data from the analogue scale mood checks were also subjected to separate 2 (Condition) × 6 (Time point in experimental sequence) ANOVAs for the ratings of happiness, sadness, and anxiety. For happiness ratings, there was no reliable overall effect of time point in sequence, $F(5, 230) = 1.5$, $p > .1$, no overall effect of condition, $F(1, 46) = 3.18$, $p = .08$, and no condition by time point interaction, $F(5, 230) = 0.43$, $p > .1$. For sadness ratings, there was a reliable overall effect of time point in sequence, $F(5, 230) = 5.05$, $p < .001$, no effect of condition, $F(1, 46) = 0.01$, $p > .1$, and no condition by time point in sequence interaction, $F(5, 170) = 1.38$, $p > .1$. For the anxiety ratings, there was also an effect of time point in sequence, $F(5, 230) = 9.73$, $p < .001$, no effect of condition, $F(1, 46) = 0.01$, $p > .1$, and, this time, a borderline condition by time point in sequence interaction, $F(5, 230) = 2.19$, $p = .056$.

The relationships between performance on normalised animal fluency and normalised AMT indices were examined to see if the effects found with self-related category generation replicated in the animal domain. There was a positive, but nonsignificant relationship between output on the fluency task and the numbers of specific memories recalled, $r(46) = .18, p > .1$, one-tailed, a larger negative correlation with omissions, $r(46) = -.26, p < .05$, one-tailed, and no relationship with the logit transformed ratio index of specificity in recall, $r(46) = .04, p > .1$, or the percentage of output that was specific, $r(46) = .09, p > .1$. The overall pattern of correlation is very similar to that found in Experiment 1. Indeed, the correlations between category fluency performance and specific memories did not differ significantly between the two experiments ($z = 0.51, p > .1$) nor did the correlations between fluency and omissions ($z = 1.06\ p > .1$). Accordingly, the normalised data from the two experiments were combined to reveal both a significant positive correlation overall between performance on the fluency task and the normalised numbers of specific memories, $r(82) = .23, p < .05$, and a negative relationship with omissions, $r(82) = -0.35, p < .001$.

Those participants who produced more examples on the category generation task produce more specific memories and make fewer omissions on the AMT task, irrespective of reference in the fluency task to self or animals. In neither experiment was generative capability per se associated with the relative proportion of specific to nonspecific responses in their output. Since Ramponi et al. (2004) had shown a positive correlation between level of recollection and schematic model differentiation, as measured by total LEAS scores, a positive relationship would be expected between LEAS and performance on the fluency task as well as specific recollections, and the logit ratios. Again using the combined normalised data from both experiments there were significant correlations between LEAS and fluency, $r(82) = .33, p < .001$, and between LEAS and the number of specific memories, $r(82) = .19, p < .05$, and a positive, but nonsignificant correlation with the logit ratio, $r(82) = .13, p = .12$. There was also a significant negative correlation between LEAS and omissions, $r(82) = -.20, p < .05$.

Discussion

As predicted, there was no difference in the pattern of autobiographical memories retrieved in close temporal proximity to either the intermixed or blocked category fluency tasks, when the superordinate themes were not self-related. Consistent with the processing mode and schematic model hypothesis, this finding suggests that an analytical mode of processing may need to be concerned with self-related material in order to have an impact on the distribution of responses in autobiographical memory recall.

GENERAL DISCUSSION

The first experiment adds considerable overall reinforcement to the rumination hypothesis. It supports a causal role for an analytic mode of processing self-related meanings in altering the balance between specific and categoric responses in autobiographical recall. In Experiment 1, an analogue of rumination involving the generation of repeated material on the same self-related theme had the effect of reducing the contribution of specific recollection and increasing the contribution of categoric output in nondysphoric individuals who are not prone to excessive levels of rumination in their everyday life. In a context where previous studies have shown that shifting depressed patients away from rumination leads to a reduction in categoric responses (e.g., Watkins & Teasdale, 2001, 2004), we believe this to be the first study providing direct evidence for the reverse effect, and, hence a bidirectional causal role of rumination in influencing memory specificity. Furthermore, the rumination task used in Experiment 1 had no effect on mood and did not depend on the existence of a dysphoric mood for its effects (unlike the rumination task used by Nolen-Hoeksema and colleagues) indicating that this rumination effect on retrieval was independent of negative mood.

In Experiment 2, there was no effect of the different intermixed and blocked fluency tasks when the material to be generated concerned animals, despite an increase in the sample size. This is consistent with the inference that an analytical mode of processing on self-related information is needed to carry over to influence the relative contributions of specific and categoric responses on the AMT at least in a nonclinical group, although this does not prove this hypothesis definitively. Even if, as hypothesised in more detail, the general parameter "rate of change" leads to attention in the wider mental landscape switching from a level of representation involving specific meanings to a level involving schematic models, it may be that the particular model content most recently "in place" needs to be self-related. This is broadly consistent with a conjoint effect of both schematic models and mode of processing, the dual setting conditions originally proposed by Teasdale and Barnard (1993) and further elaborated by Ramponi et al. (2004).

One apparent discrepancy between the current findings and the demonstrations that an analytical processing mode influences categoric memory retrieval in depressed patients (Watkins & Teasdale, 2001) concerns self-related content. In the current experiments, only self-related processing influenced autobiographical memory retrieval, whereas Watkins and Teasdale (2001) reported that shifting the mode of processing (more or less analytical) influenced categoric memory retrieval in depressed patients independent of whether the processing tasks were self-focused or not. Nonetheless, it also seems quite plausible that self-related ideation and, with that, activation of self-related schematic models, may be more likely to have occurred spontaneously in close temporal proximity to an autobiographical memory cue in depressed samples than nondepressed ones. There is an extensive literature indicating that depressed patients have elevated levels of self-focus (Ingram, 1990; Ingram & Smith, 1984; Pyszczynski & Greenberg, 1987). Any elevated naturally occurring self-focused processing in depression would have lead to the dual setting conditions being more likely to be present in depressed samples than in our normal healthy sample and hence help to account for the effect of self-relatedness in one study but not the other.

The current study further replicates previous findings indicating that categoric memory recall is not mood state-dependent. Watkins and Teasdale (2001) found that their particular induction of an analytic mode of rumination with depressed individuals did influence specificity of memory retrieval but did not affect mood, indicating that categoric memory retrieval may be independent of mood change. Simply altering the rate of change in thematic content of ideation in the present study also had no systematic effect on mood (and indeed, was partly chosen to avoid any confound with mood effects). Our paradigm was nonetheless sensitive to any potential effects on mood, as demonstrated by the presence of systematic order effects in the repeated analogue scales assessing sadness and anxiety.

The present study is subject to three qualifications. First, there is a possible alternative explanation. In Experiment 1 there was a trend for the intermixed condition to give rise to a greater output on the fluency task than the blocked condition. This leaves open the possibility that the fluency task could simply have acted to prime a slightly wider range of self-aspects and hence retrieval descriptions from which specific recollections could be generated. Although naturally a strong a priori candidate, neither the finding that condition still significantly influences the relative specificity of memory recall even when covarying for number of items generated nor the individual difference data are very consistent with this account. For example, this explanation would have to predict that those individuals who generate a larger number of examples would produce more specific memories, but this relationship should hold only in the first experiment where the fluency task is self-related. Positive but non-significant correlations were, in fact, found in both experiments and they did not differ reliably between the two experiments, leading to a significant correlation over *both* experimental sets. Indeed, specificity of recall and output on the fluency task across experiments were both correlated positively with LEAS, and LEAS also correlated negatively with omissions. The relationship between specific memories and LEAS corroborates one component of the earlier report of Ramponi et al. (2004). In addition, LEAS, fluency and specificity of recall are all interrelated to some degree. This supports the argument for a key role for differentiation of schematic models over and above the effect of the experimental manipulation, which we have argued here is best attributed to the adoption of different modes of processing. In these respects our data are wholly consistent with the two-component processing mode and schematic model hypothesis.

The second two qualifications relate to our use of a supernormal sample and concern the impact on our analyses of: (a) low levels of categoric retrieval; and (b) the effects of selecting only participants with low BDI and excluding those with a self-reported high level of rumination in everyday life. As far as the low levels of categoric retrieval is concerned, the overall pattern on different measures is, at least, internally consistent. It would, however, have affected our sensitivity to, for example, replicating the relationship between LEAS and the logit ratio reported by Ramponi et al. (2004). Here, the relationship is in the same direction as the earlier report but not significant. Indeed, the lower magnitude of these correlations is quite likely to be an unintended side effect of participant selection. The average LEAS scores in the current study are considerably higher than those reported in the Ramponi et al study. Although neither BDI nor RSQ were correlated with LEAS in that study, one effect of exclusions on *conjoint* criteria could well have been the underrepresentation in the current samples of those with low levels of differentiation in their self-related schematic models and hence the rather more modest correlations in the current between LEAS and the measures of autobiographical recollection.

The current findings are thus consistent with the suggestion that a chronic style of ruminative, analytical thinking about the self, dynamically maintained in an attempt to resolve goal discrepancies or make sense of past events may play a role in producing overgeneral memory in depression. The current results further suggest that the mode of processing, the degree of self-related processing and the extent of differentiation of schematic models of the self are all variables that contribute to the specificity of autobiographical memory recall. Potentially, these variables may help to account for, and provide new avenues of investigation into, a number of observations in the clinical literature on specificity of autobiographical memory. First, these variables provide a possible mechanism to explain the observed relationship between history of traumatic abuse and reduced specific memory in depression (e.g., de Decker, Hermans, Raes, & Eelen, 2003; Hermans et al., 2004; Kuyken & Brewin, 1995): childhood physical or sexual abuse produces increased analytical rumination about the self (e.g., "Why did this happen to me?; Conway, Mendelson, Giannopoulos, Csank, & Holm, 2004) and may lead to less differentiated models of the self. Second, this analysis may help to account for the diagnostic specificity of elevated categoric memory: Only disorders/mental states characterised by increased analytical thinking about the self *and* less differentiated self-models may display elevated categoric retrieval. Thus, by this account, one would not necessarily expect elevated categoric memory in generalised anxiety disorder (GAD), despite worry clearly involving increased analytical thinking (Borkovec, Ray, & Stöber, 1998): speculatively, the dual setting conditions may not necessarily be in place, as worry tends to be focused on external threats rather than self-related material, and anxiety disorders may not be associated with as low levels of differentiation in self-models as is depression.

As well as providing evidence consistent with the rumination hypothesis, the current findings indicate the potential value of concentrating attention on the role of generic mechanisms, like modes of processing meaning (see also

Teasdale, 1999), generic information processing parameters, like rates of change in information in the current mental landscape, or generic attributes of self-representation (as opposed to self esteem, dysfunctional attitudes etc.) in understanding psychopathology. Such an approach is consistent with a move towards greater consideration of the cognitive processes underpinning psychopathology, rather than a focus on specific cognitive content. In particular, recent work has emphasised the potential value of examining cognitive processes that are both common across multiple psychological disorders and active in the psychological healthy, that is, to look at transdiagnostic cognitive processes. A body of evidence suggests that a number of cognitive processes including attention, categoric memory retrieval, and rumination are common across a range of psychiatric diagnoses (for a review, see Harvey, Watkins, Mansell, & Shafran, 2004). More widely, a transdiagnostic approach may be of particular value in explaining comorbidity and developing understanding of deeper mechanisms that can be related to the wider psychological literature.

REFERENCES

Barnard, P. (2003). Asynchrony, implicational meaning and the experience of self in schizophrenia. In T. Kircher & A. David (Eds.), *The self in neuroscience and psychiatry*, (pp. 121–146), Cambridge, UK: Cambridge University Press.

Barnard, P. (2004). Bridging between basic theory and clinical practice. *Behaviour Research and Therapy*, 42, 977–1000.

Beck, A. T., Ward, C. H., Mendelson, M., Mock, J., & Erbaugh, J. (1961). An inventory for measuring depression. *Archives of General Psychiatry*, 4, 561–571.

Borkovec, T. D., Ray, W. J., & Stöber, J. (1998). Worry: a cognitive phenomenon intimately linked to affective, physiological and interpersonal behavioral processes. *Cognitive Therapy and Research*, 8, 561–576.

Brittlebank, A. D., Scott, J., Williams, J. M. G., & Ferrier, I. N. (1993). Autobiographical memory in depression: State or trait marker? *British Journal of Psychiatry*, 162, 118–121.

Conway, M., Mendelson, M., Giannopoulos, C., Csank, P. A. R., & Holm, S. L. (2004). Childhood and adult sexual abuse, rumination on sadness and dysphoria. *Child Abuse and Neglect*, 28, 393–410.

Conway, M. A., & Pleydell-Pearce, C. W. (2000). The construction of autobiographical memories in the self-memory system. *Psychological Review*, 107, 261–288.

Dalgleish, T., Spinks, H., Yiend, J. & Kuyken, W. (2001). Autobiographical memory style in seasonal affective disorder and its relationship to future symptom remission. *Journal of Abnormal Psychology*, 110, 335–340.

de Decker, A., Hermans, D., Raes, F., & Eelen, P. (2003). Autobiographical memory specificity and trauma in inpatient adolescents. *Journal of Clinical and Child Adolescent Psychology*, 32, 22–31.

Eldridge, M., Barnard, P., & Bekerian, D. (1994). Autobiographical memory and daily schemas at work. *Memory*, 2, 51–74.

Ellis, H. C., & Moore, B. A. (1999). Mood and memory. In M. Power & T. Dalgleish (Eds.), *Handbook of cognition and emotion* (pp. 193–210), Chicester, UK: Wiley.

Evans, J., Williams, J. M. G., O'Loughlin, S., & Howells, K. (1992). Autobiographical memory and problem solving strategies of parasuicide patients. *Psychological Medicine*, 22, 399–405.

Goddard, L., Dritschel, B., & Burton, A. (1996). Role of autobiographical memory in social problem-solving and depression. *Journal of Abnormal Psychology, 105,* 609–616.

Goddard, L., Dritschel, B., & Burton, A. (1997). Social problem-solving and autobiographical memory in non-clinical depression. *British Journal of Clinical Psychology, 36,* 449–451.

Harvey, A. G., Bryant, R. A., & Dang, S. T. (1998). Autobiographical memory in acute stress disorder. *Journal of Consulting and Clinical Psychology, 66,* 500–506.

Harvey, A., Watkins, E., Mansell, W., & Shafran, R. (2004). *Cognitive behavioural processes across psychological disorders: A transdiagnostic approach to research and treatment.* Oxford, UK: Oxford University Press.

Hermans D., van den Broeck K., Belis G., Raes F., Pieters G., & Eelen P. (2004). Trauma and autobiographical memory specificity in depressed inpatients. *Behaviour Research and Therapy, 42,* 775–789.

Ingram, R. E. (1990). Self-focused attention and clinical disorders: Review and a conceptual model. *Psychological Bulletin, 107,* 156–176.

Ingram, R. E., & Smith, T. S. (1984). Depression and internal versus external locus of attention. *Cognitive Therapy and Research, 8,* 139–152.

Just, N., & Alloy, L. B. (1997). The response styles theory of depression: Tests and an extension of the theory. *Journal of Abnormal Psychology, 106,* 221–229.

Kuehner, C., & Weber, I. (1999). Responses to depression in unipolar depressed patients: An investigation of Nolen-Hoeksema's response styles theory. *Psychological Medicine, 29,* 1323–1333.

Kuyken, W., & Brewin, C. R. (1995). Autobiographical memory functioning in depression and reports of early abuse. *Journal of Abnormal Psychology, 104,* 585–591.

Lane, R. D., Quinlan, D. M., Schwartz, G. E., Walker, P. A., & Zeitlin, S. B. (1990). The levels of emotional awareness scale: A cognitive developmental measure of emotion. *Journal of Personality Assessment, 55,* 124–134.

Lane, R. D., & Schwarz, G. E. (1987). Levels of emotional awareness: A cognitive-developmental theory and its application to psychopathology. *American Journal of Psychiatry, 144,* 133–143.

Lyubomirsky, S., & Nolen-Hoeksema, S. (1995). Effects of self-focused rumination on negative thinking and interpersonal problem solving. *Journal of Personality and Social Psychology, 69,* 176–190.

McFarland, C., & Buehler, R. (1998). The impact of negative affect on autobiographical memory: The role of self-focused attention to moods. *Journal of Personality and Social Psychology, 75,* 1424–1440.

McNally, R. J., Litz, B. T., Prassas, A., Shin, L. M., & Weathers, F. W. (1994). Emotional priming of autobiographical memory in post-traumatic stress disorder. *Cognition and Emotion, 8,* 351–367.

McNally, R. J., Lasko, N. B., Macklin, M. L., & Pitman, R. K. (1995). Autobiographical memory disturbance in combat-related posttraumatic stress disorder. *Behaviour Research and Therapy, 33,* 619–630.

Mackinger, H. F., Pachinger, M. M., Leibetseder, M. M., & Fartacek, R. R. (2000). Autobiographical memories in women remitted from major depression. *Journal of Abnormal Psychology, 109,* 331–334.

Nelson, H. (1982). *The national adult reading test (NART).* Windsor, UK: NFER.

Nolen-Hoeksema, S. (1991). Responses to depression and their effects on the duration of depressive episodes. *Journal of Abnormal Psychology, 100,* 569–582.

Nolen-Hoeksema, S. (2000). The role of rumination in depressive disorders and mixed anxiety/depressive symptoms. *Journal of Abnormal Psychology, 109,* 504–511.

Nolen-Hoeksema, S., Morrow, J., & Fredrickson, B. L. (1993). Response styles and the duration of episodes of depressed mood. *Journal of Abnormal Psychology, 102,* 20–28.

Peeters, F., Wessel I., Merckelbach, H., & Boon-Vermeeren, M. (2002). Autobiographical memory specificity and the course of major depressive disorder. *Comprehensive Psychiatry, 43,* 344–350.

Pollock, L. R, & Williams, J. M. G. (2001) Effective problem solving in suicide attempters depends on specific autobiographical recall. *Suicide and Life Threatening Behaviour*, 31, 386–396.

Pyszczynski, T., & Greenberg, J. (1987). Self-regulatory perseveration and the depresssive self-focusing style: A self-awareness theory of reactive depression. *Psychological Bulletin*, 102, 122–138.

Raes, F., Hermans, D., & Eelen, P. (2003, May). Correlates of autobiographical memory specificity in major depression: Rumination, trauma and general cognitive functioning. Presentation at the Third Special Interest Meeting on Autobiographical Memory and Psychopathology, Le Lignely, Belgium, 2003.

Ramponi, C., Barnard, P., & Nimmo-Smith, I. (2004). Recollection deficits in dysphoric mood: An effect of schematic models and executive mode? *Memory*, 12, 655–670.

Spasojevic, J., & Alloy, L. B. (2001). Rumination as a common mechanism relating depressive risk factors to depression. *Emotion*, 1, 25–37.

Teasdale, J. D. (1999). Emotional processing, three modes of mind, and the prevention of relapse in depression. *Behaviour Research and Therapy*, 37, S53–S77.

Teasdale, J. D., & Barnard, P. J. (1993). *Affect, cognition and change: Re-modelling depressive thought*. Hove: Erlbaum.

Trapnell, P. D., & Campbell, J. D. (1999). Private self-consciousness and the five-factor model of personality: Distinguishing rumination from reflection. *Journal of Personality and Social Psychology*, 76, 284–304.

Treynor, W., Gonzalez, R., & Nolen-Hoeksema, S. (2003). Rumination reconsidered: A psychometric analysis. *Cognitive Therapy and Research*, 27, 247–259.

Watkins, E. (2004). Adaptive and maladaptive ruminative self focus during emotional processing. *Behaviour Research and Therapy*, 42, 1037–1052.

Watkins, E., & Baracaia, S. (2002). Rumination and social problem-solving in depression. *Behaviour Research and Therapy*, 40, 1179–1189.

Watkins, E., & Moulds, M. (2005). Distinct modes of ruminative self-focus: Impact of abstract versus concrete rumination on problem solving in depression. *Emotion*, 5, 319–328.

Watkins, E., & Teasdale, J. D. (2001). Rumination and overgeneral memory in depression: Effects of self-focus and analytic thinking. *Journal of Abnormal Psychology*, 110, 353–357.

Watkins, E. R., & Teasdale, J. D. (2004). Adaptive and maladaptive self-focus in depression. *Journal of Affective Disorders*, 82, 1–8.

Watkins, E. R., Teasdale, J. D., & Williams, R. M. (2000). Decentering and distraction reduce overgeneral autobiographical memory in depression. *Psychological Medicine*, 30, 911–920.

Williams, J. M. C. (1996). Depression and the specificity of autobiographical memory. In D. C. Rubin (Ed.), *Remembering our past: Studies in autobiographical memory* (pp. 244–267). Cambridge, UK: Cambridge University Press.

Williams, J. M. G., & Broadbent, K. (1986). Autobiographical memory in suicide attempters. *Journal of Abnormal Psychology*, 95, 144–149.

Williams, J. M. G., & Dritschel, B. (1992). Categoric and extended autobiographical memories. In M. A. Conway, D. C. Rubin, H. Spinnler, & W. A. Wagenaar (Eds.), *Theoretical perspectives on autobiographical memory* (pp. 391–412). Dordrecht, the Netherlands: Kluwer.

Retrieval of autobiographical memories: The mechanisms and consequences of truncated search

J. Mark G. Williams, Stella Chan, Catherine Crane, and Thorsten Barnhofer
University of Oxford, UK

Jess Eade and Helen Healy
University of Wales, Bangor, UK

Five studies examined the extent to which autobiographical memory retrieval is hierarchical, whether a hierarchical search depends on central executive resources, and whether retrieving memories that are "higher" in the hierarchy impairs problem-solving ability. The first study found that random generation (assessed using a button-pressing task) was sensitive to changes in memory load (digit span). The second study showed that when participants fail to retrieve a target event, they respond with a memory that is higher up the hierarchy. The third study showed that memory is more generic only when participants use low imageable cues under cognitive load. The final two experiments showed that experimental manipulation of memory specificity affects problem solving (MEPS performance). The data are consistent with Conway and Pleydell-Pearce's hierarchical retrieval model of autobiographical memory, and suggest that overgeneral memory in nonclinical participants is associated with reduced executive capacity only when retrieval is "top-down" (generative).

The aim of this article is to elucidate the mechanisms underlying the retrieval of specific and general autobiographical memories and to examine their causal role in affecting other aspects of cognition. Our interest derives from the repeated observation that clinical groups have difficulty in recollecting specific autobiographical events. They tend to respond with memories which summarise a category of events rather than selecting one particular instance of an event. This phenomenon first reported by Williams and Broadbent (1986) has been found

---

Correspondence should be addressed to Professor Mark Williams, University Department of Psychiatry, Warneford Hospital, Oxford, OX3 7JX, UK; e-mail: mark.williams@psych.ox.ac.uk

This research was supported by the Wellcome Trust (GR06779 (University of Oxford) and by the Medical Research Council (University of Bangor; Grant No G9621313). Special thanks to Paul Wallace who carried out some of the testing in Bangor.

© 2006 Taylor & Francis
DOI: 10.1080/02699930500342522

many times in depressed and other clinical groups (see Williams, 2004 for a review). Whatever the origins of such a deficit, it has been suggested that it has a number of important consequences, for example, reducing an individual's ability to imagine a specific future (Williams et al., 1996) and prolonging episodes of affective disturbance (Brittlebank, Scott, Williams, & Ferrier, 1993; Dalgleish, Spinks, Yiend, & Kuyken, 2001; Peeters, Wessel, Merckelbach, & Boon-Vermeeren, 2003; although see Brewin, Reynolds, & Tata, 1999 for an exception). Of all the consequences of overgeneral memory, the most commonly reported has been its association with poorer interpersonal problem solving as assessed by the Means Ends Problem Solving (MEPS) task (Evans, Williams, O'Loughlin, & Howells, 1992, Goddard, Dritschel, & Burton, 1996; Pollock & Williams, 2001; Sidley, Whitaker, Calam, & Wells, 1997). Unfortunately, the majority of these studies have been correlational in nature, so the causal status of the overgenerality of memory remains unknown.

We wish to test several hypotheses regarding the mechanisms underlying overgeneral memory: that it arises because retrieval involves search through a hierarchy; that such memory represents truncated search in circumstances in which retrieval is effortful; and that when we experimentally manipulate retrieval so that individuals recall memories from different levels in the hierarchy, then we can observe changes in problem solving performance that mimic those seen in clinical groups. We start, then, with the issues of mechanism.

Previous attempts to explain overgenerality in retrieval have suggested that it is a trait avoidant cognitive style resulting from a previous trauma (Brewin, Watson, McCarthy, Hyman, & Dayson, 1998; Kuyken & Brewin, 1994). While there is accumulating evidence to support this hypothesis (see Williams 2004 for a review), it cannot be the whole story. First, regarding the state-trait issue, there is evidence that overgenerality in memory can be manipulated both by manipulations that reduce ruminative thinking (e.g., Watkins & Teasdale, 2001), and by psychological treatment (Serrano, Latorre, Gatz & Rodriguez, 2005; Williams, Teasdale, Segal, & Soulsby, 2000). Second, regarding the "avoidant" issue, such memory deficits have also been observed in the normal elderly (Winthorpe & Rabbitt, 1988) where they correlate with working memory capacity, raising the possibility that such capacity limitations might also contribute to the lack of specificity in autobiographical recall (Williams, 1996). A related phenomenon is that reported by Ellis and Ashbrook (1988), Hertel and Hardin (1990), and Hertel (1998) who suggest that depressed subjects show poor memory in nonautobiographical tasks also because of limited resources.

Why would such capacity limitations make autobiographical memory more overgeneral, rather than merely slowing retrieval? Barsalou (1988) suggested that generic concepts are often better established in memory than exemplars, so that such summarisations become increasingly more accessible (needing less cognitive effort to retrieve) than a particular event memory. In fact, there are now a number of models of autobiographical memory that assume that strategic memory retrieval is a *staged* process in which an individual first derives an intermediate description of the to-be-recalled information, and that this initial description is then used to search for candidate episodes which fit the description. According to this view, specificity of output reflects different levels in the hierarchy (see Figure 1). Such a "descriptions framework" (first proposed by Norman & Bobrow, 1979) has influenced a number of models of event retrieval (Conway, 1990; Conway & Rubin, 1993; Reiser, Black, & Abelson 1985; Williams, 1996; Williams & Hollan 1981). Its clearest recent statement is to be found in Conway and Pleydell-Pearce's (2000) model of the working self-concept and autobiographical memory. However, despite this convergence of views about the hierarchical, staged, nature of voluntary memory retrieval, there is little direct evidence for it, nor for the notion that search through the hierarchy is effortful. One exception is the study by Haque and Conway (2001) who interrupted cued autobiographical retrieval after 2, 5, or 30 seconds. They found that early interruption resulted in the output of more general memories, but only if participants were also engaged in a secondary task (the AH4 intelligence test).

In the following studies, we wished more directly to test hypotheses relating to the way individuals are proposed to search autobiographical memory. The first preparatory study examines the effects of varying memory load (digits) on a random button-pressing task to test the sensitivity of random generation as a measure of executive capacity. In our second study, we test the hierarchical model of retrieval by examining the pattern of "errors" that are made when individuals fail to hit the designated target retrieval category. We show that

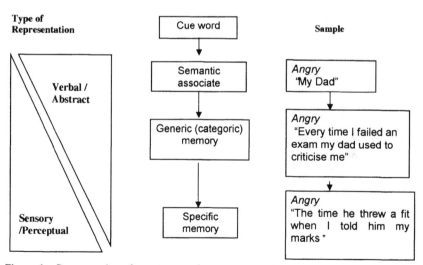

Figure 1. Representation of memory search processes (Williams, Barnhofer, Crane, Hermans, Raes, Watkins, & Dalgleish, 2006).

when participants fail to achieve the target, their errors fall systematically into the category that is "higher" in the hierarchy. We use the random button-pressing task to show that retrieving autobiographical memories in response to word cues reduces capacity in general, but that use of different targets and variation of cue imageablity do not differentially affect the secondary task.

In our third study, we examine the effect of performing the autobiographical memory task in a standard dual task paradigm: that is, with and without the secondary task of random button pressing. Low and high imageable cues are used to manipulate participants' retrieval strategy (generative vs. direct). We show that memory becomes less specific under dual task conditions only in the generative (low imageable cue) condition.

In Studies 5 and 6 we examine the effects of experimentally manipulating the "hierarchical" memory output (categoric vs. specific) on problem-solving performance. We show that whether output is manipulated by using specific vs. generic instructions (as in Study 2) or by using high vs. low imageable cues (as in Study 3) we can observe effects on problem-solving performance.

All the studies use analogue populations—students from the Universities of Bangor or Oxford, and unless otherwise stated, we used the Autobiographical Memory Task as first used by Williams and Broadbent (1986). Main effects and interactions identified in analyses of variance were followed up with planned comparisons or, where the comparisons were not specified a priori, with Bonferroni-corrected pairwise comparisons.

STUDY 1

The main goal of the first experiment was to test the sensitivity of a task that we wished to use as a measure of cognitive load: A random generation task. Random generation (of letters or numbers) has often been used as a measure of central executive capacity, since it involves holding material in working memory to avoid repetitive or habitual responding (such as "a, b, c" or "2, 4, 6"). The problem with such random number or letter generation tasks is that they involve speech, so that they cannot be used alongside other tasks that also involve verbal output, such as memory retrieval. Baddeley (1996) suggested that presenting a keyboard with 10 keys labelled 0–9 could also be used as a measure of central executive capacity. Such manual responding also demands that individuals remember their recent key presses in order to inhibit any tendency to give patterned, habitual responses.

Before using this task alongside the autobiographical memory task, we wanted to check if it was sensitive to cognitive load. To this end, participants were given four digit span tasks (with digit sequences varying in length: two, four, six, and eight). This task was performed singly and concurrently with the random key-pressing task. We predicted that the heavier processing load of increasing digit sequences should result in a systematic reduction in the randomness of responses generated concurrently.

Method

Participants

A total of 20 participants were recruited, 16 women and 4 men, and the mean age was 29 years.

Materials

A specially constructed keyboard was used to run the random key-pressing task. This keyboard measured 57 cm × 70 cm and contained two groups of five keys, one for each hand. The keys were 2 cm wide and 1.3 cm apart. The keyboard was connected to a Macintosh Computer which generated a pacing tone (one per second) and recorded each keypress. The keys were numbered 0–9 inclusive. Pilot testing had indicated that asking participants to respond with a key press at a rate of one per second yielded randomisation scores that were close to the mean for other published data (Evans, 1978).

Memory span task. This task was an immediate verbal memory task consisting of digit lists which varied from 2 to 8 digits. There were 5 conditions, baseline (no load), 2, 4, 6, and 8 digits and participants were requested to recall the different lists of digits. This task was performed singly and concurrently with the secondary task of random key pressing.

Measure of randomness. As an index of the randomisation of the 100 digits generated using the keyboard, Evans (1978) index of randomisation (RNG) was calculated.[1] This measure of randomness is adapted from Tulving's (1962) subjective organisation index of clustering in free recall and takes account of overuse of repeated pairs of sequences of digits. Responses are entered into a 10 × 10 matrix reflecting the frequency with which any digit follows any other digit in 100 consecutive responses. The (RNG) index can range in value from 0 to 1. Evans (1978) reported mean RNG from a number of samples of subjects based on 100 numbers produced at the rate of one per second as .300 ($SD = 0.045$). Higher RNG values reflect more habitual "clustering" of responses, so *lower* levels of randomness.

---

[1] There are a number of ways to assess randomness. We piloted tested 6 parameters: chi square, mean difference, auto correlation index, Evans RNG, triplets, and a phase measure. We found that Evans RNG was the most sensitive to differences between human participants and computer-generated or tabled random numbers (Healy, 1997, pp. 161–163). This replicated previous findings (Spatt & Goldenberg, 1993) so we used the RNG measure.

Procedure

The testing session began with an explanation of randomness followed by a brief practice at generating single key responses using the keyboard. Participants were given the following instructions:

> You may be familiar with the concept of randomness. For example, if you were to throw a dice many times, each of the six numbers on the dice would occur in random sequence. Similarly if you imagine that there is a hat in front of you containing these keys numbered 0–9, and that you select a key one at a time and call out the number. That key is replaced in the hat and this procedure repeated until 100 random numbers have been called. Your task is to press the numbered keys in a similar random fashion, in response to a tone that the computer makes. You must try to pace your responses with the tone. If you should find yourself ahead or behind the tone just try to get into pace with it again. Remember that 0 is a real number and use the full range of keys from 0–9 inclusive.

This explanation and instruction was followed by a brief practice at generating single key presses at the rate of one every second using the keyboard. A baseline trial was then completed whereby participants performed the random key-pressing task alone.

Digit span. The following instructions were given:

> I will be calling out different lists of numbers to you. Some of these lists contain 2 digits, others have 4, 6 and 8 digits. I will call out these digits to you and your task is to repeat the digits back to me at the same rate. For example take the 4 digit case, I will call out 7 1 4 9, and you repeat those numbers back to me. If you are unable to recall a number just say blank.

This was followed by practice trials with each of the five digit memory loads, then the task itself started, the procedure being repeated using different numbers for each trial, and with the order of the digit span task being counterbalanced with half the group commencing the digit span task in ascending order (0,2,4,6,8) and the other half commencing in reverse order (8,6,4,2,0). Participants were randomly allocated to one of two conditions: to perform the memory span task at each sequence length with or without concurrent keyboard generation (in counterbalanced order). The task continued until 130 s had elapsed, so that the maximum number of key presses was 130 for each digit span length, and so that, allowing for omissions, 100 key presses could be recorded in order to generate a reliable index of randomness in each condition. In addition, the number of omissions was recorded as an additional index of cognitive load (i.e., as an indicator of participants becoming slower at the task or deviating from the requirement to generate key presses at a regular rate).

Results and discussion

The influence of concurrent digit span on random keyboard generation was analysed in a one-way analysis of variance incorporating the five memory load conditions (see Figure 2). This demonstrated a clear effect of trial condition, $F(4, 18) = 14.03$, $p < .001$. Planned comparisons between conditions indicated that the zero load condition was more random than the 4, 6, or 8 digit condition ($p < .01$). The two digit condition was more random then than 6 or 8 digits ($p < .01$), the 2, 4 digit, and 6 digit were more random than the 8 digit ($p < .01$). In addition to variation in randomness, there was a difference across digit load conditions in proportions of omissions: baseline, $M = 1.7$ (2.9); two digit: $M = 10.4$ (7.1); four digit: $M = 12.7$ (7.5); six digit: $M = 15.8$ (6.8), and eight digit: $M = 18.9$ (7.5) $F(4, 19) = 48.8$; $MS_e = 17.5$, $p < .001$. Planned comparisons shows that omissions in the baseline condition were less than in all other conditions ($p < .001$). Omissions in the eight digit condition were greater than in the two, four, and six digit conditions ($p < .01$). There were also a difference between the six digit and the four digit conditions ($p < .01$).

These findings are consistent with our prediction following Baddeley (1996) and replicate the results of Baddeley, Emslie, Kolodny, and Duncan (1998). The greater the length of a concurrent digit sequence, the poorer the performance on the random key-pressing task as indexed both by a randomisation index and proportion of omissions. Thus, the key-pressing version of the traditional random generation task can be regarded as a sensitive measure of variation in task-processing demands. Having established that the secondary task of random key pressing is a sufficiently sensitive index of cognitive load, the following two

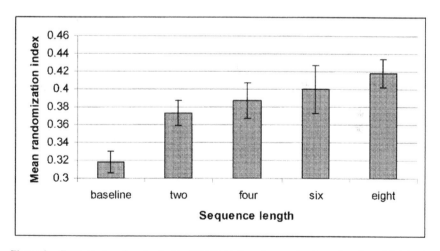

Figure 2. Evans' index of randomisation (RNG) (higher = less random) as a function of digit load.

studies use this secondary task to examine the differential effort involved in retrieving autobiographical memories.

Note that this task has the advantage for autobiographical memory studies in that it can act both as indicator of extent of central executive resources that are being used while retrieving, and can be used in a dual task paradigm to deliberately *interfere* with memory retrieval (where both single and dual conditions are used). In Study 2, we use random generation as an indication of extent of resource usage, and in Study 3, we use it in a fully dual task paradigm.

STUDY 2

There are three predictions of the hierarchical model that we wished to test in this study. First, if memory search involves "staged" progression through a hierarchy, then if search is too effortful, so that a participant cannot retrieve the type of memory required, then their response should reflect an "earlier" stage in retrieval. So if participants are unable to access a specific memory they will truncate their search at a general memory, and if even this proves difficult, will truncate the search earlier at a personal semantic memory.

Second, if less executive capacity is required to access a general memory, because it is "higher" in the hierarchy, then there should be less disruption to the random button-pressing task if participants are given the task of retrieving a general memory. Participants were asked to retrieve *general* memories for half the trials and to retrieve *specific* events for the other half. In this way, we hoped to see whether varying the "stage" in the hierarchy that was the "target" of retrieval would affect the random secondary task. We predicted that a "general" target, being higher in the hierarchy, should be easier to accomplish, and therefore be associated with greater randomness.

Third, all participants were given cue words that varied in their imageability—high versus low. We have found that highly imageable cues are more likely to produce specific memories (Williams, Healey, & Ellis, 1999). This is because the word is likely to evoke a visual image that provides a discriminable and constructible cue, an analogue representation of the object, rather than its verbal label. If such cues make it easier to search memory, then participants should find that with high imageable cues they are more able to maintain their random generation performance than if they are searching for the same target (e.g., a specific event) using a low imageable cue.

Method

Participants

There were 37 individuals taking part in this experiment, 25 women and 12 men with an average age of 28 years (18–45 years).

Materials

Autobiographical Memory Test (AMT). In this version of the AMT, participants were required to recall events that had happened to them, in response to high and low imageable cues. The time period from which events could be recalled was not specified and participants were told that the event could be important or trivial, in the recent past or a long time ago. There were two instructional conditions. In the *Specific* condition, it was emphasised that each event retrieved should be a specific event (a particular event that lasted less than one day). In the *Generic* condition, it was emphasised that what was required was a *type* of event or a series of events. A total of 40 cues was used in a completely within-subject design (four conditions: specific instructions with high and low imageable cues and generic instructions using high and low imageable cues). The cues used in the autobiographical memory tests are shown in the Appendix. All participants were given practice trials to ensure familiarity with the test.

Key-pressing task. This followed the same procedure as in Study 1, with practice trials being given to ensure familiarity with the task and each of the four conditions involving 130 s (130 potential key presses).

Procedure

Participants were given practice trials to ensure familiarity with the key-pressing task. In the AMT, participants were given 10 s to respond to each cue and if they failed to respond within that time the following cue was called after an interval of 3 s (130 s in all).[2] A baseline condition (no memory task) was given to participants before embarking on the counterbalanced experimental (memory and concurrent key-pressing task) conditions. In the concurrent task subjects were requested to press the keys as randomly as possible whilst retrieving memories in response to the cue words spoken aloud by the examiner.

Results

The patterns of memories retrieved are shown in Table 1. Participants' responses were divided into the different types of memories retrieved. These include the number of specific memories (e.g., *Happy*—the day my teacher gave me an A

---

[2] Note that this time limit is less than that usually required for the AMT. For this study, we had been concerned that a longer time interval might allow too much time when the participant would not need to be retrieving. The disadvantage of this procedure is that mental effort of retrieval is confounded with the effort of reporting. However, there is no way of avoiding this unless the randomisation task stops when the participant begin to respond. Given the need to collect 100 responses to generate a reliable index of randomness, we decided to give participants cue words in relatively quick succession.

TABLE 1
Pattern of retrieval, means and (standard deviations) in the autobiographical Memory Test (AMT): Study 2

Cue imageability	Instruction			
	Be specific		Be general	
	High	Low	High	Low
Memory output				
Omissions	0.38 (0.6)	1.75 (1.8)	0.22 (0.6)	0.84 (1.2)
Semantic	0.32 (0.7)	0.86 (1.2)	3.38 (1.8)	5.35 (2.7)
Categoric	1.95 (1.7)	2.97 (1.8)	4.76 (1.8)	3.10 (2.1)
Specific	7.35 (1.9)	4.40 (2.2)	1.59 (1.3)	0.51 (1.2)

grade), categoric memories ("every time I got good marks for my English at school"), semantic memories ("Mrs Jones, my English teacher") and omissions.[3]

Specific memories. The results of a 2 × 2 ANOVA showed a main effect of type of instruction, $F(1, 36) = 176.00, p < .001$, and a main effect of imageability, $F(1, 36) = 77.14, p < .001$. More specific memories were retrieved following specific instructions and in response to high imageable cues. A significant interaction was also found between instructions and imageability, $F(1, 36) = 19.39, p < .001$, due to the larger difference between high and low imageable cues when participants were given instructions to be specific than when given instructions to be general. Although this interaction may result from a floor effect in the specific category when participants have been asked to be general, the result of interest for our hypothesis is the significant difference between the number of specific memories under high and low imageability cue conditions.

Categoric memories (see Table 1). The results of a similar 2 × 2 ANOVA showed a significant effect of instructions, $F(1, 36) = 13.53, p < .001$, and a significant interaction was found between instruction × imageability, $F(1, 36) =$

---

[3] The following procedure was used to establish the reliability of the AMT for this series of studies. The experimenter's (H.H.) ratings for a random sample of 10 participants for a prior experiment involving 18 cues varying in imageability and valence from the same database (180 responses in all) were given to an independent rater who was blind to the experimental hypotheses. This yielded a reliability coefficient of .82, comparable with previous studies in our laboratory. This experimenter's ratings were then used for Studies 2 and 3. If there were any responses for which H.H. had doubts, she consulted with J.M.G.W. who gave a decision remaining blind to the treatment condition of the participant.

30.75, $p < .001$. Planned comparisons showed that more categoric memories were retrieved in response to high imageable cues following instructions to be general than to be specific ($p < .01$) whereas for low imageable cues this difference was not significant. Also, significantly more categoric memories were retrieved to high imageable cues than to low imageable cues following instructions to be general.

Personal semantic memories. The results of a 2 × 2 ANOVA show significant effects of both instruction, $F(1, 36) = 185.10$, $p < .001$, and of imageability, $F(1, 36) = 28.12$, $p < .001$. More personal semantic memories were retrieved in response to low imageable cues and when participants were instructed to be general. A significant interaction was found between type of instruction and imageability, $F(1, 36) = 12.82$, $p < .01$. Planned comparisons show that following instructions to be general more semantic memories were retrieved in response to low imageable cues compared to the number of semantic memories retrieved in response to high imageable cues ($p < .001$).

Omissions. A 2 (instructions -specific and general) × 2 (imageability -high and low) ANOVA where the dependent variable was the number of omissions on the autobiographical memory task showed a significant effect of imageability, $F(1, 36) = 19.58$, $p < .001$, and a significant effect of instruction, $F(1, 36) = 19.27$, $p < .001$. Overall, there were more omissions to low imageable cues and following instructions to be specific. A significant interaction was also found between instruction × imageability, $F(1, 36) = 6.88$, $p < .05$. Planned comparisons reveal that participants made a significantly greater number of omissions to low imageable cues following specific instructions compared to the other conditions ($p < .01$).

Random generation measure. A one-way ANOVA was performed where Evans' RNG was the dependent variable. There was a significant main effect for condition, $F(4, 33) = 16.20$, $p < .001$. Planned comparisons showed that the difference between baseline and cued memory trials all reached significance ($p < .01$) suggesting that the randomness at baseline (button pressing without the AMT, $M = 0.30$) was significantly greater when compared to randomness when concurrent with the AMT (overall $M = 0.37$). However, no significant differences in randomness were shown within the four autobiographical memory conditions ($Ms = 0.38, 0.37, 0.36$, and 0.37 for the four conditions: specific instructions (high and low imageability); and generic instructions (high and low imageability), respectively.

Omissions during the key-pressing task were also examined. Although omissions differed between baseline key pressing and concurrent key pressing (1% vs. 16.5%; $F(4, 31) = 42.9$, $p < .01$), there was no difference in omissions between the four different memory conditions (16.1%, 18.1%, 16.2%, and

15.9% omission for the four conditions, respectively). A 2 (Memory instruction; specific or general) × 2 (cue type; high imageable or low imageable) ANOVA with Evans' RNG as the dependent variable was not significant neither for the instruction manipulation nor the imageability manipulation ($F < 1$ in both cases.)

Discussion

The first aim of this study was to examine whether patterns of errors on the AMT would conform to a hierarchical model. We predicted that where individuals failed to retrieve a specified target memory, they would output a memory that was "higher" in the hierarchy. This is indeed the pattern of data that was obtained. If asked to be general in their retrieval output, participants were able to produce more categoric memories as requested. However, when the cues were low in imageability, retrieval appeared to be more difficult, and there was a shift to retrieve more personal semantic memories, as predicted by a hierarchical model. This pattern is also evident when participants are asked to retrieve specific memories. If given high imageable cues, participants have little difficulty in complying. If cues are low in imageability, however, there is a shift towards the retrieval of more categoric memories. For each instruction condition, therefore, the modal response is to retrieve the category of memory requested, but for low imageable cues, there is a shift towards the category that is at an earlier, "higher" stage in the memory hierarchy. So far, this is consistent with a hierarchical model.

Second, we wished to examine the effect of the retrieval of specific and general autobiographical memories on a secondary task. The hierarchical model predicts that, because the retrieval of specific autobiographical memories is a more effortful process than the retrieval of general autobiographical memories, this effort would be reflected by a decrement in randomness in memory trials where participants were instructed to retrieve specific memories. No such effect was found. We also predicted that retrieval using high imageable cues would be less effortful (as shown in less interference with random generation) than retrieval using low imageable cues. Once again, no such effect was found.

Why, given the evidence of hierarchical search in the pattern of errors, was there no effect of memory retrieval condition on the secondary task? Although a significant difference in randomness was demonstrated between baseline trials (no retrieval) and autobiographical memory trials, no difference within autobiographical memory conditions was apparent despite our knowing that the secondary task is highly sensitive to differing cognitive load (Study 1).

A first possibility is that the design of our experiment prevented any such effect from emerging. Note that we used a time limit for each memory cue of 10 s with an interval to the next cue of only 3 s. Thus memory retrieval may be confounded with memory reporting. Our intention was to keep the participants in retrieval mode for 130 s (the time need to collect 100 key presses for evaluating randomisation) by the relatively rapid presentation of cues. But with such short intervals, much of the time was taken up with reporting, rather than retrieval, and autobiographical memory theory makes no predictions about the cognitve load that is involved in reporting a memory that has already been retrieved.[4]

A second possibility is that participants "traded off" effort on one task with the other. Analysis of omissions on the autobiographical memory task is consistent with such a strategy. There were more omissions when participants were requested to retrieve specific memories in response to low imageable cues. This trial condition was predicted to be the most difficult so the increased omissions may have enabled participants to maintain performance on the key-pressing task during completion on the autobiographical memory task.

Could it be that such a "trade-off" was adopted across the board between performance on the primary autobiographical memory task and the random key-pressing task? By opting to select memories further up the hierarchy of autobiographical memory, participants may have maintained randomness by the deployment of such a "truncated search" strategy. Because we did not include a condition where the AMT was used *without* random button pressing (i.e., the full "dual task paradigm"), we cannot test this hypothesis in this study. This was the aim of Study 3.

STUDY 3

In this study, participants performed the standard autobiographical memory test (AMT) (with instructions to be specific) *both* as a single task *and* in trials combined with the concurrent key-pressing task. This allows us to see whether autobiographical memory retrieval, when accompanied by a secondary task, is more categoric than when done without an additional load. What predictions can be made for such a dual task experiment—under what circumstances do we predict interference?

Although most explanations of overgeneral memory are derived from hierarchical "descriptions theory", Conway and Pleydell-Pearce (2000) make clear that we need to make a distinction between generative (top-down) and direct (bottom-up) retrieval. Generative retrieval involves the intentional, staged search that uses abstract general descriptions referred to by Norman and Bobrow (1979) and Burgess and Shallice (1996). It is this top-down, strategic retrieval that is usually invoked to explain overgeneral memory (Williams, 1996). By contrast, direct retrieval is "bottom up", is more likely to involve sensory and perceptual cues (see Figure 1), and arises because some cues can activate event specific knowledge directly, experienced as spontaneous and unexpected recall, see Williams, 2004, for a review).

---

[4] We are grateful to an anonymous reviewer for this suggestion.

It is possible that highly imageable cues (such as *butterfly* or *mountain*) activate *direct* retrieval because they may rapidly evoke a visual image, activating a perceptual/sensory analogue of the cue's referent—such a cue is more like actually *seeing* a butterfly (see Conway & Fthenaki, 2000, for a discussion of the role of imagery in direct retrieval of autobiographical memory and its disruption by brain damage). If so, then memory cued by high imageable words will be relatively immune to disruption by secondary tasks. By contrast, if low imageable cues invoke top-down, generative retrieval, they should be susceptible to disruption. According to the hierarchical search model, such disruption should be evident in decreased specificity of the recalled memories.

The results of a previous study by Goddard, Drischel, and Burton (1998) is consistent with this hypothesis. They also used a dual task paradigm to explore the effects of cognitive load on autobiographical memory. They used a four-choice reaction time task as the concurrent task. This was found to interfere with memory retrieval, with more extended memories being recalled in the "easy" dual task condition, and more categoric memories in the "difficult" dual task condition.[5]

Method

Participants

There were 26 participants in this experiment; 19 females and 7 males ranging in age from 18 to 45 years.

Materials

The random button-pressing task was as used in Study 2.

Autobiographical memory Test (AMT). Participants were required to recall events that had happened to them, in response to high and low imageable cues under single and dual task conditions, in counterbalanced order (in a within-subject design). The time period from which events could be recalled was not specified and participants were told that the event could be important or trivial. It was emphasised that each event retrieved should be a specific event (a particular event that lasted less than 1 day). Three cues were used for each memory condition: (a) task performed alone; and (b) task combined with the key pressing. Participants were asked to retrieve specific memories of past events in response to high imageable (*butterfly, mountain, cloud, house, painting, fire*) or low imageable (*wisdom, attitude, moral, boredom, explanation, obedience*) cue

---

[5] For a reason that remained unclear, this effect was only found in male participants by Goddard et al. In the current study we were unable to recruit sufficient male participants to be able to verify whether our results interacted with gender.

words. For this study, participants were allowed 30 s to respond to each cue, the more commonly used time interval for the AMT.

Procedure

All participants were given practice trials for both key pressing and memory, alone and together, to ensure familiarity with the task. A total of 130 s were allocated for each trial of three cue word presentations (3 × 30 s each trial = 120 s, with 10 s allowed for presentation of cues).[6]

Results

Evans' index of randomisation (RNG) was treated as the dependent variable in a one way analysis of variance incorporating baseline measures of randomness and two autobiographical memory conditions. A main effect of trial condition was shown, $F(1, 22) = 15.43$, $p < .001$. Planned contrasts demonstrated significant differences between the randomness of sequences generated at baseline, without concurrent AMT ($M = 0.32$; $SD = 0.1$) and those trials where participants completed the AMT concurrently ($M = 0.39$, $SD = 0.1$; $p < .001$). As in Study 2, there were no significant differences in the randomness of sequences between the autobiographical memory tests cued by high vs. low imageable cues ($M_{high} = 0.38$, $SD = 0.1$; $M_{low} = 0.40$, $SD = 0.1$).

Key press omissions. As in Study 2, there was a large and significant difference in omission rate when key pressing was performed alone (1.3%), than when it was performed concurrently with the AMT: 9.6%; $F(4, 22) = 12.97$, $MS_e = 31.22$, $p < .001$. A 2 (memory instruction; specific or general) × 2 (imageability; high and low) ANOVA was computed with percentage of omissions as the dependent variable. There was no significant effect of instructions or cue imageability. This suggests that the amount of cognitive effort involved was the same for all retrieval conditions. The next analysis therefore focused on whether the secondary task affected memory specificity, and in which condition.

The results for specificity of autobiographical memories retrieved when the autobiographical memory task was performed as a single task and concurrently with the key pressing task are shown in Figure 3. Specificity scores were computed based on criteria specified by Baddeley and Wilson (1986): with a specific response scoring 3 points, an extended response scored 2 points, a categoric response 1 point, and omissions scored 0 (there were very few

---

[6] Note that this design does not deal with the possible confounding of retrieval and reporting noted for Study 2, though the proportion of time allocated to retrieval overreporting should be relatively greater in this present study.

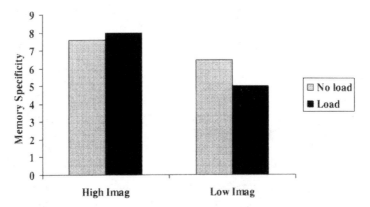

Figure 3. Effect of cognitive load (random button pressing) on specificity of autobiographical memory retrieval.

semantic associates). A 2 × 2 ANOVA was performed in which imageability (high and low) and trial condition (single and combined) were treated as within-subject variables. A main effect of imageability was shown, $F(1, 25) = 58.98$, $p < .001$, with higher specificity scores being associated with high imageable cues. There was no main effect of condition (single vs. combined; $F(1, 25) = 3.92$, $p > .05$). However, the predicted interaction between cue imageability and trial condition was significant, $F(1, 25) = 8.50$, $p < .01$. Planned comparisons showed that memories with lower specificity scores were retrieved in response to low imageable cues in dual task conditions ($M = 5.0$, $SD = 2.0$) than in single task conditions ($M = 6.5$, $SD = 1.4$; $p < .01$). Omission scores were low and not significantly different between the four conditions (less than 1% of responses).

We next examined the distribution of memory types (specific, extended, and categoric) that accounted for this pattern of data. These are shown in Table 2. As can be seen, the reduced specificity associated with low imageable cues (versus high imageable cues) under dual task conditions arose from an excess of extended memories.

Discussion

The results were consistent with the data from Goddard et al. (1998), and with our prediction that trials where participants were instructed to retrieve specific memories in response to low imageable cues (generative retrieval) would be most affected by cognitive load. Goddard et al. (1998) found a similar effect using choice reaction time as a concurrent task, but only in male participants. We found a similar effect using predominantly female participants, though one difference in outcome of the two studies was that the effect of cognitive load in the present study was to switch memory towards extended retrieval and away

TABLE 2
Pattern of retrieval (mean specificity scores and proportions) of autobiographical memory in Study 3

	Task	
Imageability	Single	Combined
High		
Specific	7.7 (85%)	8.04 (89%)
Extended	0.75 (8%)	0.26 (3%)
Categoric	0.60 (7%)	0.70 (8%)
Low		
Specific	6.5 (72%)	5.01 (56%)
Extended	0.5 (6%)	1.99 (22%)
Categoric	2.0 (22%)	2.0 (22%)

from specific retrieval when cue imageability was low. The fact that nonspecificity under these conditions was attributable to increased extended memories was unexpected, but consistent with an emerging pattern of data with nonclinical participants that nonspecificity can arise from a number of different types of response in the AMT (see general discussion). In both studies, however, cognitive load had the effect of reducing specific memory. By contrast, cognitive load had no effect when imageability was high. This is consistent with the hypothesis that high imageable cues invoke direct retrieval.

Studies 2 and 3 provide some evidence consistent with the hypothesis that memory search is a staged, hierarchical process. Although we have not found the predicted effects of memory retrieval or differential "effort" of retrieval on random button pressing as an index of executive capacity, our data suggest that if people cannot output the required memory, they tend to respond with a memory that is "higher" in the hierarchy (or earlier in the search), consistent with a truncated search model. Further, under circumstances when they are retrieving using a generative, hierarchical search, retrieval can be interfered with by a cognitive load. When such interference occurs, the result is reduced specificity.

What consequences does such truncated search have? Of all its potential effects, one of the most consistent suggestions to emerge from the literature is that overgeneral memory is associated with poorer problem solving (Evans et al., 1992; Goddard et al., 1996; Pollock & Williams, 2001; Sidley, Whitaker, Calam, & Wells, 1997; Williams, Barnhofer, Crane, & Beck, 2005). The suggestion has been that since strategic access to specific representations of past events is a critical aspect of fluent problem solving, anything that blocks such access is going to have direct effects on how easily effective solutions come to mind in such tasks as the Mean Ends Problem Solving (MEPS) task. However, with the exception of the Goddard et al. (1998) study that attempted to block access to specific memory experimentally, these studies are correlational in nature. It remains possible that overgeneral memory correlates with poor problem solving because it is a proxy for some other variable.

Perhaps the best candidate for such a third variable is rumination. Nolen-Hoeksema and colleagues have found that experimental induction of rumination reduced problem solving (Lyubomirsky & Nolen-Hoeksema, 1995) and Watkins and Baracaia (2002) found that inducing participants to ask ruminative "Why?"-type questions *during* a problem-solving task interfered with performance compared to asking "How?" questions. How might rumination affect problem solving? In an ingenious series of studies, Watkins and colleagues have shown that rumination is closely associated with categoric retrieval (Watkins, Teasdale & R.M. Williams, 2000). They find that reducing rumination by distraction or by experiential (as opposed to analytic) self-focus results in more specific memories (Watkins & Teasdale, 2001). Watkins' research raises the possibility that in addition to any direct effect of rumination on problem solving (e.g., through a reduction in available cognitive capacity, or an increase in mood disturbance), it may also affect problem solving by reducing specificity of memory: If people truncate their search through memory and output a memory that is "higher" in the hierarchy, then this may be sufficient to impair problem solving. Of course, this would not imply that there were not many others ways in which problem solving could be affected, but at the moment we have no evidence for a causal link between memory specificity and problem solving.[7]

Studies 4 and 5 examine the hypothesis that experimental manipulation of specificity of memory will affect problem solving. Study 4 was conducted several years ago, and used cue word imageability to manipulate memory specificity in a within-subject design. Because it was conducted before several recent studies, it reflects the methods used at that time to score memory and problem solving. Although the results clearly supported our predictions, we felt that we needed to replicate them using alternative ways of manipulating memory specificity and more recently developed ways of testing and scoring memory and problem solving—so we conducted Study 5 to replicate the effects. This used a between-subject design, and manipulated memory by direct instruction.

---

[7] Interestingly, although this was not known when these studies were designed, Watkins and Moulds (in press) have now found a direct link between type of self-focus and problem solving. In clinically depressed patients, a self-focus manipulation (derived from Nolen-Hoeksema & Morrow's 1991 rumination manipulation), previously found to increase specific autobiographical memory recall, improved the effectiveness of problem solving, relative to a self-focus manipulation known to reduce specific autobiographical memory recall (Watkins & Teasdale, 2001, 2004). Importantly, in this study, the specificity of mental representations for the problems produced by the different manipulations mediated their effect on problem solving, indicating a causal link between memory specificity and problem solving.

STUDY 4

Method

Participants

These were 20 undergraduates (5 women and 15 men), mean age was 25 years ($SD = 5.51$).

Design

A within-subject design was used in which all participants were given both high and low imageable cues to manipulate memory specificity. In order to maximise the influence of the induction it was interleaved with the problem-solving task.

Memory induction

Participants were given the standard instructions for the AMT (Williams & Broadbent, 1986), except that the level of specificity was left open. Each participant was given nine high imageable cue words (in 3 blocks of three words), and nine low imageable cue words (3 blocks of three words), in counterbalanced order. After each block of three words participants completed an individual MEPS item (see Table 3).

Manipulation check

To ensure that the memory manipulation had been effective, mean levels of memory specificity were compared for responses to the high and low imageability cues. Specificity of memory was scored based on a modified version of

TABLE 3
Sequence of cue words and means End Problem Solving (MEPS) task items: Study 4

Butterfly	Thought
Mountain	Greed
Cloud	Moral
MEPS Item (1)	MEPS item (4)
House	Attitude
Painting	Wisdom
Fire	Obedience
MEPS item (2)	MEPS item (5)
Grass	Explanation
Library	Boredom
Letter	Hearing
MEPS item (3)	MEPS item (6)

Baddeley and Wilson (1986): 3 points were given for a specific response, 2 points for a categoric response, 1 point for a semantic associate, with omissions scored 0 (there were very few extended memories).[8] Each participant recalled memories to nine high imageability and nine low imageability cues (max. specificity score for each condition = 27). Responses were analysed using a one-way t-test for repeated measures. As predicted, cueing by high imageability words resulted in participants recalling more specific memories ($M = 20.3$, $SD = 2.6$) than did cueing by low imageability words ($M = 13.45$, $SD = 2.06$, $t = 16.83$, $p < .0001$).

Means End Problem Solving (MEPS) Task

A written, first-person format of the MEPS was used. All participants were required to provide answers to six MEPS situations (randomly ordered: these were about having arguments with a partner, losing a watch during shopping, making friends in a new neighbourhood, having trouble getting along with a supervisor, being attracted to someone at a party, and feeling disliked by friends), presented verbally by the experimenter. In each case, the participants was given the beginning and (successful) end of the story, and asked to say how the protagonist achieved their goal. Participants were given 3 min to complete their response. Between each MEPS item, participants were presented with three cues from the Autobiographical Memory Test (AMT), counterbalancing high and low imageability, so that by the end of the experiment, three MEPS items had followed high imageable cues (specific induction) and three MEPS items had followed low imageable cues (generic induction; see Table 3).

The scoring of the MEPS test followed criteria set out by Marx, Williams, and Claridge (1992). Points were awarded for both quantitative and qualitative aspects of participants' solutions. Number of *relevant means* refers to the number of discrete steps that enabled the protagonist of the story to reach a specified goal. One point was awarded for each step. *Specificity* ratings were evaluated using a scale ranging from 1 (not at all specific) to 3 (very specific; total score for each condition = 9). *Effectiveness* was scored using a 7-point scale, ranging from 1 (not at all effective) to 7 (extremely effective; total score for each condition = 21). D'Zurilla and Goldfried's (1971) definition of effective problem solving was adopted: A solution is deemed effective if it maximises positive short- and long-term consequences and minimises negative short-and long-term consequences, both personally and socially.

---

[8] Note that this scale is different to that used in Study 3. However, note that in this case we are not interested in these data as a measure of outcome, but only to check that the induction had worked.

Results and discussion

Effect of memory induction on MEPS task performance

The effect of memory induction on problem solving was evaluated using a within-subject ANOVA. For *Relevant Means*, there was no main effect for induction, $F(1, 18) = 2.44$, $p = .14$. For *Specificity*, a significant main effect was found for induction, $F(1, 18) = 12.5$, $p = .002$. MEPS solutions following the use of high imageable cues in the memory induction phase ($M = 7.5$; $SD = 1.03$) were significantly more specific than solutions provided following induction ($M = 6.30$, $SD = 1.34$). For *Effectiveness* a significant main effect was found for induction, $F(1, 18) = 8.61$, $p = .009$, MEPS solutions provided following the use of high imageable cues in the memory induction phase ($M = 12.4$, $SD = 2.83$) were significantly more effective than solutions provided following the use of low imageable cues during memory induction ($M = 10.10$, $SD = 2.56$).

The results of this study provided good preliminary evidence that overgenerality in memory has a causal effect on the quality of problem solving. However, in this study we used imageability as our method of inducing generic vs. specific memory retrieval styles. It is possible that the mere act of being exposed to highly imageable cues has a direct effect on MEPS performance. Further, there was no independent check for the reliability of coding effectiveness of problem solving. Is this finding replicable using a different method of analogising truncated search and with the appropriate check on the reliability of problem solving performance?

STUDY 5

Method

Participants

These were 40 undergraduate and graduate students (25 women, 15 men). The mean age of the sample was 24.44 years ($SD = 3.13$). There was no significant difference in age or sex distribution between individuals allocated to the generic and specific induction conditions. One female participant allocated to the generic induction condition failed to follow the experimental instructions and was eliminated from the analyses.

Design

The study employed a mixed between (2 groups: specific and generic induction) × within (pre-post) design with problem solving being tested both before after the memory induction procedure.

Memory induction

Each participant was randomly allocated to receive either a specific or a generic memory induction with seven males allocated to each group. Participants were presented with a list of 12 cue words in a questionnaire format (4 positive, 4 negative, 4 neutral words) and asked to *write down* a memory for each one. Participants were given one minute for each cue. In the *specific* induction condition, they were asked to retrieve an event that lasted less than a day and occurred at a particular time and place. Participants were instructed that the event could have occurred at any time during their life, excluding the day of the experimental session. In the *generic* condition participants were asked to write a description of the *type of* event that the cue reminded them of. This was defined as "the sort of event that happens or has happened in the past". In both cases, examples of an appropriate and an inappropriate response were provided as outlined below:

Specific induction. For the cue word "unhappy" it would be ok to write "*Sitting having coffee on my first day at university on my own*", but it would not be ok to write "*Every time I have coffee on my own in a café*", because this does not refer to a specific event.

Generic induction. For the cue word "unhappy" it would be ok to write "*I feel bad when my brother and I don't get along*", but it would not be ok to write "*I was unhappy when my brother and I fought last night*" because this refers to one particular occasion that made you unhappy rather than the type of thing which makes you unhappy in general.

Prior to completing the task participants were given a practice item to ensure that they understood the instructions.

MEPS task

Two versions of the MEPS task were created, each with three items, with one version presented prior to ("pretest") and once following ("posttest") the manipulation of memory specificity, counterbalanced across participants. Before completion of the "pretest" participants completed one practice item to familiarise them with the task. Participants were given 2 min for each individual problem, after which they were asked by the experimenter to finish their sentence and move on to the next item.

Each problem solution was rated with respect to the number of *relevant means* it contained, its *effectiveness* (1–7 scale) and the degree of *specificity* with which the problem solution was described (in this study using a 1–7 scale). An independent rater, blind to participant group, rated a random sample of 20% of the responses. Kappa coefficients for reliability were .92 for number of relevant means, .73 for effectiveness and .60 for specificity, indicating adequate reliability on all three measures.

Manipulation check

To ensure that the memory manipulation had been effective, mean levels of memory specificity were compared in the two experimental induction conditions. The mean number of specific memories produced by participants in the specific induction condition was $M = 11.25$ ($SD = 1.21$) out of a possible 12, in contrast to a mean of $M = 0.00$ ($SD = 00$) specific memories produced by participants in the generic induction condition. The mean number of categoric memories produced by participants in the specific induction condition was $M = 0.20$ ($SD = 0.52$), in contrast to a mean of $M = 9.16$ ($SD = 3.40$) categoric memories produced by participants in the generic induction condition. The majority of noncategoric responses made by participants in the generic induction group took the form of semantic associations $M = 2.58$ ($SD = 3.49$). Univariate analysis of variance indicated that there was a significant difference between groups in memory specificity, $F(1, 37) = 492.67, p < .001$.

Results

Effect of memory induction on MEPS task performance

Table 4 shows the mean scores on each measure of problem-solving performance in the generic and specific induction groups for Study 5. To examine the effect of the memory induction on problem-solving performance a repeated measures analysis of variance was computed with time (pre-induction, post-induction) and MEPS measure (relevant means, effectiveness, specificity) as within-subjects factors, with induction group (generic, specific) and sex as the between-subjects factors. Analysis revealed a main effect of time resulting from the fact that across the sample as a whole problem-solving performance declined from the pre-induction to the post-induction test phase, $F(1, 35) = 10.31, p < .01$. However, this effect was qualified by a significant interaction between time and group, $F(1, 35) = 5.70, p < .05$, and a significant interaction between time and sex, $F(1, 35) = 6.01, p < .05$. There were no other significant two-way or three-way interactions. Post hoc Bonferroni corrected pairwise comparisons indicated that although there were no significant differences between the generic and specific groups in problem-solving performance either before or after the memory induction, the individuals receiving the generic induction declined significantly in problem solving from the pretest to the posttest ($p < .001$). In contrast, individuals completing the specific induction did not change in problem-solving performance ($p > .5$). The significant interaction between time and

TABLE 4
Means and (standard deviations) for problem-solving measures following generic or specific memory induction: Study 5

	Generic			Specific		
	Pre-	Post-	Change	Pre-	Post-	Change
No. of means	5.61 (1.10)	5.00 (1.04)	−0.61	4.98 (1.01)	5.00 (1.26)	+0.02
Effectiveness (max = 7)	4.89 (0.76)	4.40 (1.14)	−0.49	4.63 (0.70)	4.41 (1.17)	−0.22
Specificity (max = 7)	5.28 (0.73)	4.93 (0.94)	−0.35	5.03 (0.67)	5.13 (0.81)	+0.10

sex resulted from the fact that, across the group as a whole, whilst there was no significant difference between males and females pre-induction, males deteriorated in performance from pre-induction to post induction testing in general ($p < .01$), whereas females showed no significant change. As a consequence males performed significantly more poorly overall than females at post-induction testing ($p < .05$). Finally there was also a main effect of measure, $F(2, 70) = 15.20$, $p < .001$, resulting from the fact that across the study as a whole, individuals had higher scores for the measures of number of relevant means and specificity than for effectiveness. However the absence of both a two-way interaction between time and measure and a three-way interaction between time, measure, and group, suggests that the pattern of differential decline in problem solving performance from the pre-test to the post-test under generic and specific induction conditions was similar for the three measures of problem solving performance.

To examine whether memory overgenerality was in fact responsible for the decline in problem solving performance observed in the generic group, correlations were computed between the total memory specificity score of memories produced in the memory induction immediately prior to the MEPS posttest, and the measures of posttest problem-solving performance for the data in Study 5. These correlations are shown in Table 5. These confirmed that the lower the specificity of memory following the generic induction, the worse the problem-solving performance on the MEPS (number of means and effectiveness). The repeated-measures analysis of variance, described above, was repeated including memory specificity immediately prior to the MEPS posttest as a covariate. Following the addition of this covariate the main effects of time and measure, as well as the interaction between time and group were no longer significant, supporting the suggestion that induced memory overgenerality was responsible for the poorer post-induction problem-solving performance of the generic

TABLE 5
Correlations between memory specificity and post-induction measures of problem-solving effectiveness in individuals receiving the generic memory induction (n = 19)

	Post-number of means	Post-effectiveness	Post-specificity
Memory specificity score	.57**	.45*	.38

*$p \leq .05$; **$p \leq .01$.

induction group.[9] The interaction between time and sex ($p < .05$) remained significant suggesting that it may be accounted for by other factors (e.g., greater deteriorations in effort in males relative to females across the experimental session). Finally, analysis indicated a significant main effect of group, resulting from the fact that individuals allocated to the generic induction condition displayed better overall problem-solving performance than individuals allocated to the specific induction condition once memory specificity was entered as a covariate $F(1, 34) = 5.52, p < .05$.

Discussion

The aim of Studies 4 and 5 was to examine the causal relation between autobiographical memory that is "higher" in the hierarchy and problem-solving ability. Both studies found that experimental manipulation that induced participants to retrieve more or less specific memories made these participants more or less fluent in their problem-solving ability. The fact that this effect can be seen in a within-subject design shows that problem solving is extremely sensitive to temporary changes in mode of memory retrieval. Further, the fact that memory can have such an effect on problem solving when manipulated *either* by high vs. low imageable cues, *or* by directly instructing participants to retrieve specific or categoric memories suggests that the effects seen are not linked only to a particular experimental method, but validly reflect the effect of specificity of memory on problem solving.

This is, to our knowledge, the first study to show definitively that memory retrieval from higher in the hierarchy has a causal effect on problem solving. This does not, of course, mean that memory specificity is the only, or even the main way in which problem solving can become impaired. However, it shows that people need good strategic access to a specific database if their problem solving is to be fluent. If the sort of truncated search examined in Studies 2 and 3

---

[9] Ideally, a formal test of mediation would be conducted to examine the impact of memory induction condition on problem-solving performance. However, in the current study, because the memory induction was so successful, induction condition and memory specificity were completely confounded, with very little nonoverlapping variance to be explained.

becomes chronic, then it is highly likely to have important consequences for the onset and maintenance of emotional disorders.

GENERAL DISCUSSION

The aim of this series of studies was to examine the possible mechanisms underlying autobiographical memory search. There has long been an assumption that strategic search in memory is a hierarchical staged process, but with the exception of a few studies, there had been little direct evidence for this assumption. We tested the hierarchical model of retrieval by examining the pattern of "errors" that are made when individuals fail to hit the designated target retrieval category. We found that when participants fail to achieve the target type of memory, their errors fall systematically into the category that is "higher" in the hierarchy, at an earlier intermediate stage. A random generation task performed concurrently with the Autobiographical Memory Test showed that autobiographical retrieval reduced executive capacity in general, but that altering the target of retrieval (specific, generic) or cue imageablity did not differentially affect the secondary task. We speculated that this was because people traded off performance on memory in order to maintain randomness. In our third study we examined the effect of performing the autobiographical memory task in a standard dual task paradigm: that is, with and without the secondary task of random button pressing. We predicted that interference from the secondary task would be shown only when participants were engaged in top-down "generative" retrieval. Low and high imageable cues were used to manipulate participants' retrieval strategy (generative vs. direct, respectively). We found that memory became more generic under dual task conditions only in the generative (low imageable cue) condition. In our final two studies we examined the effects on problem-solving performance of experimentally manipulating the "hierarchical" memory output (categoric vs. specific). We found that when memory is manipulated to be more generic, problem solving is impaired, compared to the level of problem solving following specific retrieval or baseline performance.

Before discussing these results, it is important to point out the limitations of the studies. First, the fact that we found no effect of cue imageability on random generation, nor an effect on randomness of asking participants to retrieve specific vs. generic memories may reflect the insensitivity of the random button-pressing task. Other secondary tasks might have been used, and further research is required to check the effect of using different working memory tasks. However, the fact that randomness was found to be affected by differences in memory load (digit span) was some reassurance that the task was sufficiently sensitive to cognitive effort being expended on other tasks. Nevertheless, we must be cautious in concluding that there was unequivocal support for the hierarchical model of retrieval. Some of the results were consistent with hypotheses, others were not. Note also that these pattern of results are consistent with the view that some modes of retrieval *are* more effortful, but not necessarily because memory is hierarchical. It is possible that retrieval (or reconstruction) of some types of event simply requires more resources in *selecting* from a relatively "flat" structure (i.e., a person has difficulty in choosing from a number of response options). Nevertheless, in any circumstances in which there are response options, and some responses are easier to retrieve than another, interference is likely selectively to impair retrieval under certain conditions, and we still need to know what the *consequences* of such bias in retrieval output may be for other tasks such as problem solving.

Second, the explanation for the lack of effect of memory on randomness; that individuals were able to sustain randomness by changing the effort expended on the memory task, must remain speculative until this is studied in its own right. Such a study would need to include a range of different levels of difficulty of both primary and secondary tasks, and experimental manipulation of which task is designated as the primary task and which is secondary. Only in this way can one properly examine a hypothesis of "trade-off" between tasks.

Third, the effect of memory on problem solving was measured using the MEPS, and this task can be criticised for its artificiality. Nevertheless, performance on the MEPS has been found to correlate with the way individuals approach their real-life problems (Marx et al, 1992). Further, the association of overgeneral memory with poor planning and problem-solving in the real world has been found by Hutchings, Nash, Williams, and Nightingale (1998), who studied mothers whose young children had been referred to a Child Guidance Centre for behavioural problems. Those with overgeneral retrieval style were more likely to fail to attend their appointment. Even so, there are many other factors that are likely to affect problem solving in addition to memory. The claim of Studies 4 and 5 is not that memory is the only contributor, but that it is one of them, and it has a causal link with problem solving.

We turn now to discussion of the results. If they prove reliable in replication studies they will provide important support for Conway and Pleydell-Pearce's model, and for those models of memory that assume that voluntary retrieval is hierarchical, that it starts with elaborating the cue, and moves through generating generic descriptions to more specific mnemonic material, using both extended event time-lines (Barsalou, 1988) and categories of events (Norman & Bobrow, 1979). Note that the nonspecificity we found in Study 3 under generative retrieval/high load conditions came about as the results of increases in extended memories. To date, most interest has focused on categoric type of overgeneral memories because of the finding (e.g., Williams & Dritschel, 1988) that, in *clinical* groups, it is the categoric type of error that accounts for overgenerality (but see Williams, Williams, and Ghadiali, 1998, for an exception). However, in *nonclinical* groups the differences between different types of nonspecificity is not so clear-cut. In normal controls, nonspecificity can arise from a number of sources. Raes, Hermans, Williams, and Eelen (this Issue) suggest that different types of nonspecificity may emerge in a developmental sequence, with more adaptive (affect regulating) nonspecificity arising early. At this early stage, more avoidant nonclinical participants respond to cues with a variety of responses that simply share the characteristic of avoiding a specific response. This adaptive nonspecificity may give way later in the developmental sequence to more habitual categoric responses that are maladaptive in the long term, because inter alia of their downstream effects on problem solving. Establishing a causal link between this maladaptive "categoric" responding and problem solving was the aim of Studies 4 and 5. Together, they provided strong evidence of a direct causal link between categoric recall and impaired problem solving.

Figure 1 makes clear that both verbal/analytic subsystems and sensory/perceptual subsystems are used during retrieval (Conway & Pleydell Pearce, 2000). Early on in retrieval, more semantic processing is involved, with sensory/perceptual code being used later in the process. Conway and Pleydell-Pearce also assume, as do other models of retrieval, that setting up the retrieval specification at the earliest stage is effortful, and will use central executive capacity. Consistent with this, studies of young children and of elderly and brain damaged groups show that the ability to be specific in retrieval of events develops during the third and fourth years of life, and that this ability is impaired by reduced working memory capacity in ageing and in brain damage (Williams, 1996). The research reported here was motivated by the finding of Winthorpe and Rabbitt (1988) that elderly participants who had reduced working memory capacity (assessed using a sentence span task) were more likely to be overgeneral in their recall of events from their lives. Goddard et al. (1998) used a choice reaction time as a secondary task in normal participants and found that the secondary task increased overgeneral memories, but only when the task was more difficult.

However, it remains true that the research that has examined "reduced capacity" accounts is not yet giving a consistent picture. First, correlations between number of overgeneral memories and tasks that are sensitive to executive capacity (such as verbal fluency) are relatively low in normal participants (Williams & Dritschel, 1992) and do not differ between suicidal and matched control groups (MacLeod, Pankhania, Lee, & Mitchell, 1997; Williams & Broadbent, 1986). On the other hand, Dalgleish and colleagues (Dalgleish, 2004) have found that reduced specificity of autobiographical memory is closely associated with errors on cognitive tasks that represent "goal neglect"—the loss of task pragmatics due to reduced executive capacity. An example of this would be a person giving an illegitimate response on a verbal fluency task (*generate as many words as you can in a minute beginning with "s"*) by saying not only swim (legitimate) but then also "swimmer, swimming, swims". This represents a type of goal neglect in which a person fails to inhibit plausible but incorrect candidates. Could it be, then, that executive capacity accounts for overgeneral memory only under certain conditions?

Note that the studies that have found evidence that capacity limits are important determinants of autobiographical memory performance tend to use nonclinical participants—people who have not been referred with a clinical diagnosis. As seen in our discussion of different types of nonspecificity earlier, we see here also that, in clinical groups, a slightly different picture may emerge from that found in nonclinical groups. There is accumulating evidence that people with affective disorders (major depression, bipolar disorder), eating disorder and posttraumatic stress disorder show overgeneral memory, and that such overgenerality is associated with a history of trauma such as sexual or physical abuse (see Williams 2004 for a review). Furthermore, in these groups, there is little or no evidence that degree of memory overgenerality correlates with severity of mood disturbance (Hutchings et al., 1998; Jones et al., 1999; Kuyken & Brewin, 1995; Peeters et al., 2003; Phillips & Williams, 1997; Williams & Broadbent, 1986; and Williams et al., 1996). This suggests that in addition to the acute effects of limited executive capacity (on nonspecificity arising from a number of sources), there may also be a more trait-like effects in which overgeneral (categoric) memory occurs as the outcome of a developmental sequence that started as a functional response in order to regulate affect (Williams et al., 2006). Further research will need to be done to determine the relative contribution of affective/motivational explanations for non-specificity and the contribution of reduced executive resources.

REFERENCES

Baddeley, A. (1996). Exploring the central executive. *Quarterly Journal of Experimental Psychology, 49A*, 5–28.

Baddeley, A., Emslie, H., Kolodny, J., & Duncan, J. (1998) Random generation and the executive control of working memory. *Quarterly Journal of Experimental Psychology, 51A*, 819–852.

Baddeley, A. D., & Wilson, B. (1986). Amnesia, autobiographical memory, and confabulation. In D. C. Rubin (Ed.), *Autobiographical memory* (pp. 225–252). Cambridge, UK: Cambridge University Press.

Barsalou, L. W. (1988). The content and organization of autobiographical memories. In U. Neisser & C. E. Winograd (Eds.), *Remembering reconsidered: Ecological and traditional approaches to the study of memory* (pp. 193–243). Cambridge, UK: Cambridge University Press.

Brewin, C. R., Reynolds, M., & Tata, P. (1999). Autobiographical memory processes and the course of depression. *Journal of Abnormal Psychology, 108*, 511–517.

Brewin, C. R., Watson, M., McCarthy, S., Hyman, P., & Dayson, D. (1998). Intrusive memories and depression in cancer patients. *Behaviour Research and Therapy, 36*, 1131–1142.

Brittlebank, A. D., Scott, J., Williams, J. M. G., & Ferrier, I. N. (1993). Autobiographical memory in depression: State or trait marker? *British Journal of Psychiatry, 162*, 118–121.

Burgess, P. W., & Shallice, T. (1996). Confabulation and the control of recollection. *Memory, 4*, 359–411.

Conway, M. A. (1990). *Autobiographical memory: An introduction*. Buckingham, UK: Open University Press.

Conway, M. A., & Fthenaki, A. (2000). Disruption and loss of autobiographical memory. In F. Boller & J. Grafman (Eds.), *Handbook of neuropsychology* (2nd ed., pp. 281–312). Amsterdam: Elsevier Science.

Conway, M. A., & Pleydell-Pearce, C. W. (2000). The construction of autobiographical memories in the self- memory system. *Psychological Review, 107*, 261–288.

Conway, M. A. & Rubin, D. C. (1993). The structure of autobiographical memory. In A. F. Collins & S. E. Gathercole (Eds.), *Theories of memory* (pp. 103–137). Hove, UK: Erlbaum.

Dalgleish, T. (2004, May). *Emotional autobiographical memories, depression, and goal neglect.* Keynote address at the First European CERE conference on emotions. University of Amsterdam, The Netherlands.

Dalgleish, T., Spinks, H., Yiend, J., & Kuyken, W. (2001). Autobiographical memory style in seasonal affective disorder and its relationship to future symptom remission. *Journal of Abnormal Psychology, 110*, 335–340.

D'Zurilla, T., & Goldfried, M. R. (1971). Problem solving and behavior modification. *Journal of Abnormal Psychology, 78*, 107–126.

Ellis, H. C., & Ashbrook, P. W. (1988). Resource allocation model of the effects of depressed mood states on memory. In K. Fiedler & J. Forgas (Eds.), *Affect, cognition and social behavior* (pp. 25–43). Toronto: Hogrefe.

Evans, F. J. (1978). Monitoring attention deployment by random number generation: An index to measure subjective randomness. *Bulletin of the Psychonomic Society, 12*, 35–38.

Evans, J., Williams, J. M. G., O'Loughlin, S., & Howells, K. (1992). Autobiographical memory and problem-solving strategies of parasuicide patients. *Psychological Medicine, 22*, 399–405.

Goddard, L., Dritschel, B., & Burton, A. (1996). Role of autobiographical memory in social problem solving and depression. *Journal of Abnormal Psychology, 105*, 609–616.

Goddard, L., Dritschel, B., & Burton, A. (1998). Gender differences in the dual-task effects on autobiographical memory retrieval during social problem solving. *British Journal of Psychology, 89*, 611–627.

Haque, S., & Conway, M. A. (2001). Sampling the process of autobiographical memory construction. *European Journal of Cognitive Psychology, 13*, 529–547.

Healy, H. (1997) *Determinants of specificity in autobiographical memory.* PhD Thesis, University of Wales, Bangor, UK.

Hertel, P. T. (1998). Relation between rumination and impaired memory in dysphoric moods. *Journal of Abnormal Psychology, 107*, 166–172.

Hertel, P. T., & Hardin, T. S. (1990). Remembering with and without awareness in a depressed mood: Evidence of deficits in initiative. *Journal of Experimental Psychology: General, 119*, 45–59.

Hutchings, J., Nash, S., Williams, J. M. G., & Nightingale, D. (1998). Parental autobiographical memory: Is this a helpful clinical measure in behavioural child management? *British Journal of Clinical Psychology, 37*, 303–312.

Jones, B., Heard, H., Startup, M., Swales, M., Williams, J. M. G., & Jones, R. S. P. (1999). Autobiographical memory and dissociation in borderline personality disorder. *Psychological Medicine, 29*, 1397–1404.

Kroll, N. E. A., Markowitsch, H. J., Knight, R. T., & van Cromon, D. Y. (1997). Retrieval of old memories: the temporo-frontal hypothesis. *Brain, 1120*, 1377–1399.

Kuyken, W., & Brewin, C. R. (1995). Autobiographical memory functioning in depression and reports of early abuse. *Journal of Abnormal Psychology, 104*, 585–591.

Lyubomirsky, S., & Nolen-Hoeksema, S. (1995). Effects of self-focused rumination on negative thinking and interpersonal problem solving. *Journal of Personality and Social Psychology, 69*, 176–190.

MacLeod, A. K., Pankhania, B., Lee, M., & Mitchell, D. (1997). Parasuicide, depression and the anticipation of positive and negative future experiences. *Psychological Medicine, 27*, 973–977.

Marx, E. M., Williams, J. M. G., & Claridge, G. C. (1992). Depression and social problem solving. *Journal of Abnormal Psychology, 101*, 78–86.

Norman, D. A., & Bobrow, D. G. (1979). Descriptions: An intermediate stage in memory retrieval. *Cognitive Psychology, 11*, 107–123.

Peeters, F., Wessel, I., Merckelbach, H., & Boon-Vermeeren, M. (2003). Autobiographical memory specificity and the course of major depressive disorder. *Comprehensive Psychiatry, 43*, 344–350.

Phillips, S., & Williams, J. M. G. (1997). Cognitive impairment, depression and specificity of autobiographical memory in the elderly. *British Journal of Clinical Psychology, 36*, 341–347.

Pollock, L. R., & Williams, J. M. G. (2001). Effective problem solving in suicide attempters depends on specific autobiographical recall. *Suicide and Life-Threatening Behavior, 31*, 386–396.

Raes, F., Hermans, D., de Decker, A., Eelen, P., & Williams, J. M. G. (2003). Autobiographical memory specificity and affect regulation: An experimental approach. *Emotion, 3*, 201–206.

Reiser, B. J., Black, J. B., & Abelson, R. P. (1985). Knowledge structures in the organization and retrieval of autobiographical memories. *Cognitive Psychology, 17*, 89–137.

Serrano, J. P., Latorre, J. M., Gatz, M., & Rodriguez, J. M. (2004). Life Review Therapy using autobiographical retrieval practice for older adults with depressive symptomatology. *Psychology and Aging, 19*, 272–277.

Sidley, G. L., Whitaker, K., Calam, R., & Wells, A. (1997). The relationship between problem-solving and autobiographical memory in parasuicide patients. *Behavioural and Cognitive Psychotherapy, 25*, 195–202.

Spatt, J., & Goldenberg, G. (1993) Components of random generation ny normal subjects and patients with disexecutive syndrome. *Brain and Cognition, 23*, 231–242.

Tulving, E. (1962). Subjective organization in free recall of 'unrelated' words. *Psychological Review, 69*, 344–354.

Watkins, E., & Baracaia, S. (2002). Rumination and social problem-solving in depression. *Behaviour Research and Therapy, 40*, 1179–1189.

Watkins, E., & Teasdale, J. D. (2001). Rumination and overgeneral memory in depression: Effects of self-focus and analytic thinking. *Journal of Abnormal Psychology, 110*, 353–357.

Watkins, E., Teasdale, J. D., & Williams, R. M. (2000). Decentring and distraction reduce overgeneral autobiographical memory in depression. *Psychological Medicine, 30*, 911–920.

Williams, J. M. G. (1996). Depression and the specificity of autobiographical memory. In D.C.Rubin (Ed.), *Remembering our past: Studies in autobiographical memory* (pp. 244–267). Cambridge, UK: Cambridge University Press.

Williams, J. M. G. (2004). Experimental cognitive psychology and clinical practice: Autobiographical memory as a paradigm case. In J.Yiend (Ed.), *Cognition, emotion and psychopathology* (pp. 251–269). Cambridge, UK: Cambridge University Press.

Williams, J. M. G., Barnhofer, T., Crane, C., & Beck, A. T. (2005). Problem solving deteriorates following mood challenge in formerly depressed patients with a history of suicidal ideation. *Journal of Abnormal Psychology, 114*, 421–431.

Williams, J. M. G., Barnhofer, T., Crane, C., Hermans, D., Raes, F., Watkins, E., & Dalgleish, T. (2006). *Autobiographical memory specificity and emotional disorders*. Manuscript submitted for publication.

Williams, J. M. G., & Broadbent, K. (1986). Autobiographical memory in suicide attempters. *Journal of Abnormal Psychology, 95*, 144–149.

Williams, J. M. G., & Dritschel, B. (1992). Categoric and extended autobiographical memories. In M.A.Conway, D. C. Rubin, H. Spinnler, & W. A. Wagenaar (Eds.), *Theoretical perspectives on autobiographical memory* (pp. 391–410). Dordrecht: Kluwer.

Williams, J. M. G., Ellis, N. C., Tyers, C., Healy, H., Rose, G., & MacLeod, A. K. (1996). The specificity of autobiographical memory and imageability of the future. *Memory and Cognition, 24*, 116–125.

Williams, J. M. G., Healy, H., & Ellis, N. C. (1999). The effect of imageability and predicability of cues in autobiographical memory. *Quarterly Journal of Experimental Psychology, 52A,* 555–579.

Williams, J. M. G., Teasdale, J. D., Segal, Z. V., & Soulsby, J. (2000) Mindfulness-Based Cognitive Therapy reduces overgeneral autobiographical memory in formerly depressed patients. *Journal of Abnormal Psychology, 109,* 150–155.

Williams, M. D., & Hollan, J. D. (1981). Processes of retrieval from very long-term memory. *Cognitive Sciences, 5,* 87–119.

Williams, W. H., Williams, J. M. G., & Ghadiali, E. J. (1998) Autobiographical memory in traumatic brain injury: Neuropsychological and mood predictors of recall. *Neuropsychological Rehabilitation, 8,* 43–60.

Winthorpe, C., & Rabbitt, P. A. (1988). Working memory capacity, IQ, age, and the ability to recount autobiographical events. In M. M. Gruneberg, P. E. Morris, & R. N. Sykes (Eds.), *Practical aspects of memory: Current research and issues* (Vol. II, pp. 175–179). Chichester, UK: Wiley.

APPENDIX
Cues used in the Autobiographical Memory Test: Study 2

Instruction			
Be specific		*Be general*	
High	Low	High	Low
Factory	Knowledge	Butterfly	Obedience
Teacher	Upkeep	Mountain	Explanation
Baby	Worth	Cloud	Boredom
Nun	Malice	House	Hearing
Poetry	Ability	Painting	Legislation
Robbery	Mood	Fire	Thought
Sea	Permission	Grass	Greed
Bouquet	Law	Library	Moral
Coffee	Effort	Letter	Attitude
Rose	Duty	Lake	Wisdom

Impact of depressive symptoms, self-esteem and neuroticism on trajectories of overgeneral autobiographical memory over repeated trials

John E. Roberts and Erica L. Carlos
University at Buffalo, The State University of New York, Buffalo, NY, USA

Todd B. Kashdan
George Mason University, Fairfax, VA, USA

The present study examined trajectories of change in the frequency of overgeneral autobiographical memory (OGM) over the course of repeated trials, and tested whether particular dimensions of depressive symptomatology (somatic and cognitive-affective distress), self-esteem, and neuroticism account for individual differences in these trajectories. Given that depression is associated with impairments in effortful processing, we predicted that over repeated trials depression would be associated with increasingly OGM. Generalised Linear Mixed Models with Penalised Quasi-Likelihood demonstrated significant linear and quadratic trends in OGM over repeated trials, and somatic distress and self-esteem moderated these slopes. The form of these interactions suggested that somatic distress and low self-esteem primarily contribute to OGM during the second half of the trial sequence. The present findings demonstrate the value of a novel analytical approach to OGM that estimates individual trajectories of change over repeated trials.

Overgeneral autobiographical memory (OGM) has been repeatedly demonstrated in depressed and suicidal patients (Dalgleish, Spinks, Yiend, & Kuyken, 2001; Kuyken & Brewin, 1995; Kuyken & Dalgleish, 1995; Moore, Watts, & Williams, 1988; Williams & Broadbent, 1986; Williams & Dritschel, 1988; Williams & Scott, 1988), as well as in a number of additional clinical conditions including posttraumatic stress disorder (McNally, Lasko, Macklin, & Pitman, 1995), acute stress disorder (Harvey, Bryant, & Dang, 1998), obsessive-compulsive disorder (Wilhelm, McNally, Baer, & Florin, 1997), and possibly

---

Correspondence should be addressed to John E. Roberts, Department of Psychology, University at Buffalo, The State University of New York, Buffalo, NY, 14209, USA; e-mail: robertsj@buffalo.edu

We would like to thank Eric Grady, Eva Maron, and Michael Ammermuller for their considerable assistance in conducting the study and Craig Colder for data-analytical advice.

borderline personality disorder (Jones et al., 1999; although see also Arntz, Mereen, & Wessel, 2002; Kremers, Spinhoven & van der Does, 2004). When asked to retrieve a specific autobiographical memory (AM; one with a distinct time and place), these individuals instead tend to respond with memories that are general (ones that occurred over a period of time greater than 24 hours or actually consisted of numerous similar memories combined into one). Some data suggest that OGM prospectively predicts a more prolonged course of disorder, at least in the case of episodes of depression (Brittlebank, Scott, Williams, & Ferrier, 1993; Dalgleish et al., 2001: Peeters, Wessel, Merckelbach, & Boon-Vermeeren, 2002; although see also Brewin, Reynolds, & Tata, 1999) and acute stress disorder (Harvey et al., 1998). It may also act as a vulnerability to depressive symptoms in combination with life stressors (Gibbs & Rude, 2004).

Although OGM has been most consistently reported in depressed and suicidal patients, the fact that similar difficulties have been demonstrated in other mental disorders raises the possibility that shared features across these conditions contribute to OGM. For example, there is evidence that a major dimension of psychopathology reflects degree of internal distress (as opposed to "acting-out" behavioural problems; Krueger, 1999). These so-called internalising disorders, such as depression and various anxiety disorders, likely emerge from a common dispositional tendency that may be associated with high levels of neuroticism or low self-esteem. For example, self-esteem deficits appear to be involved in a number of disorders (Roberts, in press), while neuroticism has been proposed as a potential diathesis for both depression and anxiety (Clark, Watson, & Mineka, 1994). It may be that these shared characteristics are involved in OGM, and therefore may account for the presence of this memory anomaly across different clinical disorders. On a related note, it is unclear whether particular constellations of depressive symptoms play a greater or lesser role in OGM. For example, is OGM primarily associated with the affective components of depression, such as sad mood and low positive affect, or is it more strongly associated with somatic symptoms, such as sleep disturbance, agitation, and fatigue? In this regard, Dalgleish et al. (2001) suggest that OGM prospectively predicts the maintenance of somatic symptoms of depression, but not the affective and cognitive symptoms. The present research was designed to examine the role of self-esteem, neuroticism, and various dimensions of depressive symptomatology in predicting OGM.

In some sense it is not surprising to find that depression is associated with poor performance on the Autobiographical Memory Task (AMT), a task that asks participants to retrieve specific AMs to various cue words. It is well recognised that depression involves cognitive impairment, and numerous studies have demonstrated that depression can be associated with substantial deficits in effortful processing (see Hartlage, Alloy, Vazquez, & Dykman, 1993). Depressed individuals tend to perform poorly on a variety of demanding tasks. As summarised by Gotlib, Roberts, and Gilboa (1996), cognitive performance may suffer in depression as the result of lowered motivation (Miller, 1975), decreased cognitive capacity or resources (Ellis & Ashbrook, 1988), failure to initiate cognitive strategies (Hertel, 1994; Hertel & Hardin, 1990), failures to inhibit intrusive distracting thoughts (Hertel & Rude, 1991), or more extensive processing of certain stimuli (usually negatively valenced) at the expense of other stimuli (usually positively valenced; Williams, Watts, MacLeod, & Mathews, 1997). Any of these factors on their own or in combination could contribute to poor cognitive performance in depression.

In the context of AM, it may be that OGM is the result of some of these same factors. For example, lowered motivation, deficient attentional resources, and distracting negative thoughts all might make it difficult for depressed individuals to go through the mental operations involved in retrieving specific memories. Over the course of the task, they may fail to maintain the instruction set or find it increasingly difficult to muster the energy to retrieve specific memories. Consistent with this perspective, recent research suggests that reductions in AM specificity may be related to "secondary goal neglect" (Dalgleish, 2004). In other words, depressed individuals may sufficiently attend to the primary goal of verbalising memories from their own past experience (autobiographical), while failing to sufficiently attend to the secondary goal of retrieving *specific* memories. For example, Dalgleish (2004) reported that OGM was correlated with poor performance on the WAIS Block Design. Likewise, depressed individuals performed poorly when the instruction set was altered and they were asked to produce OGMs. In this case, they produced more specific memories than non-depressed control participants. Accordingly, it may be valuable to frame the AMT (Williams & Broadbent, 1986) as a cognitive task that requires effortful processing.

From this perspective we would expect that mental fatigue and concentration difficulties would be associated with increased frequency of OGMs and that performance would decline over repeated trials as a function of decreasing attention and concentration. In other words, we would expect a linear trend over trials in which the frequency of OGMs progressively increases. Of most relevance to the present research, we would expect individual differences in these trajectories that vary as a function of factors such as the severity and nature of symptomatology. In particular, according to this perspective, individuals with higher levels of depressive symptomatology would likely show steeper declines in performance over time and would become increasingly overgeneral. This perspective also suggests that specific symptoms of depression are going to be most strongly associated with reductions in specificity. In particular, difficulties with sustained attention, concentration, and motivation would be most closely associated with OGM, particularly over time and repeated trials.

Recent research suggests that the association between depression and reduced AM specificity can be moderated by the nature of self-focused attention (Park, Goodyer, & Teasdale, 2004; Watkins & Teasdale, 2001, 2004). When depressed individuals engage in highly analytical self-focused processing, in which they think about the causes and meaning of their internal states, they tend to maintain low levels of specificity. In contrast, when they engage in low analysis self-focused processing, in which they simply experience those internal states, they tend to become more specific. The present study tested whether these two modes of self-focused processing moderate the effects of depressive symptoms, self-esteem, or neuroticism on OGM.

The present study was designed to investigate trajectories of OGM over repeated trials, and to determine if specific dimensions of depressive symptoms, self-esteem, or neuroticism are associated with individual differences in these trajectories. Given that depression is associated with impairment in effortful processing, we predicted that these symptoms would be associated with steeper increases in OGM over repeated trials. In order to examine individual differences in trajectories of OGM over repeated trials, we treated data from the AMT (Williams & Broadbent, 1986) as multilevel in nature with repeated trials being nested within participants. Such multilevel level approaches are increasingly used to model individual growth curves (Kenny, Bolger, & Kashy, 2002). Within this framework we can examine both the estimated level of specificity at the start of the trial sequence (intercept) and the rate of change over the sequence (slope). We also tested whether the nature of self-focused attention (analytical vs. experiential) would moderate the effects of depressive symptoms, self-esteem, or neuroticism on trajectories of OGM across trials. Based on previous research demonstrating that experiential processing attenuates the effects of depression on AM specificity (Park et al., 2004; Watkins & Teasdale, 2001), we predicted that depressive symptoms would be associated with steeper increases in the frequency of OGM among those in the high analytical processing condition.

METHOD

Participants

Participants were 204 undergraduate students (112 female) at the University at Buffalo who received credit in partial fulfillment of a course requirement. Participants' mean age was 19.8 ($SD = 5.1$).

Self-report measures

Depressive symptomatology. The Beck Depression Inventory-II (BDI; Beck, Steer & Brown, 1996) was used to assess depressive symptoms. The BDI is a widely used self-report measure of depressive severity and has been shown to have strong psychometric properties (see Gotlib & Cane, 1989, for a review of this literature). In the present sample, coefficient alpha was .90.

Self-esteem. The Rosenberg Self-Esteem Scale (Rosenberg, 1979) is a 10-item scale designed to measure global self-regard (e.g., "On the whole, I am satisfied with myself"). Responses were made on 7-point Likert scales (1 = *strongly agree*; 7 = *strongly disagree*). In the present sample, coefficient alpha was .90.

Neuroticism. The Eysenck Personality Questionnaire—Revised Short Scale (Eysenck, Eysenck, & Barrett, 1985) was used to measure neuroticism. The neuroticism scale consists of 12 items, such as: "Does your mood often go up and down?" and "Are you an irritable person?" Participants indicate "yes" or "no" to each item. In the present sample, coefficient alpha was .83.

Procedures

The study was described to all participants before receiving their informed consent to participate. Participants were run individually. After completing a packet of self-report questionnaires, they were randomly assigned to either a high or low analytical processing condition (Watkins & Teasdale, 2001). In both conditions, participants read the same set of 28 items, such as "how hopeful or hopeless you are feeling", "the way your body feels right now", and "how quick or slow your thinking is right now". Participants focused on these statements for 8 min. In the high analysis condition, participants were instructed to "think about" each of the different items (e.g., "Think about your character and who you strive to be"). In the low analysis condition, participants were asked to focus their attention on the experience of the items (e.g., "Focus your attention on the experience of the physical sensations you feel in your body"). In contrast to Watkins and Teasdale (2001) we did not include a distraction condition.

Next, the AMT (Williams & Broadbent, 1986) was administered. Participants were asked to recall a specific personal memory in response to six positive, six negative, and six neutral cue words (e.g., *friendly*, *hurt*, and *uncle*, respectively). One list of 18 words was used in which we interspersed words based on valence. Specifically, we presented a positive word, followed by a neutral word, followed by a negative word, followed by a positive word, and so forth. Participants were given 30 s per cue word to recall a memory. Each memory was rated on its specificity (specific for memories with a distinct time and place and that lasted less than 1 day and general for memories that demonstrated a summary of many similar events, that lacked a distinct time and place, or that lasted for over 1 day). Categoric overgeneral memories (i.e., those that summarised many similar events) and extended overgeneral memories (i.e., those that lacked a distinct time and place or that lasted for over 1 day) were not distinguished in our coding. Participants were not prompted with a reminder to retrieve specific memories after incorrectly responding with an OGM. If a participant did not retrieve a memory in the allotted time period, it was considered an omission. If a participant responded with a semantic or verbal associate rather than a real memory, they were prompted for a memory; if they failed to respond with one, the trial was coded as an omission. Likewise, if the participant responded with a memory from that day they were asked to respond with one from at least the day before, whereas if they responded with an anticipated future event they were asked to retrieve a memory from the past. Of the 3626 scoreable AMT presentations in the sample, there were 2189 (60.4%) specific memories, 1144 (31.5%) overgeneral memories, and 293 (8.1%) omissions. A total of 46 trials could not be scored due to experimenter error. In order to determine reliability, a total of 90 responses were recoded by another rater who listened to audiotapes. Cohen's kappa was .78.

RESULTS

Factor analysis of depressive symptomatology

On average, our sample reported mild levels of depressive symptoms on the BDI ($M = 9.9$; $SD = 8.0$, range 0–49). To examine the structure of depressive symptomatology in our sample, a Maximum Likelihood Factor Analysis with Varimax Rotation was conducted on the BDI. Examination of the scree plot, as well as a parallel analysis (Horn, 1965), suggested that the data were best represented by two factors. These factors accounted for 36.2% of the total variance. Factor scales were constructed based on items that loaded greater than or equal to .4 on only a single factor. Items were summed with unit weighting. Factor 1 consisted of 12 items ($\alpha = .86$) and was labelled "Cognitive-affective distress" (items 1, 2, 3, 4, 5, 7, 8, 9, 10, 12, 13, and 14). Item content included sad mood, pessimism, feelings of failure, loss of pleasure, suicidality, and worthlessness. It accounted for 18.8% of unique variance. Factor 2 was composed of 6 items ($\alpha = .80$) and was labelled "Somatic distress" (items 11, 15, 16, 17, 19, and 20). Item content included agitation, loss of energy, sleep disturbance, irritability, concentration difficulties, and fatigue. This factor accounted for 17.4% of the unique variance.

As can be seen in Table 1, the two dimensions of depressive symptomatology were moderately to highly correlated with each other, as well as with self-esteem and neuroticism.

Multilevel analysis of trajectories

Although the number of overgeneral memories is typically summed to create a single total score in studies using the AMT, data can also be viewed as a series of repeated measures that can be modelled with multilevel data-analytical procedures (Kenny et al., 2002; Nezlek, 2001). Viewing our data in this way has the advantage of allowing the modelling of trajectories of change over our

TABLE 1
Correlation matrix, means, and (standard deviations) of dimensions of depressive symptoms, self-esteem, and neuroticism

	Cognitive-affective distress	Somatic distress	Self-esteem	M	(SD)
Cognitive-affective distress				4.8	(4.7)
Somatic distress	.66			3.9	(3.0)
Self-esteem	−.74	−.59		53.0	(10.9)
Neuroticism	.62	.55	−.61	5.5	(3.5)

Note. All correlations are statistically significant at $p < .001$.

sequence of 18 trials. Within our data, repeated trials are nested within participants. From this perspective, each individual has an intercept, reflecting the participant's estimated level of OGM at the start of the trial sequence, and a slope, reflecting the participant's estimated linear rate of change over trials. In addition to the linear slope, higher order polynomials can be estimated, most commonly the quadratic term. This term reflects the participant's estimated rate of acceleration of change at a given trial. Given that our dependent variable was dichotomous (overgeneral vs. specific),[1] primary analyses were conducted with Generalised Linear Mixed Models with Penalised Quasi-likelihood. Specifically, we used the glmPQL function of the MASS package (Venables & Ripley, 2002) run in R 2.0 (R Core Development Team, 2004). Significant interactions were graphically displayed by plotting estimated scores for each trial conditioned at 1.5 *SD* above and below the mean for the moderator variable. In the case of somatic distress, which was a positively skewed variable with a negative value at 1.5 *SD* below the mean, we plotted at a value of 0 instead.

Linear and quadratic effects of trial sequence. Preliminary analyses were conducted to test the linear and quadratic effects of trial sequence on specificity in the sample as a whole. We first tested the linear effects of trial, while statistically controlling for cue valence of stimuli (treated as a dummy variable with three levels: negative, neutral, and positive). A significant linear trend was found, $\beta = .082$, $t(3126) = 10.73$, $p < .001$, such that likelihood of retrieving an OGM increased over time. In order to test whether effects were fixed or random, we estimated models using the NLME package (Pinehiero & Bates, 2000) run in R 2.0 (R Core Development Team, 2004), and compared the fit of models in which intercepts and slopes were fixed vs. random. The linear effect of Trial had both a random intercept, Likelihood Ratio (LR) = 92.01, $p < .001$, and a random

---

[1] Omissions were excluded from the analyses reported below. Results were virtually identical when OGMs were contrasted with a category that included both specific memories and omissions.

slope, $LR = 9.76$, $p < .01$. In other words, there was significant variability across participants in terms of their baseline probability of retrieving an OGM at the first trial (intercept) and their rate of change over trials (slope). We next tested the quadratic effect of trial sequence (Trial-squared), while statistically controlling for the linear effects of trial and cue valence. The quadratic effect was statistically significant, $\beta = -0.012$, $t(3125) = 6.90$, $p < .001$. Furthermore, the model including the quadratic component provided a better overall fit than the model limited to the linear component, $LR = 38.99$, $p < .001$.

As seen in Figure 1, across participants there was an inverted U-shaped function in which the probability of recalling an OGM increased rapidly during the first half of the trial sequence, and then decelerated and began to decrease during the second half. Although this quadratic effect was statistically significant for the sample as a whole, it was also a random effect, $LR = 8.44$, $p < .05$. In other words, there was significant variability across participants in the degree to which their performance fit this quadratic curve. Our next set of analyses tested whether different dimensions of depressive symptomatology, self-esteem, and neuroticism were associated with variability in this quadratic effect, and whether mode of processing (analytical vs. experiential) would moderate these effects.

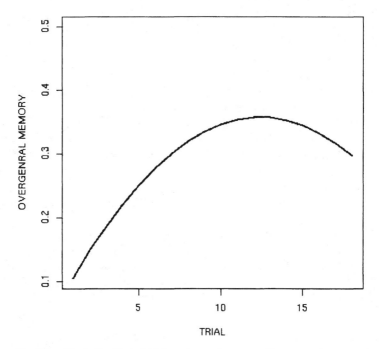

Figure 1. Quadratic effect of trial number on frequency of overgeneral memory.

Predictors of individual differences in trajectories. In order to examine factors that might moderate the quadratic effect of trial sequence, models were constructed in a stepwise manner. Step 1 included the main effects of the putative moderator (the two dimensions of depression, self-esteem and neuroticism each tested individually), Trial and cue valence (Val) dummy coded (negative, neutral, and positive). Step 2 included the two-way interaction between the putative moderator and Trial, as well as the quadratic component of trial number (Trial-squared), whereas Step 3 included the interaction between the putative moderator and the quadratic component of Trial. In each of these models, the linear and quadratic components of Trial were treated as random. Initial models included Condition (analytical vs. experiential self-focused processing) as a factor. None of the main effects of Condition or its higher order interactions with the linear or quadratic components of Trial or the dimensions of depression, self-esteem or neuroticism were statistically significant (all $ps>.10$). Therefore Condition was not included in any of the models reported below.

As can be seen in Table 2, there were significant main effects of Trial and cue valence across analyses. The probability of retrieving an OGM increased over trials, $t = 10.71$, $p < .001$. Likewise, the probability of retrieving an OGM increased with neutral cue words relative to negative cue words, $t = 3.82$, $p < .001$, as well as with positive cue words relative to negative cue words, $t = 8.15$, $p < .001$. In contrast, none of the main effects of the two dimensions of depression (self-esteem or neuroticism) were significant. Likewise, the two-way interactions between these predictors and the linear effects of Trial were not statistically significant.

The primary theoretical question of interest was whether the quadratic trend of Trial is moderated by dimensions of depressive symptomatology, self-esteem or neuroticism. This question is addressed by the interaction term between $Trial^2$ and each of these variables. Given that the quadratic term is represented by Trial × Trial, these effects are triple interactions (Trial × Trial × Putative Moderator). As can be seen at the lower row of Table 2, the $Trial^2$ × Somatic distress, $t = 3.27$, $p < .01$, and $Trial^2$ × Self-esteem, $t = 3.02$, $p < .01$, interactions were statistically significant. These results indicate that somatic distress and self-esteem each accounted for a statistically significant amount of variance across participants in the quadratic effects of trial number. In other words, the shape of these quadratic curves differed depending on participants' level of somatic distress and self-esteem.

The two significant interactions are graphically displayed in Figures 2 and 3. As can be seen in Figure 2, individuals who were low in somatic distress show a similar inverted U-shaped curve to the one seen in the sample as a whole; specifically they had a rapid increase in the frequency of overgeneral memories, followed by a deceleration and eventual decline of these memories. In contrast, individuals high in somatic distress showed a steady linear increase in the frequency of overgeneral memories over trials that was not followed by

TABLE 2
Multilevel analysis testing individual differences in trajectories of overgeneral memory over repeated trials

	Somatic distress		Distress		Cognitive-affective		Self-esteem		Neuroticism	
	β	t	β	t	β	t	β	t	β	t
Step 1: Main effects										
PM	.008	0.30	.011	0.63	-.011	1.42	-.011	1.42	-.032	1.32
Trial	.087	11.04***	.087	11.04***	.086	11.02***	.086	11.02***	.087	11.05***
Valence (neutral)	.377	3.97***	.377	3.97***	.377	3.97***	.377	3.97***	.377	3.97***
Valence (positive)	.786	8.29***	.786	8.28***	.787	8.29***	.787	8.29***	.787	8.29***
Step 2: w-way interactions										
Cue × Cue	-.013	7.17***	-.013	7.17***	-.012	6.56***	-.012	6.56***	-.013	7.15***
Cue × PM	.002	0.53	.001	0.62	-.000	0.12	-.000	0.12	-.002	0.61
Step 3: 3-way interactions										
Cue × Cue × PM	.002	3.06**	.000	1.06	-.001	2.88**	-.001	2.88**	-.001	1.39

PM, putative moderator variable; PA, positive affect; β, unstandardised beta coefficient. * $p < .05$; ** $p < .01$; *** $p < .001$.

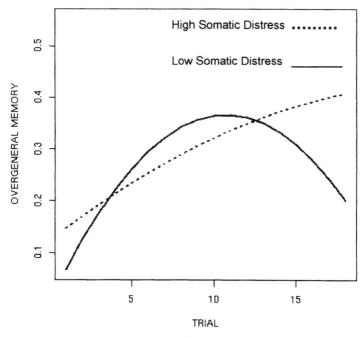

Figure 2. Depressive Somatic Distress × Trial^2 interaction on frequency of overgeneral Memory. High Somatic Distress reflects scores estimated from the full equation conditioned at 1.5 standard deviations above the mean. In contrast, because Somatic Distress had a nonmeaningful negative value at 1.5 standard deviations below the mean, low Somatic Distress was conditioned at a value of 0.

deceleration. As can be seen in Figure 3, self-esteem exhibited a similar pattern. Individuals high in self-esteem exhibited a rapid increase in overgeneral memories, followed by a deceleration and decline, whereas those with low self-esteem never decelerated.

Separate tests across cue valence. Because cue words were administered in a single fixed order, it is possible that our quadratic effects were driven by the particular words that appeared toward the end of the list. In order to address this concern, we ran follow-up analyses to test the linear and quadratic effects of Trial with each of the three valences of cue words (positive, neutral, negative) separately. Furthermore, we tested whether somatic distress and self-esteem moderated the quadratic terms. Because the original 18-item word list was subdivided into three 6-item lists, any major idiosyncrasies of word order that existed in the original list would likely be eliminated. If effects were generally similar across the three lists, then it would be difficult to argue that our findings were simply due to word order.

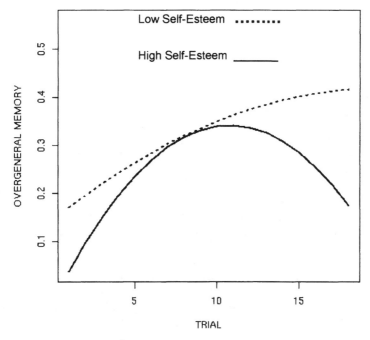

Figure 3. Self-esteem × Trial² interaction on frequency of overgeneral memory. Graph reflects scores estimated from the full equation conditioned at 1.5 standard deviations above and below the mean on Self-esteem.

The linear effect of Trial was statistically significant for positive, $t = 7.13$, $p < .001$, neutral, $t = 2.33$, $p < .05$, and negative words, $t = 8.56$, $p < .001$. Likewise, the quadratic term was statistically significant for positive, $t = 5.76$, $p < .001$, and negative words, $t = 5.59$, $p < .001$, but not for neutral words, $t = 0.76$, $p = .45$. The quadratic term was moderated by somatic distress with neutral, $t = 2.73$, $p < .01$, and negative words, $t = 1.90$, $p < .06$, but not positive words, $t = 1.21$, $p = .22$. Likewise, the quadratic term was moderated by self-esteem with positive, $t = 2.08$, $p < .05$, and negative words, $t = 2.09$, $p < .05$, but not neutral words, $t = 1.48$, $p = .14$. Overall, this pattern suggests generally similar effects across word types, and therefore does not support the word order interpretation.

DISCUSSION

The present study was designed to explore two novel questions related to overgeneral memory in depression. First, this research examined the trajectory of OGM over repeated trials and tested whether or not there was significant variability in these trajectories across participants. Second, this research tested whether particular dimensions of depressive symptomatology, self-esteem and neuroticism moderated the shape and form of these curves. In other words, if there were individual differences in these trajectories, would characteristics, such as dimensions of symptomatology account for this variability?

The sample as a whole showed both linear and quadratic effects of trial number on OGM. The linear effect suggested that participants became more overgeneral over time. However, this linear effect was qualified by a higher order quadratic effect. The latter was in the shape of an inverted U, and suggested that the frequency of OGMs rapidly increased over the first half of the trial sequence, stabilised during the middle of the sequence, and began to decrease toward the end of the sequence. Although this quadratic effect was significant for the sample as a whole, it was random. In other words, there was significant variation across participants in the magnitude and shape of this effect. The next logical question is what accounts for these individual differences? In the present study we tested whether various dimensions of depressive symptomatology, self-esteem and neuroticism, would moderate the trajectory of OGM over repeated trials.

In our sample, a Maximum Likelihood Factor Analysis with Varimax Rotation suggested that depressive symptomatology was represented by two major dimensions that we labelled cognitive-affective distress and somatic distress. Of these two dimensions, somatic distress was a statistically significant moderator of AM trajectories. Likewise, self-esteem moderated the shape of these trajectories. The form of these interactions suggests that individuals low in somatic distress or high in self-esteem exhibit a rapid increase in the frequency of overgeneral memories during the first half of the trial sequence, followed by a deceleration and decline during the second half. In contrast, among individuals high in somatic distress or low in self-esteem, frequency of OGMs progressively increases over the entire trial sequence without any period of deceleration. Consequently, performance between those low and high in somatic distress or self-esteem is fairly comparable during the first half of the trial sequence—they all rapidly increase in the frequency of retrieving OGMs. In contrast, during the second half of the sequence, participants high in somatic distress or low in self-esteem continue to accelerate in their frequency of OGMs, whereas the trend is reversed among those low in somatic distress or high in self-esteem. In contrast, interactions between the quadratic component of trial sequence and cognitive-emotional distress and neuroticism were not statistically significant.

As discussed in the introduction, it makes sense that symptoms related to somatic distress would be associated with an increased frequency of OGMs, particularly in the later half of the trial sequence. Our dimension of somatic distress included symptoms of psychomotor agitation, concentration difficulties, sleep disturbance, and fatigue that are likely to have a major impact on effortful cognitive tasks. Likewise, low self-esteem appears to impact these processes. In contrast, other types of depressive symptoms, such as those reflecting low positive affect (sad mood, loss of pleasure, loss of interest), and negatively valenced cognitions (self-criticism, feelings of failure, guilt, and punishment), and the personality dimension neuroticism were not related to trajectories of OGM in our study. These findings suggest that future research on OGM in depression might benefit from examining more fine-grained dimensions of symptomatology. Certain types of depressive symptoms appear to have a greater impact than others. In addition, certain personality correlates of depression, such as low self-esteem, appear to have greater impact than others.

As described above, the frequency of OGMs increased through Trial 10 or so in the sample as a whole, and then began to decrease. It is interesting to consider what might be happening at this point in the trial sequence. One possibility is that the effect is simply an artifact that resulted from the particular cue words that were presented in the final half of the sequence. Although we interspersed positive, negative, and neutral cue words, our study used a single list that was presented in a fixed order. Our analyses statistically controlled for word valence, but it is possible that the linear and quadratic effects of trial number were an artifact of the particular word order used. In other words, effects may have had more to do with the particular words used in the early, middle and late phases of the trial sequence, rather than trial number per se. On the other hand, this possibility would not explain why somatic distress and self-esteem moderated these effects. Furthermore, follow-up analyses demonstrated similar linear and quadratic effects in analyses conducted separately on cue words of each valence (positive, negative, neutral), and in general, somatic distress and self-esteem, moderated these quadratic effects across word types. Nonetheless, it would be important for future studies to use multiple word lists and to vary the order of word presentation across trial numbers to control for this possible confound.

What else might be happening at this point in the sequence? It is possible that participants develop a mnemonic strategy for generating responses early in the task. For example, a participant might try to generate responses based on their work experiences. As the trial sequence continues and the pool of work-related experiences becomes depleted, this particular mnemonic device is likely to become progressively less successful. Perhaps at some point many individuals learn to "shift gears" and use a different mental framework, such as generating responses based on their experiences within their families. Given that this pool of memories has not yet been tapped, it would likely prove to be more useful in generating specific autobiographical memories. This account would explain the curvilinear effect with performance steadily worsening up to a certain point and then improving. The point of inflection would be when individuals arrive at a new more effective mnemonic device. Within this account, individuals with greater somatic distress and lower self-esteem would be less able to flexibly switch from one mnemonic device to another. They would stick to their initial strategy despite its ever-decreasing utility, and consequently their performance would decrease in a linear manner with no point of inflection. This account is clearly speculative and little is known about the actual strategies participants use in the AMT. It would be valuable for future studies to test whether manipulations that change participants' mnemonic devices at various points in the trial sequence subsequently lead to increased specificity in the AMT, particularly among high somatic distress and low self-esteem participants.[2]

Interestingly, it seems likely that symptoms of somatic distress are a common feature of the various clinical disorders in which reductions in AM specificity have been demonstrated; not only would these symptoms be present in depression, they would also likely characterise posttraumatic stress disorder, obsessive-compulsive disorder, and borderline personality disorder. It may be that somatic distress with its concomitant difficulties with concentration and attention is responsible for the increased levels of OGM across these conditions. It also seems likely that low self-esteem is a common feature of these conditions that in turn could contribute to OGM across a range of mental disorders. It should also be noted that nontrauma-related anxiety disorders typically do not demonstrate OGM (e.g., Burke & Matthews, 1992; Wenzel et al., 2002; Wessel, Meeren, Peeters, Arntz, & Merckelbach, 2001) and several studies have failed to find OGM in borderline personality disorder (Arntz et al., 2002; Kremers et al., 2004). These findings are problematic for our transdiagnostic formulation as it is likely that these conditions are also marked by elevated levels of somatic distress. It would be important for future studies to directly test the degree to which symptoms of somatic distress, such as loss of energy, fatigue, concentration difficulties, and agitation, as well as low self-esteem, are associated with OGM across a range of different mental disorders. It may be that various conditions, such as borderline personality disorder and OCD, are only associated with OGM when they are marked by high levels of comorbid somatic distress symptoms or low self-esteem (see also Kremers et al., 2004; Wilhelm et al., 1997).

Previous studies have shown that OGM has important correlates and functional consequences. For example, OGM is more common among individuals with a history of childhood trauma (Dalgleish et al., 2003; de Decker, Hermans, Raes, & Eelen, 2003; Hermans et al., 2004; Kuyken & Brewin, 1995; although also see Wessel et al., 2001), leading some to speculate that OGM helps regulate negative moods resulting from these adverse experiences. Consistent with this hypothesis, a recent study found that reduced AM specificity was associated with better short-term negative mood regulation (Raes, Hermans, de Decker, Eelen, & Williams, 2003). On the other hand, there is evidence that OGM is associated with problem-solving deficits (Goddard, Dritschel, & Burton, 1996). It is possible that trajectories of change in specificity over trials might serve as a stronger predictor of these and related outcomes. It may prove valuable for future studies to estimate each participant's intercept and slope coefficients and to use these as predictor variables of these and other outcomes (see Young et al.,

---

[2] We thank Phil Barnard for suggesting this explanation to us.

1996 for an example based on individual intercepts and slopes involving the association between depressive symptomatology and hopelessness). It may be that estimated baseline levels (intercepts) and estimated rates of downward performance over trials (slopes) are differentially related to outcomes, such as mood regulation and problem solving. Future research should also examine whether the intercepts, linear slopes or quadratic terms of OGM data prospectively predict the course of depressive disorders or risk for the onset of future depressive symptoms. Such work would be informative as to whether OGM plays an etiological role in depression.

Recent research has suggested that a specific cognitive process, analytic self-focused processing (which involves analysing and trying to understand, as opposed to simply "experiencing") may contribute to difficulties retrieving specific autobiographical memories in depression (Park et al., 2004; Watkins & Teasdale, 2001, 2004). In contrast, in our study this processing style failed to interact with our two dimensions of depressive symptomatology, self-esteem or neuroticism, in predicting trajectories of OGM. Of note, past research demonstrating the effects of analytical processing was based on clinically depressed samples in contrast to our college sample. It may be that analytical processing has a greater impact on more severely depressed individuals with major depressive disorder compared to individuals with elevated levels of subclinical symptoms. Furthermore, the past studies focused on categoric overgeneral memories in particular, whereas our study collapsed across categoric and extended overgeneral memories.

In terms of methodology, our findings suggest that depression may be more strongly associated with OGM after approximately 12–14 trials. Following this logic, future research may benefit from using lengthier sequences of cue words. Traditionally, 18 cue words are presented on the AMT (Williams & Broadbent, 1986). Our results suggest that differences between individuals with high levels of somatic distress and low self-esteem only emerge with the final few cue words. Increasing the number of cue words potentially will yield a more sensitive index of OGM regardless of whether investigators explore trajectories, as we have done, or simply create an aggregate score.

Given our findings suggesting that OGM in part results from poor concentration and fatigue, it will be important for future research to determine whether OGM is distinct from more general cognitive deficits and poor performance. Does OGM predict psychopathology, early childhood abuse, mood regulation, or problem-solving controlling for performance on other effortful cognitive tasks? Would the addition of secondary cognitive tasks, which increase demand on cognitive resources, amplify the effects of depression and other mental conditions on AM specificity? Does the downward trajectory of memory specificity reflect participants' gradually forgetting the instruction to recall *specific* memories or developing secondary goal neglect? To test this latter possibility, it may be useful to examine changes in these trajectories following a reminder in which instruction are restated at some point in the series of trials. It also would be useful to examine whether the trajectories are similar when the instruction set is reversed and participants are asked to produce overgeneral memories rather than specific memories (Dalgleish, 2004). It would also be important to examine if similar trajectories arise when participants are given reminder prompts following overgeneral responses. Finally, future research should determine whether symptoms of somatic distress and low self-esteem are the key contributors to OGM in more serious diagnosable depressive disorders, and other mental conditions, such as posttraumatic stress disorder. It may be that this constellation of symptoms helps account for the range of mental disorders that are associated with OGM.

REFERENCES

Arntz, A., Meeren, M., & Wessel, I. (2002). No evidence for overgeneral memories in borderline personality disorder. *Behaviour Research and Therapy, 40*, 1063–1068.

Beck. A. T., Steer, R. A., & Brown, G. K. (1996). *Beck depression inventory manual* (2nd ed.). San Antonio, TX: Psychological Corporation.

Brewin, C. R., Reynolds, M., & Tata, P. (1999). Autobiographical memory processes and the course of depression. *Journal of Abnormal Psychology, 108*, 511–517.

Brittlebank, A. D., Scott, J., Williams, J. M., & Ferrier, I. N. (1993). Autobiographical memory in depression: State or trait marker? *British Journal of Psychiatry, 162*, 118–121.

Burke, M., & Mathews, A. (1992). Autobiographical memory and clinical anxiety. *Cognition and Emotion, 6*, 23–35.

Clark, L. A., Watson, D., & Mineka, S. (1994). Temperament, personality, and the mood and anxiety disorders. *Journal of Abnormal Psychology, 103*, 103–116.

Dalgleish, T. (2004). *Emotional autobiographical memories, depression and goal neglect.* Paper presented at the Annual Congress of the European Association for Behavioural and Cognitive Therapies, Manchester, UK.

Dalgleish, T., Spinks, H., Yiend, J., & Kuyken, W. (2001). Autobiographical memory style in seasonal affective disorder and its relationship to future symptom remission. *Journal of Abnormal Psychology, 110*, 335–340.

Dalgleish, T., Tchanturia, K., Serpell, L., Hems, S., Yiend, J., de Silva, P., & Treasure, J. (2003). Self-reported parental abuse relates to autobiographical memory style in patients with eating disorders. *Emotion, 3*, 211–222.

de Decker, A., Hermans, D., Raes, F., & Eelen, P. (2003). Autobiographical memory specificity and trauma in inpatient adolescents. *Journal of Clinical Child and Adolescent Psychology, 32*, 22–31.

Ellis, H. C., & Ashbrook, P. W. (1988). Resource allocation model of the effects of depressed mood on memory. In K. Fiedler & J. Forgas (Eds.), *Affect, cognition and social behavior.* Toronto, Canada: Hogrefe.

Eysenck, S. B. G., Eysenck, H. J., & Barrett, P. (1985). A revised version of the psychoticism scale. *Personality and Individual Differences, 6*, 21–29.

Gibbs, B. R., & Rude, S. S. (2004). Overgeneral autobiographical memory as depression vulnerability. *Cognitive Therapy and Research, 28*, 511–526.

Goddard, L., Dritschel, B., & Burton, A. (1996). Role of autobiographical memory in social problem solving and depression. *Journal of Abnormal Psychology, 105*, 609–616.

Gotlib, I. H., & Cane, D. B. (1989). Self-report assessment of depression and anxiety. In P. C. Kendall & D. Watson (Eds.), *Anxiety and depression: Distinct and overlapping features* (pp. 131–169). San Diego, CA: Academic Press.

Gotlib, I. H., Roberts, J. E., & Gilboa, E. (1996). Cognitive interference in depression. In I. G. Sarason, G. R. Pierce, & B. R. Sarason (Eds.), *Cognitive interference: Theories, methods, and findings* (pp. 347–377). Mahwah, NJ: Erlbaum.

Hartlage, S., Alloy, L. B., Vazquez, C., & Dykman, B. (1993). Automatic and effortful processing in depression. *Psychological Bulletin, 113*, 247–278.

Harvey, A. G., Bryant, R. A., & Dang, S. T. (1998). Autobiographical memory in acute stress disorder. *Journal of Consulting and Clinical Psychology, 66*, 500–506.

Hermans, D., van den Broeck, K., Belis, G., Raes, F., Pieters, G., & Eelen, P. (2004). Trauma and autobiographical memory specificity in depressed inpatients. *Behaviour Research and Therapy, 42*, 775–789.

Hertel, P. T. (1994). Depressive deficits in word identification and recall. *Cognition and Emotion, 8*, 313–327.

Hertel, P. T., & Hardin, T. S. (1990). Remembering with and without awareness in depressed mood: Evidence of deficits in initiative. *Journal of Experimental Psychology: General, 119*, 45–59.

Hertel, P. T., & Rude, S. S. (1991). Depressive deficits in memory: Focusing attention improves subsequent recall. *Journal of Experimental Psychology: General, 120*, 301–309.

Horn J. L. (1965). A rationale and test for the number of factors in factor analysis, *Psychometrika, 30*, 179–185.

Jones, B., Heard, H., Startup, M., Swales, M., Williams, J. M. G., & Jones, R. S. P. (1999). Autobiographical memory and dissociation in borderline personality disorder. *Psychological Medicine, 29*, 1397–1404.

Kenny, D. A., Bolger, N., & Kashy, D. A. (2002). Traditional methods for estimating multilevel models. In D. S. Moskowitz & S. L. Hershberger (Eds.), *Modeling intraindividual variability with repeated measures data* (pp. 1–24). Mahwah, NJ: Erlbaum.

Kremers, I. P., Spinhoven, P., & van der Does, A. J. W. (2004). Autobiographical memory in depressed and nondepressed patients with borderline personality disorder. *British Journal of Clinical Psychology, 43*, 17–29.

Krueger, R. F. (1999). The structure of common mental disorders. *Archives of General Psychiatry, 56*, 921–926.

Kuyken, W., & Brewin, C. R. (1995). Autobiographical memory functioning in depression and reports of early abuse. *Journal of Abnormal Psychology, 104*, 585–591.

Kuyken, W., & Dalgleish, T. (1995). Autobiographical memory and depression. *British Journal of Clinical Psychology, 34*, 89–92.

McNally, R. J., Lasko, N. B., Macklin, M. L., & Pitman, R. K. (1995). Autobiographical memory disturbance in combat-related posttraumatic stress disorder. *Behaviour Research and Therapy, 33*, 619–630.

Miller, W. R. (1975). Psychological deficit in depression. *Psychological Bulletin, 82*, 238–260.

Moore, R. G., Watts, F. N., & Williams, J. M. (1988). The specificity of personal memories in depression. *British Journal of Clinical Psychology, 27*, 275–276.

Nezlek, J. B. (2001). Multilevel random coefficient analyses of event- and interval-contingent data in social and personality psychology research. *Personality and Social Psychology Bulletin, 27*, 771–785.

Park, R. J., Goodyear, I. M., & Teasdale, J. D. (2004). Effects of induced rumination and distraction on mood and overgeneral autobiographical memory in adolescent Major Depressive Disorder and controls. *Journal of Child Psychology and Psychiatry, 45*, 996–1006.

Peeters, F., Wessel, I., Merckelbach, H., & Boon-Vermeeren, M. (2002). Autobiographical memory specificity and the course of major depressive disorder. *Comprehensive Psychiatry, 43*, 344–350.

Pinheiro, J. C., & Bates, D. M. (2000). *Mixed-effects models in S and S-Plus*. New York: Springer.

R Development Core Team (2004). *R: A language and environment for statistical computing*. R Foundation for Statistical Computing, Vienna, Austria. (ISBN 3-900051-00-3, URL http://www.R-project.org)

Raes, F., Hermans, D., de Decker, A., Eelen, P., & Williams, J. M. G. (2003). Autobiographical memory specificity and affect regulation: An experimental approach. *Emotion, 3*, 201–206.

Roberts, J. E. (in press). Self-esteem from a clinical perspective. In M. Kernis (Ed.), *Self-esteem: Issues and answers.* Hove, UK: Psychology Press.

Rosenberg, M. (1979). *Conceiving the self.* New York: Basic Books.

Venables, W. N., & Ripley, B. D. (2002). *Modern applied statistics with S* (4th ed.). New York: Springer.

Watkins, E., & Teasdale, J.D. (2001). Rumination and overgeneral memory in depression: Effects of self-focus and analytic thinking. *Journal of Abnormal Psychology, 110*, 353–357.

Watkins, E., & Teasdale, J. D. (2004). Adaptive and maladaptive self-focus in depression. *Journal of Affective Disorders, 82*, 1–8.

Wenzel, A., Jackson, L. C., & Holt, C. S. (2002). Social Phobia and the recall of autobiographical memories. *Depression and Anxiety, 15*, 186–189.

Wessel, I., Meeren, M., Peeters, F., Arntz, A., & Merckelbach, H. (2001). Correlates of autobiographical memory specificity: the role of depression, anxiety and childhood trauma. *Behaviour Research and Therapy, 39*, 409–421.

Wilhelm, S., McNally, R. J., Baer, L., & Florin, I. (1997). Autobiographical memory in obsessive-compulsive disorder. *British Journal of Clinical Psychology, 36*, 21–31.

Williams, J. M., & Broadbent, K. (1986). Autobiographical memory in suicide attempters. *Journal of Abnormal Psychology, 95*, 144–149.

Williams, J. M., & Dritschel, B. H. (1988). Emotional disturbance and the specificity of autobiographical memory. *Cognition and Emotion, 2*, 221–234.

Williams, J. M. G., & Scott, J. (1988). Autobiographical memory in depression. *Psychological Medicine, 18*, 689–695.

Williams, J. M. G., Watts, F. N., MacLeod, C., & Mathews, A. (1997). *Cognitive psychology and the emotional disorders* (2nd ed.). New York: Wiley.

Young, M. A., Fogg, L. F., Scheftner, W., Fawcett, J., Akiskal, H., & Maser, J. (1996). Stable trait components of hopelessness: Baseline and sensitivity to depression. *Journal of Abnormal Psychology, 105*, 155–165.

Reduced autobiographical memory specificity and affect regulation

Filip Raes and Dirk Hermans
University of Leuven, Belgium

J. Mark G. Williams
University of Oxford, UK

Paul Eelen
University of Leuven, Belgium

The effect of specificity of autobiographical memory (AM) retrieval on the affective impact of an emotional event was examined. In Study 1 ($N = 90$) the impact of a negative and positive experience was compared between student participants who habitually retrieve autobiographical memories (AMs) in a specific way and participants who generally retrieve less specific memories. In Study 2 ($N = 48$) the effect of an experimentally induced (specific vs. overgeneral) retrieval style on the impact of a negative experience was studied in student participants who habitually retrieve less specific memories. Study 1 replicated the finding of Raes, Hermans, de Decker, Eelen, & Williams (2003) that a negative event leads to *less* subjective distress in low-specific participants as compared with high-specific participants. However, both groups did not differ in their affective reaction to a positive event. Important, reduced memory specificity was associated with "repressive coping", providing further evidence for the idea that reduced memory specificity is used as an avoidant or repressive-defensive mechanism to regulate negative affect (Williams, 1996). In Study 2, participants who were induced to retrieve memories in an overgeneral way experienced *more* distress following a negative event as compared with participants who were induced to retrieve memories in a specific way. Results are discussed in the context of recent findings concerning AM specificity and emotion regulation (Philippot, Schaefer, & Herbette, 2003). Directions for further research are suggested.

Correspondence should be addressed to Filip Raes, Department of Psychology, University of Leuven, Tiensestraat 102, B-3000 Leuven, Belgium; e-mail: filip.raes@psy.kuleuven.be

Thanks are due to Tom Beckers, Wim de Neys, and Ilse Van Diest for their assistance in data collection (Study 1) and to Linda Geypen and Annemie Defranc for rating the SCT responses (Study 2). We also thank anonymous reviewers for their many helpful comments and suggestions.

Some people find it relatively easy to think of a specific or single past event in response to cue words (e.g., "When I buried my pet under the apple tree in our garden when I was six" to the word *sad*). Others, however, find this far more difficult or retrieve more general or "categoric" rather than specific events from their autobiographical memory (AM) (e.g., "Every time I attend a funeral"). Past research has shown that depressed people as well as people with a history of trauma display difficulty with recalling personal past events in a specific way, a phenomenon referred to as *overgeneral memory* (OGM; for reviews see Hermans et al., 2004; Williams, 2004, respectively).

In trying to offer an explanation as to which function OGM serves, Williams (1996) formulated the *affect regulation hypothesis* (Williams, 1996). This hypothesis states that some people, in particular those who have experienced adversities in their childhood, may have learned that by retrieving memories in a less specific or overgeneral categoric way, they are able to regulate or minimise to some extent the negative affect attached to specific negative or traumatic events. In this view, specific memories are assumed to evoke more intense, primary emotion. Less specific or categoric memories also "have their emotional consequences, but, although painful, these are less-focused, secondary emotions" (Williams, Stiles, & Shapiro, 1999, p. 301). Williams also refers to the negative affect resulting from specific and categoric memories as respectively "sharp pain" vs. "dull ache" (Williams, 1996, p. 261). This reduced specificity of AM, albeit advantageous in the short term through the avoidance of intense or painful emotions, is further thought to put people at risk for developing an emotional disorder in the long term, such as depression (cf. Brittlebank, Scott, Williams, & Ferrier, 1993).

Correlational research (survey studies) offered support for Williams' affect regulation claim, showing an association between past trauma experience and reduced memory specificity (e.g., Dalgleish et al., 2003; de Decker, Hermans, Raes, & Eelen, 2003; Kuyken & Brewin, 1995; see Hermans et al., 2004, for a review). First experimental evidence for the affect regulation account of reduced memory specificity was provided by Raes, Hermans, de Decker, Eelen, and Williams (2003), who found that student groups distinguished on the basis of their specificity of memory reacted differently to a negative event. Using a written format of a cue word procedure, known as the Autobiographical Memory Test (AMT; Williams & Broadbent, 1986), Raes et al. (2003) selected participants that were either high- or low-specific with regard to their retrieval of autobiographical memories (AMs). High-specific were those participants that retrieved a specific memory to each of 10 cue words, whereas low-specific participants retrieved only six or fewer specific memories. It was decided in that study to use the number of specific memories as an index of OGM because: (1) to date, most published studies have used the raw number of specific memories as their main dependent variable or primary index of OGM in statistical analyses; and (2) in student, nonclinical populations, there is a marked low prevalence of overgeneral categoric memories. (For example, in a group of 405 students, the mean number of categoric memories on a 10-item AMT was only 0.20, $SD = 0.52$.) Thus, to select students on the basis of the number of categoric memories would prove a very difficult enterprise, given the overall low rate of categoric memories generated by students in response to AMT cue words.

Following this preexperimental selection procedure, participants of the high- and low-specificity group in the Raes et al. (2003) study were then randomly allocated to either a stress or no-stress condition, in which they had to solve a number of very difficult or very simple tangram puzzles, respectively. Afterwards, participants filled out the Impact of Puzzle task Scale (IPS; Raes et al., 2003), which is a 15-item scale measuring subjective distress as a result of the puzzle task, and is modelled after the Impact of Event Scale (IES; Horowitz, Wilner, & Alvarez, 1979; for more details, see Raes et al., 2003). Visual analogue scales were also administered, assessing the amount of intrusive thoughts for the puzzle task and the extent of unpleasantness of such thoughts. It was found that the stressful puzzle task led to more subjective distress in high-specific than in low-specific individuals. Furthermore, after the negative event, high-specific people thought more frequently about it and thought it more unpleasant and disturbing to find themselves thinking back to the negative event. The results illustrate the pay-off for individuals who retrieve memories in a less specific way: They are less emotionally aroused by a negative event. These results, thus, are consistent with Williams' (1996) affect regulation hypothesis of OGM.

Although in line with Williams' (1996) affect regulation account, the findings of Raes et al. (2003) are markedly contradictory to results recently obtained by Philippot and colleagues (Philippot, Schaefer, & Herbette, 2003). Philippot and co-workers observed the opposite pattern: Compared to students who were induced into an overgeneral mode of accessing AMs, students who were primed into a specific access mode to AM reported *less intense emotions* during subsequent emotion induction (through film excerpts or mental imagery). In these studies, participants were primed by reactivating two specific vs. two overgeneral personal memories for 20 seconds each.

Philippot et al. (2003) coined the notion of a *strategic inhibition hypothesis* in explaining their results. This hypothesis argues that when one voluntarily searches for a specific emotional AM (i.e., generative retrieval; Conway & Pleydell-Pearce, 2000), the parallel activation of the related emotion during retrieval may disrupt or hinder the effortful control processes that modulate this staged type of retrieval. [Note that in Philippot et al.'s (2003) account emotionality is thought to be directly related to categoric or generic information.] Therefore, to avoid such hindrance in the search for a specific memory, a parallel inhibition is believed to be operative in inhibiting the associated emotion. Thus, the control processes can be efficiently employed to access a specific memory, instead of stopping short at a general level. However, if a person recalls personal memories in an overgeneral categoric way, and is not in a specific retrieval mode (so the effortful searching process is not active), there will be no inhibition of emotion. Therefore remaining at an overgeneral or categoric level results in more intense emotion.

In order to further elucidate these contradictory findings in the literature with respect to AM specificity and emotion regulation [Raes et al. (2003) vs. Philippot et al. (2003)], Study 1 of the current paper is designed to investigate the replicability of the initial findings of Raes et al. (2003). Based on Philippot et al.'s strategic inhibition hypothesis and the experimental findings of these authors (Philippot et al., 2003), it is predicted that reduced AM specificity is related to enhanced emotional arousal. However, based on Williams' (1996) affect regulation hypothesis and the Raes et al. (2003) study, one would expect reduced AM specificity to be associated with less emotional arousal as compared with high AM specificity.

If people who have lower specificity are less emotionally affected by a negative experience, as shown by the Raes et al. (2003) study, this raises two further important questions that are addressed in Study 1 of the present paper. First, we do not know whether the effects of attenuated affect generalise to positive affect. That is, do people who habitually retrieve low-specific memories report fewer *positive feelings* following a positive event than people who habitually retrieve highly specific memories. This was investigated in the first study by adding a positive condition (success experience) to the design of our previous study (Raes et al., 2003). Although the affect regulation hypothesis proposed the regulation of negative affect as the origin of reduced memory specificity, once it has generalised to positive memories, it predicts that positive feelings would be attenuated as well (Williams, 1996). Second, it is possible that the basic findings of Raes et al. (2003) were due to a, yet unknown, *third variable*. Such a variable would then be associated with both AM specificity and affective reactivity to an emotional (negative) event, and might thus be driving the central effects observed by Raes et al. (2003).[1] In addressing this issue, we added in Study 1 a set of instruments measuring likely candidates to act as such a third variable. In this respect we included instruments measuring variables such as working memory capacity, general personality dimensions, trait anxiety, and contingent self-esteem (or "conditional" self-esteem, i.e., self-esteem that is highly dependent or based on the approval of others or oneself). It might be, for example, that high-specific individuals' self-esteem is more dependent on others' approval or feedback, and because of that they react

---

[1] Note that in the Raes et al. (2003) study no differences were found for high- and low-specific individuals on a measure of conscientiousness (i.e., the Conscientiousness subscale of the NEO-Five Factory Inventory; Costa & McCrae, 1992; Hoekstra et al., 1996), nor on a measure of the motive to success and the motive to avoid failure (i.e., the Achievement Motives Scale; Lens & Baeyens, 1991; Nygård & Gjesme, 1973).

with more affect to a failure than do low-specific individuals. Or possibly, low-specific individuals are lower in trait anxiety or neuroticism, and therefore, self-report less subjective distress following a failure as compared to high-specific individuals. A working memory task was added in the light of an alternative, more cognitive account of reduced memory specificity. This cognitive hypothesis states that lack of cognitive resources, in particular central executive capacity, would hinder the search and elaboration of specific AMs (Kuyken & Brewin, 1995; see also Kuyken, in press). Possibly then, low-specific individuals in the Raes et al. (2003) study retrieved fewer specific memories, not because of an affect regulative motive, but because of poor central executive functioning.

A variable that is of particular interest with respect to this third variable issue is *repressive coping*. Individuals who use a repressive coping style are said to avoid negative affect, and are operationally defined as scoring high on a defensiveness measure in combination with low trait anxiety scores (Weinberger, Schwartz, & Davidson, 1979). Two identifying features of repressors have emerged from past research. They appear to have difficulties in recalling negative AMs (e.g., Davis, 1987; Davis & Schwartz, 1987; Myers & Brewin, 1994; Myers, Brewin, & Power, 1992; Newman & Hedberg, 1999; but see d'Argembeau, Comblain, & van der Linden, 2003) and they typically report low levels of subjective distress in stressful or self-threatening situations (e.g., Pauls & Stemmler, 2003; Weinberger et al., 1979). The similarity with low-specific individuals (Raes et al., 2003) is striking and gave rise to the hypothesis that reduced memory specificity would be linked to a repressive coping style. Singer and Salovey (1993) found that in a group of repressors, when asked to write down 10 self-defining memories, their memories were significantly less specific than those of self-assured participants (i.e., participants scoring low on both distress and restraint scales). Singer and Salovey did not use, however, the standard AMT (Williams & Broadbent, 1986; see below). This AMT is now frequently used in both experimental research as well as in clinical studies with various psychiatric populations (major depression, PTSD, schizophrenia, borderline personality disorder, Williams, 2004). The present study examines the specific possibility that individuals' low specificity in memories on this AMT is linked to a repressive coping style.

In summary, Study 1 examines: (1) whether low memory specificity is predictive of reduced negative affect following a negative experience (cf. Raes et al., 2003), *and* whether it is also predictive of an attenuation of positive feelings following a positive experience; (2) whether this effect of memory specificity on the impact of an emotional event is independent of other possible differences between high- and low-specific individuals (third variable issue); and, in particular (3) whether reduced memory specificity is related to a repressive coping style.

STUDY 1

Method

Participants

A written 10-item AMT was collectively administered to 425 first-year psychology students. Mean specificity score was 7.69 ($SD = 1.78$). On the basis of their specificity scores on this written AMT, 45 high- and 45 low-specific students (all women) were invited to participate in the experiment in return for course credit (Mage $= 18.41$ years; $SD = 2.36$). High-specific students are defined as those who retrieved a specific memory for each of the 10 cue words, whereas low-specific students were those who retrieved only six or fewer specific memories.

Materials

Autobiographical Memory Test (AMT; Williams & Broadbent, 1986). To test AM specificity the same written and oral versions of the AMT were used as in the Raes et al. (2003) study. Participants were asked to write down a specific memory (written AMT) or to describe a *specific* memory (oral AMT) for each of 10 cue words (i.e., a memory referring to one particular occasion or event that happened on a particular day at least 1 week before). Different cues were used in the oral and written version and were embedded in the frame sentence: "Can you write down/describe one specific moment or event that the word X reminds you of?" They were given 60 s to write down or to describe a memory in response to each cue word. Each response was coded as either a specific memory or a nonspecific memory. Nonspecific memories were further qualified as either an overgeneral categoric memory ("watching football on TV"), an overgeneral extended memory (e.g., "when I was still in college"), no memory (e.g., semantic associates), omission, same event (referring to an event already mentioned), or incorrect specific (referring to an event of the past week). Using this scoring procedure, previous studies at our laboratory obtained good reliability (Pousset, Raes, & Hermans, 2004; Raes et al., 2003) with interrater agreement ranging from 92% to 99% ($K = .83 - .96$). The dependent variable was the number of specific responses. If participants' first response to a cue in the oral AMT was not a specific memory, they were prompted: "Can you think of a specific time—one particular episode?" (Williams, 2000; Williams & Broadbent, 1986). However, only first responses were taken into account.

Tangram Puzzle Task (TPT). This task consists of different puzzle pieces that need to be correctly assembled to form complex patterns. Three versions were used. In the *negative experience* condition, the patterns were presented as homogeneous black figures. The TPT was presented in this version as an intelligence test; participants were told that they should be able to assemble at least six puzzles within 15 min, which is impossible. In the *neutral experience* condition, white lines indicated the position of the puzzle pieces. In this version, the TPT was presented as a filler task that needed to be validated. Participants were given 15 min and were asked to work on these puzzles at a relaxed pace. In the *positive experience* condition, the position of only a few puzzle pieces was indicated using white lines. As in the negative condition, the TPT was presented as an intelligence test. All puzzles were solvable, but somewhat more challenging than those in the easy version. Participants had to assemble 18 patterns. After every three puzzles which were correctly assembled, they were told that they had performed better compared to a norm group, to attain a gradual build up of positive feelings while doing the TPT.

Impact of Puzzle task Scale (IPS). To assess subjective distress, we used a modified Impact of Puzzle task Scale (IPS; Raes et al., 2003). Thirty items were rated on a 4-point scale (*not at all* to *very much*), for the extent to which they are experienced during the task. Fifteen items ask about *n*egative aspects (nIPS; e.g. "I was no longer able to think clearly", "I tried not to get upset"). Sample items for the 15-item *p*ositive aspects (pIPS) are "I experienced a pleasant, kind of excited feeling" and "I felt somewhat euphoric".

Visual Analogue Impact Scales (VAIS). By placing a cross along two 0–100 horizontal lines (*not at all* to *very much*), participants indicated: (1) to what extent they were still thinking about the TPT afterwards (VAIS-I; Intrusion); and (2) to what extent they experienced this "thinking back" as unpleasant (VAIS-U; Unpleasantness).

Positive and Negative Affect Schedule Scales (PANAS Scales; Watson, Clark, & Tellegen, 1988). Ten positive (Positive Affect; PA) and ten negative mood descriptors (Negative Affect; NA) are rated on a 5-point scale (*very slightly or not at all* to *very much*) for the extent to which they are experienced at the present moment (State version). The PANAS Scales have good reliability and validity (Watson et al., 1988).

State-Trait Anxiety Inventory, Trait version (STAI-T; van der Ploeg, Defares, & Spielberger, 1980). The STAI measures trait anxiety. This questionnaire has good validity and reliability (van der Ploeg et al., 1980).

Contingent Self-Esteem Scale (CSES; Paradise & Kernis, 1999). The CSES assesses the degree to which people's self-esteem is dependent on the approval of others or oneself (e.g., "An important indicator of my feelings of worth is how I perform up to my self-set standards"). Fifteen items are rated on a 5-point scale (*completely disagree* to *completely agree*). Past studies have shown adequate internal consistency (Kernis & Paradise, 2002) and reliability of the Dutch version used in the present study was satisfactory (Vansteenkiste, 2002).

Marlowe-Crowne Social Desirability Scale (MC; Crowne & Marlowe, 1964). To measure defensiveness we used the Dutch adaptation of the MC by Denayer (1974) which has good reliability and validity.

NEO-Five factor Inventory (NEO-FFI, Costa & McCrae, 1992). General personality dimensions were assessed using the Dutch version by Hoekstra, Ormel, and de Fruyt (1996), meeting good reliability and validity standards.

Group Administrable Adaptation of the Operation Span Test (GOSPAN; de Neys, d'Ydewalle, Schaeken, & Vos, 2002). The GOSPAN, which is a computerised and group administrable adaptation of the operation span task (OSPAN; Turner & Engle, 1989) with adequate reliability and validity, was used to measure working memory capacity. In the GOSPAN, participants are presented three series of 2–6 operation word strings on a computer screen. First, participants have to indicate whether a given operation is correct or false (e.g., "IS (4:2)–1 = 5?"). Next, the corresponding word is presented (e.g., "BALL"). After each set of operation-word strings, participants have to recall the list of presented words.

Procedure

Participants were tested individually. The experiment was presented as consisting of three separate validation studies. In the first part, participants were administered the MC and CSES. The second part consisted of the Tangram Puzzle Task. Participants in each specificity group were randomly assigned to either the negative, neutral, or positive experience condition. PANAS Scales (State version) were completed before and after the puzzle task (manipulation check). Next, the oral AMT was administered (third part). Upon completion of the impact and visual analogue scales, participants were debriefed. The STAI-T, NEO-FFI, and GOSPAN were collectively administered to all first year psychology students before the experiment (mean interval of time of 0.5 month).

Data analysis

Following reliability checks on the AMT, and manipulation checks on the experimental induction of mood using the TPT, the main dependent variables (reaction to the puzzles) were analysed using 2 (high vs. low specificity) × 3 (negative vs. neutral vs. positive condition) ANOVAs. One degree of freedom tests were then used to test the significance of the simple two by two interactions, focusing on the negative and positive conditions seperately. Next, the high- and low-specific participants were compared on the set of variables that was included in light of the third variable issue. Finally, the relationship between repressive coping and reduced memory specificity was examined using multiple regression analysis.

Results

Memory style as a stable characteristic

The number of specific first responses on the oral AMT was significantly correlated with the number of specific responses on the written AMT, $r(90) = .65$, $p < .001$ (mean time interval of 1.5 months). This suggests that AM specificity is relatively stable over time and over mode of retrieval (written versus oral).

Manipulation check

A one-way ANOVA on PANAS NA change scores revealed a main effect of condition, $F(2, 87) = 10.69$, $p < .001$ ($M_{NEG} = 2.77$, $SD = 4.71$; $M_{NEU} = -1.07$, $SD = 2.03$; $M_{POS} = -0.23$, $SD = 2.81$). Post hoc Tukey's HSD test showed a significantly greater increase in negative affect (NA) in the negative condition than in the neutral and positive condition. The NA change scores in the neutral and positive condition did not differ significantly. A one-way ANOVA on the PANAS positive affect (PA) change scores revealed a main effect of condition, $F(2, 87) = 23.73$, $p < .001$ ($M_{NEG} = -6.13$, $SD = 4.73$; $M_{NEU} = -2.70$, $SD = 4.06$; $M_{POS} = 1.70$, $SD = 4.43$). Post hoc Tukey's HSD test showed that mean PA change scores differed significantly between all conditions. In the negative condition, there was a greater decrease in PA as compared with the neutral condition. In the neutral condition there was a decrease in PA, which significantly differed from the increase in PA in the positive condition. These analyses confirm that the TPT manipulation successfully produced the desired emotional experiences (negative, neutral, positive).

Affective reaction to the puzzles

Table 1 presents the mean scores and standard deviations on the impact measures for the two specificity groups as a function of condition (negative vs. neutral vs. positive experience).

First, we discuss the results for the affective impact of the *negative experience* (i.e., difficult TPT condition). A 2 (high vs. low specificity) × 3 (negative vs. neutral vs. positive experience) ANOVA on the impact scale scores (*negative aspects*; nIPS) yielded a significant higher order interaction, $F(2, 84) = 7.27$, $p < .01$. One degree of freedom contrasts revealed, as predicted, a significant 2 (high vs. low specificity) × 2 (negative vs. neutral experience) interaction, $F(1, 56) = 13.71$, $p < .001$. Further contrasts showed that high-specific participants experienced significantly more subjective distress in the negative condition than

TABLE 1
Mean scores (and standard deviations) on impact measures for the high- and low-specific groups as a function of condition

Measure	Negative		Neutral		Positive	
	HS	LS	HS	LS	HS	LS
nIPS	24.00 (9.67)	13.33 (8.63)	4.07 (4.93)	6.40 (4.42)	8.27 (6.72)	6.87 (4.50)
pIPS	4.80 (3.53)	10.40 (9.92)	19.47 (9.15)	16.13 (10.00)	32.60 (13.18)	26.87 (11.85)
VAIS-I	59.60 (26.34)	34.80 (27.37)	34.67 (20.26)	32.00 (23.31)	40.73 (26.32)	42.13 (26.46)
VAIS-U	50.67 (24.17)	25.60 (20.67)	10.40 (13.09)	19.07 (20.86)	9.60 (14.86)	17.47 (20.01)

HS, high-specific group; LS, low-specific group; nIPS, impact of Puzzle task Scale (negative aspects); pIPS, Impact of Puzzle task Scale (positive aspects); VAIS, Visual Analogue Impact Scales; VAIS-I, Intrusion; VAIS-U, Unpleasantness.

low-specific participants, $F(1, 56) = 16.11$, $p < .001$, whereas both groups did not differ in the neutral condition, $F < 1$.

The same 2 × 3 interaction was only marginally significant for the *positive aspects* impact scale scores (pIPS), $F(2, 84) = 2.64$, $p < .08$. Further analyses revealed that the simple 2 (high vs. low specificity) × 2 (*negative* vs. neutral experience) interaction was marginally significant, $F(1, 56) = 2.95$, $p < .09$. High-specific participants experienced significantly fewer positive feelings in the negative condition than in the neutral condition, $F(1, 56) = 15.90$, $p < .01$, whereas this difference was not significant for low-specific participants, $F(1, 56) = 2.43$, $p = .12$.

The 2 × 3 ANOVA on the *Intrusion ratings* (VAIS-I) did not reveal a significant interaction, $F(2, 84) = 2.36$, $p = .10$. Further analyses showed that the 2 (high vs. low specificity) × 2 (negative vs. neutral experience) interaction tended towards significance, $F(1, 56) = 2.91$ $p = .09$. High-specific participants experienced significantly more intrusive thoughts in the negative condition than in the neutral condition, $F(1, 56) = 7.38$, $p < .01$, whereas this difference was not significant for low-specific participants, $F(1, 56) < 1$.

The 2 × 3 ANOVA on the *Unpleasantness ratings* (VAIS-U) did reveal a significant interaction, $F(2, 84) = 7.45$, $p < .01$. One degree of freedom contrasts showed a significant 2 (high vs. low specificity) × 2 (negative vs. neutral experience) interaction $F(1, 56) = 11.43$, $p < .01$. Further contrasts showed that high-specific participants rated thoughts about their puzzle performance as more unpleasant in the negative condition than in the neutral condition, $F(1, 56) = 32.58$, $p < .001$, whereas this difference was not present for the low-specific participants, $F(1, 56) < 1$.

Second, we discuss the results for the affective impact of the *positive experience*. One degree of freedom contrasts did not reveal a significant 2 (high vs. low specificity) × 2 (positive vs. neutral experience) interaction on the impact scale scores (*negative aspects*; nIPS), $F(1, 56) = 1.13$, $p = .29$. Also for the the *positive aspects* impact scale scores (pIPS), the expected 2 (high vs. low specificity) × 2 (positive vs. neutral experience) interaction was not significant, $F(1, 56) < 1$. For the *Intrusion ratings* (VAIS-I) and *Unpleasantness ratings* (VAIS-U), again, the same two by two interactions were not significant, both Fs < 1.

Group differences on other variables

High-specific and low-specific participants did not differ on the following measures: STAI-T, GOSPAN, and NEO-FFI subscales Openness, Extraversion, Agreeableness, and Conscientiousness. They did differ significantly, however, on contingent self-esteem (CSES), $t(88) = 3.14$, $p < .01$ ($M_{HS} = 54.11$, $SD = 5.43$; $M_{LS} = 50.13$, $SD = 6.52$), and Neuroticism (NEO-FFI), $t(79) = 2.43$, $p < .05$ ($M_{HS} = 3.16$, $SD = 0.70$; $MLS = 2.78$, $SD = 0.72$).[2] Most importantly, however, when simultaneously controlled for the measures on which the two specificity groups differed (as covariates), all the significant results reported above under "Affective reaction to the puzzles" remained significant.[3] We must note, however, that although widely applied, the use of ANCOVA to control or correct for other significant differences between preformed (or non-randomly assigned) groups has been criticised (e.g., Miller & Chapman, 2001). Therefore, we also conducted a multiple regression analysis in the negative experience condition with the impact scale scores (*negative aspects*; nIPS) as the dependent variable, and memory specificity (the average of specificity on the written AMT and specificity score on oral AMT), neuroticism and contingent self-esteem as the three predictor variables. Memory specificity came out as the only significant predictor, $\beta = .41$; $t(25) = 2.06$, $p < .05$.

Repressive coping

We conducted a multiple regression analysis with memory specificity as the dependent variable (average of specificity on the written AMT and specificity score on oral AMT) and trait anxiety × defensiveness, trait anxiety, and defensiveness as the three predictor variables. Recall that "repressive coping" is defined as a combination of low trait anxiety and high defensiveness. If repressive copers indeed retrieve less specific memories, we should expect the interaction term to be predictive of memory specificity. The regression evidenced a rather poor fit ($R^2_{adj} = 13\%$), but the overall relationship was

---

[2] Degrees of freedom vary because of missing values.

[3] The same was true when negative and positive affect scores (PANAS) at baseline (i.e., before the puzzle task) were covaried out. In fact, high- and low-specific participants did not differ at baseline for state negative and positive affect.

significant, $F(3, 78) = 5.04$, $p < .01$. Most important, the interaction term was a significant predictor, $\beta = -1.12$; $t(78) = -2.00$, $p < .05$, indicating that repressive coping style is having an effect. Following Mendolia (2002), we also calculated a continuous measure of repressive coping, which is called the Index of Self-regulation of Emotion (ISE). For each participant, this ISE is calculated by subtracting the defensiveness score (MC) from the trait anxiety score (in our study: STAI-T). This difference is then subtracted from the highest possible positive score to invert the scores: 80 − (STAI-T − MC), such that scoring high on this ISE represents more repressive coping. When this ISE was then used to predict memory specificity, it came out as a significant (negative) predictor, $\beta = -.30$; $t(80) = -2.78$, $p < .01$, clearly indicating that the more a repressive coping style is being used, the less specific AMs are retrieved. Similar evidence comes from a simple t-test comparing our high- and low-specific group on this ISE, with the low-specific group scoring higher than the high-specific group, $t(80) = -2.26$, $p < .05$. Importantly, when controlled for repressive coping (as a covariate), the significant results reported under "affective reaction to the puzzles" remained significant. In the light of the problematic nature of the use of ANCOVA to correct for group differences on potential covariates (see above), we also conducted a multiple regression analysis in the negative experience condition with the impact scale scores (*negative aspects*; nIPS) as the dependent variable, and memory specificity (the average of specificity on the written AMT and specificity score on oral AMT), and repressive coping as the two predictor variables. Memory specificity came out as the only significant predictor, $\beta = .50$; $t(26) = 2.63$, $p < .05$.

Although repressive coping and reduced AM specificity are associated, further analyses showed that the relation between repressive coping and impact scale scores (*negative aspects*; nIPS) was in the predicted direction, but that this association was not significant, $\beta = -.22$; $t(27) = -1.15$, $p = .26$. Following Baron and Kenny (1986), such relation would be a necessary condition to be met in order to establish a mediating role for reduced AM specificity of the relation between repressive coping and decreased emotional responding.

Discussion

The results of the present study replicate the findings of Raes et al. (2003) that a negative event leads to more distress in high-specific than in low-specific participants and that, afterwards, high-specific people tend to find thoughts about the negative experience intruding more frequently and rate these intrusions as more unpleasant. Recall that this was independent of higher levels of self-reported neuroticism and contingent self-esteem in high-specific individuals. The results, then, provide further evidence for Williams' (1996) affect regulation thesis that reduced specificity in memory retrieval might be used as a functional strategy to protect oneself from distress following a negative experience.

The present study also examined the relationship between AM specificity and repressive coping style. The primary reason to include a measure of repressive coping was, as mentioned in the introduction, to test the hypothesis that repressive coping would be associated with reduced AM specificity, and—subsequently—to examine whether reduced AM specificity would still predict emotional responding to a negative event once repressive coping is controlled for. This hypothesis was distilled from previous studies, reviewed in the introduction, showing that this coping style is related to: (1) difficulties in the recall of specific emotional AMs; and (2) relative lower levels of self-reported distress following self-threatening or stressful events. Also, given Williams' (1996) affect regulation hypothesis stating that reduced AM specificity may serve a cognitive avoidance function, we expected such relation between repressive-defensive coping and lack of AM specificity. Results indeed showed that AM specificity was inversely related to a repressive coping style. To our knowledge, this is the first time that an association has been reported between reduced memory specificity, as measured with the standard AMT cue word procedure, and repressive coping style.

Given this association, repressive coping appeared a likely candidate to act as a third variable accounting for the association between reduced AM specificity and decreased emotional responding. However, even when controlled for repressive coping, results showed that reduced AM specificity was still significantly related to lower levels of emotional distress in the present study.

Further analyses showed that one of the conditions to establish mediation of AM specificity did not hold, namely a significant relation between the independent variable (i.e., repressive coping) and the dependent variable (i.e., emotional distress following a stressful event). Whereas previous studies had shown that repressive coping is inversely related to self-reported negative affect following self-threatening or stressful experiences (e.g., Pauls & Stemmler, 2003; Weinberger et al., 1979), such an association was not found in the present study. One possible reason that may account for the absence of an association between repressive coping and decreased emotional responding to a stressful task, may be the relative low sample size. Another reason could be the fact that we selected participants on the basis of their level of memory specificity and not on the basis of their tendency to use a repressive coping style. That is, we did not identify separate groups based on their profile on the defensiveness measure and trait anxiety. Although the present study showed an association between repressive coping style and reduced AM retrieval on the AMT as a first exploratory step, future research should take on a more direct test of the relationship between repressive coping, AM specificity, and emotional responding using larger samples and/or select participants based on the extent to which they adopt a repressive coping style.

It was further hypothesised that reduced specificity would also attenuate positive feelings following a positive event. We predicted this on the assumption that lack of specificity, although initially developed as a means of regulating negative affect in a person's life, also generalises to positive events and positive memories (Williams, 1996). Results were, however, not in line with this prediction: High specificity did not lead to more positive feelings following a positive experience, as compared to low specificity. Possibly, such effects on positive affect only become apparent over the long term, in the presence of pathology or experience of severe traumatic events. Another possibility is that in the case of positive experiences repressive copers use strategies, other than reduced memory specificity, to counteract the attenuating effect of reduced memory specificity and/or to maximise positive feelings following a positive event. One would then expect reduced memory specificity and repressive coping to be related differently to positive emotions following a positive event. Accordingly, a multiple regression was post hoc conducted regressing postive feelings following a positive experience (pIPS) on both repressive coping (ISE) and memory specificity (average of specificity on written AMT and specificity score on oral AMT). Indeed, this analysis showed that repressive coping and memory specificity were, respectively, a significant and marginally significant predictor of positive feelings following a positive (success) experience (pIPS), $\beta = .49$; $t(23) = 2.58$, $p < .05$, and $\beta = .34$; $t(23) = 1.78$, $p < .09$, respectively. Thus, note that more repressive coping is predictive of *more* and lower specificity predictive of *less* intense positive feelings. That repressive coping is positively related to positive affect in the positive condition is also in line with a recent model of repression (Mendolia, 1999, 2002). Mendolia's model of repression states that the emotional distancing or avoidance in repressors from an emotional event only occurs when the emotional event is perceived to threaten self-concept, and that repressors in the case of a non-self-threatening emotional event (cf. the positive condition in our study with positive success feedback), will respond with *more* (positive) emotion.

The limited cognitive resource account (Kuyken, in press; Kuyken & Brewin, 1995) states that OGM, at least in part, is due to depleted cognitive resources. However, this cognitive account of reduced AM specificity was not supported. High- and low-specific participants did not differ in their scores on a working memory task.

The main finding of our previous study (Raes et al., 2003) and of Study 1 of the present paper is that the intensity of negative emotions (distress) as a result of a failure experience is positively related to AM specificity: The more specific people are in their retrieval of memories, the *more intense* negative *emotions* they report resulting from the failure experience. These findings are in line with Williams' (1996) affect regulation account, but, as mentioned earlier, contrary to findings reported by Philippot and colleagues (Philippot et al., 2003) who observed that a specific mode of accessing AMs results in relative *less intense emotions* during subsequent emotion induction.

One important difference between our studies and those of Philippot is that ours use a split-group, semi-experimental, or correlational design, whereas those of Philippot use a completely experimental design in which participants are randomly allocated to either a specific or overgeneral access mode condition. Indeed, when Philippot and colleagues post hoc allocated participants in a subsequent unpublished study as either high- or low-specific using our criteria on an AMT that was administered before the experiment, results were such that low-specific students tended to report less negative emotions following a failure task (P. Philippot, personal communication, 19 January 2004). All this seems to suggest that chronic or "trait" vs. manipulated memory specificity results in quite different effects on the intensity of emotional reactions. In this respect, Philippot et al. (2003, p. 271) note that in the field of emotion regulation it is no exception that experimental manipulation effects show opposite patterns to those from correlational effects.

However, this trait vs. state issue does not readily explain the divergent effects. We propose that an explanation for the contradictory findings possibly lies in the fact that low-specific individuals in our studies are not necessarily equivalent to the individuals who are primed with overgeneral categoric memories in Philippot's studies. Recall that low-specific participants were selected according to the criterium of retrieving only six or fewer specific memories. We did so following other AMT studies of which most have used the raw number of specific memories on the AMT as the main dependent variable (see above).

However, when we post hoc examined which nonspecific memories these low-specific individuals had retrieved, we noticed that it were mainly omissions ($M = 2.00$; $SD = 1.65$) rather than overgeneral categoric memories that had a low prevalence rate (e.g., "Every time I attend a funeral"; $M = 0.42$; $SD = 0.62$). In particular, such overgeneral categoric memories are generally regarded as representing OGM in depression (e.g., Barnhofer, de Jong-Meyer, Kleinpass, & Nikesch, 2002; Williams & Dritschel, 1988). It was also this *categoric* retrieval style that was experimentally induced in Philippot's studies. We, however, selected low-specific participants on the basis of a low number of *specific* memories.

We thus suggest that "trait" low specificity, as defined in our studies, is mostly concerned with accessing or retrieving fewer specific memories (cf. omissions) and, as such, may form part of a defensive strategy against too intense negative emotions (cf. the link with repressive coping). Recalling fewer specific memories, thus, appears to enable people to suffer less distress and experience fewer intense emotions following a stressful experience. Overgeneral categoric retrieval on the other hand arouses *more* intense emotions as suggested by the findings of Philippot et al. (2003). The bottom line is that one can be low-specific in the sense of having difficulty recalling specific events from one's past, without necessarily being overgeneral in a categoric sense, that is, summarising memories. All this suggests that the affect regulating quality in avoiding specific memories (Williams, 1996) lies not so much in categoric retrieval, as well in not accessing highly specific memories. Overgeneral categoric memory, on the other hand, does not seem to have affect regulating qualities. On the contrary, categoric nonspecificity appears to lead to enhanced emotional reactivity.

In line with this reasoning, one would expect low-specific individuals to report *more* intense negative affect in response to a negative experience when they are experimentally induced to retrieve memories in a *categoric* way (cf. Philippot et al., 2003), as compared to when they have to perform the standard AMT first (i.e., when they are asked to retrieve specific memories). This was investigated in a second study. Previous studies have suggested that low-specific individuals avoid specific memories (as an affect regulating mechanism) by retrieving fewer specific memories, without therefore necessarily retrieving overgeneral categoric memories. If a categoric access mode to AM is indeed associated with more intense affect, it would be interesting to see if it can override a habitual repressive-defensive retrieval style in this group of people when confronted with a negative event.

STUDY 2

Method

Design

The overall design was a 2 (specific vs. overgeneral memory induction) × 2 (negative vs. neutral experience) between-subjects design, resulting in four groups: specific induction-negative experience, specific induction-neutral experience, overgeneral induction-negative experience, and overgeneral induction-neutral experience.

Participants

On the basis of their specificity scores on a written 10-item AMT, collectively administered to all first-year psychology students, 48 low-specific students (all women) were invited to participate in the experiment in return for course credit (M_{age} = 18.25 years; SD = 1.19). Of the 48 low-specific participants, 24 retrieved 6 or less specific memories on the written screening AMT [cf. low-specific participants as operationalised in Study 1 and in the Raes et al. (2003) study], and 24 retrieved 7 specific memories on the screening AMT. As a score of 7 is still under the mean, the latter participants are regarded as "moderate" low-specific participants. Low-specific and moderate low-specific participants were equally and randomly allocated to each of the four groups in Study 2. The moderate low-specific participants were included for experimental reasons, but it had no effect on the results, so no further mention will be made of this topic.

Materials

Retrieval style induction. We used an adaptation of Williams et al. (1996) retrieval style induction procedure. This procedure proved successful in manipulating the level of specificity with which participants recall autobiographical material (Williams et al., 1996). We used a list of 18 cues (9 positive and 9 negative words). In the specific induction group, participants were instructed to retrieve a specific memory in response to each of the 18 cue words ("Describe one specific occasion or moment in your past when you felt X"). It was clearly emphasised that it should be a single event that happened to them on a particular place and at a particular time in the past, and did not last longer than one day. Participants were given two examples of a specific memory (e.g., "I felt unhappy, that first day at campus in the student's restaurant, drinking a coffee all by myself", to the cue *unhappy*). In the overgeneral induction group, participants were instructed to give a "type of event" that each of the 18 cues brought to mind ("Describe a type or sort of event that makes you feel X"). Participants were given two examples of what was meant with a "type or sort of event" (e.g., "I feel unhappy, every time my brother and I have a quarrel", in response to the cue *unhappy*). It was explained to them that by type of event we meant the sort of thing that happens to them or has happened to them in the past ("categoric memory"). For both the specific and the overgeneral induction group, participants were allowed to practice with two sample cues before the 18 test words were administered. Participants were given 60 seconds to describe a specific memory (specific induction group) or a summary or category of events (overgeneral induction group). If their first response did not meet the criteria for either a specific memory (specific induction group) or a categoric memory (overgeneral induction group) they were prompted to continue their search for such a memory. The prompting procedure was repeated until a memory of the requested type was retrieved. After 60 seconds, the experimenter proceeded to the next cue.

Tangram Puzzle Task (TPT). The negative and neutral conditions of Study 1 were used. Given that our main interest was to investigate the impact of the experimental manipulation on the impact of a negative experience, the positive condition was not included.

Sentence Completion Task (SCT). Participants were asked to complete 14 sentence beginnings in a written format (e.g., "I hope I'll never...", "In my opinion, creativity is..."). The SCT was used as a filler task to bridge the time between the TPT and the administration of posttest impact and intrusion measures. In addition, the SCT was used as an extra manipulation check for retrieval style induction.

Impact measures. The 15-item negative aspects Impact of Puzzle task Scale (nIPS), the Visual Analogue Impact Scales VAIS-Intrusion and VAIS-Unpleasantness, and the State version of the Positive and Negative Affect Schedule Scales (PANAS Scales; Watson et al., 1988) were used as in Study 1.

Procedure

Participants were randomly allocated to one of the four groups and were tested individually.

The experiment was presented as consisting of three separate validation studies. The first study was introduced as a validation study of a cue word memory task (induction phase). The second study consisted of the Tangram Puzzle Task, an alleged intelligence test. PANAS Scales (State version) were completed before and after the puzzle task (manipulation check). Next, the SCT was completed (third study; filler task). Upon completion of the impact and visual analogue scales, participants were debriefed.

Data analysis

Following manipulation checks of the mood induction procedure and of the experimental induction of retrieval styles, the main dependent variables (reaction to the puzzles) were analysed using 2 (specific vs. overgeneral induction group) × 2 (condition: negative vs. neutral experience) ANOVAs.

Results

Manipulation checks

A one-way ANOVA on PANAS NA change scores revealed a main effect of condition, $F(1, 46) = 17.99$, $p < .001$ ($M_{NEG} = 3.42$, $SD = 5.07$; $M_{NEU} = -1.25$, $SD = 1.82$). A one-way ANOVA on the PANAS PA change scores revealed a main effect of condition, $F(1, 46) = 11.47$, $p < .01$ ($M_{NEG} = -5.71$, $SD = 5.23$; $M_{NEU} = -1.29$, $SD = 3.68$). These results show that we successfully induced a negative experience.

A one-way ANOVA on the number of first responses on the 18-item AMT that are specific showed that in the specific induction group more specific memories were retrieved (as a first response) than following the overgeneral induction procedure, $F(1, 46) = 1037.37$, $p < .001$ ($M_{SIG} = 14.67$, $SD = 2.20$; $M_{OIG} = 0.08$, $SD = 0.28$). Also, a one-way ANOVA on the number of first responses that were of the categoric overgeneral type, indicated that in the overgeneral induction group more categoric responses were retrieved (as a first response) than following the specific induction procedure, $F(1, 46) = 6625.96$, $p < .001$ ($M_{OIG} = 17.46$, $SD = 0.66$; $M_{SIG} = 0.50$, $SD = 0.78$). This is the first confirmation that the manipulation had succeeded in producing more categoric/

generic memories following the overgeneral induction procedure, and more specific memories following the specific induction procedure.

The response to one of the sentences of the Sentence Completion Task (SCT) was used as an extra manipulation check of retrieval style induction. Participants were explained that it concerned a study on style, imagination, and creativity. One of the sentences probed for the past ("Last year..."). Two independent raters scored the written responses to this sentence stem on a 5-point specificity scale, with higher scores representing higher specificity.[4] The average of the scores of the two raters, who showed sufficiently high interrater agreement ($r = .89$, $p < .001$), was taken as an additional specificity check score. As expected, the participants of the overgeneral retrieval style induction group obtained a lower specificity score than those who were induced into a specific retrieval style, $t(46) = 2.96$, $p < .01$ ($M_{OIG} = 2.56$, $SD = 1.06$; $M_{SIG} = 3.46$, $SD = 1.03$). Again, this convincingly shows that the retrieval style manipulation was successful.

The affective impact of a negative experience

Table 2 presents the mean scores and standard deviations on the impact measures for both induction groups in function of condition.

A 2 (specific vs. overgeneral) × 2 (negative vs. neutral experience) ANOVA on the impact scale scores (*negative aspects*; nIPS) yielded the predicted significant interaction, $F(1, 44) = 5.43$, $p < .05$. One degree of freedom contrasts showed that in the negative experience condition participants from the overgeneral induction group experienced more distress as compared with participants who were induced into a specific retrieval style, $F(1, 44) = 7.58, p < .01$. In the neutral experience condition, both induction groups did not differ, $F < 1$.

The 2 × 2 ANOVA on the *Intrusion ratings* (VAIS-I) also revealed a significant interaction, $F(1, 44) = 4.54$, $p < .05$. One degree of freedom contrasts showed that participants who were induced into an overgeneral retrieval mode experienced significantly more intrusive thoughts in the negative condition than in the neutral condition, $F(1, 44) = 20.27$, $p < .001$, whereas this difference was not significant for participants of the specific induction group, $F(1, 44) < 2.22, p = .14$.

Similarly, the 2 × 2 ANOVA on the *Unpleasantness ratings* (VAIS-U) revealed a significant interaction, $F(1, 44) = 5.15, p < .05$. Participants that were

---

[4] 1 = no memory, mere association (e.g., "Last year... I would never have predicted to be where I am now"); 2 = an overgeneral categoric or summary-type memory (e.g., "Last year... I felt sad on many occasions"); 3 = an overgeneral memory that extends over the entire past year ("Last year... I was still at St. Michael's high school"); 4 = a particular event that does not extend over the entire past year, but lasted longer than a day, *and* that did not happen repeatedly (e.g., "Last year... I spent a week with a colleague in North Wales); 5 = a specific event, that did not last longer than a day (e.g., "Last year... I had a wonderful time at the surprise party for my 18th birthday").

TABLE 2
Mean scores (and standard deviations) on impact measures for the specific and overgeneral induction groups as a function of condition

	Negative		Neutral	
Measure	SIG	OIG	SIG	OIG
nIPS	11.83 (8.21)	19.00 (8.90)	3.92 (3.42)	2.50 (2.07)
VAIS-I	43.92 (24.45)	58.08 (25.59)	29.67 (24.20)	15.00 (19.00)
VAIS-U	35.00 (28.48)	55.33 (20.66)	17.42 (16.56)	10.17 (16.15)

SIG, = specific induction group; OIG, overgeneral induction group; nIPS, Impact of Puzzle task Scale (negative aspects); VAIS, Visual Analogue Impact Scales; VAIS-I, Intrusion; VAIS-U, Unpleasantness.

induced into an overgeneral retrieval mode rated thoughts about their puzzle performance as more unpleasant in the negative condition as compared with participants that were induced into a specific retrieval style, $F(1, 44) = 5.60$, $p < .05$. In the neutral experience condition, both induction groups did not differ, $F < 1$.

Discussion

Results replicated the finding of Philippot et al. (2003) that the induction of a *categoric* memory retrieval mode leads to relatively *more* intense negative affect following a negative experience. Although our methods for retrieval mode and emotion induction differ from those used by Philippot et al. (2003), the fact that both result in similar findings is an indication of the robustness of the phenomenon. Philippot et al. (2003) proposed the *strategic inhibition hypothesis* to account for their pattern of findings (see above).

We would like to advance here an alternative, but not mutually exclusive account for the emotion enhancing effect of catgoric memory retrieval. This being an attempt to knit the findings of Study 2 and those of Philippot et al. (2003), together with an increasing body of evidence suggesting a link between depressive rumination and overgeneral categoric memory retrieval (Park, Goodyer, & Teasdale, 2004; Ramponi, Barnard, & Nimmo-Smith, 2004; Watkins & Teasdale, 2001, 2004; Watkins, Teasdale, & Williams, 2000). We suggest that a possible alternative explanation for the emotion enhancing effect of categoric memories, observed by Philippot et al. (2003) as well as in Study 2, lies it its association with ruminative or abstract vs. nonruminative or concrete thinking. Williams (1996) already suggested that OGM may be related to rumination. He proposed that ruminative thinking might be maintaining or contributing to OGM. In this respect, Williams coined the notion of *mnemonic interlock*, referring to an overelaboration of categoric self-describing labels or memories (e.g., "I've always failed"). He suggests that such overelaboration of summary-type labels or memories is "encouraged *and by itself encouraging* ruminative self-focus" (Williams, 1996, p. 261; our emphasis). So far, although experimental studies have only provided evidence for the effect of rumination on OGM (Park et al., 2004; Watkins & Teasdale, 2001, 2004; Watkins, et al., 2000), it is generally assumed that OGM and rumination are *mutually* reinforcing. So it is not unlikely that the experimental induction of an overgeneral categoric access mode to AM, may have established a ruminative mind-set in participants prior to the experience of an emotional event. Indeed, in Study 2, participants who were induced into an overgeneral retrieval mode reported more intrusive thoughts afterwards in the negative condition than in the neutral condition, whereas this difference was not present for participants of the specific induction group. Rumination is generally regarded as a highly verbally based style of thinking during which generic, relatively abstract self-related information (vs. concrete and event-specific material) is cognitively rehearsed. So the idea is that when participants experienced the experimental failure while this ruminative mind-set was activated (through the induction of a categoric retrieval style), this may have caused the intensification of negative feelings and thoughts following this failure experience, as compared to the specific retrieval group. Also, from a vast amount of research it is known that rumination (vs. distraction) prolongs or worsens negative feelings (for a recent review, see Nolen-Hoeksema, 2004).

GENERAL DISCUSSION

In two studies, the effect of specificity of autobiographical memory retrieval on affective impact of an emotional event was examined. Results of Study 1 replicated the earlier finding that people who habitually retrieve few specific memories report relatively fewer negative feelings following a failure experience. Furthermore, Study 1 extended this finding by demonstrating an association with repressive or defensive coping, which fits with Williams' (1996) affect regulation account of reduced AM specificity. These findings, however, are opposite to those recently reported by Philippot and colleagues (2003), who found that people report more intense emotion when primed with overgeneral memories than when primed with specific memories. In Study 2, these results were extended to a different paradigm to that of Philippot et al. (2003). Above, we suggested how this intensification of emotion after overgeneral AM retrieval induction might be explained by a ruminative mind-set, installed by this overgeneral or generic access to AM.

We suggested that the seemingly contradictory findings between our previous study (Raes et al., 2003) and Study 1 (present paper) on the one hand, and Philippot et al. (2003) and Study 2 (present paper) on the other hand, may be resolved by distinguishing between two types of "low specificity". One can be low-specific: (1) because one retrieves relatively few specific memories—without therefore necessarily recalling past events in an overgeneral way; or (2) because one retrieves relatively more overgeneral categoric memories. The current studies, together with the work of Philippot and others, offer preliminary support for this "two types explanation".

But how, then, do the two "styles" relate to one another? One way in which the two might relate is in a developmental psychopathological sense. In this view, the overgeneral retrieval style that is observed in depressed individuals could be seen as a counterproductive outgrowth of something that started as a functional strategy, namely the blocking or avoiding of specific memories. The latter can be observed in low-specific students, and pays off in the short term as they experience fewer intense negative emotions (Raes et al., 2003; Study 1 of the present paper). In the long-term, however, this strategy might backfire and develop into what is regarded as a vulnerability or depressogenic factor, namely a categoric retrieval style. Such an overgeneral style, in which memories are recalled in a categoric, summarised form is no longer characterised by the benefits of the avoidant retrieval style at the outset. On the contrary, it puts one at risk for developing emotional problems, in particular, depression. This fits with the affect regulation hypothesis. Following the argument that was developed here, the only part of the hypothesis that possibly may need alteration is where it states that avoiding memories by remaining at a categoric level is affect reducing. More likely, the affect regulating quality in avoiding specific memories lies not so much in categoric retrieval, as in not accessing (highly specified) memories.

How does the avoidance of specific memories (without clear categoric memories) over time then develop into a depressotypic categoric retrieval style? One possibility is that after some time, as suggested by the affect regulation theory, an associative network will exist of intertwined self-descriptive categoric memories due to (increasing) ruminative thinking (i.e., mnemonic interlock).[5] But how is the avoidance of certain thoughts or memories then assumed to increase ruminative thinking over time? For Wegner (e.g., Gold & Wegner, 1995) one of the origins of ruminative thinking is chronic suppression or avoidance of thoughts about events that have occurred in the past. The ironic or paradoxical effect of suppressing unwanted thoughts resulting in the re-emergence of what is suppressed, the so-called rebound effect, is convincingly supported by a number of studies (e.g., Wegner & Wenzlaff, 1996).

Thus, in the short term, or in the face of an experimental (minor) stressor, this strategy of reduced specificity is useful to regulate affect (via cognitive avoid-

---

[5] Another, not necessarily competing possibility, is that through the avoidance of specific retrieval, the specific or contextual features of memories are not consolidated. As a consequence, over time, memories will be recalled in a categoric or summarised form.

ance). However, in the long term or in the face of severe traumatic experiences (e.g., child sexual abuse), significant life events or real-life stressors, this strategy will not suffice, and even backfires. A similar idea has been put forward by Hayes, Wilson, Gifford, Follette, and Strosahl (1996, p. 1157): "In many instances, there is nothing harmful about seeking relaxation or putting off distracting thoughts or avoiding physical pain. Ironically, however, these healthy forms of experiential avoidance apply most clearly when the experiences involved are not intense and clinically relevant".

Another study worth mentioning in this respect, is that by Wenzlaff and Luxton (2003) in which they found evidence that thought suppression over time can indeed enhance or promote depressive rumination when people experience high levels of real-life stress. In a longitudinal study, they selected high- and low-suppressors, who both had low levels of depression and rumination. However, 10 weeks later, high-suppressors who reported to have experienced high levels of stress evidenced significant increases in ruminative thinking and dysphoria, relative to the low-suppressors and also to the high-suppressors who had experienced relatively low levels of stress.

Another way in which the relationship between two types or styles of low specificity might be conceptualised is that both are (relatively) independent of one another. A small subsample of people—like the low-specific students in our studies—just happen to retrieve relatively fewer specific memories in response to cue words, without therefore necessarily evidencing a categoric memory retrieval style. It is this subsample who employs a repressive coping style, of which the particular memory retrieval style probably forms part. On the other hand, there are people who recall past events in a rather general way, like depressed people. The evidence so far suggests that this is maladaptive, or might even represent a vulnerability marker for depression. Why then do we not observe this vulnerability marker (i.e., categoric memories) in large groups of students (cf. the overall low rate of categoric memories generated by students in response to AMT cue words)? One would expect overgeneral catgeoric memory to be more frequent in these groups, given that the disorder for which it is regarded as a vulnerability index (i.e., depression) is so highly prevalent. One reason for OGM to be low prevalent in nonclinical populations might be the nature of the AMT procedure. It might very well be that even if some students have the tendency to think of their past in general terms, they still manage to come up with specific memories to cue words when asked to do so. But, once depressed, this overgeneral retrieval style might become like a dominant response style, more and more difficult to inhibit. This implies that even when students come up with specific memories to cues, it might nevertheless be that some of them actually do have a tendency to recall past material in a generalised way. Perhaps, then, this vulnerabilty needs to be detected by another method than the AMT in nonclinical participants (in order to overcome the floor effect of categoric memories in existing studies using nonclinical participants).

There are several limitations of the presented studies that warrant consideration. First, affect regulation was not directly measured. Rather, affect was assessed, per se, that is, by means of a single scale which was administered at the end of each of the studies. Second, affect regulation was treated as a result of AM retrieval style. However, the reverse might also be the case, in that specificity of AM retrieval style is an outcome of individual differences in emotion regulation, and not (only) a predictor. Although this is less likely to be the case in Study 2 (in which AM retrieval style was experimentally manipulated prior to induction of failure and the assessment of resulting distress), this may nevertheless entail a valid alternative, yet not mutually exclusive explanation for the Study 1 data. It might be that particular affect regulation strategies impact the extent of specificity with which events are encoded or consolidated and thus later retrieved from AM. For example, data by Schimmack and Hartmann (1997) suggest that repressive copers may retrieve fewer specific unpleasant emotion memories, partly because they experience fewer negative emotions when faced with negatively toned events (thus resulting in fewer unpleasant AMs available). A third limitation is that our two studies solely focused on nonclinical female students, thereby limiting the generalisability of the findings to males and clinical samples. Also, Study 2 only used participants who habitually retrieve few specific memories in response to cue words, with resulting reduced generalisability of the findings. Thus, future research is needed to determine the extent to which the present results would generalise to a broader range of individuals. Fourth, sample sizes were relatively small, which limits statistical power. This is especially important to bear in mind with regard to the results for the positive or success condition in Study 1. Therefore, conclusions with respect to the absence of any effect of memory specificity for the positive condition in Study 1 should be treated with caution, since power was low.

Despite these limitations, the data described here indicate that it may be important to distinguish between two types of nonspecific AM retrieval; that is, nonspecificity due to: (1) recall of few specific memories (i.e., omissions); and nonspecificity that is attributable to (2) recall of overgeneral categoric memories. Also, the present findings, together with previous work (Philippot et al., 2003; Raes et al., 2003) suggest that both types are oppositely related to emotional responding: Whereas nonspecificity of type (1) is associated with decreased emotional responding, type (2) nonspecificity is associated with heightened emotional responding. It was further suggested that the relationship between the two types may be conceptualised in at least two ways. It might be that both are related in a developmental way in which type (1) over time develops into type (2) with short-term advantages turning into long-term disadvantages. Or, both types of nonspecific AM recall may simply constitute two distinct phenomena. Regarding the latter case, it was mentioned that OGM (i.e., categoric retrieval) may then need to be detected in nonclinical populations using other means than the AMT (see above). So one possible avenue for future research will be the development of a more sensitive method to tap OGM in nonclinical samples, or to adapt the AMT for that purpose. Also, if both types indeed represent two separate memory phenomena, then the present results constitute an important note of caution for the interpretation of AMT data in nonclinical populations. Namely, this would imply that retrieving few specific memories is not necessarily the same as retrieving overgeneral categoric memories. To date, researchers often use the number of specific memories as a primary index for OGM and so have we (see Study 1 of the present paper and Raes et al., 2003). Future research is sorely needed to further clarify the precise relationship between both types of nonspecific AM retrieval.

The importance of assessing known vulnerability markers for emotional disorders, such as OGM, in nonclinical groups should be clear in terms of prevention issues. Future research should therefore further elucidate whether the AMT is truly a suitable method for this purpose or whether it is picking up something different in these groups. Longitudinal studies might inform us whether OGM, in a *preclinical phase*, expresses itself in a different way, namely, as the relative inability to retrieve specific memories, evidencing itself in omissions, rather than in overgeneral categoric memories.

REFERENCES

Barnhofer, T., de Jong-Meyer, R., Kleinpass, A., & Nikesch, S. (2002). Specificity of autobiographical memories in depression: An analysis of retrieval processes in a think-aloud task. *British Journal of Clinical Psychology, 41,* 411–416.

Baron, R. M., & Kenny, D. A. (1986). The moderator-mediator variable distinction in social psychological research: Conceptual, strategic, and statistical considerations. *Journal of Personality and Social Psychology, 51,* 1173–1182.

Brittlebank, A. D., Scott, J., Williams, J. M. G., & Ferrier, I. N. (1993). Autobiographical memory in depression: State or trait marker? *British Journal of Psychiatry, 162,* 118–121.

Conway, M. A., & Pleydell-Pearce, C. W. (2000). The construction of autobiographical memories in the self-memory system. *Psychological Review 107,* 261–288.

Costa, P. T., & McCrae, R. R. (1992). *Revised NEO personality inventory (NEO-PI-R) and the five factor inventory (NEO-FFI): Professional manual.* Odessa, FL: Psychological Assessment Resources.

Crowne, D. P., & Marlowe, D. (1964). *The approval motive: Studies in evaluative dependence.* New York: Wiley.

Dalgleish, T., Tchanturia, K., Serpell, L., Hems, S., Yiend, J., de Silva, P., & Treasure, J. (2003). Self-reported parental abuse relates to autobiographical memory style in patients with eating disorders. *Emotion, 3,* 211–222.

D'Argembeau, A., Comblain, C., & van der Linden, M. (2003). Phenomenal characteristics of autobiographical memories for positive, negative, and neutral events. *Applied Cognitive Psychology, 17,* 281–294.

Davis, P. J. (1987). Repression and the inaccessibility of affective memories. *Journal of Personality and Social Psychology, 53,* 585–593.

Davis, P. J., & Schwartz, G. E. (1987). Repression and the inaccessibility of affective memories. *Journal of Personality and Social Psychology, 52,* 155–162.

de Decker, A., Hermans, D., Raes, F., & Eelen, P. (2003). Autobiographical memory specificity and trauma in inpatient adolescents. *Journal of Clinical Child and Adolescent Psychology, 32*, 23–32.

Denayer, L. (1974). *Sociale wenselijkheidsschalen: Aanpassing van de Marlowe-Crowne schaal voor EHSO* [Social desirability scales: Adaptation of the Marlowe-Crowne Scale for senior high school]. Unpublished master's thesis, University of Leuven, Belgium.

de Neys, W., d'Ydewalle, G., Schaeken, W., & Vos, G. (2002). A Dutch, computerized, and group administrable adaptation of the operation span test. *Psychologica Belgica, 42*, 177–190.

Gold, D. B., & Wegner, D. M. (1995). Origins of ruminative thought: Trauma, incompleteness, nondisclosure, and suppression. *Journal of Applied Social Psychology, 25*, 1245–1261.

Hayes, S. C., Wilson, K. G., Gifford, E. V., Follette, V. M., & Strosahl, K. (1996). Experiential avoidance and behavioural disorders: A functional dimensional approach to diagnosis and treatment. *Journal of Consulting and Clinical Psychology, 64*, 1152–1168.

Hermans, D., van den Broeck, K., Belis, G., Raes, F., Pieters, G., & Eelen, P. (2004). Trauma and autobiographical memory specificity in depressed inpatients. *Behaviour Research and Therapy, 42*, 775–789.

Hoekstra, H., Ormel, H., & de Fruyt, F. de (1996). *Handleiding NEO persoonlijkheidsvragenlijsten NEO-PI-R en NEO-FFI* [Manual of the NEO personality questionnaires NEO-PI-R en NEO-FFI]. Lisse: Swets & Zeitlinger.

Horowitz, M., Wilner, N., & Alvarez, W. (1979). Impact of Event Scale: A measure of subjective stress. *Psychosomatic Medicine, 41*, 209–218.

Kernis, M. H., & Paradise, A. W. (2002). Distinguishing between secure and fragile forms of high self-esteem. In E. L. Deci & R. M. Ryan (Eds.), *Handbook of self-determination research* (pp. 339–360). Rochester, NY: University of Rochester Press.

Kuyken, W. (in press). The autobiographical memory paradox in depression. *The Psychologist*.

Kuyken, W., & Brewin, C. R. (1995). Autobiographical memory functioning in depression and reports of early abuse. *Journal of Abnormal Psychology, 104*, 585–591.

Lens, W., & Baeyens, H. (1991). *Dutch version of the achievement motives scale.* Unpublished manuscript, University of Leuven, Belgium.

Mendolia, M. (1999). Repressors' appraisals of emotional stimuli in threatening and nonthreatening positive emotional contexts. *Journal of Research in Personality, 33*, 1–26.

Mendolia, M. (2002). An index of self-regulation of emotion and the study of repression in social contexts that threaten or do not threaten self-concept. *Emotion, 2*, 215–232.

Miller, G. A., & Chapman, J. P. (2001). Misunderstanding analysis of covariance. *Journal of Abnormal Psychology, 110*, 40–48.

Myers, L. B., & Brewin, C. R. (1994). Recall of early experience and the repressive coping style. *Journal of Abnormal Psychology, 103*, 288–292.

Myers, L. B., Brewin, C. R., & Power, M. J. (1992). Repression and autobiographical memory. In M. A. Conway, D. C. Rubin, H. Spinnler, & W. Wagenaar (Eds.), *Theoretical perspectives on autobiographical memory* (pp. 375–390). Dordrecht, The Netherlands: Kluwer.

Newman, L. S., & Hedberg, D. A. (1999). Repressive coping and the inaccessibility of negative autobiographical memories: Converging evidence. *Personality and Individual Differences, 27*, 45–53.

Nolen-Hoeksema, S. (2004). The response styles theory. In C. Papageorgiou & A. Wells (Eds.), *Depressive rumination: Nature, theory, and treatment* (pp. 107–124). Chichester, UK: Wiley.

Nygård, R., & Gjesme, T. (1973). Assessment of achievement motives: Comments and suggestions. *Scandinavian Journal of Educational Research, 17*, 319–327.

Paradise, A. W., & Kernis, M. H. (1999). *Development of the contingent self-esteem scale.* Unpublished data, University of Georgia.

Park, R. J., Goodyer, I. M., & Teasdale, J. D. (2004). Effects of induced rumination and distraction on mood and overgeneral autobiographical memory in adolesecent major depressive disorder and controls. *Journal of Child Psychology and Psychiatry, 45*, 996–1006.

Pauls, C. A., & Stemmler, G. (2003). Repressive and defensive coping during fear and anger. *Emotion, 3*, 284–302.

Philippot, P., Schaefer, A., & Herbette, G. (2003). Consequences of specific processing of emotional information: Impact of general versus specific autobiographical memory priming on emotion elicitation. *Emotion, 3*, 270–283.

Pousset, G., Raes, F., & Hermans, D. (2004). *Correlates of autobiographical memory specificity in a non-clinical student population.* Unpublished manuscript.

Raes, F., Hermans, D., de Decker, A., Eelen, P., & Williams, J. M. G. (2003). Autobiographical memory specificity and affect regulation: An experimental approach. *Emotion, 3*, 201–206.

Ramponi, C., Barnard, P. J., & Nimmo-Smith, I. (2004). Recollection deficits in dysphoric mood: An effect of schematic models and executive mode? *Memory, 12*, 655–670.

Schimmack, U., & Hartmann, K. (1997). Individual differences in the memory representation of emotional episodes: Exploring the cognitive processes in repression. *Journal of Personality and Social Psychology, 73*, 1064–1079.

Singer, J. A., & Salovey, P. (1993). *The remembered self: Emotion and memory in personality.* New York: The Free Press.

Turner, M. L., & Engle, R. W. (1989). Is working memory capacity task dependent? *Journal of Memory & Language, 28*, 127–154.

van der Ploeg, H. M., Defares, P. B., & Spielberger, C. D. (1980). *Handleiding bij de Zelf-Beoordelings-Vragenlijst (ZBV). Een Nederlandstalige bewerking van de Spielberger state-trait anxiety inventory (STAI-DY)* [Manual of the self-assessment questionnaire (SAQ). A Dutch revision of the Spielberger state-trait anxiety inventory (STAI-DY)]. Lisse, The Netherlands: Swets & Zeitlinger.

Vansteenkiste, M. (2002). *Dutch version of the contingent self-esteem scale.* Unpublished manuscript, University of Leuven, Belgium.

Watkins, E., & Teasdale, J. D. (2001). Rumination and overgeneral memory in depression: Effects of self-focus and analytic thinking. *Journal of Abnormal Psychology, 110*, 353–357.

Watkins, E., & Teasdale, J. D. (2004). Adaptive and maladaptive self-focus in depression. *Journal of Affective Disorders, 82*, 1–8.

Watkins, E., Teasdale, J. D., & Williams, R. M. (2000). Decentring and distraction reduce overgeneral autobiographical memory in depression. *Psychological Medicine, 30*, 911–920.

Watson, D., Clark, L. A., & Tellegen, A. (1988). Development and validation of brief measures of positive and negative affect: The PANAS Scales. *Journal of Personality and Social Psychology, 54*, 1063–1070.

Wegner, D. M., & Wenzalff, R. M. (1996). Mental control. In E. T. Higgins & A. W. Kruglanski (Eds.), *Social psychology: Handbook of basic principles* (pp. 466–492). New York: Guilford Press.

Weinberger, D. A., Schwartz, G. E., & Davidson, R. J. (1979). Low-anxious, high-anxious, and repressive coping styles: Psychometric patterns and behavioral responses to stress. *Journal of Abnormal Psychology, 88*, 369–380.

Wenzlaff, R. M., & Luxton, D. D. (2003). The role of thought suppression in depressive rumination. *Cognitive Therapy and Research, 27*, 293–308.

Williams, J. M. G. (1996). Depression and the specificity of autobiographical memory. In D. C. Rubin (Ed.), *Remembering our past. Studies in autobiographical memory* (pp. 244–267). Cambridge, NY: Cambridge University Press.

Williams, J. M. G. (2000). *Autobiographical memory test: Report of the AMT consensus meeting.* Institute of Medical and Social Care Research, University of Wales, Bangor.

Williams, J. M. G. (2004). Experimental cognitive psychology and clinical practice: Autobiographical memory as a paradigm case. In J. Yiend (Ed.), *Cognition, emotion and psychopathology* (pp. 251–269). Cambridge, UK: Cambridge University Press.

Williams, J. M. G., & Broadbent, K. (1986). Autobiographical memory in suicide attempters. *Journal of Abnormal Psychology, 95*, 144–149.

Williams, J. M. G., & Dritschel, B. (1992). Categoric and extended autobiographical memories. In M. A. Conway, D. C. Rubin, H. Spinnler, & W. A. Wagenaar (Eds), *Theoretical perspectives on autobiographical memory* (pp. 391–412). Dordrecht: Kluwer Academic.

Williams, J. M. G., Ellis, N. C., Tyers, C., Healy, H., Rose, G., & MacLeod, A. K. (1996). The specificity of autobiographical memory and imageability of the future. *Memory and Cognition, 24*, 116–125.

Williams, J. M. G., Stiles, W. B., & Shapiro, D. A. (1999). Cognitive mechanisms in the avoidance of painful and dangerous thoughts: Elaborating the assimilation model. *Cognitive Therapy and Research, 23*, 285–306.

Retrieval-induced forgetting of autobiographical memory details

Ineke Wessel
University of Groningen, The Netherlands

Beatrijs J. A. Hauer
University of Maastricht, The Netherlands

Several studies suggest that intrusive and overgeneral autobiographical memory are correlated. Thus, paradoxically, in some patients a hyperaccessibility of memory for one (series of) event(s) goes hand-in-hand with a scarcity of memories for other personal experiences. This clinical observation is reminiscent of the laboratory phenomenon of retrieval-induced forgetting (RIF). This refers to the finding that repeatedly recalling some experimental stimuli impairs subsequent recall of related (i.e., tied to the same retrieval cue) stimuli. RIF of emotional autobiographical memories might provide an experimental model for the clinical memory phenomena in question. The present paper reports two experiments that explored the merits of applying the retrieval practice paradigm to relatively broad categories of autobiographical memories. Both studies found a significant RIF effect in that practised memories were recalled better than unrelated unpractised (baseline) memories. In addition, unpractised memories that were related to the practised memories were recalled more poorly than baseline memories. Implications of these findings for modelling the co-occurrence of intrusive and overgeneral memories are discussed.

Overgeneral autobiographical memory refers to the phenomenon that some patients are relatively unable to come up with memories of personally experienced events that are tied to a specific time and place (Williams, 1996). In contrast, intrusive memory is characterised by the unbidden occurrence of

---

Correspondence should be addressed to Ineke Wessel, Department of Clinical and Developmental Psychology, University of Groningen, Grote Kruisstraat 2-1, 9712 TS Groningen, The Netherlands; e-mail J.P.Wessel@rug.nl

Preparation of this article was supported by grant 452-03-329 of the Foundation for Behavioural and Educational Sciences of the Netherlands Organisation for Scientific research (NWO) awarded to Dr Wessel.

We gratefully acknowledge Marten van der Braak, Stefan Nouwen, and Laura Klein for their assistance in the data collection and scoring. Johan Verwoerd and Peter de Jong are thanked for their comments on an earlier draft of this article.

© 2006 Taylor & Francis
DOI:10.1080/02699930500342464

recollections of a personally experienced event, that interrupts daily activity and is difficult to control (e.g., Brewin, Christodoulides, & Hutchinson, 1996). Interestingly, there is evidence that intrusive memories and overgeneral memories are correlated in various clinical samples (Brewin, Reynolds, & Tata, 1999; Brewin, Watson, McCarthy, Hyman, & Dayson, 1998; Kuyken & Brewin, 1995; Stokes, Dritschel, & Bekerian, 2004; Wessel, Merckelbach, & Dekkers, 2002). Although some studies failed to find such a link (de Decker, Hermans, Raes, & Eelen, 2003; Henderson, Hargreaves, Gregory, & Williams, 2002; Hermans et al., 2004), these observations raise the question of what mechanisms might be involved. An account that specifically addresses the role of intrusive memory in overgeneral memory holds that the occurrence (Brewin et al., 1999) or the avoidance (Kuyken & Brewin, 1995) of intrusions occupies working memory and thus leaves fewer resources for retrieval of other memories. As Brewin and colleagues (1999, p. 515) put it: "this interference may simply result from the presence of other information competing for limited space in working memory". Thus, intrusive memories would easily get in the way of other autobiographical memories (AMs).

An alternative account would be that intrusive memory not only consumes working memory resources, but also contributes to a decreased availability for recall of other competing AMs. In the experimental memory literature, it has been suggested (Anderson, 2003; Levy & Anderson, 2002) that the effects of competition at retrieval go further than merely prohibiting weaker memory representations to access consciousness. Retrieval competition may also affect the *availability* of these other memories in that activation levels of their representations are reduced (i.e., inhibition). Evidence for this suggestion comes from studies employing the retrieval practice paradigm. In the typical study (Anderson, Bjork, & Bjork, 1994), participants learn a list of category names (fruit, furniture), each in conjunction with up to six different exemplars (e.g., fruit-apple; fruit-strawberry; furniture-chair, furniture-closet). In a later retrieval practice phase, the crucial cued recall manipulation (e.g., fruit-a...) induces participants to repeatedly retrieve only half of the exemplars of only half of the categories. In a later category-cued recall test, participants are instructed to again retrieve *all* exemplars of the earlier study list. Of course, results typically show a practice effect such that recall of practised exemplars (fruit-apple) is enhanced relative to exemplars from unrelated, unpractised categories (furniture). More interestingly, however, recall of exemplars from practised categories that were not part of the retrieval practice phase (i.e., unpractised related exemplars, e.g., fruit-strawberry) is impaired relative to the exemplars from unrelated, unpractised categories (furniture). This latter effect has been dubbed retrieval-induced forgetting (RIF). One interpretation (e.g., Anderson, 2003) is that RIF signals inhibition of the representations of related unpractised exemplars in long-term episodic memory. Since the initial demonstration of RIF employing category-exemplar pairs (Anderson et al., 1994), the effect has been found in a number of subsequent studies employing various types of stimuli (e.g., homographs, propositions, geometric shapes, slides, stories) and themes (e.g., personality traits, burglaries; see for an overview Levy & Anderson, 2002). Thus, there is good evidence in the experimental psychology literature that repeated retrieval of some memories has a detrimental effect on recall of related memories.

The phenomenology of RIF bears resemblance to observations in the clinical literature that intrusive memories and overgeneral memories are correlated. That is, intrusive memory involves the frequent retrieval of certain memories whereas overgeneral memory refers to a relative inability to come up with specific memories of other personally experienced events. This raises the question whether similar mechanisms as in RIF studies are involved here. Perhaps then, the retrieval practice paradigm might provide an experimental analogue for the clinically observed link between intrusive and overgeneral memories. Interestingly, the method was recently successfully applied to AMs. Barnier and colleagues (Barnier, Hung, & Conway, 2004) asked their participants to generate AMs in response to affectively laden cue-words (e.g., horrified, happy). Each word was a cue to four unique AMs, thus resembling the semantic categories with several exemplars that were employed in earlier studies. Next, the AMs were used in a Retrieval Practice experiment. The results showed that fewer unpractised related than unpractised unrelated memories were recalled. Thus, RIF was observed for complex, emotional memories and this may serve as the starting point for further inquiries of whether RIF might be involved in psychopathological memory phenomena, such as the co-occurrence of intrusive memories and overgeneral memories. Of course, in its original form the basic retrieval practice procedure is artificial. Our goal is to modify the paradigm in a systematic fashion such that ultimately, it more closely resembles the real-life observations of interest. The present paper reports two experiments that were intended as a first step in that direction.

EXPERIMENT 1

In an earlier study of elderly concentration camp survivors (Wessel et al., 2002), scores on a measure of intrusive memories (Impact of Event Scale, IES; Horowitz, Wilner, & Alvarez, 1979) were correlated with fewer specific AMs in response to negative cues, but not in response to positive cues (see Kuyken & Brewin, 1995, for a similar finding). As the IES specifically targets intrusive memories of negative shocking events, the question rises whether the accompanying lack of AM specificity in response to negative cues may be interpreted as a RIF-like phenomenon. One problem with such an interpretation is that these earlier studies measured AMs using a broad range of cues, whereas retrieval practice studies rely on relatively narrow categories (e.g., Anderson et al., 1994; Barnier et al., 2004). Therefore, Experiment 1 explored the merits of applying the retrieval practice paradigm to the relatively broad categories of "positive" and "negative" AMs.

In order to explore this, healthy participants were asked to generate both positive and negative AMs, each memory pertaining to a unique event. Several weeks later, these AMs were used as stimuli in a retrieval practice experiment. The expectation was that overall, recall of unpractised AMs that were related to practised AMs would be impaired compared to unpractised unrelated AMs. In addition, it was expected that the retrieval practice manipulation would equally affect recall of positive and negative AMs. That is, if it is repeated retrieval that affects the recall of other AMs, then this should occur for related memories of the same category, irrespective of the valence of that category.

Method

Participants

Participants were 48 second-year psychology students (9 men) at the University of Maastricht. At the time of testing they had not had any courses on memory. They received €15 for participating. The experiment was approved by the ethics committee of the Department of Psychology at the University of Maastricht.

General overview of procedure

The study consisted of two sessions. In session 1, AMs were collected in order to serve as idiosyncratic stimuli in session 2. Session 2 was a Retrieval Practice (RP) experiment consisting of: (1) a study; (2) a RP; (3) a distracter; and (4) a test phase.

Materials

AM collection. Booklets were constructed consisting of 12 pages with "negative memory" and 12 pages with "positive memory" printed at the top of the pages. Each page had the words "where", "when", "who", and "what" printed in the left margin. At the bottom of the page, three 11-point Likert scales asked for emotional intensity (anchored 0 = *not at all intense* and 10 = *extremely intense*), negative valence (anchored 0 = *neutral* and 10 = *extremely negative*) and positive valence (anchored 0 = *neutral* and 10 = *extremely positive*) of the memories. Half of the booklets asked for the 12 negative AMs first, whereas the other half of the booklets began asking for 12 positive AMs.

Study phase. Ten positive and 10 negative AMs of comparable emotional intensity were selected from the session 1 booklets. In the study booklets these AMs were typed on separate pages in random order. The appropriate valence category label (i.e., either "positive memory" or "negative memory") was at the top of each page.

RP phase. For RP booklets, a set of five different AMs was selected from one of the two valence categories. Autobiographical memory selection was random, with the restriction that the mean emotional intensity ratings of the to-be-practised AMs did not differ from those of the unpractised AMs in that category. Retrieval cues for each AM were printed on separate pages. Retrieval cues were the valence category label (i.e., either "positive memory" or "negative memory") at the top of the page, and the original information in the "where" and "when" units of the original AMs. This information provided a unique cue to ensure that the target AM was indeed retrieved during practice. In addition, the words "who" and "what" were printed on the left margin. This resulted in a set of 5 pages containing unique retrieval cues for different AMs. The set was presented three times, such that the order of pages was random within each set. This resulted in 15 page RP booklets. Care was taken to ensure that the same AM was not practised twice in succession (e.g., by being the last AM in one set and the first AM in the consecutive set). Half of the booklets cued positive AMs, the other half of the booklets cued negative AMs.

Distracter phase. As a distracter, parts of Raven's Advanced Progressive Matrices (Raven, 2000) were used.

Test phase. Category-cued recall booklets contained separate pages showing a valence category label at the top and the words "where", "when", "who", and "what" in the left margin. Half of the booklets began with 10 pages referring to the positive category, followed by 10 pages asking for negative memories. This order was reversed for the other half of the booklets.

Procedure

Participants were tested in groups (maximum of 10 participants). At the outset of session 1, participants were told that they would participate in two unrelated experiments on emotion and memory, with the first looking at autobiographical memory and the second at memory for visual material. The purpose of this cover story was to prevent rehearsal of the AMs between sessions. Next, participants were instructed to write down 12 positive and 12 negative specific memories of personally experienced events in the AM collection booklets. They were told to provide each memory only once and report memories that differed from each other as much as possible. There was no time limit for filling in the booklets. Session 2 took place 3 weeks later. Participants were told about the cover story and its purpose. Next they participated in the RP experiment. In the study and RP phases, a beep delivered by a Compaq Laptop computer signalled when participants were to turn the page in their booklet and continue with the next AM. In the study phase, they were instructed to to study each page for 15 s. In the RP phase, they were to write down the correct AM in response to the retrieval cues in the RP booklet. Time to respond was 60 s per memory. The duration of the subsequent distracter phase was 5 minutes. In the final test phase, participants were instructed to fill in the category-cued recall booklet by writing down the details of all AMs that they had studied in the initial phase of the RP experiment. There was no time limit for the test phase. Order of testing was counterbalanced such that half of the sample received the booklet that started with the category that was practised during the RP phase, whereas the other half of the sample started category cued recall with the unpractised category.

Data scoring

Two raters (I.W. and B.H.) compared testing and study AMs while they were unaware of which valence category and which particular AMs were rehearsed during the RP phase. Information reported in the when, where, who and what units was scored separately. If information given at category-cued recall testing matched the information in the study AM, that unit was given 1 point. The wording would not have to be identical, as long as the information was similar in essence and no elements were lost or added. A unit received 0.5 points when some information was lost (e.g., "summer of 1995" instead of "July 1995") or new elements were added. A unit of information that was not reported or was completely false received 0 points. Thus, scores for each AM ranged between 0 and 4. Next, for each rater, separate scores for AMs that were practised in the RP phase (Rp+), unpractised AMs from the practised valence category (Rp−) and AMs from the unpracticed valence category (nRp) were summed and transformed into proportions. In order to determine interrater reliability, Intraclass Correlation Coefficients (ICCs; Fleiss, 1986) were calculated. ICCs were excellent (i.e., .96, .99, and .97 for Rp+, nRp, and Rp−, respectively), and therefore the data were averaged across raters.

Results

Retrieval practice phase

The mean correct recall percentages in the retrieval practice phase were 95.28 ($SD = 8.13$) and 95.69 ($SD = 8.08$) for who and what information, respectively. Means for the group with a positive RP phase (who: $M = 95.83$, $SD = 8.06$; what: $M = 95.56$, $SD = 8.34$) and the group with a negative RP phase (who: $M = 94.72$, $SD = 8.34$; what: $M = 95.83$, $SD = 7.82$) did not significantly differ, $t(46) = 0.47$ and $t(46) = -0.12$ for who and what information, respectively.

TABLE 1
Overall mean correct recall proportions, means correct recall proportions in Rp valence category, and output group in Experiment 1 (standard deviations in parentheses)

		$Rp+$	nRp	$Rp-$
Overall		0.71 (0.21)	0.57 (0.20)	0.54 (0.22)
Rp valence category	Positive Rp+	0.74 (0.20)	0.56 (0.18)	0.57 (0.20)
	Negative Rp+	0.68 (0.22)	0.58 (0.22)	0.50 (0.24)
Output group	Early Rp+	0.75 (0.17)	0.58 (0.19)	0.57 (0.21)
	Early Rp−	0.67 (0.24)	0.57 (0.22)	0.50 (0.23)

Rp, Retrieval Practice; Rp+, memories practised in the Retrieval Practice phase; Rp−, unpractised memories that are related to Rp+ memories; nRp, unpractised memories that are unrelated to Rp+ memories.

Test phase

Correct recall. Table 1 summarises the relevant means and standard deviations for Rp+, nRp and RP− AMs recalled during the test phase. A 2 (RP Valence: positive vs. negative) × 3 (Retrieval Practice: Rp+ vs. nRp vs. Rp−) analysis of variance (ANOVA) with repeated measures on the last factor rendered a significant main effect of Retrieval Practice, multivariate $F(2, 45) = 34.49, p < .001$. An a priori t-test showed that the retrieval practice manipulation was successful in that Rp+ AMs were better recalled than nRp AMs, $t(47) = 7.18, p < .001$, one-tailed. More importantly, a second a priori t-test revealed that correct recall was significantly lower for Rp− than nRp AMs, $t(48) = 1.72, p < .05$, one-tailed. Contrary to expectations, the RP Valence × Retrieval Practice interaction was also significant, $F(2, 45) = 5.29, p < .01$. In order to break down this interaction, separate ANOVAs were carried out. First, a 2 (RP valence: positive vs. negative) × 2 (Retrieval Practice: Rp+ vs. nRp) analysis rendered a significant Retrieval Practice main effect, multivariate $F(1, 46) = 57.78, p < .001$, and a significant RP Valence × Retrieval Practice interaction, $F(1, 46) = 6.74, p < .05$, suggesting a larger practice effect for positive than negative AMs.

Second, a 2 (RP Valence: positive vs. negative) × 2 (Retrieval Practice: nRp vs. nRp−) analysis revealed a borderline significant main effect for retrieval practice, multivariate $F(1, 46) = 3.29, p = .08$, and a significant RP Valence × Retrieval Practice interaction, $F(1, 46) = 6.45, p < .05$. Paired t-tests revealed that Rp+ AMs were recalled significantly better than nRp AMs in both Rp valence conditions, $t(23) = 3.38, p < .01$ and $t(23) = 7.60, p < .001$ for negative and positive conditions, respectively. Cued recall of Rp− items was significantly lower than nRp AMs in the negative valence condition, $t(23) = 2.96, p < .01$, but not in the positive valence condition, $t(23) = -0.53, p = .60$. Thus, it appears that the RIF effect was restricted to negative AMs.

Valence groups did not significantly differ with regard to Rp+ AMs, $t(46) = 1.13, p = .26$, Rp− AMs, $t(46) = 1.25, p = .22$, and nRp AMs, $t(46) = −0.43, p = .67$. t-Tests showed that the differential RIF effect in the valence groups could not be attributed to differences in emotional intensity ratings[1] (ts > −1.09 and ≤ 0.04).

Output interference. Next, we explored whether the origins of the RIF effect could be traced back to a noninhibitory account, such as output interference. This refers to the phenomenon that practised items have a high probability to be recalled first, and that this interferes with retrieval of (unpractised) items later in the recall sequence (Anderson, 2003). To explore this, we recorded the position of each AM in the recall sequence. A t-test showed that the mean position of Rp− AMs ($M = 6.04, SD = 1.25$) was indeed significantly higher than that of Rp+ AMs ($M = 4.05, SD = 1.03; t(47) = −6.49, p < .001$). In order to determine whether initial recall of Rp+ AMs blocked retrieval of Rp− AMs, we followed a procedure employed in earlier studies (e.g., Barnier et al., 2004; Macrae & Roseveare, 2002). First, we calculated difference scores by subtracting the mean position of Rp+ AMs from the mean position of Rp− AMs. Thus, the higher this difference score, the earlier Rp+ AMs were recalled relative to Rp− AMs. We then used this difference score for a median split in each of the two testing order counterbalancing groups (i.e., recall test of Rp AMs first or recall test of nRp AMs first). The halves of these groups with the lowest scores were combined into an early Rp− group, whereas the half of these groups with the higher scores formed an early Rp+ group. Recall data (see Table 1) were subjected to a 2 (Output Group: early Rp+ vs. early Rp−) × 3 (Retrieval Practice: Rp+ vs. nRp vs. Rp−) ANOVA with repeated measures on the last factor. Neither the Output Group main effect, nor the Output Group × Retrieval Practice interaction reached significance, $F(1, 46) = 0.85, p = .36$, and $F(2, 45) = 1.83, p = .17$, respectively. Thus, output order was unlikely to be responsible for the present findings.

Discussion

Overall, the present results replicate the basic findings of RIF studies that recall of unpractised-related AMs was worse than that of unpractised-unrelated AMs. However, the crucial overall difference between nRp and Rp− AMs (RIF effect) was small (i.e., 3%), especially given that findings with nonidiosyncratic stimuli typically range from 9% to 20% (Anderson, 2003). One reason for this

---

[1] Emotionality ratings were as follows. In the positive Rp+ group means were 5.40 ($SD = 2.01$), 5.70 ($SD = 2.16$) and 5.34 ($SD = 2.19$) for Rp+, nRp, and Rp−, respectively. In the negative Rp+ group means were 5.83 ($SD = 1.32$), 5.68 ($SD = 1.63$) and 5.93 ($SD = 1.43$) for Rp+, nRp, and Rp−, respectively.

small overall effect lies in its interaction with valence: that is, negative but not positive Rp− AMs were recalled worse than baseline (nRp) AMs. It is important to note that in the negative Rp condition, the Rp− AMs were negative and the comparison nRp AMs were positive (and vice versa in the other condition). Thus, the control (nRp) category was always of a different valence than the critical Rp category. It may be argued that negative nRp AMs provided an inappropriate baseline for their positive Rp counterparts and vice versa. Yet, the finding that baseline (nRp) AMs were comparable with respect to correct recall percentages and emotional intensity ratings speaks against this notion. Nevertheless, the question rises whether RIF would be found when baseline and Rp− AMs are of the same valence. In Experiment 2 this question was addressed.

EXPERIMENT 2

In Experiment 2, the procedure of Experiment 1 was modified such that Rp and nRp categories consisted of AMs of the same valence (i.e., negative). More specifically, in order to obtain sets of AMs that would fit into relatively broad categories, participants retrieved negative AMs in response to two types of cue words (nouns and adjectives). These combinations of cue words and AMs were grouped into the categories of "situations" and "traits" for the retrieval practice procedure. During retrieval practice, combinations of category names and cue words (e.g., "trait-sneaky") were used to promote retrieval of the target Rp+ AMs. Expectations were that overall, retrieval practice would result in recall differences between the critical Rp− and baseline (nRp) categories. No effect of Rp category (situations or traits) was expected.

Method

Participants

A total of 40 psychology students (16 men) at Maastricht University participated in the study in exchange for course credit. They were all tested at the start of their first year (prior to any courses on memory). None had participated in Experiment 1.

General overview of procedure

As in Experiment 1, participants participated in an AM-collection session and an RP experiment (session 2) consisting of four phases.

Materials

Similar materials were used as in Experiment 1, with the following modifications.

Session 1 AM collection. The AM collection booklets contained 20 pages, each with a negatively valenced cue word printed at the top. Ten cues were nouns and 10 were trait adjectives.[2] Below these cue words, the words "where", "when", "who", and "what" were printed in the left margin. At the bottom of each page, four 100 mm Visual Analogue Scales (VASs) asked for judgements of emotional intensity (anchored 0 = *not at all* to 100 = *extremely*) and valence (anchored 0 = *extremely negative* and 100 = *extremely positive*). Emotionality and valence was rated for both the time of experiencing the event (retrospective ratings) and the time of recalling it (i.e., in session 1; current ratings).

Study phase. The booklet contained the 20 AMs that were collected in session 1, now labelled with one of two broad category names: situations (nouns, e.g., *situation-theft*) and traits (adjectives, e.g., *trait-sneaky*). The category label was pasted above the cue words in the original AM collection booklets. The VASs were removed.

RP phase. Combinations of category labels and cue words were used as retrieval cues for five different AMs. Retrieval cues were printed at the top of each page in the RP booklet, followed by the words "where", "when", "who", and "what" in the left margin. As in Experiment 1, the set of five retrieval cues was presented for three times. Half of the booklets cued AMs in the situation category, the other half cued AMs in the trait category. Counterbalancing of cuewords resulted in 20 different versions of the RP booklets (10 for situations and 10 for traits).

Test phase. Category-cued recall booklets contained category labels at the top of each page followed by the words "where", "when", "who", and "what" in the left margin. There were separate booklets for situations and for traits. Each booklet contained 15 pages so that participants could not infer the maximum number of 10 target AMs by counting the pages. As in Experiment 1, order of testing was counterbalanced.

Procedure

The procedure was similar to that of Experiment 1, with the following modifications. At the start of session 1, participants were instructed to provide specific negative AMs in response to the cue words in their booklets. Specific

---

[2] Nouns were: theft (*diefstal*), lie (*leugen*), disappointment (*teleurstelling*), quarrel (*ruzie*), accident (*ongeluk*), heartache (*liefdesverdriet*), stench (*stank*), danger (*gevaar*), blunder (*blunder*), and loss (*verlies*). Adjectives were: selfish (*egoïstisch*), stupid (*dom*), mean (*gierig*), impudent (*brutaal*), indecisive (*besluiteloos*), stubborn (*koppig*), pessimistic (*pessimistisch*), sneaky (*achterbaks*), arrogant (*arrogant*) and domineering (*bazig*).

memories were defined as pertaining to a specific place and time (within 1 day). Participants were explicitly told that it was satisfactory to report seemingly trivial events, as long as the memories were emotionally negative to them. Each memory was to be reported only once.

In the session 2 study phase, participants were explicitly instructed to study each AM in the context of the corresponding category label and cue word (e.g., *situation-theft*) for 30 s. In the RP phase, time to respond was 75 s for the first presentation of the five retrieval cues and 60 and 45 s for the second and third presentations, respectively. The distracter phase was 10 minutes. Finally, during the test phase, participants were given 15 minutes per test booklet (i.e., situations and traits).

Data scoring

Rp+, Rp− and nRp memories reported in the cued recall test phase were scored by an independent rater following the procedure described in Experiment 1. During scoring, it appeared that some memories were reported in the wrong cued recall booklet (i.e., participants reported memories that were originally studied as belonging to the trait category in the situations booklet during recall and vice versa). Therefore, apart from correct recall proportions in the correct category, we also calculated correct recall proportions irrespective of category (i.e., the booklet the memories were reported in).

Results

Retrieval practice phase

Overall, mean recall performance in the retrieval practice phase was 88.83 ($SD = 11.69$). Groups with a situations RP phase ($M = 88.67$, $SD = 12.6$) and a traits RP phase ($M = 89.0$, $SD = 11.03$) did not significantly differ, $t(38) = -0.09$, $p = .93$.

Test phase

Recall in correct category. Table 2 summarises the means and standard deviations of the correct recall proportions for AMs reported in the correct cued recall category and for all AMs that were reported, irrespective of category. Including recall order (practised category first or nonpractised category first) as a factor in the analyses did not reveal any significant main or interaction effects. Thus, the data were collapsed across this factor in subsequent analyses. A 2 (Rp category: traits vs. situations) × 3 (Retrieval Practice: Rp+ vs. nRp vs. Rp−) analysis of variance (ANOVA) with repeated measures on the last factor rendered a significant effect of retrieval practice, multivariate $F(2, 37) = 21.07$, $p < .001$. A priori *t*-tests revealed that Rp+ AMs were significantly better recalled

TABLE 2
Mean correct recall proportions (and standard deviations) in the correct category and irrespective of category in Experiment 2

		$Rp+$	nRp	$Rp-$
Correct category	Overall	0.77 (0.17)	0.58 (0.17)	0.47 (0.24)
	Situations Rp+	0.79 (0.18)	0.52 (0.17)	0.46 (0.25)
	Traits Rp+	0.74 (0.17)	0.63 (0.15)	0.48 (0.24)
Irrespective of category	Overall	0.78 (0.14)	0.60 (0.17)	0.53 (0.21)
	Situations Rp+	0.80 (0.14)	0.54 (0.17)	0.51 (0.22)
	Traits Rp+	0.75 (0.15)	0.66 (0.14)	0.56 (0.20)

Rp, Retrieval Practice; Rp+, Memories practised in the Retrieval Practice phase; Rp−, unpractised memories that are related to Rp+ memories; nRp, unpractised memories that are unrelated to Rp+ memories.

than nRP AMs, $t(39) = 5.56$, $p < .001$, one-tailed, and that participants recalled significantly fewer Rp− than nRp AMs, $t(39) = 3.12$, $p < .01$, one-tailed.

Contrary to expectations, the RP category by Retrieval Practice interaction was significant, multivariate $F(2, 37) = 4.03$, $p < .05$. Separate ANOVAs were carried out in order to break down this interaction. A 2 (RP category: situations vs. traits) × 2 (Retrieval Practice: Rp+ vs. nRp) ANOVA showed a significant Retrieval Practice main effect, multivariate $F(1, 38) = 34.94$, $p < .001$, and a significant RP category × Retrieval Practice interaction, multivariate $F(1, 38) = 6.11$, $p < .05$. Paired t-tests revealed that Rp+ AMs were recalled significantly better than nRp AMs for both the situations, $t(19) = 6.23$, $p < .001$, and traits, $t(19) = 2.31$, $p < .05$, RP groups. Independent t-tests showed that groups did not significantly differ regarding Rp+ AMs, $t(38) = 0.86$. However, the traits RP group recalled nRp AMs significantly better than the situations RP group, $t(38) = -2.18$, $p < .05$. A 2 (RP category: situations vs. traits) × 2 (Retrieval Practice: nRp vs. Rp−) ANOVA showed a significant Retrieval Practice main effect, multivariate $F(1, 38) = 1.84$, $p < .001$. The RP category × Retrieval Practice interaction was not significant, multivariate $F(1, 38) = 1.84$, $p = .18$.

Recall irrespective of category. The question rises to what extent the difference between nRp and Rp− recall performance indicates genuine RIF in the sense that Rp− AMs became less accessible or available for recall. Therefore, analyses were repeated for correct recall proportions including the AMs that were reported in the wrong category. The 2 (RP category: traits vs. situations) × 3 (Retrieval Practice: Rp+ vs. nRp vs. Rp−) ANOVA with repeated measures on the last factor yielded a significant main effect of Retrieval Practice, multivariate $F(2, 37) = 21.78$, $p < .001$. An a priori t-test showed that the correct recall proportion for nRp AMs was higher than that of

Rp− AMs, $t(39) = 2.42$, $p < .05$, one-tailed. Thus, overall, the relatively poor recall of Rp− AMs cannot be attributed entirely to a greater tendency to recall those AMs in the wrong category.

Again, the RP category × Retrieval Practice interaction was significant, $F(2, 37) = 5.24$, $p < .05$. Follow-up analyses showed a similar pattern as the analyses for correct recall proportions in the correct category.

Emotionality and valence. To check whether the differential recall of nRp AMs in the Rp groups might be attributed to differences in emotionality and valence, session 1 ratings for nRp AMs were subjected to independent t-tests.[3] Valence ratings did not differ between RP groups. However, the retrospective emotionality ratings were significantly lower in the situations Rp+ group ($M = 50.60$, $SD = 13.03$) than in the traits Rp+ group ($M = 65.49$, $SD = 13.68$), $t(38) = -3.53$, $p < .01$. (Note that nRp AMs in the situations group were traits AMs and vice versa.) The difference in current emotionality ratings of nRp AMs was borderline significant ($M = 33.75$, $SD = 15.83$ and $M = 43.30$, $SD = 15.96$ for the traits and situations RP groups, respectively), $t(38) = -1.9$, $p = .07$.

Output interference.[4] To see whether the RIF effect could be attributed to output interference, the position of each AM in the recall sequence was recorded. A t-test showed that the mean position of Rp+ AMs ($M = 3.57$, $SD = 1.15$) was lower than that of Rp− AMs ($M = 4.91$, $SD = 1.77$), $t(37) = -3.44$, $p < .01$. In order to check whether initial recall of Rp+ AMs hampered later recall of Rp− AMs, output order preference groups were created following the procedure of Experiment 1, resulting in an early Rp+ group ($n = 19$) and an early Rp− group ($n = 19$). Recall data (see Table 3) were subjected to a 2 (Output Group: early Rp+ vs. early Rp−) × 3 (Retrieval Practice: Rp+ vs. nRp vs. Rp−) ANOVA with repeated measures on the last factor. Analysis of the correct recall proportion for correctly categorised AMs revealed a significant effect of Retrieval Practice, multivariate $F(2, 35) = 19.23$, $p < .001$ and a significant Output Group × Retrieval Practice interaction, multivariate $F(2, 35) = 4.45$, $p < .05$. Contrary to an explanation in terms of output interference, however, the direction of this interaction was such that differences between nRp and Rp− items were largest in the early Rp− group. In addition, it should be noted that the early Rp− group also recalled significantly more Rp− AMs in the inappropriate nRp category ($M = 0.14$, $SD = 0.22$) than the early Rp+ group ($M = 0.01$, $SD = 0.05$, $t_{\text{adjusted df}}(19.54) = -2.43$, $p < .05$). Therefore the analyses were repeated for correct recall proportions irrespective of category.

---

[3] Mean emotionality and valence ratings were calculated for all Rp+, nRp, and Rp− AMs. No other comparisons between the traits and situations Rp groups were significant.

[4] Two participants in the situations Rp group did not report Rp− memories at all, leaving 38 participants for this analysis.

TABLE 3
Mean correct recall proportions (and standard deviations) in the correct category and irrespective of category for output order preference groups in Experiment 2

	Early Rp+ (n = 19)			Early Rp− (n = 19)		
	Rp+	nRp	Rp−	Rp+	nRp	Rp−
Correct category	0.72	0.56	0.56	0.81	0.62	0.43
	(0.19)	(0.15)	(0.22)	(0.16)	(0.15)	(0.21)
Irrespective of category	0.74	0.60	0.58	0.82	0.64	0.52
	(0.15)	(0.14)	(0.20)	(0.13)	(0.15)	(0.18)

Rp+, Memories practised in the Retrieval Practice phase; Rp−, unpractised memories that are related to Rp+ memories; nRp, unpractised memories that are unrelated to Rp+ memories.

The Output Group × Retrieval Practice interaction was not significant, multivariate $F(2, 35) = 1.93$, $p = .16$. Taken together, output interference does not seem to be responsible for the present results.

Discussion

Overall, the present findings show RIF in that unpractised related AMs were more poorly recalled than unpractised unrelated AMs. The effect was substantially larger (11% for correctly categorised AMs) than in Experiment 1. These results could be partly traced back to a noninhibitory phenomenon: Some AMs were reported in the incorrect category at cued recall. Nevertheless, after ignoring what category AMs were reported in at recall, the overall difference between nRp and Rp− AMs was still a significant 7%.

It should be noted that differences between AMs in the baseline (nRp) categories appeared to be responsible for reducing the magnitude of the overall RIF effect. Baseline AMs in the situations category were rated as more emotional in session 1 and were better recalled in session 2 than traits AMs. These differences were less prominent for Rp+ and Rp− AMs. Thus, despite efforts to make the Rp categories as similar as possible, the categories may not have provided an appropriate baseline for each other.

GENERAL DISCUSSION

The goal of the present studies was to further explore the retrieval-induced forgetting effect in autobiographical memory. The results of both experiments show that overall, unpractised AMs that were related to practised AMs were more poorly recalled than unpractised unrelated (baseline) AMs. These findings are in line with earlier studies demonstrating RIF that relied on nonidiosyncratic stimuli (see Levy & Anderson, 2002). In addition, these findings replicate and extend earlier findings that RIF occurs for AMs (Barnier et al., 2004). In the study by Barnier and colleagues (2004), narrow categories of AMs were used (e.g., four AMs in reaction to the cue "horrified"). The present observation that RIF did occur for relatively broad categories of AMs suggests that the paradigm may contribute to clarifying the mechanisms involved in everyday and perhaps even psychopathological memory phenomena.

Yet, the present findings also suggest that a consequence of modifying the retrieval practice paradigm to more closely resemble real life is that the magnitude of RIF effects is smaller than in situations that allow for more rigorous experimental control. Anderson (2003) noted that the magnitude of RIF depends on the extent to which the memories that share a retrieval cue compete during retrieval practice. For example, in experiments employing semantic category-exemplar pairs (e.g., Anderson et al., 1994), the effect is larger for strong (i.e., prototypical) exemplars (e.g., fruit-orange) than for weak exemplars (e.g., fruit-guava). Anderson's (2003) interpretation is that strong exemplars provide more competition at retrieval practice than weak exemplars, rendering more inhibition of the former than the latter. Taxonomic categories have the advantage that they consist of a finite number of members, that differ in the extent to which they are prototypical for that category. Clearly, broad categories of AMs consist of a larger number of members and it is not immediately obvious how to select strong exemplars. Another reason for the relatively small magnitude of the present effects may well lie in systematic differences between the categories that were employed. In both experiments the unpractised (nRp) baseline AMs belonged to a different category than the practised AMs. In Experiment 2 the baseline (nRp) AMs in the different categories differed in terms of recall performance and emotionality ratings, suggesting that despite similar valence ratings, traits, and situations AMs provided a suboptimal baseline for each other. However, in Experiment 1 the baseline AMs were comparable on the dimensions of emotionality and recall. Interestingly, the RIF effect occurred for negative AMs, and not for positive AMs. At present, we have no obvious explanation for this finding. Future research may further clarify the role of valence in RIF.

On a more theoretical note, the question rises precisely what mechanism underlies RIF effects. One dominant view in the literature on RIF (e.g., Anderson, 2003; Levy & Anderson, 2002) is that the long-term memory representations of unpractised related exemplars are (temporarily) inhibited in the sense that activation levels are decreased. However, because inhibition is difficult to measure directly, alternative noninhibitory accounts have been put forward (e.g., MacLeod, Dodd, Sheard, Wilson, & Bibi, 2003). One such possibility is output interference, referring to the phenomenon that practised items have a high probability to be recalled first, and that this interferes with retrieval of (unpractised) items later in the recall sequence (Anderson, 2003). The results showed that in the present experiments, output interference was an unlikely alternative explanation. Yet, that does not mean that noninhibitory processes can be ruled out altogether.

The present experiments were inspired by the notion that RIF (or even inhibition) might play a role in the clinical situation in which intrusive memories and overgeneral memories co-occur. How does this idea compare to other explanations regarding the origins of overgeneral memory? One influential account is the affect regulation hypothesis (Williams, 1996, see also Raes, Hermans, de Decker, Eelen, & Williams, 2003) that holds that the retrieval of categoric AMs would serve a protective function, in that the sharp affect that accompanies retrieval of specific (traumatic) memories is avoided. Such an account does not readily accommodate findings that intrusive memories and overgeneral memories are linked. For example, if categoric retrieval mainly serves a protective function, why would it fail for exactly those AMs that are most distressing in those who suffer from them? An advantage of the present idea is that its starting point lies in what is known about normal memory phenomena. In this sense, overgeneral memory is viewed as an (unwanted) by-product of the repetitive execution of the retrieval process that characterises intrusive memory. Perhaps retrieving the same set of AMs over and over again results in an ongoing state of reduced accessibility or availability of closely related AMs. Such impairment might spread to more distant AMs.

Taken together, the retrieval practice paradigm may provide a starting point for providing an experimental analogue for the clinical situation in which overgeneral memory is correlated with intrusive memory. Yet, several issues need to be addressed in future studies before it can be inferred that RIF indeed plays a role in that situation. To begin with, a limitation of the present method is that practised (Rp+) AMs do not closely resemble the characteristics of intrusive memory. The retrieval practice procedure consists of repeatedly retrieving several (five in these experiments) different AMs in an intentional manner, triggered by abstract verbal cues. By contrast, clinical research (see Ehlers, Hackmann, & Michael, 2004) suggests that patients with posttraumatic stress disorder (PTSD, in which intrusive memory is a hallmark symptom (American Psychiatric Association, 1994) experience only a few different intrusions (i.e., two on average; Hackmann, Ehlers, Speckens, & Clark, 2004). In addition, a prominent feature of intrusive memories is that they are perceived as uncontrollable and that their retrieval is involuntary rather than intentional, frequently brought about by sensory cues. It would be interesting to see if inducing involuntary recall of only one AM (e.g., through thought suppression, Wegner, 1989) hampers specificity of other AMs. Furthermore, it remains to be seen how the RIF effect compares to the relative inability to be specific as in the clinical phenomenon of overgeneral autobiographical memory. Especially in the case of Experiment 2, there were indications that retrieval practice affected the association between cue word and AM rather than the ability to retrieve the target AM itself. That is, some of the memories in that experiment were recalled in the incorrect category, indicating that participants forgot the source of those AMs rather than the AMs themselves. In that respect, the situations and traits labels in Experiment 2 were rather artificial. Future research may concentrate on employing AMs that naturally fall into obvious categories (such as positive and negative memories). A related problem that needs to be addressed is that the present method does not take discrepancies in recall of details between sessions into account. That is, if an error is made in session 1, this would constitute the study material for the retrieval practice experiment, irrespective of whether the correct detail is recalled at the time of study. Providing participants with the opportunity to correct their AMs at time of study may solve this problem. Finally, the present experiments involved healthy undergraduate participants, limiting the generalisability of the results. Future studies should explore whether retrieval-induced forgetting of AMs occurs in different samples. Overall, the conceptualisation of overgeneral memory as the result of processes involved in intrusive memory raises interesting possibilities. Addressing these issues is a challenge for future research.

REFERENCES

Anderson, M. C. (2003). Rethinking interference theory: Executive control and the mechanisms of forgetting. *Journal of Memory and Language, 49*, 415–445.

Anderson, M. C., Bjork, R. A., & Bjork, E. L. (1994). Remembering can cause forgetting: Retrieval dynamics in long-term memory. *Journal of Experimental Psychology: Learning, Memory, and Cognition, 20*, 1063–1087.

American Psychiatric Association. (1994). *Diagnostic and statistical manual of mental disorders* (4th ed.). Washington DC: Author.

Barnier, A. J., Hung, L., & Conway, M. A. (2004). Retrieval-induced forgetting of emotional and unemotional autobiographical memories. *Cognition and Emotion, 18*, 457–477.

Brewin, C. R., Christodoulides, J., & Hutchinson, G. (1996). Intrusive thoughts and intrusive memories in a nonclinical sample. *Cognition and Emotion, 10*, 107–112.

Brewin, C. R., Reynolds, M., & Tata, P. (1999). Autobiographical memory processes and the course of depression. *Journal of Abnormal Psychology, 108*, 511–517.

Brewin, C. R., Watson, M., McCarthy, S., Hyman, P., & Dayson, D. (1998). Memory processes and the course of anxiety and depression in cancer patients. *Psychological Medicine, 28*, 219–224.

de Decker, A., Hermans, D., Raes, F., & Eelen, P. (2003). Autobiographical memory specificity and trauma in inpatient adolescents. *Journal of Clinical Child and Adolescent Psychology, 32*, 22–31.

Ehlers, A., Hackmann, A., & Michael, T. (2004). Intrusive re-experiencing in post-traumatic stress disorder: Phenomenology, theory, and therapy. *Memory, 12*, 403–415.

Fleiss, J. L. (1986). *The design and analysis of clinical experiments*. New York: Wiley.

Hackmann, A., Ehlers, A., Speckens, A., & Clark, D. M. (2004). Characteristics and content of intrusive memories in PTSD and their changes with treatment. *Journal of Traumatic Stress, 17*, 231–240.

Henderson, D., Hargreaves, I., Gregory, S., & Williams, J. M. G. (2002). Autobiographical memory and emotion in a nonclinical sample of women with and without a reported history of childhood sexual abuse. *British Journal of Clinical Psychology, 41*, 129–142.

Hermans, D., van den Broeck, K., Belis, G., Raes, F., Pieters, G., & Eelen, P. (2004). Trauma and autobiographical memory specificity in depressed inpatients. *Behaviour Research and Therapy, 42*, 775–789.

Horowitz, M., Wilner, N., & Alvarez, W. (1979). Impact of event scale: A measure of subjective stress. *Psychosomatic Medicine, 41*, 209–218.

Kuyken, W., & Brewin, C. R. (1995). Autobiographical memory functioning in depression and reports of early abuse. *Journal of Abnormal Psychology, 104*, 585–591.

Levy, B. J., & Anderson, M. C. (2002). Inhibitory processes and the control of memory retrieval. *Trends in Cognitive Sciences, 6*, 299–305.

MacLeod, C. M., Dodd, M. D., Sheard, E. D., Wilson, D. E., & Bibi, U. (2003). In opposition to inhibition. In B. H. Ross (Ed.), *The psychology of learning and motivation* (pp. 163–214). San Diego, CA: Academic Press.

Macrae, C. N., & Roseveare, T. A. (2002). I was always on my mind: The self and temporary forgetting. *Psychonomic Bulletin and Review, 9*, 611–614.

Raes, F., Hermans, D., de Decker, A., Eelen, P., & Williams, J. M. G. (2003). Autobiographical memory specificity and affect regulation: An experimental approach. *Emotion, 3*, 201–206.

Stokes, D. J., Dritschel, B. H., & Bekerian, D. A. (2004). The effect of burn injury on adolescents' autobiographical memory. *Behaviour Research and Therapy, 42*, 1357–1365.

Raven, J. (2000). The Raven's progressive matrices: Change and stability over culture and time. *Cognitive Psychology, 41*, 1–48.

Wegner, D. M. (1989). *White bears and other unwanted thoughts: Suppression, obsession, and the psychology of mental control.* New York: Penguin.

Wessel, I., Merckelbach, H., & Dekkers, T. (2002). Autobiographical memory in Dutch-Indonesian survivors of the World War II era. *Journal of Traumatic Stress, 15*, 227–234.

Williams, J. M. G. (1996). Depression and the specificity of autobiographical memory. In D. Rubin (Ed.), *Remembering our past: Studies in autobiographical memory* (pp. 271–296). Cambridge, UK: Cambridge University Press.

Autobiographical memory in depressed and nondepressed patients with borderline personality disorder after long-term psychotherapy

Ismay P. Kremers
Leiden University, The Netherlands

Philip Spinhoven, and A. J. Willem Van der Does
Leiden University and Leiden University Medical Centre, The Netherlands

Richard Van Dyck
VU University and VU Medical Centre, Amsterdam, The Netherlands

The present study investigated whether scores on the Autobiographical Memory Test (AMT) in 55 patients with borderline personality disorder (BPD) were modified after long-term psychotherapy and whether the pretreatment AMT scores would predict improvement in depression severity or BPD symptom severity at the end of treatment. In addition, it was analysed whether changes in ratings of mood, thought suppression, dissociation, and BPD symptom severity following treatment were associated with changes in AMT scores. Only patients with BPD and a comorbid diagnosis of depression at time 1, generated significantly more specific memories and fewer categoric memories after 15 months of therapy. Moreover, these changes were unrelated to type of therapy and changes in depression severity, borderline symptom severity, dissociation, or thought suppression. The AMT scores at initial assessment did not predict depression severity at 15 months. The percentage of negative specific memories tended to predict BPD symptom severity.

Correspondence should be addressed to Dr Philip Spinhoven, Leiden University, Department of Psychology. Wassenaarseweg 52, 2333 AK Leiden, The Netherlands.
E-mail: spinhoven@fsw.leidenuniv.nl

Ismay P. Kremers is now at the Departments of Internal Medicine and Geriatrics, University of Groningen Medical Center, Groningen, The Netherlands.

The present study was supported by a grant from the fund for evaluative research in medicine of the Dutch Healthcare Insurance Board, awarded to A. Arntz (principal investigator, Maastricht University), R. Van Dyck (VU-Medical Centre), and Ph. Spinhoven (Leiden University). We wish to thank J. Giesen-Bloo, M. Nadort, the research assistants, and all therapists for their invaluable help.

© 2006 Taylor & Francis
DOI:10.1080/02699930500342662

Overgeneral memory has been demonstrated in suicidal patients (Williams & Dritschel, 1988), but also in depressed patients (e.g., Kuyken & Dalgleish, 1995; Williams & Scott, 1988), patients with bipolar disorder (Scott, Stanton, Garland, & Ferrier, 2000), patients with obsessive-compulsive disorder who also had a comorbid diagnosis of depression (Wilhelm, McNally, Baer, & Florin, 1997) and patients who experienced traumatic events during childhood or adulthood (e.g., de Decker, 2001; Henderson, Hargreaves, Gregory, & Williams, 2002).

Autobiographical memory in patients with borderline personality disorder

According to Conway (1997; Conway & Pleydell-Pearce, 2000) autobiographical memory (AM) is hierarchically structured, with more general information (lifetime periods) at the top, intermediate knowledge (general or extended events) at the second level, and more specific information (event-specific knowledge) at the lowest level. Conway (1997) and Williams (1996) suggested that in case of traumatic events, nonspecific memories serve as a way to control affect by minimising negative emotions that come with the memories of traumatic and negative events. As patients with borderline personality disorder (BPD) report high rates of childhood trauma (Zanarini, 1997), one would expect that they would also have trouble remembering specific events. Results are contradictory, however (Arntz, Meeren, & Wessel, 2002; Jones et al., 1999; Renneberg, Theobald, Nobs, & Weisbrod, 2005). Recently, it was found that an overgeneral style of memory retrieval among outpatients with BPD was restricted to patients who had major depression (Kremers, Spinhoven, & van der Does, 2004).

Stability of autobiographical memories

According to some studies, overgenerality is a trait-like phenomenon that is unrelated to mood severity. Williams and Dritschel (1988) studied the mood state dependency of the phenomenon in patients who had taken an overdose between 1 and 10 days prior to testing and ex-patients who had taken an overdose between 3 and 14 months prior to testing. Mood and memory specificity levels in patients and ex-patients did not differ. Because the variance of mood scores in both groups was large, correlations were calculated between level of mood disturbance and AM specificity scores. Overgeneral recall appeared to be mood-state independent, because there were no significant correlations. This conclusion was supported by several other studies (Brittlebank, Scott, Williams, & Ferrier, 1993; Mackinger, Pachinger, Leibetseder, & Fartacek, 2000b; Phillips & Williams, 1997). More recently, Peeters, Wessel, Merckelbach, and Boon-Vermeeren (2002) found AMT scores to be relatively stable over time in a sample of depressed outpatients, despite a decrease in depression severity after 7 months of treatment. The treatment was a combination of antidepressant medication and supportive psychotherapy. The suggestion that overgenerality is a trait marker was also raised by Brittlebank et al. (1993). They found that overgeneral recall did not change in depressed inpatients- and outpatients during a 7 month treatment with psychotropic medication. However, their last assessment included only 13 patients.

It can be concluded that AM specificity seems to be a relative stable cognitive style. However, there is also evidence that change is possible if appropriate interventions are used (Park, Goodyer, & Teasdale, 2004; Watkins & Teasdale, 2001, 2004; Watkins, Teasdale, & Williams, 2000; Williams, Teasdale, Segal, & Soulsby, 2000). Watkins and colleagues (2000) administered the AMT to dysphoric and depressed patients. Patients were allocated to rumination or distraction conditions followed by either a decentring question or a control question condition. Relative to rumination, distraction reduced overgeneral recall, and relative to control questions, decentring questions reduced overgeneral recall. Thus, even brief cognitive interventions like decentring and distraction may reduce overgeneral memory, albeit temporarily. In the only clinical study to date, Williams et al. (2000) found that overgeneral recall was also modifiable by psychotherapy. In recovered depressed patients who had been treated with Mindfulness-Based Cognitive Therapy (MBCT), the tendency to retrieve events in an overgeneral style was reduced, regardless of changes in depressive symptoms. To summarise, overgeneral memory style seems to be a relatively stable characteristic but is amenable to certain interventions.

Autobiographical memory as a predictor

If autobiographical memory is a trait-like phenomenon and related to depression, it may also predict the course and outcome of depression. Indeed, Brittlebank et al. (1993) found that overgeneral autobiographical memory in response to positive cue words correlated with severity of depression at follow-up. Dalgleish, Spinks, Yiend, and Kuyken (2001) found that the number of overgeneral memories in reaction to positive cues predicted depression scores at follow-up in patients with seasonal affective disorder, also after correcting for initial symptom levels. However, this was dependent on the measure that was used to rate depressive symptomatology. In addition, Mackinger and colleagues (Mackinger et al., 2004; Mackinger, Loschin, & Leibetseder, 2000a) found that AM specificity predicted the remissive course of depression during detoxification therapy in alcohol-dependent men as well as postnatal affective changes in a nonclinical sample of women. Harvey, Bryant, and Dang (1998) concluded that difficulties in recalling specific memories in response to positive cue words predicted symptoms of posttraumatic stress disorder 6 months later in survivors of motor vehicle accidents. In addition, Peeters et al. (2002) discovered that depressed outpatients with specific memories in reaction to negative cues had a better prognosis after 7 months of treatment. Only one study could not confirm the predictive function of overgeneral memories in depressed patients (Brewin, Reynolds, & Tata, 1999). Some possible explanations for the discrepant results were raised by the authors (use of inpatients, smaller proportion of overgeneral memories at baseline), but more research is needed to fully explain these findings.

Present study

In the present study the AMT scores in patients with BPD were investigated over time. The literature review showed that autobiographical memory appeared to be stable, except when specific interventions were used. The modification of AM specificity by psychotherapy has only been investigated in one clinical trial in formerly depressed patients treated with MBCT (Williams et al., 2000). Since we know from our former study that only patients with BPD and a comorbid diagnosis of depression have trouble remembering specific events, we wanted to know whether depressed and nondepressed patients with BPD differed from each other in percentage of specific and categoric memories over a course of 15 months of psychotherapy. The course of specific and categoric memories in depressed and nondepressed borderline patients was investigated as part of a multicentre treatment trial in which the effects of two well-defined forms of psychotherapy, that is, psychoanalytic transference focused psychotherapy (TFP) and schema focused cognitive behaviour therapy (CBT) were studied (Clarkin, Yeomans, & Kernberg, 1999; Giesen-Bloo et al., in press; Young, 1994). The therapy focused on BPD, not on depression. We hypothesised that the percentage of categoric memories would be reduced after both forms of psychotherapy, because both in TFP and CBT the therapist explicitly instructed the patient to focus on subjective experiences without trying to judge, avoid, or suppress them. In TFP the patient was encouraged to notice his/her transference reactions in the therapy situation and in past situations in a nonjudgemental way in order to achieve a better integration of positive and negative images of the self and significant others. In CBT patients were explicitly instructed to monitor their experiences and cognitions using diaries and during experiments and exercises in therapy sessions or homework assignments. These core procedures in both therapies may have encouraged patients to remember in a more specific way by reducing the tendency to truncate the memory retrieval process at a more general level.

The second aim of this study concerns correlates of overgeneral memory. Former studies found no relationship between overgenerality and mood. However, studies did find a relationship between dissociation and AM specificity. Harvey et al. (1998) found specificity of AM to be negatively correlated with dissociation in participants with acute stress disorder. In addition, Jones et al. (1999) found a positive correlation between overgenerality and dissociation in patients with BPD. In a nonclinical sample however, Wessel, Merckelbach,

Kessels, and Horselenberg (2001) found no differences on autobiographical memory specificity between college students who were either high or low on dissociation. Others concluded that avoidance of intrusive memories was related to overgenerality of memories (Kuyken & Brewin, 1995). This latter finding, together with the suggestion that dissociative symptoms were the result of efforts to forget (van den Hout, Merckelbach, & Pool, 1996) made us decide to study not only the association of changes in ratings of mood and dissociation with changes in specific and categoric memories in patients with BPD, but also the effect of changes in thought suppression on changes in memory specificity.

Finally, we investigated whether pretreatment AMT scores predicted depression severity or BPD symptoms after 15 months of therapy. Until now, the predictive validity of scores on the AMT for the outcome of a well-defined form of psychotherapy has never been investigated. Therefore, it is relevant to study whether AMT scores predict the outcome of well-defined forms of psychotherapy into more detail. When AMT scores indeed predict reduction of depression severity or BPD symptoms after psychotherapy in patients with BPD, either positively or negatively, this will be of importance for the clinical treatment of patients with BPD.

METHOD

Participants

Eligible participants were outpatients with DSM-IV borderline personality disorder who participated in a multicentre treatment trial (Giesen-Bloo et al., in press). Included were patients with a primary diagnosis of borderline personality disorder at time 1 (T 1) as assessed with the Structured Clinical Interview for DSM-IV Personality Disorders (SCID-II; First, Spitzer, Gibbon, & Williams, 1994), aged between 18 and 60 years, and Borderline Personality Disorder Severity Index-score (see below) above 20 at T 1. Presence of a depression at T 1 was assessed with the SCID-I (First, Spitzer, Gibbon, & Williams, 1997). Exclusion criteria were a psychotic disorder, a bipolar disorder, an antisocial personality disorder, a dissociative identity disorder, and attention-deficit hyperactivity disorder before the age of 7 years.

Therapy and therapists

Treatment sessions were held twice weekly. Therapists received intensive training and supervision from experts. Treatment integrity was assured by participation of the therapists in a pilot study, and by weekly local and twice a year intercentre supervision.

Measures

Autobiographical Memory Test (AMT). The modified autobiographical memory test by McNally, Lasko, Macklin, and Pitman (1995) was used. Respondents were asked to mention a specific moment at which they exhibited the trait that was written on a card. All 10 cue words were personality traits or mood states, whereas in the version that was introduced by Williams and Broadbent (1986) nouns were also presented and respondents were asked to mention a specific moment in reaction to the cue words. In the present study, a specific memory was defined as a memory that referred to a particular event in the past that happened on one particular day, lasting no longer than one day. We used three sets of 10 words each: 5 positive and 5 negative. The words were friendly, guilty, rude, honest, helpful, jealous, clever, selfish, humorous, hostile (T 1); happy, clumsy, loyal, cruel, tolerant, disciplined, cowardly, distrustful, kind, lazy: time 2 (T 2); interested, nervous, obstinate, generous, relaxed, irritated, grateful, sad, angry, and polite: time 3 (T 3). Words were read aloud and at the same time were shown on a card. The cue words were presented after three practice words. The task was started only after it was clear, during the practice phase, that the respondent understood the purpose of the task. Respondents were allowed 60 s to remember an event and if they did not come up with one, the next word was presented. Answers were recorded on audiotape. The following scoring categories were used: (a) specific (particular event at one particular day); (b) categoric (repeated events); (c) extended (event lasted longer than one day); (d) interviewer forgot or skipped one particular cue word by accident, the audiotape was unintelligible, or the respondent gave an answer that was a statement or a verbal association instead of a memory; and (e) response failure (omissions, i.e., when the respondent said nothing). The first author scored the tapes and a trained rater scored a random sample of 20% independently in order to assess the interrater-reliability. A kappa of .88 was obtained for the three most important categories: specific, categoric and omissions. Because of the low frequency of memories in the categories (c) and (d) these categories were not further analysed. The proportion of memories was calculated by dividing the number of the particular memories by the total number of cue words minus the omissions.

Beck Depression Inventory (BDI). The BDI (Beck, Ward, Mendelson, Mock, & Erbaugh, 1961; Bouman, Luteijn, Albersnagel, & Van der Ploeg, 1985), a 21-item self-report questionnaire was used to measure the severity of depressive symptoms during the past week.

Borderline Personality Disorder Severity Index (BPDSI). The BPDSI (Arntz et al., 2003, adapted from Weaver & Clum, 1993), a semistructured interview, was administered, to assess the frequency and severity of manifestations of BPD during the last 3 months. The interview consisted of nine subscales. In the present study the sum score of these subscales was used. Giesen-Bloo, Wachters, Schouten, and Arntz (2005) showed that the discriminant, construct and concurrent validity were good.

Dissociative Experiences Scale (DES). The DES (Carlson & Putnam, 1993; Draijer & Boon, 1993), a 28-item self-report scale to measure the proneness to experience dissociative phenomena, was employed to rate how often (the percentage of time) participants experienced each item. The average score across all items was the total score.

White Bear Suppression Inventory (WBSI). The WBSI (Muris, Merckelbach, & Horselenberg, 1996; Wegner & Zanakos, 1994), a 15-item self-report questionnaire, was administered to measure the tendency to suppress negative and unwanted thoughts. The sum score was the total score.

Procedure and design

After a complete description of the study, written informed consent was obtained from all participants. The study was approved by the Medical Ethical Committee. To examine whether AMT scores changed after psychotherapy, depressed and nondepressed patients with BPD were administered the AMT on three occasions: before start of treatment (T 1), 9 months later (T 2), and again 6 months later (T 3). Initially, patients were tested in one or two sessions in the third month of treatment. Several months into the study, the assessment procedure was rescheduled to take place immediately before the start of treatment. Analyses showed no significant differences on any AMT measure between the 31 patients assessed before start of treatment and the 24 patients assessed after 3 months.

RESULTS

Respondents

At T 1, 83 patients were tested, 47 of whom had a comorbid depression. Forty-one patients were randomly assigned to TFP, and 42 patients to CBT. At T 3, the AMT was readministered to 59 patients (71%). Four tape recordings failed, leaving 55 respondents with scores on all three AMT assessments, 37 of whom had a depression at T 1. Five participants were male. There were no significant differences on AMT scores at baseline between patients who were still in therapy after 15 months and patients who dropped out of therapy before T 3, but patients who dropped out of treatment were more often nondepressed and more often followed TFP.

TABLE 1
Baseline characteristics for depressed and nondepressed patients with Borderline Personality Disorder

Variable	BPD/D+ (N = 37)	BPD/D− (N = 18)
	M (SD)	M (SD)
Age	29.8 (8.6)	31.7 (7.9)
Education[a]		
Low	21	12
High	16	4
BDI	30.5 (9.8)	23.1 (8.7)
DES	19.3 (14.2)	18.6 (14.3)
WBSI	61.8 (7.9)	60.5 (10.7)
BPDSI	34.5 (7.6)	30.8 (8.0)

Note: Minor discrepancies in column totals are due to missing values.

[a] Low education, high school or lower; High education, more than high schools.

BPD/D+, depressed patients with BPD; BPD/D−, nondepressed patients with BPD; BDI, Beck Depression Inventory; DES, Dissociative Experiences Scale; WBSI, White Bear Suppression Inventory; BPDSI, Borderline Personality Disorder Severity Index.

Twenty-two completers received TFP and 33 patients CBT. Table 1 shows no significant differences in mean ages of the depressed and nondepressed groups, $t(1, 53) = -0.79, p = .43$. These groups also did not differ on level of education ($\chi^2 = 1.58, p = .21$), baseline DES scores, $t(1, 53) = 0.17, p = .87$, baseline WBSI scores $t(1, 53) = 0.50, p = .62$, or BPDSI scores at baseline, $t(1, 53) = 1.66, p = .10$). As expected, depressed patients had higher BDI scores at baseline than nondepressed patients, $t(1, 53) = 2.71, p < .01$. Unsurprisingly, BDI scores in the nondepressed group were also rather high.

Differential treatment effect on AMT scores

To investigate a possible differential effect of TFP and CBT, repeated-measures ANOVAs were conducted with time and valence as within-subjects variables and depression diagnosis and therapy condition as the between-subject variables. Separate analyses were conducted for specific and categoric memories. There were no significant interactions with therapy condition for specific or categoric memories (p-values ranging from .29 to .99). We therefore decided to conduct all analyses across therapy conditions.

Changes in specific memories after therapy

A repeated-measures ANOVA with time and valence as within-subjects variables and depression diagnosis as the between-subject variable was carried out on the percentage of specific memories. Table 2 shows that there was a significant main effect of time for specific memories, $F(1, 53) = 18.90, p < .001$. Follow-up simple contrasts indicated a significant decrease in percentage of specific memories between T 1 and T 2 ($p < .05$) and a significant increase in percentage of specific memories between T 1 and T 3 ($p = .001$). The significant interaction between time and group showed that this pattern was different for both diagnostic subgroups, $F(1, 53) = 6.77, p < .01$. Follow-up simple contrasts indicated a significant interaction from T 1 to T 2 ($p < .01$) and from T 1 to T 3 ($p = .001$). The BPD patients with depression showed an increase in percentage of specific memories from T 1 to T 3, whereas nondepressed BPD patients showed a decrease in percentage of specific memories from T 1 to T 2. Both groups had nearly identical scores at T 2 and T 3.

The main effect of valence for specific memories was almost significant, $F(1, 53) = 2.91, p = .09$: slightly more specific memories were recalled in reaction to positive words than in reaction to negative words. In addition, the interaction between time and valence was significant for specific memories, $F(1, 53) = 5.44, p < .01$. Follow-up simple contrasts indicated a significant interaction from T 1 to T 2 ($p < .01$) and not from T 1 to T 3 ($p = .92$). The percentage of specific memories in reaction to negative words increased between T 1 and T 2, whereas the percentage of specific memories in reaction to positive words did not increase. There were no significant interactions between valence and group for specific memories, $F(1, 53) = 1.32, p = .26$ or between time, valence, and group, $F(1, 53) = 0.17, p = .85$.

TABLE 2
Means (and standard deviations) of percentages of specific and categoric memories of depressed and nondepressed patients with Borderline Personality Disorder

	Negative cues			Positive cues		
	Time 1	Times 2	Times 3	Time 1	Time 2	Time 3
Spec.						
BPD/D−	75.0 (17.3)	53.5 (24.5)	77.8 (27.3)	76.7 (18.5)	71.1 (21.9)	76.7 (22.0)
BPD/D+	59.1 (24.3)	52.2 (22.9)	79.5 (20.3)	54.8 (24.2)	64.3 (25.4)	76.8 (22.9)
Categ.						
BPD/D−	16.7 (17.1)	22.2 (20.5)	14.4 (21.5)	10.0 (14.1)	14.4 (15.0)	14.4 (17.9)
BPD/D+	26.4 (22.8)	33.0 (25.9)	13.0 (17.3)	30.0 (24.5)	17.3 (22.2)	14.1 (17.6)

Spec, percentage of specific memories; Categ, percentage of categoric memories; BPD/D−, nondepressed patients with BPD; BPD/D+, depressed patients with BPD.

A complementary pattern was observed for categoric memories, however contrast tests were not significant.

Symptoms

Paired *t*-tests showed that mean scores on the DES, WBSI, BDI, and BPDSI were significantly lower after 15 months of therapy than at the start of treatment (see Table 3).

To check whether the change in percentage of specific and categoric memories was independent of the change in scores on the BDI, DES, WBSI, and BPDSI, several repeated-measures ANOVAs were performed with standardised residual change scores for the BDI, DES, WBSI, and BPDSI, respectively on T 3 as a covariate. These standardised residual gain scores were calculated by statistically correcting, for instance, BDI T 3 scores for BDI T 1 scores by multiple regression analysis. With regard to the BDI scores, there was still a significant main effect of time for specific memories, $F(1, 53) = 14.52$, $p < .001$. The significant interaction between time and group also remained, $F(1, 53) = 11.54$, $p = .001$. All effects involving valence became non-significant or remained nonsignificant. With regard to the DES, WBSI, and BPDSI scores, very similar results were found.

In addition, with regard to the BDI scores, the main effect of time for categoric memories remained, as well as the significant interaction between time and group, and the nonsignificant interactions between valence and group and between time, valence, and group. The significant main effect of valence disappeared after correcting for depressive symptoms as well as the significant interaction between time and valence. Again, the results after correcting for DES, WBSI, and BPDSI scores were quite similar.

TABLE 3
Mean scores of symptom measures and thought suppression before start of therapy and 15 months later

	Time 1	*Time 3*
DES	19.1 (14.1)**	14.4 (12.2)**
WBSI	61.4 (8.9)**	57.5 (11.9)**
BDI	28.1 (10.0)**	23.8 (12.5)**
BPDSI	33.3 (7.9)***	21.5 (10.8)***

DES, Dissociative Experiences Scale; WBSI, White Bear Suppression Inventory; BDI, Beck Depression Inventory; BPDSI, Borderline Personality Disorder Severity Index.
**p < .01; ***p < .001.

Prediction of treatment outcome with baseline AMT scores

Separate hierarchical regression analyses for specific and categoric memories were used to see whether pretreatment AMT scores predicted BDI and BPDSI scores at the end of treatment after correcting for initial symptom levels. First, the prediction of depression severity was studied. Predictors were: BDI at baseline (step 1) and AMT scores at baseline: Percentage of positive and negative specific or categoric memories (step 2). Including the AMT scores in the regression model did not make a significant contribution, F-change $(1, 54) = 2.90$, $p = .10$ (positive specific memories); F-change $(1, 54) = 2.38$, $p = .13$ (negative specific memories); F-change $(1, 54) = 2.63$, $p = .11$ (positive categoric memories) and F-change $(1, 54) = 0.58$, $p = .45$ (negative categoric memories).

The same analyses were done with BPD symptom severity as dependent variable. Most of the AMT scores did not make a significant contribution, F-change $(1, 54) = 0.21$, $p = .65$ (positive specific memories), F-change $(1, 54) = .29$, $p = .59$ (positive categoric memories), and F-change $(1, 54) = 1.67$, $p = .20$ (negative categoric memories). When we examined the specific memories in reaction to a negative cue word then the contribution of these memories was almost significant: F-change $(1, 54) = 3.47$, $p = .07$, $\beta = -.23$, $t(54) = -1.86$, $p = .07$.

DISCUSSION

Stability of autobiographical memories in patients with BPD

The present study examined whether the percentage of specific and categoric memories in depressed and nondepressed patients with BPD changed after psychotherapy (i.e., psychoanalytic transference-focused psychotherapy or schema-focused cognitive behaviour therapy). The present study is a replication of the study of Williams and colleagues (2000) where it was found that overgeneral recall in ex-patients was modifiable by psychotherapy. The present study was the first in which the course of overgeneral recall in patients after long-term psychotherapy was studied. The results showed that in patients with BPD the percentage of specific memories increased and the percentage of categoric memories decreased irrespective of treatment condition. It is important to note that the increase in specificity was associated with a decrease in categoric memories. This means that the increase in specificity was a genuine increase in specificity rather than an increase in overall number of memories. Of course, since we did not study a control group, we do not know whether therapy has caused these changes.

An interesting result is that the increase in specific memories and the reduction in categoric memories was true only for the depressed patients with BPD: The nondepressed patients with BPD did not change in the percentage of specific and categoric memories between the start of therapy and 15 months later. This means that the overgeneral memory bias in depressed patients with BPS was eliminated after 15 months of psychotherapy. Unfortunately, we were not able to administer the SCID-I again after 15 months of therapy, so it is not known whether the patients who were diagnosed with a depression at T 1, and who became more specific, actually still met the DSM criteria for a depression after 15 months of therapy. Possibly, it is only the treatment of depression that results in an increase in specific memories and a decrease in categoric memories and not the treatment of BPD. This would support the idea that a comorbid diagnosis of depression is related to overgeneral memories in BPD (Kremers et al., 2004), just as it is in obsessive-compulsive disorder (Wilhelm et al., 1997). Of course, the nondepressed patients with BPD were already specific at the start of treatment and therefore had less room for improvement than the depressed patients.

Nondepressed patients with BPD showed a significant decrease in percentage of specific memories between T 1 and T 2. This may be explained by hypothesising an adaptive role of overgeneral memory (de Decker, 2001; Kenealy, Beaumont, Lintern, & Murrell, 2000; Raes, Hermans, de Decker, Eelen, & Williams, 2003; Startup et al., 2001; Swales, Williams, & Wood, 2001). In the first months of therapy patients may have trouble integrating and dealing with all the intense feelings and emotions that are provoked and therefore feel more vulnerable. An overgeneral mode of retrieval could protect oneself against negative emotions. Of course, this reasoning is tentative and needs more investigation.

Autobiographical memory and psychological symptoms

Congruent with what other researchers found, the increase in specific memories and the decrease in categoric memories was independent of a change in BDI scores (cf. Watkins & Teasdale, 2001; Watkins et al., 2000; Williams et al., 2000). Of note are the rather high BDI scores in BPD patients without a diagnosis of depression at baseline. These high scores possibly reflect depressive reactions during the last week which, because of their more transient character, do not qualify as a depressive disorder according to DSM-IV criteria. Indeed, several authors have pointed out that mood instability is characteristic of BPD (Stone, 1980; Zanarini, Gunderson, Frankenburg, & Chauncey, 1990).

In addition, the increase in specific memories and the decrease in categoric memories was not related to improvement in dissociation or suppression. The present study was the first to study these relationships in a clinical setting. When patients tried to avoid distressing emotions, for instance through dissociation or active thought suppression, this could result in more overgeneral memories (cf. Harvey et al., 1998; Jones et al., 1999; Kuyken & Brewin, 1995; Williams, Stiles, & Shapiro, 1999b). In the present study, this was not the case. In addition, the improvement was not dependent on the change in BPD symptoms reported by patients. So, the affect-regulation hypothesis, as stated in the introduction does not help to explain the results of the present study. Possibly, the defensive function of an overgeneral memory style might not be adequate when traumatic events as complex and severe as often is the case in patients with BPD are involved.

The presence of a depression was related to improvement in AMT scores, whereas BDI scores were unrelated to improvement. Dalgleish et al. (2001) suggested that the association between memory specificity and depressive symptomatology depended on the measure that was used. They found a non-significant relationship between scores on the AMT and the BDI and a significant relation between scores on the AMT and the Hamilton Rating Scale for Depression (HRSD; Hamilton, 1960). This pattern would follow if autobiographical memory specificity were not related to the cognitive symptoms of depression (on which the BDI is focused to a large extent), but rather to its somatic-vegetative symptoms which form part of the diagnostic criteria for a depressive disorder and on which the HRSD is focused primarily.

Mood, dissociation, thought suppression, and BPD symptoms were related to cue valence effects on AMT scores. Categoric memories were more often recalled in reaction to negative words and specific memories in response to positive words, but after correction for the influence of BDI, DES, WBSI, or BPDSI scores, these effects disappeared. The relevance of cue word valence is still subject to discussion. Some studies supported the idea that positive words elicited fewer specific memories in clinical groups (Harvey et al., 1998; Puffet, Jehin-Marchot, Timsit-Berthier, & Timsit, 1991; Williams & Broadbent, 1986; Williams & Scott, 1988), other studies found the opposite (Jones et al., 1999; Mackinger et al., 2000b) and still other studies found no effect of valence at all (Brittlebank et al., 1993; Goddard, Dritschel, & Burton, 1996; McNally et al., 1995).

Autobiographical memory as a predictor

Pretreatment AMT scores were not able to predict depression severity (BDI) after 15 months of therapy, in contrast to several other studies (Brittlebank et al., 1993; Dalgleish et al., 2001; Peeters et al., 2002, but see Brewin, Reynolds, & Tata, 1999). Perhaps, this contradiction can be explained by lack of power in the present study. Interestingly, the percentage of specific memories in reaction to negative words tended to predict BPD symptom severity: Patients, who remembered more negative specific memories, reported less severe BPD symptoms after 15 months of treatment. Positive memories did not predict reduction of BPD symptom severity. A possible explanation for the valence effect in the present study is that during therapy the focus was on negative experiences. When patients already have the capability of more fully experiencing negative events, part of the goal of therapy is reached.

To date it is unknown which processes underlie the predictive value of (positive or negative) specific (or categoric) memories for outcome as observed in the present or previous studies. There is a dearth of studies investigating when and why AMT scores are relevant in predicting outcome.

Methodological issues

The findings from this study need to be considered in the light of some limitations. First, the sample consisted uniquely of outpatients, who functioned well enough to be able to follow psychotherapy for at least 15 months twice a week: this sample is not representative of all patients with BPD. In addition, the patients who dropped out of treatment were more often nondepressed and more often followed TFP, resulting in a selection of patients who were included in the present follow-up study. However, results cannot be explained through selective drop-out: AMT scores at baseline did not differ between dropouts and patients who remained in therapy. Another limitation concerns the repeated administration of the AMT: It is possible that the improvement on the AMT over time was the result of a practice effect. In addition, it is possible that there was an effect of the word sets used. It is possible that the sets differed in imageability, richness, and frequency (Baddeley, 1997; Williams, Healy, & Ellis, 1999b). Thus it would be useful to study repeated AMT administrations in a control sample using the same word sets that we used. Another issue is the use of the AMT version as modified by McNally et al. (1995). The difference was that in the original version (Williams & Broadbent, 1986) the memory did not need to refer to the subject him/herself, whereas in the McNally version the cue words as well as the instruction were self-referent. It is possible that the sensitivity of the test was affected by this modification. On the other hand, the test appears to be sensitive enough to detect differences between depressed and nondepressed patients with and without BPD. McNally et al. (1995) also found differences in memory specificity among Vietnam combat veterans with and without PTSD using this adapted form of the AMT. Finally, the absence of a control group is unfortunate. Inclusion of a control group would have made it possible to study the effect of treatment itself.

Conclusion

In conclusion, in outpatients with BPD who also have a comorbid diagnosis of depression, the percentage of specific memories increased and the percentage of categoric memories decreased after psychotherapy and these changes were independent of changes in mood, dissociation, thought suppression, and BPD symptoms. The AMT scores at initial assessment did not predict depression severity at 15 months. The percentage of negative specific memories tended to predict BPD symptom severity.

REFERENCES

Arntz, A., Meeren, M., & Wessel, I. (2002). No evidence for overgeneral memories in borderline personality disorder. *Behaviour Research and Therapy, 40*, 1063–1068.

Arntz, A., van den Hoorn, M., Cornelis, J., Verheul, R., Van den Bosch, W. M. C., & De Bie, A. J. H. T. (2003). Reliability and validity of the Borderline Personality Disorder Severity Index. *Journal of Personality Disorders, 17*, 54–59.

Baddeley, A. (1997). Recollection and autobiographical memory. In A. Baddeley (Ed.), *Human memory: Theory and practice* (pp. 211–228). Hove, UK: Psychology Press.

Beck, A. T., Ward, C. H., Mendelson, M., Mock, J., & Erbaugh, J. (1961). An inventory for measuring depression. *Archives of General Psychiatry, 4*, 561–571.

Bouman, T. K., Luteijn, F., Albersnagel, F. A., & van der Ploeg, F. A. E. (1985). Enige ervaringen met de Beck Depression Inventory (BDI) [Some experiences with the Beck Depression Inventory]. *Gedrag-Tijdschrift voor Psychologie, 13*, 13–24.

Brewin, C. R., Reynolds, M., & Tata, P. (1999). Autobiographical memory processes and the course of depression. *Journal of Abnormal Psychology, 108*, 511–517.

Brittlebank, A. D., Scott, J., Williams, J. M. G., & Ferrier, I. N. (1993). Autobiographical memory in depression: State or trait marker? *British Journal of Psychiatry, 162*, 118–121.

Carlson, E., & Putnam, F. W. (1993). An update on the Dissociative Experiences Scale. *Dissociation, 6*, 16–27.

Clarkin, J. F., Yeomans, F. E., & Kernberg, O. F. (1999). *Psychotherapy for borderline personality*. New York: Wiley.

Conway, M. A. (1997). Past and present: recovered memories and false memories. In M. A. Conway (Ed.), *Recovered memories and past memories* (pp. 150–191). Oxford, UK: Oxford University Press.

Conway, M. A., & Pleydell-Pearce, C. W. (2000). The construction of autobiographical memories in the Self-Memory System. *Psychological Review, 107*, 261–288.

Dalgleish, T., Spinks, H., Yiend, J., & Kuyken, W. (2001). Autobiographical memory style in seasonal affective disorder and its relationship to future symptom remission. *Journal of Abnormal Psychology, 110*, 335–340.

de Decker, A. (2001). *Autobiographical memory in traumatized adolescents*. Unpublished doctoral dissertation, University of Leuven, Belgium.

Draijer, N., & Boon, S. (1993). The validation of the Dissociative Experiences Scale against the criterion of the SCID-I, using receiver operating characteristics (ROC) analysis. *Dissociation, 6*, 28–37.

First, M. B., Spitzer, R. L., Gibbon, M., & Williams, J. B. W. (1994). *Structured clinical interview for DSM-IV Personality disorders (SCID-II)*. New York: New York State Psychiatric Institute, Biometrics Research Department.

First, M. B., Spitzer, R. L., Gibbon, M., & Williams, J. B. W. (1997). *Structured clinical interview for DSM-IV axis I disorders (SCID-I/P)*. New York: New York State Psychiatric Institute, Biometrics Research Department.

Giesen-Bloo, J. H., Van Dyck, R., Spinhoven, P., van Tilburg, W., Dirksen, C., van Asselt, Th., et al. (in press). Outpatient psychotherapy for borderline personality disorder: A randomized clinical trial of schema focused therapy versus transference focused psychotherapy. *Archives of General Psychiatry*.

Giesen-Bloo, J. H., Wachters, L. M., Schouten, E., Arntz, A. R. (2005). *Assessment of Borderline personality disorder with the borderline personality disorder severity Index-IV: Psychometric evaluation and dimensional structure*. Manuscript submitted for publication.

Goddard, L. & Dritschel, B., & Burton, A. (1996). Role of autobiographical memory in social problem solving and depression. *Journal of Abnormal Psychology, 105*, 609–616.

Hamilton, M. (1960). A rating scale for depression. *Journal of Neurology, Neurosurgery and Psychiatry, 23*, 56–62.

Harvey, A. G., Bryant, R. A., & Dang, S. T. (1998). Autobiographical memory in acute stress disorder. *Journal of Consulting and Clinical Psychology, 66*, 500–506.

Henderson, D., Hargreaves, I., Gregory, S., & Williams, J. M. G. (2002). Autobiographical memory and emotion in a non-clinical sample of women with and without a reported history of childhood sexual abuse. *British Journal of Clinical Psychology, 41*, 129–141.

Jones, B., Heard, H., Startup, M., Swales, M., Williams, J. M. G., & Jones, R. S. P. (1999). Autobiographical memory and dissociation in borderline personality disorder. *Psychological Medicine, 29*, 1397–1404.

Kenealy, P. M., Beaumont, J. G., Lintern, T., & Murrell, R. (2000). Autobiographical memory, depression and quality of life in multiple sclerosis. *Journal of Clinical and Experimental Neuropsychology, 22*, 125–131.

Kremers, I. P., Spinhoven, Ph., & van der Does, A. J. W. (2004). Autobiographical memory in depressed and non-depressed patients with borderline personality disorder. *British Journal of Clinical Psychology, 43*, 17–29.

Kuyken, W., & Brewin, C. R. (1995). Autobiographical memory functioning in depression and reports of early abuse. *Journal of Abnormal Psychology, 104*, 585–591.

Kuyken, W., & Dalgleish, T. (1995). Autobiographical memory and depression. *British Journal of Clinical Psychology, 34*, 89–92.

Mackinger, H. F., Leibetseder, M. M., Kunz-Dorfer, A. A., Fartacek, R. R., Whitworth, A. B., & Feldinger, F. F. (2004). Autobiographical memory predicts the course of depression during detoxification therapy in alcohol dependent men. *Journal of Affective Disorders, 78*, 61–65.

Mackinger, H. F., Loschin, G. G., & Leibetseder, M. M. (2000a). Prediction of postnatal affective changes by autobiographical memories. *European Psychologist, 5*, 52–61.

Mackinger, H. F., Pachinger, M. M., Leibetseder, M. M., & Fartacek, R. R. (2000b). Autobiographical memories in women remitted from major depression. *Journal of Abnormal Psychology, 109*, 331–334.

McNally, R. J., Lasko, N. B. Macklin, M. L., & Pitman, R. K. (1995). Autobiographical memory disturbance in combat-related posttraumatic stress disorder. *Behaviour Research and Therapy, 33*, 619–630.

Muris, P., Merckelbach, H., & Horselenberg, R. (1996). Individual differences in thought suppression. The White Bear Suppression Inventory: Factor structure, reliability, validity and correlates. *Behaviour Research and Therapy, 34*, 501–513.

Park, R. J., Goodyer, I. M., & Teasdale, J. D. (2004). Effects of rumination and distraction on mood and overgeneral autobiographical memory in adolescent major depressive disorder and controls. *Journal of Child Psychology and Psychiatry, 45*, 996–1006.

Peeters, F., Wessel, I., Merckelbach, H., & Boon-Vermeeren, M. (2002). Autobiographical memory specificity and the course of major depressive disorder. *Comprehensive Psychiatry, 43*, 344–350.

Phillips, S., & Williams, J. M. G. (1997). Cognitive impairment, depression and the specificity of autobiographical memory in the elderly. *British Journal of Clinical Psychology, 36*, 341–347.

Puffet, A., Jehin-Marchot, D., Timsit-Berthier, M., & Timsit, M. (1991). Autobiographical memory and major depressive states. *European Psychiatry, 6*, 141–145.

Raes, F., Hermans, D., De Decker, A., Eelen, P., & Williams, J. M. G. (2003). Autobiographical memory specificity and affect regulation: An experimental approach. *Emotion, 3*, 201–206.

Renneberg, B., Theobald, E., Nobs, M., & Weisbrod, M. (2005). Autobiographical memory in borderline personality disorder and depression. *Cognitive Therapy and Research, 29*, 343–358.

Scott, J., Stanton, B., Garland, A., & Ferrier, I. N. (2000). Cognitive vulnerability in patients with bipolar disorder. *Psychological Medicine, 30*, 467–472.

Startup, M., Heard, H., Swales, M., Jones, B., Williams, J. M. G., & Jones, R. S. P. (2001). Autobiographical memory and parasuicide in borderline personality disorder. *British Journal of Clinical Psychology, 40*, 113–120.

Stone, M. H. (1980). *The borderline syndromes: Constitution, personality, and adaptation.* New York: McGraw-Hill.

Swales, M. A., Williams, J. M. G., & Wood, P. (2001). Specificity of autobiographical memory and mood disturbance in adolescents. *Cognition and Emotion, 15*, 321–331.

van den Hout, M., Merckelbach, H., & Pool, K. (1996). Dissociation, reality monitoring, trauma and thought suppression. *Behavioural and Cognitive Psychotherapy, 24*, 97–108.

Watkins, E., & Teasdale, J. D. (2001). Rumination and overgeneral memory in depression: Effects of self-focus and analytic thinking. *Journal of Abnormal Psychology, 110*, 353–357.

Watkins, E., & Teasdale, J. D. (2004). Adaptive and maladaptive self-focus in depression. *Journal of Affective Disorders, 82*, 1–8.

Watkins, E., Teasdale, J. D., & Williams, R. M. (2000). Decentring and distraction reduce overgeneral autobiographical memory in depression. *Psychological Medicine, 30*, 911–920.

Weaver, T. L., & Clum, G. A. (1993). Early family environments and traumatic experiences associated with borderline personality disorder. *Journal of Consulting and Clinical Psychology, 61*, 1068–1075.

Wegner, D. M., & Zanakos, S. (1994). Chronic thought suppression. *Journal of Personality, 62*, 615–640.

Wessel, I., Merckelbach, H., Kessels, C., & Horselenberg, R. (2001). Dissociation and autobiographical memory specificity. *Clinical Psychology and Psychotherapy, 8*, 411–415.

Wilhelm, S., McNally, R. J., Baer, L., & Florin, I. (1997). Autobiographical memory in obsessive-compulsive disorder. *British Journal of Clinical Psychology, 36*, 21–31.

Williams, J. M. G. (1996). Depression and the specificity of autobiographical memory. In D. C. Rubin (Ed.), *Remembering our past: Studies in autobiographical memory* (pp. 244–267). Cambridge, UK: University Press.

Williams, J. M. G., & Broadbent, K. (1986). Autobiographical memory in suicide attempters. *Journal of Abnormal Psychology, 95*, 144–149.

Williams, J. M. G., & Dritschel, B. H. (1988). Emotional disturbance and the specificity of autobiographical memory. *Cognition and Emotion, 2*, 221–234.

Williams, J. M. G., Healy, H., & Ellis, N. C. (1999a). The effect of imageability and predictability of cues in autobiographical memory. *Quarterly Journal of Experimental Psychology, 52A*, 555–579.

Williams, J. M. G., & Scott, J. (1988). Autobiographical memory in depression. *Psychological Medicine, 18*, 689–695.

Williams, J. M. G., Stiles, W. B., & Shapiro, D. A. (1999b). Cognitive mechanisms in the avoidance of painful and dangerous thoughts: Elaborating the assimilation model. *Cognitive Therapy and Research, 23*, 285–306.

Williams, J. M. G., Teasdale, J. D., Segal., Z. V., & Soulsby, J. (2000). Mindfulness-based cognitive therapy reduces overgeneral autobiographical memory in formerly depressed patients. *Journal of Abnormal Psychology, 109*, 150–155.

Young, J. E. (1994). *Cognitive therapy for personality disorders: a schema-focused approach* (rev. ed.). Sarasota, FL: Professional Resource Press.

Zanarini, M. C. (Ed.) (1997). *Role of sexual abuse in the etiology of borderline personality disorder.* Washington, DC: American Psychiatric Press.

Zanarini, M. C., Gunderson, J. G., Frankenburg, F. R., & Chauncey, D. L. (1990). Discriminating borderline personality disorder from other Axis II disorders. *American Journal of Psychiatry, 147,* 161–167.

Facets of autobiographical memory in adolescents with major depressive disorder and never-depressed controls

Willem Kuyken and Rachael Howell
University of Exeter, UK

Adolescence is a crucial developmental window because it involves elaboration of the self-concept, the laying down of lifelong autobiographical memories, and the development of emotional resilience during a time of substantial risk for mood problems. Autobiographical memory retrieval plays an important role in depression both in adults (van Vreeswijk & de Wilde, 2004) and adolescents (Kuyken, Howell, & Dalgleish, 2005; Park, Goodyer, & Teasdale, 2002). This study examined facets of autobiographical memory associated with memory retrieval in never-depressed and currently depressed adolescents: personal importance, imagery, recency, source monitoring, and field-observer perspective. Compared with never-depressed adolescents, adolescents with depression were significantly more likely to retrieve memories from an observer perspective and more recent time period, preferentially rehearsed negative memories and rated their memories as more personally important. Depressed adolescents who reported a history of trauma retrieved more vivid autobiographical memories than depressed adolescents not reporting such a history, had rehearsed them more frequently, and reported more confidence in their veracity.

Adolescence is a crucial developmental phase during which a more explicit, stable, and coherent sense of self emerges (Harter, 1999). Adolescence is also the developmental window for the emergence of mood disorders from almost no point prevalence in early adolescence to point prevalence rates comparable to adults by late adolescence (Kessler, Avenevoli, & Merikangas, 2001). Several theoreticians have argued that adolescence is about pulling together autobiographical memories (AMs) with current experiences and future aspirations into a more coherent sense of self, a process that enhances resilience (Erikson,

---

Correspondence should be addressed to Willem Kuyken, Mood Disorders Centre, School of Psychology, University of Exeter, Exeter EX4 4QG, UK; e-mail: w.kuyken@exeter.ac.uk

The authors are grateful to the young people who participated in our research and the colleagues who assisted with recruitment. We acknowledge the research assistance of Rachel Day and Claire Fothergill.

1968; Harter, 1999). There is accumulating evidence that a high density of personally important and vivid AMs are laid down in adolescence that endure into adulthood and are important for emotional health (Habermas & Bluck, 2000). Recent evidence suggests that in depressed adolescents emotional memories become less accessible in terms of their specificity (Park et al., 2002), a phenomenon that may compromise resilience. However, there is almost no research about other facets of autobiographical memory that we know are important in nonclinical populations (Baddeley, 1990). This study is an exploratory examination of some of the key facets of emotional and self-defining AMs in depressed and never-depressed adolescents.

In children and adolescents the development of meta-cognitive abilities, the ability to monitor the source of AMs and a more stable and coherent self-concept increasingly support the development of autobiographical memory (Welch-Ross, 1995; Welzer & Markowitsch, 2005). In adolescents' autobiographical memory functioning is likely to impact on their current functioning *and* their healthy psychological development. It is now a well-established finding that AM retrieval is compromised in depression, in particular through difficulty retrieving specific AM (e.g., "I felt ashamed when I cheated on my boyfriend") and instead generating a high proportion of memories that are categorical (e.g., "when I have let people down"). This is true for memories cued in response to emotion words (van Vreeswijk & de Wilde, 2004) and for self-defining memories (Moffitt, Singer, Nelligan, Carlson, & Vyse, 1994). Recently, this broad finding has been replicated with adolescents (Kuyken et al., 2005; Park et al., 2002), suggesting that difficulty accessing event specific autobiographical knowledge begins at least as early as adolescence.

A reported history of significant trauma also appears to compromise the ability to retrieve specific AMs (Hermans et al., 2004; Kuyken & Brewin, 1995), which has been replicated with adolescents reporting trauma (de Decker, Hermans, Raes, & Eelen, 2003). One theoretical account suggests that traumatic memories are not integrated with the current working self, nor integrated with more verbally accessible event specific knowledge, but are oriented by early warning schemas that are perceptually primed to threat and associated with fear (Ehlers et al., 2002). The way in which trauma affects other emotional or self-defining memories is as yet little understood.

While the specificity of AM has been extensively researched, the general memory research literature indicates several facets of AM that are important and are under-researched in depression. The valence, personal salience, vividness, age of memory, and frequency of rehearsal are key facets of AM retrieval (Baddeley, 1990). It is a well-replicated finding that people who are depressed find it easier to recall negative memories compared to people who are not depressed (e.g., Clark & Teasdale, 1982). In a nonclinical population, comparisons of positive, negative, and traumatic memories suggested positive memories were clearer and contained more visual material (Byrne, Hyman, &

Scott, 2001). To try and explain these effects, it has been suggested that to maintain a positive working self people selectively rehearse pleasant memories, an ability that is compromised in people experiencing high levels of dysphoria or distressing intrusive memories (Joormann & Siemer, 2004; Taylor & Brown, 1994; Walker, Skowronski, & Thompson, 2003). Selective rehearsal of positive memories ensures that these memories persist with more detail and are therefore more accessible than unpleasant memories. To date, no study has examined whether these effects are observable in depressed adolescents or among those depressed adolescents reporting a history of trauma.

More recent AMs are more likely to be recalled than distant AMs (the "recency effect") (e.g., Berntsen & Rubin, 2002). A range of explanations of the recency effect have been examined empirically. More recent memories are more vivid and detailed, probably simply because this detail is forgotten in older memories, are more closely linked with current goals, and have been more recently rehearsed (D'Argembeau & van der Linden, in press). To date, no research has examined if this tendency to preferentially retrieve recent memories is more pronounced for people experiencing depression, which would be a form of impoverished accessibility. This would be particularly important in adolescence where formative memories are being encoded and rehearsed.

In a seminal study a distinction was drawn between memories retrieved with the person seeing the memory as if with their own eyes (field perspective) and memories where the memory is retrieved with the person as a "fly on the wall" (observer perspective) (Nigro & Neisser, 1983). Field memories tended to be more frequent (field 51%; observer 36%, unclassifiable 12%), more recent and associated with more emotion. An emerging explanation has been that repeated retrieval and rehearsal transform field memories into observer memories (Robinson & Swanson, 1993). A variety of theorists have commented that adolescence is the period when the "I-self" begins to be more fully aware of an objectified "Me-self" with the potential to monitor and evaluate the Me-self (see Harter, 1999). In a series of correlational and experimental studies with young adults, dissonance between current and past self-concept was associated with a tendency to retrieve more observer memories (Libby & Eibach, 2002; Libby, Eibach, & Gilovich, 2005). There is also evidence that situations involving self-focus (e.g., a public presentation) invoke a higher likelihood of memories retrieved as observer memories (Robinson & Swanson, 1993). Adolescence is a time when the self-concept is undergoing significant change and development, a process that is likely to be disrupted in adolescents diagnosed with depression. If the thesis that a consonant self is associated with greater numbers of field memories, we should anticipate a higher proportion of observer memories in depressed adolescents, a group struggling to generate a consonant self.

Imagery is integral to effective AM retrieval, as the reconstructive process is thought to involve the building of mental images. Autobiographical memories, particularly more recent memories, are often rated as highly vivid (Brewer & Pani, 1996), and memories rich in imagery have a shallower retention function (Rubin & Kozin, 1984). Memory cues that are easy to image make memory retrieval easier and are more likely to yield specific memories probably because imagery is a fast and efficient form of summarising large amounts of information (Williams, Healy, & Ellis, 1999). Trauma memories in particular tend to more vivid (Wenzel, Pinna, & Rubin, 2004), although we know little about how reported trauma affects facets of other emotional and self-defining memories. To date, no research has examined if the vividness of AMs is impoverished in people suffering depression let alone among adolescents suffering depression.

Autobiographical memory retrieval is fallible and vulnerable to a range of distortions and problems. Accurate AM depends critically on the ability to recall precisely when and where a specific event occurred, a process referred to as source memory (see Schacter, 1996). Being able to distinguish real from imagined events is in large part a function of how well source information is encoded (Johnson, Hashtroudi, & Lindsay, 1993). Imagined events (e.g., results of repeated ruminative thinking) lack detailed contextual detail (Johnson, Foley, Suengas, & Raye, 1988). Depression is a disorder marked by self-focused, repetitive thinking, divorced from event-specific autobiographical knowledge (Mor & Winquist, 2002), that might lead to source monitoring problems in AM retrieval. One way of identifying source monitoring problems is through reduced overall confidence in the integrity of memories and reduced ability to accurately date memories (Schacter, 1996). In parallel ways, intrusive traumatic memories, poorly integrated with the self-system, might also lead to source monitoring problems. Source monitoring is a faculty that develops during childhood and adolescence (Welch-Ross, 1995) and it is possible that depression could interrupt normal development of this ability.

While we have reviewed these memory characteristics separately, they are systematically interrelated. In many studies, the personal importance, vividness, and emotionality of memories are highly correlated (e.g., Rubin & Kozin, 1984; Wright & Nunn, 2000). Personally important memories become stable, vivid, and therefore intrinsically highly accessible. One classic view of highly accessibly memories are "flashbulb memories" (Brown & Kulik, 1977), which tend to be personally consequential, vivid, and unique. Personal relevance and emotionality are two characteristics that make memories most accessible, and it is possible that self-defining memories have some of the qualities of flashbulb memories. To our knowledge no research has explored whether these established relationships in personally important memories between vividness and emotionality extend to adolescents diagnosed with depression.

Focus of study and research questions

Autobiographical memory in adults and adolescents with depression tends to be characterised as over-general, a form of inaccessibility to event-specific autobiographical information. In nonclinical populations there are substantial individual differences in key facets of AMs: their personal importance, vividness, rehearsal, valence, recency, date accuracy, and confidence in accuracy. Surprisingly, we know very little about these facets of AM in adolescents with depression even though they may be crucial to the emerging self-concept and skills in emotion regulation. Our study sought to extend important findings from the general AM literature to better understand AM functioning in a group at a crucial stage in developing resilience/vulnerability for depression: 12 to 18-year-olds. Specifically, we examined the personal importance, vividness, rehearsal, memory valence, recency, date accuracy, and confidence of AMs among adolescents diagnosed with depression, comparing their memories with never depressed adolescents. Because trauma has also been shown to affect memory retrieval we wanted to examine among the depressed adolescents whether trauma compromised these facets of autobiographical memory.

METHOD

Participants

A total of 65 adolescents (aged 12–18) were recruited through schools, child and adolescent mental health services, children's homes, advertisements placed in libraries, youth centres, coffee bars, and local media (newspapers, radio, and television). Depression status was assessed against the *Diagnostic Statistical Manual for Mental Disorders*, 4th edition (DSM-IV; American Psychiatric Association, 1994) criteria for major depressive disorder. *The Beck Depression Inventory*, 2nd edition (BDI-II; Beck, Steer, & Brown, 1996) assessed depression severity. The sample comprised two groups: adolescents who currently met DSM-IV criteria for major depression ($N = 34$), and adolescents who had never been depressed ($N = 31$). Exclusion criteria were: substance abuse within the past 12 hours, and incapacity to participate because of an acute, unstable or severe mental or physical health problem. The two groups were comparable on age and sex: depressed age $M = 16.12$, $SD = 1.41$, 29 (85%) female; never depressed age $M = 15.71$, $SD = 1.66$, 22 (71%) female.

Participants' reports of trauma were screened using the Trauma History Questionnaire (THQ) and where necessary through follow-up questioning. A self-reported history of significant trauma was judged present if the event(s) met the DSM-IV Criterion A for posttraumatic stress disorder (PTSD), that is, "the person experienced, witnessed or was confronted with an event or events that involved actual or threatened death or serious injury, or a threat to the physical integrity of self or others and the response involved intense fear, helplessness, or horror" (American Psychiatric Association, 1994, p. 424). Reliability of ratings between research assistants' ratings of trauma and the first author for a random sample of 10 participants was 90% (Cohen's kappa = .8). Examples of trauma meeting Criterion A were involvement in serious car accidents, being physically assaulted, sexual abuse, witnessing deaths, accidents, or severe violence.

Materials and measures

Beck Depression Inventory. The BDI-II (Beck et al., 1996) is a 21-item self-report instrument developed to measure severity of depression in adults and adolescents. Higher scores represent greater depression severity (range 0–63), and minimal, mild, moderate, and severe symptom severity ranges have been specified.

Trauma History Questionnaire (THQ; Green, 1996). This lists 23 traumatic events in three categories. For each event, participants indicate lifetime occurrence, frequency, and age at first occurrence, and where appropriate, relationship to the perpetrator. Psychometric data on the THQ has shown high test-retest reliability of items (mean 0.70). The THQ was used as an initial screen for traumatic stressors.

Children's Impact of Event Scale (CIES; Smith, Perrin, Dyregrov, & Yule, 2003; Yule, Tenbruggencate, & Joseph, 1994). This is an 8-item self-report measure of intrusion and avoidance of traumatic events for children. The CIES was adapted from the original 15-item Impact of Event Scale (Horowitz, Wilner, & Alvarez, 1979). Each item is scored on a 4-point scale: High scores indicate higher levels of intrusion and avoidance of the traumatic event, within the past week. The scale has been found to have criterion validity with the diagnosis of PTSD and has been used successfully with children as young as 9 years. Participants completed the CIES in relation to the event specified in the THQ which continued to trouble them the most. A cut-off score of 17 has been found to work efficiently at discriminating PTSD cases, with 90% of children correctly classified (Smith et al., 2003).

Autobiographical Memory Test (AMT; Williams, 2000). Participants were asked to retrieve memories in response to 10 emotionally valenced cue words: five positive (happy, hopeful, excited, proud, and loved) and five negative (lonely, frightened, sad, angry, and ashamed). To ensure cues were appropriately positively and negatively valent and appropriate to adolescents the words were selected from the list of cues used in previous AM research (Williams, 2000) and emotion words previously generated by children and adolescents (Doost,

Moradi, Taghavi, Yule, & Dalgleish, 1998). This version of the AMT has been successfully used with adolescent clinical populations (de Decker et al., 2003; Swales, Williams, & Wood, 2001). Participants were shown the word on printed flash cards (black print on white paper) and given 30 seconds to retrieve a specific AM (a time and place when something happened to them in 1 day). Words were presented with positive and negative words alternating. If participants did not retrieve a specific memory they were prompted ("can you think of a specific time—one particular event"). If participants did not retrieve a specific memory in the time available (30 seconds), an omission was recorded and the experimenter proceeded to the next cue word. To ensure that participants understood the instructions, two practice cues were given (relieved and tired). Work to date with the AMT has largely restricted itself to examining the latency and specificity of memory retrieval. To address the aims of this study we asked participants after retrieving all the memories to go back and to rate each specific memory along a number of Likert dimensions: personal importance (1, not important to 7, one of the most important events *that has ever happened to me*), vividness (1, no image to 7, as if I were seeing it now), confidence of description (1, not at all to 7, completely confident), pleasantness (1, one of the most *unpleasant* events that has ever happened to me to 4, fairly neutral to 7, one of the most *pleasant* events that has ever happened to me), and the number of times they had thought about the memory since it happened (1, first time I've remembered it; 2, infrequently—about 5; 3 sometimes—about 10; 4 often—20; 5 very often—30 or more). Participants were asked to date their memory, and then indicate the accuracy of their dating (1, accurate to the day; 2, accurate to the week; 3, accurate to the month; 4, accurate to the season/quarter; 5, accurate to the year; 6, accurate to 5 years; 7 accurate to 10 years). Test-retest reliability and checks on dating accuracy suggest this method is effective (Rubin, Wetzler, & Nedes, 1986). In this sample, the median accuracy of dating memories was within 1 week. Participants were also asked if they recalled the event from a field (i.e., seeing scene through their own eyes) or observer perspective (seeing the scene from an observer's perspective).

The Self-defining Memory Task (Singer & Moffitt, 1992), generates self-defining memories. Participants were asked to generate memories in response to the following instructions:

> I would like you to think of a memory that defines you in some way. Try to think of this as the sort of memory you might tell someone who really wanted to get to know you. It is the sort of memory you think illustrates the kind of person you feel you really are inside. It is the sort of memory that you think tells powerfully how you have become the person you are at the moment. It might be the sort of memory from your life that you remember very clearly and that still feels important to you.

After they had generated a first memory, they were encouraged to think of another self-defining memory using the following prompt: "Now I would like you to think of another memory that defines you in some way". If a generic memory was recalled the participant was prompted for a specific memory with the following instruction: "Can you think of a particular time?". Memories were spoken out loud, and later transcribed verbatim. Self-defining memories were rated along the same dimensions as emotional memories (above), but in addition participants were asked to indicate on a 7-point scale how much the memory "defines you as a person" (1, not at all to 7, completely).

Verbal Fluency Task (VFT; Benton, 1968; Tombaugh, Kozac, & Rees, 1999). This was used as a measure of executive functioning. Participants were asked to generate as many words as possible beginning with the letter "B" in 60 seconds. Names, repeated words, and word variations (e.g., belonging, belongings) were not included in the final count.

Procedure

Invitations to participate were made directly to young people as well as through parents and workers in health and social care. Recruitment targeted currently depressed adolescents and controls through the wording of advertisements and dialogue with referring services. Following informed consent and assent procedures to a broader study of "Adolescents at Risk for Depression", adolescents completed the face-to-face interviews normally at the University or occasionally at other locations, such as their homes. Interviews lasted between $1\frac{1}{2}$ to 2 hours and participants were remunerated approximately $10. After demographic and background information was collected, the memory tasks were completed. Participants' reports of trauma were screened using the THQ and where necessary through follow-up questioning. A self-reported history of significant trauma was judged present if the event(s) met the DSM-IV Criterion A for PTSD. If the THQ screened positive for trauma, then the CIES was completed. Next, the BDI-II was completed, followed by an interview to establish the presence/absence of current and past depression. Depression status was assessed using the modules for mood disorders from the *Structured Clinical Interview (SCID) for the Diagnostic Statistical Manual for Mental Disorders* (4th revised edition) (DSM-IV; American Psychiatric Association, 1994; First, Spitzer, Gibbon, & Williams, 1995). SCID interviewers were psychology graduates trained by doctoral level psychologists. Questions were asked about past number of psychiatric hospital admissions, past suicide attempts, and past self-injury. The procedure concluded with the verbal fluency task.

RESULTS

Preliminary analyses

Much of the AM data uses nominal but sequentially ordered scales representing quantitative continuous attributes (e.g., frequency of memory rehearsal) comprising either five (accuracy) or seven levels. Given the exploratory nature of this study a primarily nonparametric statistical approach will be taken. However, some analyses require a multivariate approach, and in these cases subsequent nonparametric approaches will be used to check the integrity of the main components of the analysis and are reported as a footnote if these are substantially different.

For emotion memories mean ratings for positive and negative memories were computed for each of the memory characteristics (personal importance, vividness, rehearsal, confidence, accuracy, pleasantness). In addition, the proportion of total number of memories recalled that were field memories was computed for both positive and negative cues. Finally, the ages of memories in days was computed. When approximate dates were given algorithms were used (e.g., a week ago → 7 days; 3 months ago → 3 × 30 = 90 days; Spring 3 years ago, data collected in spring, → 3 × 365 = 1095 days). The dataset was cleaned, and because missing data were rare and the study is exploratory no strategies for missing data were employed beyond reporting the accurate N for each analysis (Tabachnick & Fidell, 2001). To ensure that the five positive memory cues and five negative memory cues were generating memories subjectively rated as pleasant or unpleasant, descriptive statistics for pleasantness ratings were calculated for the two sets of cues (Table 1). The design was effective in differentially producing positive and negative memories Wilcoxon's $T = 7.01$, $p < .0001$, $N = 65$. For the two self-defining memories, mean ratings from the two memories were computed for each of the memory characteristics (personal importance, vividness, rehearsal, confidence, pleasantness). To ensure that the self-defining memory task did lead to retrieval of memories subsequently rated as "defined me as a person" descriptive statistics were computed, $M = 5.03$, $SD = 1.02$, range 2–7, suggesting that participants regarded these memories as self-defining. Moreover, self-defining memories were rated as more personally important than memories generated in response to emotion cue words (Table 1), Friedman chi-square $(df = 2) = 95.2$, $p < .0001$, $N = 64$. The content of the self-defining memories was highly variable, spanning interpersonal (both family and friends), health, school, and hobbies.

As would be expected, the depressed group reported significantly more psychiatric history and trauma than the never depressed group. Within the depressed sample, 11 (32%) had experienced one episode of depression, 9 (27%) had experienced two episodes, and 12 (35%) had experienced three or more

TABLE 1
Descriptive statistics, means, (standard deviations), and 95% confidence intervals for emotion and self-defining memories in never-depressed (N = 31) and currently depressed adolescents (N = 34)

	Never-depressed			Currently depressed		
	Emotion memories		Self-defining memories	Emotion memories		Self-defining memories
Memory characteristics	Positive	Negative		Positive	Negative	
Age	521 (371)	829 (706)	1251 (1093)	216 (281)	400 (502)	1193 (1075)
	385–657	570–1088	850–1651	118–315	225–575	812–1574
Personal importance	4.15 (0.99)	3.78 (1.01)	4.82 (1.16)	4.91 (1.04)	4.13 (1.18)	5.32 (1.59)
	4.15–4.87	3.41–4.15	4.4–5.25	4.55–5.27	3.72–4.54	4.76–5.88
Vividness	5.54 (0.83)	5.37 (0.79)	5.39 (1.04)	5.53 (0.88)	5.37 (0.81)	5.08 (1.07)
	5.24–5.85	5.08–5.66	5.01–5.77	5.22–5.83	5.05–5.68	5.42–6.18
Confidence	5.87 (0.76)	5.71 (0.89)	5.84 (0.84)	5.69 (0.88)	5.57 (1)	6.05 (1.06)
	5.69–6.24	5.39–6.04	5.53–6.15	5.39–6.0	5.22–5.92	5.67–6.42
Pleasantness	5.55–0.88	2.47 (0.56)	3.71 (1.32)	5.52 (0.74)	2.21 (0.6)	3.36 (1.47)
	5.34–5.76	2.27–2.68	3.23–4.19	5.26–5.78	2.0–2.42	2.84–3.88
Rehearsal	2.84 (0.84)	2.83 (0.80)	3.37 (1.10)	2.70 (0.87)	3.2 (0.87)	3.69 (0.96)
	2.53–3.15	2.53–3.12	2.97–3.77	2.4–3.0	2.9–3.51	3.36–4.03
Accuracy	2.31 (0.78)	2.81 (0.87)	a	2 (0.83)	2.48 (1.71)	a
	2.02–2.60	2.5–3.13		1.71–2.29	1.89–3.08	

Note: Age in days; personal importance (1–7); vividness (1–7); confidence (1–7); pleasantness (1–7, 4 neutral), rehearsal (1–5), accuracy (1 = to the day to 7 = within 10 years).
^a Data not collected.

episodes.[1] Four (12%) had been hospitalised for depression, 16 (47%) had made suicide attempts and 25 (74%) had self-harmed. The severity of depressive symptoms in the depressed sample was on the borderline between moderate and severe symptoms (BDI-II: $M = 28.68$; $SD = 12.49$), while in the never depressed group all were in the asymptomatic range (BDI-II: $M = 4.58$; $SD = 3.81$). The number and proportion of adolescents reporting significant trauma were as follows: depressed 22 (65%), never-depressed 3 (10%). Among the currently depressed sample reporting a history of significant trauma, the rates of trauma symptoms were significant with the mean Impact of Event Scale (IES) score falling significantly above the recommended cut-off for probable PTSD in 18 (53%) of the sample compared to none of the never depressed sample.

---

[1] Data on number of episodes was missing for two participants, because the SCID was not completed in full for previous episodes of depression.

The depressed and never-depressed samples were comparable on age, gender distribution and verbal fluency.[2] Any impact of demographic factors and verbal fluency on the AM variables was examined for the sample as a whole and for the depressed and never-depressed groups separately. For the sample as a whole, only one relationship reached significance. More pleasant self-defining memories were associated with greater verbal fluency, $r_s = .26$, $p < .05$, $N = 65$. There were no significant differences on any AM characteristics by gender. For the never-depressed group, younger participants tended to retrieve more field perspective self-defining memories, $r_s = -.44$, $p < .05$, $N = 31$. There were no significant differences on any AM characteristics by gender. For the currently depressed group, two relationships reached significance. Older participants recalled less unpleasant negative memories, $r_s = .53$, $p < .01$, $N = 34$. Also, older participants rehearsed negative memories less often, $r_s = -.38$, $p < .05$, $N = 34$. In the depressed group some interesting gender differences emerged. Male participants tended to rate the accuracy of the dates they gave for their positive memories higher, Mann-Whitney $U = 28$, $p < .05$, $df = 33$. Female participants tended to have rehearsed negative memories more, Mann-Whitney $U = 29$, $p < .05$, $df = 33$. Subsequent analyses addressing the study's research questions involving AM variables associated with age, gender, or verbal fluency statistically covaried age or verbal fluency or were rerun for female participants alone to ensure effects were not artefacts of these variables.

Autobiographical memory characteristics and depression

The descriptive statistics for AM characteristics for the memories are shown in Table 1. A series of mixed 3 (memory type: positive, negative, self-defining) × 2 (Group: never depressed, currently depressed) ANOVAs were computed on the following dependent variables: memories' age, personal importance, vividness, confidence, pleasantness, rehearsal, and accuracy.[3] The ANOVA for *age of memory* revealed a significant effect of group, $F(1, 62) = 4.5$, $p < .05$, with the depressed adolescents retrieving more recent memories than the never-depressed adolescents. There was a main effect of memory type, $F(2, 62) = 25.98$, $p < .0001$, with the means suggesting that positive memories tend to be most recent, negative memories intermediate, and self-defining memories most remote. The memory type by group interaction was not significant, $F(2, 62) = 1.15$. Box plots of the recency finding showed very clearly that the depressed group tends to recall memories from within the last year while the never-depressed group tends

---

[2] Verbal fluency for the sample as a whole: $M = 11.84$, $SD = 3.83$.

[3] F-tests with values < 1 are not reported.

to recall events from the previous three years. The ANOVA for *personal importance* revealed a significant effect for Group, $F(1, 62) = 6.73, p < .05$, and memory type, $F(2, 62) = 18.35, p < .0001$, but no interaction. Depressed adolescents rated their memories as more personally important than never depressed adolescents, and descriptive statistics suggest that self-defining memories and positive memories were rated as more important than negative memories.

The ANOVA for memory *vividness* showed no significant effects for group $F(1, 62) = 1.56$, nor memory type $F(2, 62) = 1.1$, nor interaction $F(2, 62) = 1.16$. The descriptive statistics suggest that the majority of the memories are recalled rich in imagery, but not with the intensity of reliving it. The ANOVA for *confidence in memories* showed no significant effects for group, a trend for memory type, $F(2, 62) = 3.01, p = .05$, and no interaction, $F(2, 62) = 1.76$. The descriptive statistics suggest that rates of confidence in memories are high, but not absolute.

The ANOVA for *memory pleasantness* showed a trend for group $F(1, 60) = 2.92, p = .09$, a trend for memory type, $F(2, 60) = 2.77, p = .07$, and no significant interaction, with the currently depressed reporting marginally less pleasant memories and the positive, self-defining, and negative memories showing decreasing pleasantness ratings.[4] Interestingly, the descriptive statistics for pleasantness suggest that the mean rating of the self-defining memories was around or just below the neutral range. The ANOVA for *rehearsal* showed no effect for group, $F(1, 62) = 4.5, p < .05$, an effect for memory type, $F(2, 62) = 3.88, p < .05$, and a trend for an interaction, $F(2, 62) = 2.93, p = .053$. Self-defining memories were rehearsed most frequently. The plots of marginal means suggested a visibly marked interaction for positive and negative memories so a follow-up 2 (memory type: positive and negative) × 2 (group, depressed, never depressed) ANOVA was computed. This replicated the effect for memory type, $F(1, 62) = 6.87, p < .05$, and showed a significant memory type by group interaction, $F(2, 62) = 8.08, p < .01$. This analysis added that depressed participants rehearsed negative memories significantly more often than positive memories.[5] The descriptive statistics suggest that emotion memories tend to have been rehearsed relatively infrequently (about 10 times), while self-defining memories had been rehearsed more often, with depressed adolescents most frequently indicating they had rehearsed their self-defining memories "often" (about 20 times).

The ANOVA for *accuracy* showed a main effect for memory type, $F(1, 63) = 6.83, p < .05$, but no effect for group, $F(1, 63) = 2.44$, nor for the interaction. Positive memories were more likely to be rated as accurate to within a day than

---

[4] Age and verbal fluency were covaried in this analysis.

[5] Age was covaried in these two analyses. The analyses were replicated for only female participants, and the pattern of findings was identical.

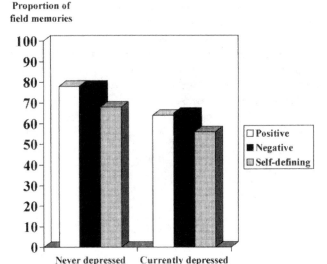

Figure 1. The proportion of field memories for positive, negative, and self-defining memories in never-depressed and currently depressed groups.

negative memories, which were more typically rated as accurate within a month.[6]

The proportion of field memories for positive, negative, and self-defining memories are shown in Figure 1. The ANOVA for *proportion of field memories* suggested a significant main effect for memory type, $F(2, 62) = 3.39$, $p < .05$, and group, $F(1, 62) = 4.49$, $p < .05$, but no interaction. Emotion memories were significantly more likely to be field memories than self-defining memories and never-depressed adolescents were significantly more likely to report field memories than depressed adolescents. When adolescents' age was added as a covariate the main effect for memory type no longer reached significance, suggesting that the greater proportion of observer self-defining memories is an artefact of participants' age (older participants' memories are more often observer memories). Importantly, the main effect for group remained significant.

In summary, this series of analyses shows a pattern of findings consistent with some of the study's predictions. Compared with never-depressed controls, depressed adolescents' AMs tended to be from the observer perspective, more recent, marginally less pleasant, and rated as more personally important. Consistent with autographical memory research, positive memories were most recent

---

[6] This analysis was replicated for only female participants, and the pattern of findings was identical.

and accurately dated while self-defining memories were most important, frequently rehearsed, and reconstructed from an observer perspective. Depressed adolescents rehearsed negative memories more often than never-depressed controls, a pattern not seen with positive memories.[7]

The findings concerning the recency effect, field/observer perspective, personal importance, and group are striking. To examine how these memory characteristics are related to psychiatric symptoms and other memory characteristics two-tailed Spearman rank correlations were computed for the currently depressed adolescents. Because very few interaction effects were observed for memory type by group, and to avoid the possibility of false positives associated with excessive numbers of correlations, memory characteristics for positive, negative, and self-defining cues were combined (Table 2). These correlations suggest that more personally important memories are more vivid, remembered with more confidence and more likely to be dated accurately. In this sample of currently depressed adolescents neither depression history nor depression severity were associated with any characteristic of memory. When these same correlations were computed for the never-depressed sample, the pattern of findings was identical with two exceptions. Higher

TABLE 2
Spearman correlations for autobiographical memory characteristics for currently depressed adolescents

	1	2	3	4	5	6	7	8	9	10
1. No. major depressive episodes	–									
2. BDI-II	.26	–								
3. Age of memories	.04	–.18	–							
4. Personal importance of memories	.06	–.11	–.13	–						
5. Vividness of memories	.07	.1	–.1	.37*	–					
6. Confidence in memories	–.08	.11	–.14	.42*	.61***	–				
7. Pleasantness of memories	.13	–.13	–.22	.20	–.04	–.21	–			
8. Rehearsal of memories	–.01	.24	–.1	.15	.43*	.19	.14	–		
9. Accuracy of memories	–.13	–.08	.11	.51**	–.09	–.11	–.15	–.08	–	
10. Proportion of field perspective memories	.27	–.01	–.15	–.04	0	–.28	.09	0	.14	–

Notes: BDI-II, Beck Depression Inventory (2nd ed.). ***$p < .001$; **$p < .01$; *$p < .05$ (2-tailed).

---

[7] Nonparametric Mann-Whitney tests with memory characteristics as the dependent variables and depression status as the independent variables confirmed all the main effects.

depressive symptoms were associated with more observer perspective memories, $r_s = -.46, p < .05, N = 31$, and more personally important memories were associated with more pleasant memories, $r_s = .46, p < .05, N = 31$.

Autobiographical memory characteristics and trauma

To examine if a history of trauma affects the accessibility and quality of AM among the depressed adolescents a series of mixed 3 (memory type: positive, negative, self-defining) × 2 (Group: no reported trauma, reported significant trauma) ANOVAs were computed on the following dependent variables: memories' age, personal importance, vividness, confidence, pleasantness, rehearsal, and accuracy. The ANOVA for *age of memory* revealed no significant effect of group, but a main effect of memory type, $F(2, 31) = 14.17, p < .0001$. The descriptive statistics suggest that positive and negative memories tend to be dated most recent and self-defining memories dated as most remote. The memory type by group interaction was not significant. The ANOVA for *personal importance* revealed no significant effect for group, a significant effect for memory type, $F(2, 31) = 6.07, p < .001$, and no interaction effect.[8] Depressed adolescents rated their self-defining memories and positive memories as more important than their negative memories.

The ANOVA for memory *vividness* showed a significant effect for group, $F(1, 31) = 13.65, p < .01$, but not for memory type, $F(2, 31) = 1.66$, nor for the interaction. The descriptive statistics suggest that the adolescents reporting trauma rate their memories as more vivid than adolescents reporting no trauma. The ANOVA for *confidence in memories* showed a significant effect for group, $F(1, 31) = 11.87, p < .01$, no effect for memory type, $F(2, 31) = 1.61$, and no interaction, $F(2, 31) = 1.2$. The descriptive statistics suggest that the adolescents reporting trauma are more convinced of the veracity of their memories than adolescents reporting no trauma.

The ANOVA for *memory pleasantness* showed no effect for group, an effect for memory type, $F(2, 29) = 3.13, p = .052$, and no interaction, $F(2, 29) = 1.31$, with the descriptive statistics suggesting that pleasant memories were rated more pleasant than the self-defining memories, which in turn were rated as more positive than the negative memories.[9] The ANOVA for *rehearsal* showed a significant effect for group, $F(1, 32) = 17.13, p < .001$, no effect for memory type, $F(2, 31) = 2.05$, and no interaction. The traumatised adolescents had rehearsed their memories significantly more often than nontraumatised adolescents.[10] The ANOVA for *accuracy* showed no effect for memory type $F(1, 32) =$

---

[8] Only *f*-values > 1 are reported.
[9] Age and verbal fluency were covaried in this analysis.
[10] Age was covaried in these two analyses. The analyses were replicated for only female participants, and the pattern of findings was identical.

1.56, no effect for group, and no interaction of memory type by group.[11] A further ANOVA for proportion of field perspective memories suggested no main effect for memory type, no effect for group, and no interaction. In summary, adolescents reporting a history of significant trauma rated their memories as more vivid, were more confident of their veracity, and had rehearsed them more frequently.

Among the depressed plus trauma participants, the levels of trauma symptoms were marked with the mean CIES score falling significantly above the recommended cut-off of 17 for probable PTSD: M 26.38 (SD 11.06). To examine in the group of depressed adolescents reporting significant trauma the impact of trauma symptoms on these memory characteristics, Spearman two-tailed rank correlations were computed. Higher levels of PTSD symptoms (total IES score) were associated with more vivid positive ($r_s = .52, p < .05, N = 21$) and self-defining memories ($r_s = .45, p < .05, N = 21$) but not more vivid negative memories ($r_s = -.13, N = 21$). Trauma symptoms were not significantly associated with confidence, veracity, or rehearsal of AMs.

DISCUSSION

This is the first study that we are aware of that has extended an important line of research on the inaccessibility of specific autobiographical memory in depression through overgeneralisation (van Vreeswijk & de Wilde, 2004) to other facets of AM. We have shown that adolescents diagnosed with depression, compared to never-depressed controls, retrieve a higher proportion of observer perspective memories, recall more recent memories, rate their memories as more personally important, and preferentially rehearse negative memories. We found no evidence for source monitoring problems. Replicating the consistent findings from the nonclinical literature (Rubin & Kozin, 1984), depressed adolescents' AMs that are personally important also tend to be rated as more vivid and accurate. Among depressed adolescents a reported history of trauma appeared to make memories more vivid.

How can these findings be explained? Our finding that depressed adolescents report significantly more observer perspective memories can be reconciled with studies showing that when people retrieve memories that are dissonant with their working self-concept they are more likely to visualise them from an observer perspective (Libby & Eibach, 2002). Depression, and particularly adolescent depression, is characterised by: (1) heightened self-awareness; (2) objectifying the self; and (3) dissonance between the actual and ideal self (Beck, 1967; Garber, Weiss, & Shanley, 1993; Higgins, 1996). The "depressive paradox"

---

[11] This analysis was replicated for only female participants, and the pattern of findings was identical.

involves attempts to resolve this dissonance using strategies that exacerbate negative mood such as ruminative self-focus on *an objectified self* ("I feel so bad, why do I feel so bad all the time, what is wrong with me?") (Nolen-Hoeksema, 1991) and avoiding strategies that process negative feelings, such as "mindful experiencing" ("feeling down and tired, this will pass and I will be OK") (Teasdale, 1999). The reconstruction of AMs depends on the influences of the current working self. Higher rates of observer memories have been linked to increased self-focus (Robinson & Swanson, 1993), a tendency towards dispositional attributions (Frank & Gilovich, 1989), and to dissonance between current and ideal selves (Libby & Eibach, 2002), conditions that are all present in depression. Why should this lead to reconstructing observer perspective memories? We propose that the modus operandi of the working self in depression tends towards objectifying the self as falling short and tends away from accepting the self as an active, experiencing agent. This modus operandi is more likely to prime retrieval to reconstruct memories from an observer perspective in which the objectified self can be evaluated. There is evidence that the negative working self in depression is maintained through a tendency to ruminate nonproductively on unpleasant, objectified, and dissonant memories (Park, Goodyer, & Teasdale, 2004; Teasdale & Green, 2004; Watkins & Teasdale, 2001). While in never-depressed populations preferential retrieval of positive memories maintains a positive working self it is plausible that in depression the converse is true, namely, that a negative working self is maintained through preferential retrieval of negative AMs in which the self is seen as falling short (Taylor & Brown, 1994; Walker et al., 2003). This explanation is consistent with our finding that depressed adolescents preferentially rehearse negative memories and that they rate their memories as particularly personally important, possibly because they are being used in the service of resolving dissonance. On the other hand, it could be that they have objectively experienced more personally consequential emotional experiences as part of their trajectory to depression, a finding consistent with the considerable evidence linking negative life events with depression (e.g., Kessler, Davis, & Kendler, 1997). Nonetheless, their relationship to these experiences will very likely impact on the course of depression.

How can we explain our finding of an exacerbated recency effect in depression? The recency effect in AM is a well-replicated phenomenon with one third to two thirds of all AMs retrieved typically being from the previous year (Rubin et al., 1986). The most parsimonious explanation is that cognitive resources are depleted in depression and because recent memories are easier to retrieve depressed adolescents' retrieval strategy is set to "easiest mode of retrieval". However, we did not find that verbal fluency was associated with memory recency, which might be expected if limited working memory was a limiting mechanism. Another explanation is that more recent memories are more likely to be consonant with current working goals, which in depressed adolescents, are likely to have been shaped by recent events surrounding the current episode of depression. Whatever the explanation, our finding that the recency effect is particularly marked in depressed adolescents is important because it suggests that depressed adolescents are drawing on a more limited range of emotional memories. Moreover, these memories will be sampled from the period leading up to and part of the current episode. We would hypothesise that this would negatively affect their emotion regulation and problem solving.

Our study examined self-defining memories as a form of "flashbulb memory" in depressed adolescents. Self-defining memories were personally important, frequently rehearsed, relatively remote and likely to be observer perspective memories. Self-defining memories tended to be rated as either neutral or somewhat unpleasant, suggesting that they are personally consequential but affectively mixed events. Examples included coping with a school transition, the relief that followed Mum returning after walking out following an argument with dad and going on holiday with a friend for the first time. These characteristics of self-defining memories are likely to make them highly accessible in depressed adolescents and future work will need to examine in what ways these memories are related to self-monitoring, emotion regulation, the self-concept, and problem solving.

Consistent with what we know from the general AM literature, we found that depressed adolescents' AM characteristics were highly interrelated. Personally consequential memories were more vivid and rehearsed more frequently. Previous research suggests that it is the personal importance ascribed to a memory that is primary in determining the richness of encoding and therefore its longer-term retention function (Wright & Nunn, 2000).

A history of trauma is common in depression (Kessler et al., 1997), and frequently associated with enduring PTSD symptoms that adversely affects AM functioning (Kuyken & Brewin, 1995). Among the adolescents diagnosed with depression, a history of significant trauma was associated with more vivid and well rehearsed memories, which were retrieved with greater confidence about their veracity. Intriguingly, it is as if reports of trauma are associated with reports of positive and self-defining memories rather like flashbulb memories, making them more rather than less accessible. It is possible that much of the emotional event-specific knowledge in AM is stored with stronger sensory-perceptual content, accounting for its vividness, rehearsal, and enhanced confidence. Young people exposed to trauma may have enhanced orienting schema to emotion in general and threat in particular and a survival strategy may be to encode emotional experiences particularly carefully as longer-term strategies for navigating emotional situations are being learned (Ehlers et al., 2002). The working self as a whole is a work in progress, and it is the working self that is thought to be able to integrate traumatic memories with other event-specific knowledge and inhibit unwanted memories from awareness (Ehlers & Clark, 2000). This preliminary finding is at odds with the adult literature (e.g., van der

Kolk & Fisler, 1995) and requires replication before a developmental hypothesis can be elaborated further. Moreover, our design did not include a group of never-depressed adolescents reporting significant trauma, which is crucial to establishing whether these putative mechanisms are particular to depression.

This work was conducted as an exploratory study and therefore raises further avenues of exploration. The novel findings require replication, and extension to an adult population of people diagnosed with depression. Further work could usefully examine the significance and role of self-defining memories in adolescent depression, perhaps linking them to the development of a coherent and elaborated self-concept, emotion regulation, and social problem solving. The hypotheses about the role of observer memories in the course of depression require empirical testing. Finally, experimental studies manipulating the factors thought to moderate memory retrieval (e.g., recency, rehearsal) and examining the impact on emotion regulation would begin to test the explanatory accounts of the functions of AM and pave the way for downstream clinical implications. Although we did not find any evidence for source monitoring errors in adolescents with depression, we used only one methodological approach (accuracy of dating), and further research should aim to triangulate this finding using alternative methods (Johnson et al., 1993).

This work extends the literature on memory in depression generally and adolescents specifically and suggests that the retrieval of event-specific knowledge may be compromised in a range of ways. Not only is the richness of event-specific knowledge inaccessible because of the high proportion of overgeneral memories (Park et al., 2002), but when specific memories are recalled they are more recent and seen from an observer perspective. Given that depressed adolescents also tend to rehearse their negative memories more often and regard them as particularly personally important it is possible that these other facets of AM play an important role in the development of the self-concept and emotional resilience. Adolescence is a crucial developmental window for a range of reasons: the self-concept goes through a period of crucial maturation, AMs are encoded which will be preferentially retrieved throughout life, and first onset of potentially lifelong mood disorders are troublingly common. The limited research in this area to date suggests that depressed adolescents' AMs are less accessible and when specific memories are retrieved they tend to be from a limited window of time and seen from the perspective of an objectified self.

REFERENCES

American Psychiatric Association. (1994). *Diagnostic and statistical manual of mental disorders*. (4th rev. ed.) Washington, DC: Author.

Baddeley, A. (1990). Recollection and autobiographical memory. In A. Baddeley (Ed.), *Human memory: Theory and practice* (pp. 293–318). Hove, UK: Lawrence Erlbaum Associates Ltd.

Beck, A. T. (1967). *Depression: Clinical, experimental and theoretical aspects*. New York: Harper & Row.
Beck, A. T., Steer, R. A., & Brown, G. K. (1996). *The Beck depression inventory* (2nd ed.). San Antonio, TX: Psychological Corporation.
Benton, A. L. (1968). Differential behavioural effects in frontal lobe disease. *Neuropsychologia, 6*, 53–60.
Berntsen, D., & Rubin, D. C. (2002). Emotionally charged autobiographical memories across the life span: The recall of happy, sad, traumatic, and involuntary memories. *Psychology and Aging, 17*, 636–652.
Brewer, W. F., & Pani, J. R. (1996). Reports of mental imagery in retrieval from long-term memory. *Consciousness and Cognition, 5*, 287.
Brown, R., & Kulik, J. (1977). Flashbulb memories. *Cognition, 5*, 73–99.
Byrne, C. A., Hyman, I. E., & Scott, K. L. (2001). Comparisons of memories for traumatic events and other experiences. *Applied Cognitive Psychology, 15*, S119–S133.
Clark, D. M., & Teasdale, J. D. (1982). Diurnal-variation in clinical depression and accessibility of memories of positive and negative experiences. *Journal of Abnormal Psychology, 91*, 87–95.
D'Argembeau, A., & van der Linden, M. (in press). Phenomenal characteristics associated with projecting oneself back into the past and forward into the future: Influence of valence and temporal distance. *Consciousness and Cognition, 13*, 844–858.
de Decker, A., Hermans, D., Raes, F., & Eelen, P. (2003). Autobiographical memory specificity and trauma in inpatient adolescents. *Journal of Clinical Child and Adolescent Psychology, 32*, 22–31.
Doost, H. T. N., Moradi, A. R., Taghavi, M. R., Yule, W., & Dalgleish, T. (1998). The development of a corpus of emotional words produced by children and adolescents. *Personality and Individual Differences, 27*, 433–451.
Ehlers, A., & Clark, D. M. (2000). A cognitive model of posttraumatic stress disorder. *Behaviour Research and Therapy, 38*, 319–345.
Ehlers, A., Hackmann, A., Steil, R., Clohessy, S., Wenninger, K., & Winter, H. (2002). The nature of intrusive memories after trauma: the warning signal hypothesis. *Behaviour Research and Therapy, 40*, 995–1002.
Erikson, E. H. (1968). *Identity, youth, and crisis*. New York: Norton.
First, M. B., Spitzer, R. L., Gibbon, M., & Williams, J. B. W. (1995). *Structured clinical interview for DSM-IV. Axis I disorder with psychotic screen*. New York: New York Psychiatric Institute.
Frank, M., & Gilovich, T. (1989). Effect of memory perspective on retrospective causal attributions. *Journal of Personality and Social Psychology, 57*, 399–403.
Garber, J., Weiss, B., & Shanley, N. (1993). Cognitions, depressive symptoms, and development in adolescents. *Journal of Abnormal Psychology, 102*, 47–57.
Green, B. L. (1996). The Trauma History Questionnaire. In B. H. Stamm (Ed.), *Measurement of stress, trauma, and adaptation* (pp. 366–369). Lutherville, MD: Sidran Press.
Habermas, T., & Bluck, S. (2000). Getting a life: The emergence of the life story in adolescence. *Psychological Bulletin, 126*, 748–769.
Harter, S. (1999). *The construction of the self: A developmental perspective*. New York: Guilford Press.
Hermans, D., van den Broeck, K., Belis, G., Raes, F., Pieters, G., & Eelen, P. (2004). Trauma and autobiographical memory specificity in depressed inpatients. *Behaviour Research and Therapy, 42*, 775–789.
Higgins, E. T. (1996). The "self digest": Self-knowledge serving self-regulatory functions. *Journal of Personality and Social Psychology, 71*, 1062–1083.
Horowitz, L. M., Wilner, N., & Alvarez, W. (1979). Impact of event scale: A measure of subjective distress. *Psychosomatic Medicine, 41*, 209–218.
Johnson, M. K., Foley, M. A., Suengas, A. G., & Raye, C. L. (1988). Phenomenal characteristics of memories for perceived and imagined autobiographical memories. *Journal of Experimental Psychology: General, 117*, 371–376.

Johnson, M. K., Hashtroudi, S., & Lindsay, D. S. (1993). Source monitoring. *Psychological Bulletin, 114*, 3–28.

Joormann, J., & Siemer, M. (2004). Memory accessibility, mood regulation, and dysphoria: Difficulties in repairing sad mood with happy memories? *Journal of Abnormal Psychology, 113*, 179–188.

Kessler, R. C., Avenevoli, S., & Merikangas, K. R. (2001). Mood disorders in children and adolescents: An epidemiologic perspective. *Biological Psychiatry, 49*, 1002–1014.

Kessler, R. C., Davis, C. G., & Kendler, K. S. (1997). Childhood adversity and adult psychiatric disorder in the US National Comorbidity Survey. *Psychological Medicine, 27*, 1101–1119.

Kuyken, W., & Brewin, C. R. (1995). Autobiographical memory functioning in depression and reports of early abuse. *Journal of Abnormal Psychology, 104*, 585–591.

Kuyken, W., Howell, R., & Dalgleish, T. (2006). *Over-general Autobiographical Memory, Trauma, and Depression in Adolescence.* Manuscript under review.

Libby, L. K. & Eibach, R. P. (2002). Looking back in time: Self-concept change affects visual perspective in autobiographical memory. *Journal of Personality and Social Psychology, 82*, 167–179.

Libby, L. K., Eibach, R. P., & Gilovich, T. (2005). Here's looking at me: The effect of memory perspective on assessments of personal change. *Journal of Personality and Social Psychology, 88*, 50–62.

Moffitt, K. H., Singer, J. A., Nelligan, D. W., Carlson, M. A., & Vyse, S. A. (1994). Depression and memory narrative type. *Journal of Abnormal Psychology, 103*, 581–583.

Mor, N., & Winquist, J. (2002). Self-focused attention and negative affect: A meta-analysis. *Psychological Bulletin, 128*, 638–662.

Nigro, G., & Neisser, U. (1983). Point of view in personal memories. *Cognitive Psychology, 15*, 467–482.

Nolen-Hoeksema, S. (1991). Responses to depression and their effects on the duration of depressive episodes. *Journal of Abnormal Psychology, 100*, 569–582.

Park, R. J., Goodyer, I. M., & Teasdale, J. D. (2002). Categoric overgeneral autobiographical memory in adolescents with major depressive disorder. *Psychological Medicine, 32*, 267–276.

Park, R. J., Goodyer, I. M., & Teasdale, J. D. (2004). Effects of induced rumination and distraction on mood and overgeneral autobiographical memory in adolescent Major Depressive Disorder and controls. *Journal of Child Psychology and Psychiatry, 45*, 996–1006.

Robinson, J. A., & Swanson, K. L. (1993). Field and observer modes of remembering. *Memory, 1*, 169–184.

Rubin, D. C., & Kozin, M. (1984). Vivid memories. *Cognition, 16*, 81–95.

Rubin, D. C., Wetzler, S. E., & Nedes, R. D. (1986). Autobiographical memory across the lifespan. In D.C.Rubin (Ed.), *Autobiographical memory* (pp. 202–221). Cambridge, UK: Cambridge University Press.

Schacter, D. L. (1996). *Searching for memory: The brain, the mind, and the past.* New York: Basic Books.

Singer, J. A., & Moffitt, K. H. (1992). An experimental investigation of specificity and generality in memory narratives. *Imagination, Cognition and Personality, 11*, 233–257.

Smith, P., Perrin, S., Dyregrov, A., & Yule, W. (2003). Principal components analysis of the impact of event scale with children in war. *Personality and Individual Differences, 34*, 315–322.

Swales, M. A., Williams, J. M. G., & Wood, P. (2001). Specificity of autobiographical memory and mood disturbance in adolescents. *Cognition and Emotion, 15*, 321–331.

Tabachnick, B. G., & Fidell, L. S. (2001). *Using multivariate statistics* (4th ed.). Needham Heights, MA: Allyn & Bacon.

Taylor, S. E., & Brown, J. D. (1994). Positive illusions and well-being Revisited – Separating fact from fiction. *Psychological Bulletin, 116*, 21–27.

Teasdale, J. D. (1999). Emotional processing, three modes of mind and the prevention of relapse in depression. *Behaviour Research and Therapy, 37*, S53–S77.
Teasdale, J. D., & Green, H. A. C. (2004). Ruminative self-focus and autobiographical memory. *Personality and Individual Differences, 36*, 1933–1943.
Tombaugh, T. N., Kozac, J., & Rees, L. (1999). Normative data stratified by age and education for two measures of verbal fluency: FAS and animal naming. *Archives of Clinical Neuropsychology, 14*, 167–177.
van der Kolk, B. A., & Fisler, R. (1995). Dissociation and the fragmentary nature of traumatic memories: Overview and exploratory study. *Journal of Traumatic Stress, 8*, 505–525.
van Vreeswijk, M. F., & de Wilde, E. J. (2004). Autobiographical memory specificity, psychopathology, depressed mood and the use of the Autobiographical Memory Test: a meta-analysis. *Behaviour Research and Therapy, 42*, 731–743.
Walker, W. R., Skowronski, J. J., & Thompson, C. P. (2003). Life Is pleasant – and memory helps to keep it that way! *Review of General Psychology, 7*, 203–210.
Watkins, E., & Teasdale, J. D. (2001). Rumination and overgeneral memory in depression: Effects of self-focus and analytic thinking. *Journal of Abnormal Psychology, 110*, 353–357.
Welch-Ross, M. K. (1995). An integrative model of the development of autobiographical memory. *Developmental Review, 15*, 338–365.
Welzer, H., & Markowitsch, H. J. (2005). Towards a bio-psycho-social model of autobiographical memory. *Memory, 13*, 63–78.
Wenzel, A., Pinna, K., & Rubin, D. C. (2004). Autobiographical memories of anxiety-related experiences. *Behaviour Research and Therapy, 42*, 329–341.
Williams, J. M. G. (2000). *Autobiographical memory test*. 2000. Unpublished manuscript.
Williams, J. M. G., Healy, H. G., & Ellis, N. C. (1999). The effect of imageability and predicability of cues in autobiographical memory. *Quarterly Journal of Experimental Psychology, 52A*, 555–579.
Wright, D. B., & Nunn, J. A. (2000). Similarities within event clusters in autobiographical memory. *Applied Cognitive Psychology, 14*, 479–489.
Yule, W., Tenbruggencate, S., & Joseph, S. (1994). Principal components-analysis of the impact of events scale in adolescents who survived a shipping disaster. *Personality and Individual Differences, 16*, 685–691.

Effects of age, dysphoria, and emotion-focusing on autobiographical memory specificity in children

Lyndsey E. Drummond, Barbara Dritschel, and Arlene Astell
School of Psychology, University of St. Andrews, UK

Ronan E. O'Carroll
Department of Psychology, University of Stirling, UK

Tim Dalgleish
Emotion Research Group, Medical Research Council, Cognition and Brain Sciences Unit, Cambridge UK

Overgeneral autobiographical memory (OGM) is strongly associated with depression in adults and appears to reflect a stable cognitive bias. However, it is not known whether this bias exists in children or what factors contribute to its development. We examined the roles of age, dysphoria, and a new variable, emotion-focusing (EF), on the production of specific autobiographical memory (AM) in children, using the standard Autobiographical Memory Test (AMT; Williams & Broadbent, 1986). Results show that older children are more specific than younger children, irrespective of cue valence. Dysphoria was linked to less specific retrieval of positive memories in children. A three-way interaction between age, valence, and dysphoria was also found, such that older dysphoric children demonstrated a difficulty in retrieving specific negative memories. In addition, emotion-focusing was associated with specific AM recall, especially to negative cues. Results are discussed with reference to the development of depressogenic biases.

Depression in adults is reliably associated with an overgeneral autobiographical memory (OGM) retrieval style (van Vreeswijk & de Wilde, 2004). Evidence suggests that overgeneral retrieval exists as part of a stable, dysfunctional cognitive style and is somewhat independent of current mood (e.g., Brittlebank, Scott, Williams, & Ferrier, 1993; Mackinger, Pachinger, & Leibertseder, 2000).

Correspondence should be addressed to Lyndsey Drummond, School of Psychology, University of St. Andrews, St. Mary's Place, Fife KY16 9JU, UK; e-mail: led@st-andrews.ac.uk

This research was supported by a Research Studentship awarded by Lyndsey Drummond by the University of St. Andrews. Tim Dalgleish is supported by the UK Medical Research Council.

This has led a number of theorists to assert that the roots of this bias may lie in childhood. Williams (1996) proposed that an OGM style may develop from early childhood as a means of coping with negative affect. Individuals, for example, who have experienced trauma during childhood, have greater difficulty in retrieving specific memories in adulthood, even for events unrelated to the trauma (e.g., Kuyken & Brewin, 1995). Adolescents exposed to family violence during childhood, and reporting comorbid depression, also exhibit an OGM bias as evidenced in interview data concerning family conflict (Orbach, Lamb, Sternberg, Williams, & Dawud-Noursi, 2001). Although links between development of an OGM style and depression have been made in theory, to date there are no studies examining OGM bias in children. Importantly, if overgeneral recall does reflect a stable bias, it could be a useful marker of cognitive vulnerability to depression in children.

We have some insight into the development of the OGM bias from investigations involving adolescents (de Decker, Hermans, Raes, & Eelen, 2003; Park, Goodyer, & Teasdale, 2002; Swales, Williams, & Wood, 2001). In these studies, as expected from the adult literature, clinically depressed adolescents are more overgeneral in their responses to cue words than nondepressed controls. However, in the Swales et al. study there was also a positive correlation within the clinical population, with the more depressed and hopeless adolescents demonstrating greater specificity to negative cues. This is in the opposite direction to that which would be expected from previous findings with depressed adults (van Vreeswijk & de Wilde, 2004). Post hoc analyses attributed this finding to a repeated memory phenomenon, whereby a subset of parasuicidal adolescents recalled the same negative traumatic event to more than one cue word. The researcher was the therapist in this study, which may also be pertinent to the result. Repeated specific recall can be addressed with clear participant instruction to prevent or judge repetition.

Existing studies examining AM retrieval in children have tended to concentrate on the *onset* of AM recall in preschool to early school age children and have used different methodologies from those used in the adult literature. This developmental literature reveals that specific questions can yield specific AM responses even in very young children. However, overall, young children's preferred mode of memory reporting is general (Nelson, 1993). Greater detail, structure and reference to temporal markers are then observed in AMs as a function of increasing age (Howe & Courage, 1997). These findings are discussed in terms of language acquisition (Nelson, 1993) and self-concept formation (Howe & Courage, 1997) rather than in terms of specificity or generality per se. However, improvement in knowledge base, strategy use, language skill, self-concept, and storage capacity, with age (for a full review see Howe & Courage, 1997), are likely to facilitate AM response specificity. By age 7, the quality of children's AM recall is considered comparable with adult functioning (Gathercole, 1998). The present study therefore sought to test an early to middle-school age child population on the standard AMT cueing task in order to bridge the gap in the AM and depression literature, and to look for evidence of the development of or onset of an overgeneral retrieval style prior to its establishment in adolescence. The use of the AMT cueing methodology then makes direct comparison between child and adult retrieval styles possible, providing a clear baseline from which to examine any effects of mood.

We considered that age and dysphoria might also interact to affect AM production. In a 5-year longitudinal study of 8–13-year-olds, Nolen-Hoeksema, Girgus, and Seligman (1992) found that as children age, cognitive style as measured by the Children's Attributional Style Questionnaire (Kaslow, Tannenbaum, & Seligman, 1978), became a significant predictor of depression. In contrast, only negative life events predicted depression in the younger group. Authors suggest the reason for this apparent increasing role of cognitive style in depression with age may be due to cognitive capacities increasing with age, or because cognitive styles become more stable across later childhood. Similar data exist, showing an increasing relationship between depression and mood congruent memory bias with age (Neshat-Doost, Taghavi, Moradi, Yule, & Dalgleish, 1998). If age, mood, and cognition do interact in this way, the association between dysphoria and overgeneral retrieval may manifest itself differently in younger as opposed to older children.

A further factor that might interact with age and dysphoria to influence AM retrieval is cue valence. In the adult literature, overgeneral recall can occur more in response to positive (as opposed to negative) cue words (e.g., Williams & Broadbent, 1986) or it can show the reverse effect (e.g., Mackinger, 2000). Inconsistent valence effects in depressed groups may be attributable to variance in the relative causal contribution of affect regulation (Williams, 1996), temporary memory system disruption caused by schema activation (Dalgleish et al., 2003) or mood congruency (see Williams, Watts, MacLeod, & Matthews, 1997). All are likely to play a role. It is also possible that age further influences this valence effect. Drummond, Dritschel, Astell, and O'Carroll (2005) tested children aged 6–11 years and a young adult comparison group on perception of facial affect. Ability to recognise facial emotion increased with increasing chronological age in this study. The results showed that there was no significant difference between adults and children on recognition of happy or neutral faces. However, there was a significant difference between children and adults on rating of sad faces. Children were significantly poorer than adults on identification of negative facial affect. Children made many 'sad as neutral' type errors, suggesting there might be an important developmental effect of processing of negatively valenced material in children. An aim of the present study was to further investigate this issue.

Finally, this study is the first to introduce the idea of *emotion focusing* (EF) as a possible additional variable influencing the overgeneral effect. Motivation for studying this variable comes from Williams (1996) who argued that OGM may in part, be attributable to preferential encoding of situations according to their emotional content. Williams, Teasdale, Segal, & Soulsby (2000) restated that trauma in early childhood may result in a cognitive style in which individuals habitually focus on, or are hypersensitive to, the affective features of events. The extent to which individuals focus on (encode) the emotional features of their environment is an important factor that has hitherto been neglected in both child and adult investigations of AM retrieval. EF was therefore used in this study to denote individuals' predisposition to focus on the emotional features of their environment. For example, given a typical scenario of a university library during an exam period, one individual may encode the fact that several students at their desks look terrified and tearful, while another individual, viewing the same scene, may notice instead that there is a pile of precariously stacked books against a chair leg. The first individual will be effectively cued to remember the library event by the word 'fear' while the second individual would be better cued by the phrase 'safety hazard' and would probably not remember the event based on an emotional descriptor.

Regarding AM predictions concerning EF, Williams (1996) suggested that people who have a greater tendency to encode the emotional content of situations would be more likely to demonstrate overgeneral recall than those who do not. This argument is based on the assumption that focusing on emotion promotes schematic level encoding. OGM would then result in individuals who were sensitised to emotion during childhood and therefore may encode emotion preferentially, for example, in the case of early childhood trauma. This hypothesised link between EF, overgeneral recall, and vulnerability to depression has not as yet been investigated.

Other theoretical accounts of cognition-emotion relations may however, make different predictions. For example, cognitive theories of depressed mood and/or AM (Beck, Rush, Shaw, & Emery, 1979; Bower, 1981; Conway & Pleydell-Pearce, 2000; Foa & Kozak, 1986; Power & Dalgleish, 1997; Teasdale & Barnard, 1993) would suggest that, to the extent that a specific autobiographical event is encoded in emotional terms, the presence of a congruent emotional cue word (such as in the AMT) would be more likely to elicit retrieval of that event from memory. The rationale here is that retrieval of AMs is facilitated by the presence of any information that maps on to the underlying representational content of that memory. Consequently, because high EF individuals would habitually lay down AM representations with a greater proportion of emotional content, the presentation of emotional cues should be more likely to activate those representations, leading to facilitated generation of specific memories. An alternative hypothesis for the effect of EF on AM retrieval is therefore, that individuals' predisposition to focus on the emotional features of their environment may result in more specific AM recall to emotional cue words. People who are depressed may preferentially encode negative affective aspects of events, such that depressed high emotion-focusers would be highly specific to negative cues. It is currently not known whether EF is associated with overgeneral or specific valenced recall. The final aim of the present study was therefore to investigate the influence of EF, and the putative interactions of EF, age, valence, and dysphoria, on AM retrieval in children.

Although OGM is characteristically discussed as a retrieval phenomenon, it is also useful to consider it as a possible encoding phenomenon. It is not clear that children or adults encode all information in a given context and then later suppress specific aspects at retrieval. Instead, some individuals may avoid or preferentially encode specific features (or emotional features) of events such that it effects specific representations in memory. This would mean that both encoding and storage (not just retrieval) are important in understanding the overgeneral bias. Whether considered in isolation or interacting with other factors, such as age, dysphoria, or valence, EF may significantly influence the nature of AM recall and thereby, the development of depressive associated biases.

In sum, the overall aim of this study was to extend the adult AM literature to a child population. To our knowledge, no one study has looked at the interaction of age, dysphoria, and valence as factors known to influence AM. Nor has any study looked at child AM using the standard cueing task, or considered EF as a contributing factor. The specific hypotheses were therefore as follows.

Hypothesis 1. Age, valence, and dysphoria will interact to influence AM specificity in children. Younger children will be less specific than older children. Age and valence will interact such that young children will demonstrate reduced specificity especially to negative cue words. Dysphoria in children will be associated with reduced specificity and the effects of dysphoria will be valence specific. The effects of dysphoria may increase with age. These effects will remain after controlling for any effects of general scholastic ability.

Hypothesis 2. Emotion-focusing will explain a significant proportion of the variance in AM specificity. EF will be associated with either increased or reduced AM specificity. EF will also interact with age, valence or dysphoria, factors already known to influence AM retrieval. The effects of EF will occur independent of scholastic ability or age.

METHOD

Participants

A total of 70 children (35 girls) took part in this study. Of the participants, 35 were aged 7–8 years ($M = 7.86$, $SD = 0.40$). The remaining 35 participants were aged 10–11 years ($M = 10.6$, $SD = 0.72$). The gender ratio across age groups was similar with 17 females in the younger group and 18 females in the older group. As previously discussed, children aged 7–8 years were chosen as the youngest age group for which AM retrieval is believed to be commensurate with adult functioning. Children aged 10–11 were then chosen to provide a discrete age comparison group and to form a good bridge with previous adolescent literature (e.g., Park et al., 2002). These two age groups ensured the best chance of detecting any deviance in normal child AM development, if any exists. There were 14 dysphoric participants (8 from the younger group and 6 from the older group). The remaining participants (27 and 29 respectively) were categorised as nondysphoric. 'Dysphoric' in this study means reporting a depressive mood (as indicated by a score of 7 or above on the Child Depression Inventory; Kovacs, 1992, see the next section).

All participants were volunteers recruited from a London, UK junior school. The school was initially contacted to sanction the research proposal. Research approval was then obtained from the relevant ethical bodies. Permission to conduct research was sought from individual classroom teachers, followed by a letter of consent to parents and finally written consent from the children themselves. The sample was ethnically mixed. No individual with special educational needs was included in this study. No child with any known history of trauma or emotional disturbance, as established from school records and teacher reports, was included. We elected to use this criterion since a history of trauma is known to influence AM recall (e.g., de Decker et al., 2003) and there would have been insufficient children with a history of trauma to examine any such influences systematically.

Materials and measures

Autobiographical Memory Test (AMT; Williams & Broadbent, 1986). The task comprised 10 emotional words, 5 positively valenced (*happy, surprised, safe, successful, interested*) and 5 negatively valenced (*sad, lonely, hurt, careless, angry*). Words were presented to participants on 120 mm × 100 mm laminated cards and participants were asked to retrieve a specific memory for each cue word. All participants completed three practice trials involving neutral words, with feedback, to ensure that all participants understood and were able to complete the requirements of the task. Every child retrieved at least one specific memory during the practice trial. Participants were informed that that they would be prompted to provide a specific memory if an overgeneral response was given (i.e., a memory that was not of a particular event on a given day). In addition, clear instruction was given requesting the child not to give the same memory to more than one cue word, to avoid the phenomenon of "repeated memories" discussed earlier. The presentation of cue words was mixed across valence. Participants were given 60 s to retrieve a memory. Failure to respond was coded as an omission; failure to retrieve a memory was coded as a 'no memory'. Failure to retrieve a memory resulted in the allocation of an overgeneral response categorisation for that cue word. All participant responses were recorded on audiotape and later coded for specificity.

Two independent raters coded the AM responses as either specific, overgeneral (OGM; extended or categoric; where an extended memory is of a single event lasting more than one day and a categoric memory is a generic collection or class of events) or as 'no memory'. The mean numbers of specific first response memories for each child, as a proportion of all responses, were used as the data for analysis. An example of scoring of an OGM response to the cue word "Lonely" was, "When I was in Year Two I used to sit on the lonely bench every playtime". This was coded as overgeneral because it is a categoric memory. A specific memory response to the same cue was, "On Friday – When I was at home. I had no-one to play with 'cause my brothers were out at a friends and I wasn't allowed to go". This memory was coded as a specific response because the memory is of a particular place and time (of less than 1 day). Over 85% interrater reliability was achieved on coding of these responses. This reliability estimate is comparable to reliability rates found in the adult literature (e.g., Williams & Broadbent, 1986).

Validity of the AMT for use in children was established in several ways. No child failed to retrieve a specific AM to at least one practice cue word and some of the experimental cue words. Some children in the youngest age group were unsure of the meaning of the words "successful" or "careless" ($N = 4$). In these instances, the experimenter explained the meaning of the word by invariably saying "good at something" or "clumsy". This was sufficient for all children to acknowledge their understanding of the word and quickly retrieve a valid memory (specific/overgeneral). There were only seven 'no memory' responses in total, which were distributed across age (three from older children) and cues. There were no omissions or memory repetitions. Content validity was also examined by having two raters judge whether the content of the reported memory was appropriate to the cue word used to elicit the memory. All children recalled appropriate content memories. High content validity was confirmed by over 95% interrater agreement on memory content appropriateness on a random 50% of the sample.

Emotion-focusing (EF). A measure of EF was constructed using combined results from two tasks: Card Sorting and Image Description. The Card Sorting Task consisted of a set of 12 cards (90 mm × 60 mm) each portraying an adult face displaying one of three different emotional facial expressions (happy, neutral, or sad). The faces were arranged in a 6 × 2 formation and consisted of an equal gender mix, mixed age, and appearance (e.g., hair length, colour). The faces were not of mixed race due to limited availability. All photographs were drawn from a sample set of faces, which had previously been used and received over 75% interrater agreement concerning the emotion being portrayed (Le Gal

& Bruce, 1999). First, the experimenter verified that each child understood the nature of grouping and physically demonstrated that the cards could be sorted into two groups, using gender as the most obvious sorting category. Once established, the cards were then replaced and the children were required to sort the cards according to their own sorting category, verbalising the decision as soon as one was made. A score of 1 was given when the child sorted the faces according to affect (emotion). A score of 0 was given for any other (nonemotional) sorting category. The sorting categories suggested by children were emotion (happy and sad faces), hair colour, hair length, age, face-shape, and subjective attractiveness.

The second EF task was the Image Description Task. This involved a picture-cueing methodology. A series of 11 photographic images of socioemotional behavioural settings (e.g., family laughing around a dinner table; child being admonished by parent figure), were drawn from a developmental psychology stimulus pool. The 11 images were presented to the participants as 200 mm × 150 mm laminates, and depicted for example, "Parents standing over a baby, smiling". All but one of the cards involved a child protagonist. Protagonists were of mixed age and race. Participants were simply asked to "Tell me what you see" in response to being shown each pictorial card. The participant responses were recorded and later coded for emotional description. Subjects were given a score of 1 if an emotional adjective or adverb was used in the description of the card, for example "happy, excited, loving". A score of 0 was given for each card where no emotional description was given, for example "a baby, a mum and a dad". Two raters examined participant responses in terms of these categories. When emotion was implied but an emotional adjective was not directly used (e.g., "running hard" or "dad is making up with son for missing him play football"), it was decided that a strict criterion would be used and only an emotional descriptive would result in an emotional classification. That is, inference of emotion was not sufficient to classify as an emotional description. Using this criterion, 100% interrater category agreement was achieved.

From these two tasks a combined measure of EF was constructed whereby the sample was divided into high, medium, or low emotion-focusers according to the following criteria. The criteria for low EF was that the participant neither sorted the cards by emotion nor used emotion descriptions in over 75% of the images in the image description task. The criteria for medium EF was that the participant either sorted the cards by emotion or described over 75% of the images in terms of emotion. The criteria for high EF required the participant to both sort the cards by emotion and describe over 75% of the images in terms of emotion. This classification was considered statistically reasonable in the absence of any other theoretical or empirical constraints.

Child Depression Inventory (CDI). The shortened version of the Child Depression Inventory (CDI-S; Kovacs, 1992) was completed. This measure consists of 10 mood-related items with three possible responses per item. Participants are directed to indicate which of each of the three statements best applies to them over the last 2 weeks. The statements are read out loud to the participants and participants are required to tick the most appropriate statement to them. According to CDI guidelines (Kovacs, 1992) participants with a CDI score of 7 or above are classed as dysphoric and those with scores below 7 are classed as nondysphoric. The word 'dysphoric' is used in this study rather than 'depressed' simply to stress that the current authors felt the measure best reflects a depressive mood or emotional state characterised by depression, which can be transient, rather than a depression disorder, which should be formally diagnosed.

General ability. A measure of scholastic ability was constructed for each child using a combination of teacher report and age appropriate National Curriculum Attainment levels. This is a method of ability grouping commonly used in British primary school education. From these two sources, children were divided into high, medium, and low ability groups. Where discrepancy existed between groupings based on optional SAT levels (e.g., high attainment in maths but medium attainment in English), the teacher's summative assessment on overall ability was used as the final criterion. Although Standard IQ measures are more commonplace and therefore easier to interpret across studies, the measure of scholastic ability was favoured to respect testing time constraints, to avoid unnecessary stress caused to individuals by IQ testing in a young and partly dysphoric sample, and to utilise teacher reports of child potential for an arguably stronger index of actual ability.

Procedure

Participants were tested individually and face-to-face, in a quiet testing environment within the school. Participants were first asked to complete the AMT, followed by the two EF tasks and the CDI. Task order was fixed to avoid possible contamination effects of the CDI or EF on the AMT. Once the participants had completed all four experimental tasks they were thanked for their participation and fully debriefed. After the testing session an indicator of general scholastic ability was obtained from school records and in consultation with the appropriate class teacher.

RESULTS

The numbers of specific AMs by age, dysphoria, and cue valence are shown in Table 1. In keeping with predictions, the data in Table 1 indicate that young nondysphoric children are less specific to negative cues than to positive cues. Furthermore, young dysphoric children appear to recall more specific negative memories and fewer specific positive memories compared to their nondysphoric age equivalents. The data also indicate that dysphoric children in the older group

TABLE 1
Means (and standard deviations) of positive and negative specific autobiographical memories (AMs) recalled by dysphoric and nondysphoric children, grouped by age

Cue valence	AMs recalled								
	7–8 years ($n = 35$)			10–11 years ($n = 35$)			Total ($n = 70$)		
	Positive	Negative	Total	Positive	Negative	Total	Positive	Negative	Total
Nondysphoric ($n = 56$)	2.97 (1.27)	0.93 (1.25)	3.90 (2.08)	4.48 (0.85)	4.22 (1.15)	8.70 (1.30)	3.70 (1.32)	2.51 (2.04)	6.21 (2.98)
Dysphoric ($n = 14$)	1.67 (1.21)	2.00 (2.37)	3.67 (3.14)	2.88 (0.64)	3.00 (1.51)	5.88 (1.55)	2.36 (1.10)	2.57 (1.91)	4.93 (2.53)
Total ($n = 70$)	2.74 (1.34)	1.11 (1.51)	3.86 (2.24)	4.11 (1.05)	3.94 (1.33)	8.06 (1.80)	3.43 (1.38)	2.53 (2.00)	5.96 (2.92)

are less specific than older nondysphoric children to both positive and negative cues, suggesting evidence of the OGM bias.

A three-way ANOVA with Age (7–8 yrs and 10–11 yrs), Dysphoria (high and low), and Valence (positive and negative) was conducted to examine this assumption. General Ability (high, medium, and low) was initially included as a covariate but was not significant, $F(1,65) = 1.56$, $p = .22$. Reported analyses are therefore without this covariate. The ANOVA revealed a significant main effect of Age, $F(1,66) = 38.80$, $p < .001$, such that older children were more specific than younger children. Results also revealed a main effect of Dysphoria, $F(1,66) = 7.38$, $p = .01$, such that overall dysphoric children were less specific than nondysphoric children. There was also a Valence trend, $F(1,66) = 3.77$, $p = .056$, in that children tended to recall fewer specific negative memories than positive. However, these main effects were qualified by a three-way interaction between Age × Valence × Dysphoria on AM recall, $F(1,66) = 4.4$, $p = .04$.

In order to deconstruct this three-way interaction, 3 two-way ANOVAs were conducted. The first examined the relationship between Age and Dysphoria on recall to positive cues, the second looked at the relationship between Age and Dysphoria on recall to negative cues. A third ANOVA was conducted to directly examine the relationship between Age and Valence on AM recall. In the first 2 × 2 ANOVA (Age × Dysphoria) on specific positive recall there remained a main effect of Age, $F(1,65) = 8.25$, $p < .001$, such that younger children recalled fewer specific positive memories than older children and a main effect of Dysphoria, $F(1,65) = 20.75$, $p < .001$, such that dysphoric children recalled fewer specific memories to positive cues than nondysphoric. There was no significant interaction between Age and Dysphoria on positive recall, $F(1,65) = 0.26$, $p = .63$.

In the second 2 × 2 ANOVA (Age × Dysphoria) on specific negative recall there remained a main effect of Age, $F(1,65) = 27.31$, $p < .001$, such that younger children recalled fewer specific negative memories than older children. There was no main effect of Dysphoria, $F(1,65) = 0.04$, $p = .85$. However, there was a significant interaction between Age and Dysphoria, $F(1,65) = 7.79$, $p = .007$, such that nondysphoric children's recall of negative memories significantly improved across age, $t(54) = 10.21$, $p < .001$, while dysphoric children's negative specific recall, though higher than nondysphorics in the younger group, stayed static across age, $t(12) = 0.97$, $p = .35$. Moreover, by age 10–11 years, dysphoric children recalled significantly fewer specific memories to negative cues than their nondysphoric age equivalents, $t(33) = 2.4$, $p = .02$, in keeping with an OGM bias.

In order to directly examine the relationship between Age and Valence a 2 × 2 ANOVA (Age × Valence) was conducted. Results show a main effect of Age, $F(1,68) = 74.92$, $p < .001$, a main effect of Valence, $F(1,68) = 20.17$, $p < .001$, and a significant interaction between Age and Valence, $F(1,68) = 13.22$, $p < .001$, such that older children were more specific than younger children to both positive, $t(68) = 4.77$, $p < .001$, and negative cues, $t(68) = 8.32$, $p < .001$. However, children in the younger group recalled significantly fewer memories to negative cues compared to positive, $t(34) = 5.45$, $p < .001$. This valence difference was not significant in the older group, $t(34) = 0.64$, $p = .53$.

In summary, and as can be seen in Table 1, age affected positive and negative recall such that older children were more specific to both. Dysphoria exerted a main effect on positive recall such that dysphoric children retrieved fewer specific positive memories than nondysphoric children. The three-way interaction above was attributable to age and dysphoria interacting to influence the recall of negative memories. Young nondysphoric children showed low specificity to negative cues. Older nondysphoric children showed relatively high negative specificity. In contrast, young dysphoric children showed higher specificity to negative cues than their same age counterparts and yet specificity to negative cues in the older dysphoric group was comparatively low.

The following analyses addressed the second study hypothesis, which was that EF would contribute to AM specificity and may interact with other factors to influence specificity. This is the first study to examine EF. It was therefore important to first establish that EF was not simply a correlate of another variable, such as age or scholastic ability, which would reduce the usefulness of EF as a measure. There was, however, no correlation between EF and Age ($r_s = .13$, $n = 70$, $p = .27$); General Scholastic Ability ($r_s = .08$, $n = 70$, $p = .51$); or Dysphoria ($r_s = .12$, $n = 70$, $p = .30$) in this sample.

Subsequently, an enter-stepwise regression model was conducted on total specific AMs such that Age and Dysphoria were entered in a first step and EF was added in a second step, to investigate whether EF accounted for unique variance in AM specificity, over and above any effects of age and dysphoria. Age and Dysphoria accounted for significant variance in AM specificity, $F(2, 69) = 45.69, p < .001$, Adjusted $R^2 = .56$. The inclusion of EF resulted in a significant additional 12% of variance being explained (R^2 change = .12, $F = 25.05, p > .001$). The final model included Age as the best independent predictor of specificity ($r = .72, n = 70, \beta = .66, p < .001$), followed by EF ($r = .47, n = 70, \beta = .35, p < .001$), and then Dysphoria ($r = .07, n = 70, \beta = -.27, p < .001$). All three variables contributed to a significant final model accounting for 68% of the variance in specificity, $F(3, 69) = 49.75, p < .001$, Adjusted $R^2 = .68$. There was no collinearity between variables (VIF < 2).

Given that EF was shown to be an important predictor of AM specificity, we repeated the analyses used to test Hypothesis 1, this time including EF as an additional factor. Two 3 × 2 × 2 ANOVAs with EF (high, medium, and low), Age (7–8 yrs and 10–11 yrs), and Dysphoria (dysphoric and nondysphoric) were therefore conducted, first for positive and then for negative valence. This was done to test the hypothesis that EF would interact with other factors known to influence AM performance.

Once again results of the analysis of positive recall showed the main effects of Age, $F(1, 58) = 18.68, p < .001$, and Dysphoria, $F(1, 58) = 28.95, p < .001$. As can be seen in Table 2, there was no main effect of EF on positive recall, $F(2, 58) = 1.79, p = .18$. However, a significant interaction was found between EF and Age on positive recall, $F(2, 58) = 4.29, p = .018$, such that older children were more specific than younger children in the low and medium EF categories, $t(17) = 3.04, p = .007$, and $t(28) = 4.13, p < .001$, respectively. However, in the high EF group there was no significant difference between younger and older children's specific positive recall, $t(19) = -0.91, p = .38$. Young children were just as likely to produce a specific positive memory as older children in this group. There was no significant three-way interaction between EF, Age and Dysphoria, $F(2, 58) = 0.25, p = .78$, and no interaction between EF and Dysphoria, $F(2, 58) = 1.02, p = .37$.

When EF was included in an analysis of specific negative recall, there remained a main effect of Age, $F(1, 58) = 35.18, p < .001$, with no main effect of Dysphoria, $F(1, 58) = 1.41, p = .24$. However, EF exerted a main effect on negative recall, $F(2, 58) = 17.02, p < .001$, such that high emotion-focusers were more specific to negative cues compared to low, $t(38) = 6.12, p < .001$, or medium, $t(48) = 3.70, p < .001$, emotion-focusers. EF did not interact with Age to affect negative recall, $F(2, 58) = 1.74, p = .18$, nor was there any three-way interaction between EF, Dysphoria, and Age, $F(2, 58) = 1.22, p = .30$. Of interest to us was whether EF and Dysphoria would interact significantly to influence negative specificity, however, no such interaction was found, $F(2, 58) = 1.68, p = .20$.

TABLE 2
Means (and standard deviations) of positive and negative specific AMs recalled by children within emotion focusing (EF) and age categories

	Emotion focusing (EF)								
	Low (n = 19)			Medium (n = 30)			High (n = 21)		
Age (yrs)	7–8 (n = 12)	10–11 (n = 7)	Total (n = 19)	7–8 (n = 16)	10–11 (n = 14)	Total (n = 30)	7–8 (n = 7)	10–11 (n = 14)	Total (n = 21)
Negative	0.5 (1.00)	2.42 (1.27)	1.21 (1.44)	0.75 (0.86)	4.00 (1.18)	2.27 (1.93)	3.00 (2.00)	4.64 (0.84)	4.10 (1.51)
Positive	2.25 (1.42)	4.14 (1.06)	2.95 (1.58)	2.87 (1.15)	4.36 (0.74)	3.57 (1.22)	3.29 (1.50)	3.86 (1.29)	3.67 (1.35)

DISCUSSION

The results of this study show that age, dysphoria, and cue valence interact to influence AM specificity in children. Older children are more specific than younger children especially to negative cues. Dysphoric children are overgeneral to positive cues and there is an interaction between age, dysphoria, and cue valence such that older dysphoric children are also overgeneral to negative cues. Regarding EF, high emotion-focusers produce specific AMs and EF significantly predicts unique variance in AM specificity. Each of the main findings is discussed in turn and possible mechanistic implications are considered.

First, as predicted, older children were able to produce a specific memory more readily than younger children. This suggests that between 7 and 11 years of age, a child's autobiographical recall develops from a general to a more specific memory style. This is consistent with the finding in the developmental literature that memorial ability develops with age (Howe & Courage, 1997; Nelson, 1993). As predicted, this effect of age on specificity was further influenced by cue valence. Younger children produced fewer specific memories in response to negative cues than to positive. This difference was not apparent with the older children, who presented approximately equal numbers of positive and negative specific memories. This age by valence effect has not been previously demonstrated and it suggests that it is particularly children's specific negative recall, which improves with age. It is clear that the development of cognitive processing of valenced stimuli in children is an interesting and previously neglected area of research, which could hold clues to the origins of information processing biases associated with depression. In addition, if AM in a normal population develops from a general to a specific retrieval style with age, the question remains whether in a depressed population memory fails to develop into a specific style or whether depressed individuals regress back to an overgeneral style.

Our results are the first to provide direct evidence that dysphoria is linked to OGM in children. Dysphoric children retrieved significantly fewer specific positive AMs than non-dysphoric children, irrespective of age. This is consistent with the well-documented adult AM literature, and with adolescent findings in general. Moreover, age and dysphoria interacted to affect specific negative retrieval, such that there was an effect of dysphoria on negative recall in the older group. Dysphoric children in the older group retrieved significantly fewer specific negative memories compared to their nondysphoric age equivalents. What is more, when we examined the pattern of negative AM retrieval across groups more closely, we found that the younger dysphoric children retrieved more specific negative memories than their nondysphoric age-group counterparts. However, while nondysphoric negative recall significantly improved across age group, the same was not true for dysphoric children. By age 10–11 years, therefore, dysphoric children were retrieving significantly fewer specific negative memories than nondysphoric older children. Thus, though dysphoric children demonstrate reduced specificity for both negative and positive cues, the effects of dysphoria on negative recall are only really apparent in the older group.

It may be that dysphoria affects positive and negative recall through different underlying mechanisms or processes. For instance, dysphoria may be affecting positive recall via mood congruency, which is a relatively autonomous mechanism based on spreading activation and therefore less dependent on age or cognitive ability than other possible mechanisms. In contrast, the impact of dysphoria on negative recall may be more schema dependent, and therefore its effect on recall is not observed until later in childhood when schemas are more firmly in place. In keeping with this schema explanation, repeated experience of dysphoric mood may allow negative biases to become more engrained and better established in older dysphoric children. In younger dysphoric children, however, negative schemas may be less well defined and therefore exert less influence on information processing. This interpretation though speculative, is supported by results from Nolen-Hoeksema et al. (1992), which showed that effects of cognition on depression increased with increasing age. This interpretation is also consistent with results from Neshat-Doost et al. (1998) who found evidence suggestive of an age-related increase in the elaboration of negative self-referent schematic representations in depressed youth. Predictions from kindling and sensitisation theory would also lend credence to this type of interpretation (see for example, Segal, Williams, Teasdale, & Gemar, 1996).

Alternatively, it may be that a young child's negative AM response style is already so highly overgeneral that dysphoria can exert little additional effect. It would therefore not be until later in childhood, when children have typically developed a more specific retrieval style, that the overgeneral effect of dysphoria on negative recall would become apparent. Interestingly, this relative difficulty in retrieving specific negative memories in older dysphoric children is not in keeping with the finding that depressed adolescents demonstrate highly specific recall to negative cues (e.g., Park et al., 2002). Further research is needed to track the evolution of the OGM bias and to clarify the differences in valence specific AM styles in children, adults, and adolescents.

Our study has also introduced the idea of emotion focusing as a potential vulnerability marker for depression. EF significantly contributed to predicting variance in AM specificity, even above the predictive value of age and dysphoria. Our results indicate that high emotion-focusers demonstrate specific memory recall to emotional cue words. Thus, an emotion-focuser who preferentially focuses on emotion in the environment may form memory representations with relatively high emotional content. When these individuals are then asked to recall events in response to emotional cue words, specific retrieval is then relatively easy for these individuals. EF could be important, especially if attempts are made to assist people in recalling specific AM information, something that is a core component of some cognitive-based clinical treatments.

Emotion encoding does not appear to correspond with overgeneral retrieval as expected by Williams (1996). However, it is proposed that with the addition of an environmental stressor, EF may emerge as a vulnerability factor for depression, more in keeping with the trauma-induced EF hypothesis proposed by Williams. EF is clearly a meaningful new measure for use with children and adults and warrants further investigation.

It is important to note that EF was not correlated with any measured independent variable in this study. Although there was an interaction between age and EF on positive recall, there was no collinearity with this variable. EF was not a product of age nor was there any correlation between scholastic ability or dysphoria, and EF. Therefore the variability accounted for by EF in this study is clearly not attributable in any straightforward way to the effects of dysphoria, age, or ability. Further longitudinal studies are required to look more closely at the relationship between negative life events, EF, and AM retrieval over time. It may be, for example, that EF interacts with ruminative style to affect AM and depressive mood.

Furthermore, in order to develop the measure of EF a greater range of stimuli could be added to the image description element, or a more sophisticated coding system could be introduced, whereby different levels of description are recognised. It might also be helpful under some circumstances to accept inference of emotion if it is found, for example, to be a typical descriptive style of some groups. In addition, high emotion focusing was associated with AM specificity. It would be interesting to test individuals on nonemotional cue words (in addition to emotional cue words), to test whether high EF individuals still demonstrate specific recall outwith their area of focal interest. EF is a new measure so no data are available to validate its use and the division used here to differentiate high, medium, and low EF was selected only as a prudent statistical division. In future, more sophisticated coding and classification categories could be explored.

Regarding other caveats or limitations of the present study, it was important in investigating the possible mechanisms through which overgeneral recall may develop and act as a vulnerability marker for the etiology or maintenance of depression, that we test a sample vulnerable to clinical depression but not suffering from it. However, it is not clear in the literature what the precise relationship is between dysphoria and depression. We would also anticipate that with the addition of clinical data and larger sample sizes, interactions, such as that between age and dysphoria, may become significant and a relationship between EF and depression would perhaps emerge. Although the present results are nonetheless interesting, replication with greater sample sizes would add to the strength of the findings; for example, some subgroups in the $3 \times 2 \times 2$ ANOVA design were small, thus leading to reduced power in our investigation of the higher order EF interactions. Finally, as noted, this is the first study to use the standard AMT in this age range. Although all children retrieved appropriate content memories to all cue words and were able to produce specific memories to at least some cue words, the lack of established validity and reliability data for this measure in children should be acknowledged as a limitation of the study.

In conclusion, this study highlights the importance of testing AM in children. Present results also demonstrate the usefulness of testing children with valenced emotional stimuli. As already highlighted, a key finding was that younger children tended to retrieve relatively fewer specific memories, particularly in response to negative cue words, whereas dysphoric children demonstrated reduced specific positive recall. It may be of interest in future studies to track this valence effect through development to see what role it may play in the later onset of depression. An understanding of the nature and development of normal valenced biases in childhood clearly has important implications for understanding the development of depressogenic biases. This study has attempted to examine the development of valenced AM specificity as one such bias. Looking at AM specificity from this developmental perspective should help us better understand the existence of OGM in adults and in psychopathology. The results of the current study also suggest that dysphoria affects AM in children, not by increasing availability of negative memories but by decreasing the availability of specific positive memories. It is unclear what underlying processes are responsible for such effects in the AM literature. It is likely though that more than one mechanism, bias, or effect is in operation at any given time. Further work is needed to unravel the contributions and roles of associated variables. Moreover, examining differential bias across age is essential. It may be, for example, that such depressive biases originate with deficits in processing of positive information but spread to include negative information processing biases with age, or failing intervention.

REFERENCES

Beck, A. T., Rush, A. J., Shaw, B. F., & Emery, G. (1979). *Cognitive therapy of depression*, New York: Guilford Press.
Bower, G. H. (1981). Mood and memory. *American Psychologist, 36*, 129–148.
Brittlebank, A. D., Scott, J., Williams, J. M. G., & Ferrier, I. N. (1993). Autobiographical memory in depression: State or trait marker? *British Journal of Psychiatry, 162*, 118–121.
Conway, M. A., & Pleydell-Pearce, C. W. (2000). The construction of autobiographical memories in the self-memory system. *Psychological Review, 107*, 261–288.
Dalgleish, T., Yiend, J., Tchanturia, K., Serpell, L., Hems, S., De Silva, P., & Treasure, J. (2003). Self-reported parental abuse relates to autobiographical memory style in patients with eating disorders. *Emotion, 3*, 211–222.
de Decker, A., Hermans, D., Raes, F., & Eelen, P. (2003). Autobiographical memory specificity and trauma in inpatient adolescents. *Journal of Clinical Child and Adolescent Psychology, 32*, 22–31.
Drummond L. E., Dritschel, B., Astell, A., & O'Carroll, R. E. (2005). *The influence of age and affect on the perception of facial emotion: A study of 6–11 year olds*. Manuscript submitted for publication.
Foa, E. B., & Kozak, M. J. (1986). Emotional processing of fear-exposure to corrective information. *Psychological Bulletin, 99*, 20–35.
Gathercole, S. E. (1998). The development of memory. *Journal of Child Psychology and Psychiatry, 39*, 3–27.
Howe, M. L., & Courage, M. L. (1993). On resolving the enigma of infantile amnesia. *Psychological Bulletin, 113*, 305–326.
Howe, M. L., & Courage, M. L. (1997). The emergence and early development of autobiographical memory. *Psychological Review, 104*, 499–523.
Kaslow, N. J., Tannenbaum, R. L., & Seligman, M. E. P. (1978). *The KASTAN: A children's attributional styles questionnaire*. Unpublished manuscript, University of Pennsylvania, USA.
Kovacs, M. (1992). *Children's depression inventory*. New York: Multi-Health Systems.
Kuyken, W., & Brewin, C. R. (1995). Autobiographical memory functioning in depression and reports of early abuse. *Journal of Abnormal Psychology, 104*, 585–591.
Le Gal, T., & Bruce, V. (1999). *Cognitive aspects of emotional expression processing*. Unpublished doctoral dissertation, University of Stirling, Stirling, UK.
Mackinger, H. F., Pachinger, M. M., Leibetseder, M. M., & Fartacek, R. R. (2000). Autobiographical memories in women remitted from major depression. *Journal of Abnormal Psychology, 109*, 331–334.
Nelson, K. (1993). The psychological and social origins of autobiographical memory. *Psychological Science, 4*, 7–14.
Neshat-Doost, H. T., Taghavi, M. R., Moradi, A. R., Yule, W., & Dalgleish, T. (1998). Memory for emotional trait adjectives in clinically depressed youth. *Journal of Abnormal Psychology, 107*, 642–650.
Nolen-Hoeksksema, S., Girgus, J. S., & Seligman, M. E. P. (1992). Predictors and consequences of childhood depressive symptoms- A 5-year longitudinal study. *Journal of Abnormal Psychology, 101*, 405–422.
Orbach, Y., Lamb, M. E., Sternberg, K. J., Williams, J. M. G., & Dawud-Noursi, S. (2001). The effects of being a victim or witness of family violence on the retrieval of autobiographical memories. *Child Abuse and Neglect, 25*, 1427–1437.
Park, R. J., Goodyer, I. M., & Teasdale, J. D. (2002). Categoric overgeneral autobiographical memory in adolescents with major depressive disorder. *Psychological Medicine, 32*, 267–276.
Power, M., & Dalgleish. T. (1997). *Cognition and emotion: From order to disorder*. Hove, UK: Psychology Press.

Segal, Z.V., Williams J. M. G., Teasdale, J. D., & Gemar, M. (1996). A cognitive science perspective on kindling and episode sensitization in recurrent affective disorder. *Psychological Medicine, 26*, 371–380.

Swales, M. A., Wood, P., & Williams, J. M. G. (2001). Specificity of autobiographical memory and mood disturbance in adolescents. *Cognition and Emotion, 15*, 321–331.

Teasdale, J. D., & Barnard, P. J. (1993). *Affect, cognition and change: Re-modelling depressive thought*. Hove, UK: Lawrence Erlbaum Associates Ltd.

van Vreeswijk, M. F., & de Wilde, E. J. (2004). Autobiographical memory specificity, psychopathology, depressed mood and the use of the Autobiographical Memory Test: A meta-analysis. *Behaviour Research and Therapy, 42*, 731–743.

Williams, J. M.G. (1996). Depression and the specificity of autobiographical memory. In D. Rubin (Ed.), *Remembering our past: Studies in autobiographical memory* (pp. 244–267). Cambridge, UK: Cambridge University Press.

Williams, J. M. G., & Broadbent, K. (1986). Autobiographical memory in suicide attempters. *Journal of Abnormal Psychology, 95*, 144–149.

Williams, J. M. G., Teasdale, J. D., Segal, Z. V., & Soulsby, J. (2000). Mindfulness-based cognitive therapy reduces overgeneral autobiographical memory in formerly depressed patients. *Journal of Abnormal Psychology, 109*, 150–155.

Williams, J. M. G., Watts, F. N., MacLeod, C., & Matthews, A. (1997). *Cognitive psychology and emotional disorders* (2nd ed.). Chichester, UK: Wiley.

Autobiographical memory in dysphoric and non-dysphoric college students using a computerised version of the AMT

Kathleen Newcomb Rekart and Susan Mineka
Northwestern University, Evanston, IL, USA

Richard E. Zinbarg
Northwestern University and The Family Institute at Northwestern University, Evanston, IL, USA

On autobiographical memory tests (AMTs) using positive and negative cue words, research has consistently found that depressed individuals (relative to non-depressed controls) are more likely to recall overgeneral memories (OGMs) and are less likely to recall specific memories. A total of 56 undergraduates who scored high or low on a measure of depression were shown positive and negative word cues and event cues in a computerised AMT. Dysphoric college students made significantly fewer specific and more categoric (overgeneral) responses than controls, but did not differ from controls in terms of extended responses. Results suggest that the difference in memory specificity between low and high dysphoric students generalises across word and event cues and that a computerised version of the AMT can be used as an alternative to interviews as a form of administration.

Extensive work over the past two decades has documented that depressed individuals show a trait-like tendency to retrieve more *overgeneral* and fewer *specific* autobiographical memories when prompted to be specific (see van Vreeswijk & de Wilde, 2004, for a meta-analysis). In the typical paradigm in this literature, the experimenter presents the participant with a single word as a memory cue and then the participant is expected to give a specific autobiographical memory related to that cue word. Several researchers have attempted to extend this work beyond adult clinical samples and found that clinically depressed adolescents were also less specific (Park, Goodyear, & Teasdale, 2002) and more categoric (overgeneral) in their responses (Swales, Williams, & Wood, 2001) than controls. Nonclinical samples of adolescents

---

Correspondence should be addressed to Kathleen Newcomb Rekart, Northwestern University, Department of Psychology, 2029 Sheridan Road, Evanston, IL 60208-2710, USA. E-mail: Kathleen.Rekart@med.va.gov

have also been studied. For example, Moffitt et al. (1994) coded the written memories of college students and found that individuals scoring high on a measure of depressed mood (relative to those scoring low on this measure) recalled a greater percentage of positive summary memories (similar to categoric memories) than single event memories (similar to specific memories). Similarly, Goddard, Dritschel, and Burton (1997) studied college students and Ramponi, Barnard, and Nimmo-Smith (2004) studied community volunteers and found that participants scoring high (> 14 and > 9, respectively, for the two studies) on the Beck Depression Inventory (BDI Beck, Ward, Mendelson, Mock, & Erbaugh, 1961); were significantly less specific than controls scoring low (< 8 and < 9, respectively, in the two studies) on the BDI.

Within research on OGM, there are two main subtypes of overgeneral memories including categoric memories (a recall of a summary of events,—e.g., "every time I went to the dentist") and extended memories (a recall of a memory that lasted more than one day, e.g., "my vacation to Florida"). Although this distinction has not been widely studied, there is evidence that depressed patients differ from controls only with respect to the number of categoric responses. For example, a reanalysis of the data of Williams and Dritschel (1988) showed that the association between OGM and depression in their clinical sample was completely a function of an excess of categoric errors (Williams, 1996); no group differences were seen in extended memories. Mackinger, Pachinger, Leibetseder, and Fartacek (2000) also found that group differences were statistically significant only for specific and categoric responses, but not for extended responses. Thus, these two types of overgenerality appear to be differentially related to depression.

The OGM effect has also been observed in clinical samples when the cueing methods were varied. Moore, Watts, and Williams (1988) presented social contexts (e.g., "a neighbour helped me"; "my partner criticised me") to depressed participants and matched controls and found that the proportion of overgeneral responses were significantly greater for the depressed group compared to controls. In a study of suicidal patients, Williams and Dritschel (1988) presented positive and negative word cues with activities (e.g., happiness—going for a walk), testing the hypothesis that providing an additional activity cue would facilitate retrieval. They found no difference in the pattern of results, with suicidal patients still producing more overgeneral memories. However, it is unclear whether the OGM effect would be observed with different cueing in a nonclinical sample.

The present research was designed to both replicate and extend previous findings concerning OGM and depression in a nonclinical sample of dysphoric college students. To replicate previous research we expected that when instructed to generate specific autobiographical memories, dysphoric college students would be more likely to generate overgeneral responses than controls. To extend previous research, we used a computerised self-report task adapted from

Williams' autobiographical memory test (AMT; Williams & Broadbent, 1986), which has many benefits for researchers. Unlike the traditional AMT in which an experimenter presents cues to participants and records their memories, the current study presented cues on the computer screen and had participants type their own responses. As a result, the computerised AMT is less time-consuming and labour-intensive for the experimenter and allows for a standardised administration of the stimuli and greater participant privacy when generating personal memories. In addition, participants' typed responses are immediately available in an easy-to-read format for the researcher. Thus, participants' responses do not need to be transcribed, and this typed format obviates problems reading participants' handwritten responses on paper-and-pencil based AMT questionnaires. We hoped to determine whether a computerised task would be sensitive enough to replicate the basic OGM effect in a group of dysphoric students.

Finally, we also conducted a variation on Williams and Dritschel's (1988) AMT paradigm in a nonclinical sample to observe whether context cues aided specific memory retrieval in a nonclinical sample. For half the trials, we presented dysphoric and nondysphoric college students with cue words (e.g., "happy", "sorry"). For the other half of the trials, we cued participants with general events and contexts (e.g., "getting a gift", "making a mistake") and tested whether dysphorics were less specific and more overgeneral for both word cues and event cues. We hypothesised that unlike in clinical samples, dysphorics might be better able to generate specific events in their lives when cued with a context or general events than with words.

METHOD

Participants

A total of 56 participants (17 male) were recruited from the Northwestern University Department of Psychology subject pool ($N = 209$) based on pretesting at the beginning of the quarter (Spring quarter, 2003) using the Mood and Anxiety Symptoms Questionnaire (MASQ; Watson et al., 1995). Participants scoring in the bottom 20% on a composite of the two depression subscales (General Distress: Depression and Anhedonic Depression) made up the Non-Dysphoric group ($n = 27$; 9 male) and participants scoring in the top 20% of the composite of the depression subscales were chosen to comprise the Dysphoric group ($n = 29$; 8 male).

Materials

Mood and Anxiety Symptom Questionnaire (MASQ; Watson et al., 1995). The MASQ we used consists of 65 symptoms and cognitions that are associated with anxiety and depression according to the revised third edition of the DSM (DSM-III-R). Participants indicated to what extent they had experienced each symptom (1 = *not at all*, 5 = *extremely*) "during the past week including today". The General Distress: Depressive Symptoms subscale (GD: Depression; 12 items) contains several indicators of depressed mood and other symptoms of mood disorder and the Anhedonic Depression Scale includes 7 Loss of Interest items reflecting anhedonia, disinterest, and low energy (e.g., "felt like nothing was enjoyable") and 14 reverse-scored High Positive Affect items assessing positive emotional experiences (e.g., felt cheerful, optimistic, looked forward to things with enjoyment). As mentioned above, we selected participants on the basis of a composite of the GD: Depression subscale and the Anhedonic Depression scale. Coefficient alpha for this composite in our sample equalled .97. Omega$_{hierarchical}$ (McDonald, 1999; Zinbarg, Revelle, Yovel, & Li, 2005; Zinbarg, Yovel, Revelle, & McDonald, in press) estimates based on 946 participants who have completed this composite as a preselection measure in five studies we have conducted range from .54 to .72.

Expanded Autobiographical Memory Test. Two types of stimuli (each with 20 items) were used in the current study. For word cues, the 10 positive and negative word cues from the original AMT (Williams & Broadbent, 1986; happy, sorry, safe, angry, interested, clumsy, successful, hurt, surprised, lonely) were used along with 10 additional depression-relevant positive and negative words obtained both from depression measures and from studies on cognition and emotion (Bradley & Matthews, 1983; Greenberg & Alloy, 1989; Zuckerman & Lubin, 1985; proud, sad, excited, rejected, cheerful, failure, pleased, hopeless, lively, guilty). For event cues, 20 positive and negative general events and contexts were gathered from the memories of college students responding to the original AMT cues in a pilot study. The most common specific memories and contexts cued by the positive and negative cue words were transformed into general events or activities (e.g., "making a new friend", "making a mistake", "celebrating a birthday", "getting a bad grade").[1] Words and events were matched for valence by 12 independent raters.

Procedure

Participants were tested in individual laboratory sessions that lasted about 1 hour. All stimuli were presented on a Dell Dimension 8200 computer utilising MediaLab (Jarvis, 2002). Instructions were obtained from J.M.G. Williams

---

[1] Event cues were as follows: "making a new friend", "making a mistake", "being some place comfortable", "having a fight with someone", "starting a new hobby", "breaking something", "getting a good grade", "being made fun of", "learning some unexpected news", "getting left out of something", "completing a project", "feeling misunderstood", "getting a gift", "ending of a relationship", "doing a fun activity", "getting a bad grade", "celebrating a birthday", "experiencing a failure", "starting a new relationship", "making a bad decision".

(personal communication, 12 October, 2002) and were adapted to account for a computerised administration format with cue words and phrases:

> The focus of this study is events that have happened in your life. You will be shown some words or phrases on the computer screen. For each word or phrase, think of an event that happened to you that the word or phrase reminds you of. The event could have happened recently (yesterday, last week) or a long time ago. It might be an important event, or a trivial event.
>
> Just one more thing: The memory you recall should be a specific event. So in response to the word 'fun' or the phrase 'going on a trip'—it would not be OK to say, 'I always enjoy going on trips', because that does not mention a specific event. But it would be OK to say 'I had a fun when I went to Six Flags' [a local amusement park] (because that is a specific event). It is also important to try to recall a different memory or event for each cue word or phrase.'

Participants were assigned to either Words First or Events First conditions using block random assignment; each participant eventually responded to all of the cues. Because the task was computerised there were no practice trials. At the end of the memory task, participants were given the MASQ a second time; it was given after the task rather than before so as to reduce any possibility of priming certain memories.

RESULTS

Coding responses

We divided the participants' typed responses among four independent coders who were blind to condition; they scored the participants' typed responses following criteria previously used by Williams and Dritschel (1992) and Ramponi et al. (2004). A memory was classified as *specific* if the event lasted less than a day and occurred at one particular time and place. For example, in response to the cue *happy*, the response "I was happy when my boyfriend gave me a sapphire ring" was coded as specific. A response was coded as *extended* if the event described lasted longer than a day. For example, to the same cue, the response "my trip to Europe" was coded as extended. The response was coded as *categoric* if it described a summary of multiple occurrences. For example, the response "whenever I go to a movie" was coded as categoric. The response was coded as a *semantic association* if it did not describe a past event, for example "The song "Happy Birthday' springs to mind". Finally *omissions* were scored if a participant typed a response like "I don't know" or "I can't think of anything". In order to establish interrater reliability, all four raters independently coded the same 100 randomly selected memory responses from the responses obtained from this sample and a sample for an earlier pilot study, kappa = .60. Discrepancies were resolved by discussion and when the group reached consensus, final consensus scores for the interrater reliability subsample of 100 memories were entered into the analysis.

Mood measures

The dysphoric group scored significantly higher ($M = 106.31$, $SD = 25.65$) on the composite of the MASQ depression subscales readministered at the time of AMT testing than the non-dysphoric group ($M = 65.04$, $SD = 21.27$), $t(54) = -6.53$, $p < .001$.[2]

Memory responses

The proportions of memories that were specific, extended, and categoric were calculated for each cue type by dividing the total number of each particular response type by the total number of typed responses for each cue category (specific, extended, categoric, semantic associates, and omissions). The mean proportions of specific, extended, and categoric response types by group for word cues and event cues, are summarised in Table 1.

To examine the OGM effect as a function of depression and cue type, we conducted three separate 2 Group (Dysphoric vs. Non-Dysphoric) × 2 Cue Type (Words vs. Events) mixed design ANOVAs with group as the between-subjects factors, with cue type as the within-subject factors, and with the proportion of specific, extended, and categoric responses generated as the three dependent variables.[3]

TABLE 1
Means (and standard deviations) of proportion of responses by group for word and event cues

Response	Cue type	Group	
		Non-Dysphoric	Dysphoric
Specific	Words	0.83 (0.11)	0.74 (0.16)
	Events	0.84 (0.11)	0.71 (0.12)
Extended	Words	0.07 (0.06)	0.09 (0.07)
	Events	0.06 (0.05)	0.08 (0.07)
Categoric	Words	0.08 (0.09)	0.17 (0.14)
	Events	0.08 (0.06)	0.18 (0.10)

---

[2] Given that some participants (Ps) were not tested for as long as one month following pre-testing, it is not surprising that some Ps no longer scored in the top or bottom 20% on the relevant MASQ scales. When these Ps were omitted from the analyses, 24 Ps remained in the dysphoric group and 16 in the non-dysphoric group. All effects remained significant.

[3] A preliminary ANOVA revealed that there were no significant main effects or interactions with Cue Order, $ps > .05$, thus this variable will not be discussed further.

Replicating the OGM Effect

To test whether the present study replicated the basic OGM effect, the main effects of Group (Dysphoric vs. Non-Dysphoric) for specific, extended, and categoric responses were examined. There was a significant main effect of Group for specific responses, $F(1, 54) = 15.43, p < .001$. As can be seen in Table 1, the dysphoric group generated fewer specific responses than the non-dysphoric group. For extended responses, the main effect of Group was not significant, $F(1, 54) = 2.48, p = .12$. Finally, there was a significant main effect of Group for categoric responses, $F(1, 54) = 16.60, p < .001$. As can be seen in Table 1, the dysphoric group generated more categoric responses than the non-dysphoric group.

OGM for word and event/context cues

The impact of Cue Type (Word vs. Event) on the OGM effect was also tested. The Group × Cue Type interactions were examined for specific, extended, and categoric responses.

The Group × Cue Type interaction was not significant for specific responses, $F(1, 54) = 1.25, p = .28$. In the light of the significant main effect of group, planned comparisons revealed that the dysphoric group was significantly less specific than the non-dysphoric group when cued with word cues [$M_{Dysphoric} = 0.74, SD = 0.16, M_{Non-Dysphoric} = 0.83, SD = 0.11; t(54) = 2.40, p < .05$] and with general event cues [$M_{Dysphoric} = 0.71, SD = 0.12, M_{Non-Dysphoric} = 0.84, SD = 0.11; t(54) = 4.17, p < .001$].

For extended responses, the Group × Cue Type interaction was not significant, $F < 1$. The dysphoric group made non-significantly more extended responses than the non-dysphoric group for both word cues [$M_{Dysphoric} = 0.09, SD = 0.07, M_{Non-Dysphoric} = 0.07, SD = .06; t < 1$] and general event cues [$M_{Dysphoric} = 0.08, SD = 0.07, M_{Non-Dysphoric} = 0.06, SD = .05; t(54) = -1.48, p = .15$].

Finally, the Group × Cue Type interaction was not significant for categoric responses, $F < 1$. Planned comparisons also revealed that the dysphoric group was significantly more categoric than the non-dysphoric group when cued with word cues [$M_{Dysphoric} = 0.17, SD = 0.14, M_{Non-Dysphoric} = 0.08, SD = 0.09; t(54) = -2.83, p < .01$] and with general event cues [$M_{Dysphoric} = 0.18, SD = 0.10, M_{Non-Dysphoric} = 0.08, SD = 0.06; t(54) = -4.27, p < .001$].

DISCUSSION

Although the overgeneral memory effect is generally studied in clinically depressed patients, results of this study are consistent with several other studies showing the OGM effects also occur in subclinical depression (e.g., Goddard et al., 1997; Moffitt et al., 1994; Ramponi et al., 2004). The significant main effects of group status for specific responses and categoric responses revealed that overall dysphoric participants were less specific and more categoric in their memory responses than controls. Results of this study also replicate previous research showing that the tendency for depressed individuals to make more overgeneral responses than controls seems most reliable for categoric overgeneral responses as opposed to extended responses (e.g., Park et al., 2002; Williams, 1996). Results also extended previous work demonstrating the OGM effect with different cueing techniques (cue words or general events) in a nonclinical sample.

Additionally, although the Williams and Broadbent's (1986) AMT has generally been administered by interview (see van Vreeswijk & de Wilde, 2004) or by paper-and-pencil questionnaire format (e.g., Henderson, Hargreaves, Gregory, & Williams, 2002; Merkelbach, Muris, & Horselenbera, 1996), results of this study also suggest that, at least when sampling from student populations as we did, the OGM effect can be studied with a computerised administration of the cue words in which participants type in their own responses. This form of administration allows for a standardised presentation of memory cues. The absence of the experimenter in the room also allows for greater participant privacy when generating personal memories.

However, there are several limitations of the current study. We selected a sample of college students scoring high and low on a measure of depression and presented participants with cues developed for the purposes of this study; thus our results are in need of replication. In addition, it is unclear the extent to which event categories complicated the memory search process because event cues decreased the participants' flexibility in searching for an appropriate memory (i.e., there might be more events during which a particular person felt "angry" than situations in which this person "had a fight with someone"). Nevertheless, the findings were as predicted.

Another potential shortcoming is that it is unclear whether the computerised procedure influenced the results. Unlike with the interview format, ratings of memories had to rely solely on the participants' first typed responses, which did not afford the rater the opportunity to follow-up potentially ambiguous responses with clarifying queries. This may have reduced the reliability of coders' ability to detect subtle differences between, for example, a specific memory that lasted less than a day versus an extended memory that lasted 2–3 days (e.g., "when I fought with Jill last weekend" or "when I visited with my grandmother last summer").

Moreover, because participants completed the task on the computer, there were also no interactive practice trials. It is unclear whether the lack of practice trials influenced the results. One possibility is that some participants did not understand the instructions; however, the proportion of specific response was 78%, which suggests that most participants did grasp the goal of the task. Ramponi et al. (2004) observed a similar proportion (76%) of specific responses in their sample of dysphoric and non-dysphoric college students using the traditional AMT. However, even if the interpretation of group differences in our sample was not adversely affected by the lack of practice trials, in patient samples this might be a problem. Thus this issue would need to be examined before recommending use of the computerised format in research on patient samples.

In sum, despite its limitations, the current investigation successfully replicated and extended previous research examining the relationship between depression and categoric (overgeneral) autobiographical memory. It replicated previous research both by producing evidence that OGM is associated with dysphoria in a nonclinical sample, and by demonstrating that results were stronger for categoric than for extended responses. It also extended previous research by demonstrating OGM using a computerised AMT with both word cues and event cues.

REFERENCES

Beck, A., Ward, C., Mendelson, M., Mock, J., & Erbaugh, J. (1961). An inventory for measuring depression. *Archives of General Psychiatry, 4*, 561–571.

Bradley, B., & Mathews, A. (1983). Negative self-schemata in clinical depression. *British Journal of Clinical Psychology, 22*, 173–181.

Goddard, L., Dritschel, B., & Burton, A. (1997). Social problem solving and autobiographical memory in non-clinical depression. *British Journal of Clinical Psychology, 36*, 449–451.

Greenberg, M. S. & Alloy, L. B. (1989). Depression versus anxiety: Processing of self- and other-referent information. *Cognition and Emotion, 3*, 207–223.

Henderson, D., Hargreaves, I., Gregory, S., & Williams, J. M. G. (2002). Autobiographical memory and emotion in a nonclinical sample of women with and without a reported history of childhood sexual abuse. *British Journal of Clinical Psychology, 41*, 129–142.

Jarvis, B. G. (2002). *MediaLab Research Software, Version 2002*. New York: Empirisoft.

Mackinger, H. F., Pachinger, M. M., Leibetseder, M. M., & Fartacek, R. R. (2000). Autobiographical memories in women remitted from major depression. *Journal of Abnormal Psychology, 109*, 331–334.

McDonald, R. P. (1999). *Test theory: A unified treatment*. Mahwah, NJ: Erlbaum.

Merckelbach, H., Muris, P., & Horselenberg, R. (1996). Correlates of overgeneral memories in normal subjects. *Behavioural and Cognitive Psychotherapy, 24*, 109–115.

Moffitt, K. H., Singer, J. A., Nelligan, D. W., Carlson, M. A., et al. (1994). Depression and memory narrative type. *Journal of Abnormal Psychology, 103*, 581–583.

Moore, R. G., Watts, F. N., & Williams, J. M. G. (1988). The specificity of personal memories in depression. *British Journal of Clinical Psychology, 27*, 275–276.

Park, R. J., Goodyer, I., & Teasdale, J. (2002). Categoric overgeneral autobiographical memory in adolescents with major depressive disorder. *Psychological Medicine, 32*, 267–276.

Ramponi, C., Barnard, P. J., & Nimmo-Smith, I. (2004). Recollection deficits in dysphoric mood: An effect of schematic models and executive mode? *Memory, 12*, 655–670.

Swales, M. A., Williams, J. M. G., & Wood, P. (2001). Specificity of autobiographical memory and mood disturbance in adolescents. *Cognition and Emotion, 15*, 321–331.

van Vreeswijk, M. F., & de Wilde, E. J. (2004). Autobiographical memory specificity, psychopathology, depressed mood and the use of the Autobiographical Memory Test: A meta-analysis. *Behaviour Research and Therapy, 42*, 731–743.

Watson, D., Clark, L. A., Weber, K., Assenheimer, J. S., et al. (1995). Testing a tripartite model: II. Exploring the symptom structure of anxiety and depression in student, adult, and patient samples. *Journal of Abnormal Psychology, 104,* 15–25.

Williams, J. M. G. (1996). Depression and the specificity of autobiographical memory. In Rubin (Ed.), *Remembering our past: Studies in autobiographical memory* (pp. 244–267). New York: Cambridge University Press.

Williams, J. M. G., & Broadbent, K. (1986). Autobiographical memory in suicide attempters. *Journal of Abnormal Psychology, 95,* 144–149.

Williams, J. M. G., & Dritschel, B. H. (1988). Emotional disturbance and the specificity of autobiographical memory. *Cognition and Emotion, 2,* 221–234.

Williams, J. M. G., & Dritschel, B. H. (1992). Categoric and extended autobiographical memories. In M. A. Conway, D. C. Rubin, H. Spinnler & W. A. Wagenaar (Eds.), *Theoretical perspectives on autobiographical memory* (pp. 391–412). Dordrecht: Kluwer.

Zinbarg, R., Revelle, W., Yovel, I., & Li, W. (2005). Cronbach's α, Revelle's β, and McDonald's ω_h: Their relations with each other and two alternative conceptualizations of reliability. *Psychometrika, 70,* 123–133.

Zinbarg, R., Yovel, I., Revelle, W., & McDonald, R. (in press). Estimating generalizability to a universe of indicators that all have an attribute in common: A comparison of estimators for ω_h. *Applied Psychological Measurement.*

Zuckerman, M., & Lubin, B. (1985). *Manual for the multiple affect adjective check list—Revised.* San Diego, CA: Edits.

Suicide attempts: Patients with and without an affective disorder show impaired autobiographical memory specificity

Max M. Leibetseder
Social Medical Services, Salzburg, Austria

Rudolf R. Rohrer
Paracelsus Private Medical University, Salzburg, Austria

Herbert F. Mackinger
University of Salzburg, Austria

Reinhold R. Fartacek
Paracelsus Private Medical University, Salzburg, Austria

A number of studies have shown reduced recall of specific autobiographical memories (AMs) in patients after attempted suicide, but in all of them the study samples were confounded with diagnoses of affective disorders. The present study aims to demonstrate impaired specific autobiographical memory in patients after a suicide attempt without a diagnosis of an affective disorder. Four groups were compared: (1) patients with an actual major depression and a suicide attempt; (2) patients after a suicide attempt without a lifetime history of an affective diagnosis; (3) patients currently suffering from major depression without a suicide attempt; and (4) control persons not suffering from either of the two conditions during their entire life. Individuals with major depression and a suicide attempt showed reduced specificity of AM and, most importantly, patients with a suicide attempt—despite the absence of an affective disorder—were equally impaired with recall of specific AMs as were patients with major depression. The authors propose that reduced specific AM is a common vulnerability factor that can lead either to the development of an affective disorder and/or to a suicide attempt.

Correspondence should be addressed to Professor H. F. Mackinger, Department of Psychology, University of Salzburg, A-5020 Salzburg, Hellbrunnerstrasse 34, Austria; e-mail: herbert.mackinger@sbg.ac.at

We thank the Medizinische Forschungsgesellschaft Salzburg for financial support of the study (Grant No. 031095/ho). We also thank the patients for their participation in the study. We further appreciate the invaluable comments made by the reviewers and editor

An autobiographical memory (AM) refers to the recollection of a personal event. In assessing AM, individuals are presented emotional cue words with the instruction to recall related specific events from their past. Such an event is considered *specific* if it occurred within one day and does not occur repeatedly. According to Williams (1996) nonspecific recalls can either be non-autobiographical (e.g., the assassination of Kennedy), extended (e.g., my vacation in Spain), or categorical (e.g., a sum of recurring events, like attending sport events). Presentation of results in the literature is irregular: Some authors refer to the reduced number of specific AMs, others to an increased recall of categorical events, which is also termed "overgenerality".

An increasing number of studies has been able to demonstrate that certain individuals have difficulties in retrieving specific AMs. Reduced specific AM has been found in various clinical groups, most prominently in patients suffering from an affective disorder, but also in patients after attempted suicide, with posttraumatic stress disorder, acute stress disorder, and borderline personality disorder (Dalgleish et al., 2005). In studies with patients who have attempted suicide, however, suicide attempt was confounded with the presence of an affective disorder.

Williams and Broadbent (1986) compared 25 inpatients after self-poisoning to two control samples and found significantly increased overgeneral memory within the first group. As the authors report, about two thirds of the suicide attempters were temporarily suffering from a major depressive disorder. Therefore one cannot say whether reduced specific AM was attributable to the particular affective state the patients were in, or to their suicide attempt. Similarly, Williams and Dritschel (1988) compared two groups of patients after deliberate self-poisoning, and their results showed that overgeneral memory seem to pertain over a longer period of time.

Williams and Scott (1988) compared 20 patients with major depression to a group of nondepressed patients. In a second step, the authors split the major depression group and formed two subgroups, consisting of individuals with a history of suicide attempts and those without. These subgroups did not differ from each other with respect to AM. The authors concluded that overgeneral memory within a group of depressive patients can therefore not be attributed to the inclusion of patients after a suicide attempt.

A study by Pollock and Williams (2001) compared a group of patients after a suicide attempt, a group of mixed psychiatric patients, and a non-psychiatric control group. Again, patients with a history of suicide attempts were more general with respect to AM recall. Unfortunately, the authors did not mention whether the suicide attempters were classified in one of the categories for affective diagnoses. Their reported mean score on the Beck Depression Inventory (BDI; Beck, Ward, Mendelson, Mock, & Erbaugh, 1961) of 29.2 ($SD = 9.2$) is indicative of severe depression, however.

Evans, Williams, O'Loughlin, and Howells in their 1992 study came closest to a homogenous group of "parasuicide-only" patients. Only one out of 12 patients with a parasuicidal incident fulfilled the criteria for a depressive disorder according to the DSM-III (American Psychiatric Association, 1980). The group of parasuicides was significantly more general than a matched group of surgical control patients.

By and large all studies on patients suffering from an affective disorder found a reduced ability to recall specific AMs (Brittlebank, Scott, Williams, & Ferrier, 1993; Evans et al., 1992; Kuyken & Dalgleish, 1995; Moore, Watts, & Williams, 1988; Puffet, Jehin-Marchot, Timsit-Berthier, & Timsit, 1991; Sidley, Calam, Wells, Hughes, & Whitaker, 1999; Sidley, Whitaker, Calam, & Wells, 1997; Wessel, Meeren, Peeters, Arntz, & Merckelbach, 2001; Williams & Dritschel, 1988), whereas correlations between specific AMs and severity of depression were negligible. Therefore, with Wessel et al. (2001, p. 417) it can be concluded that "... clinical diagnosis rather than self-reported depression severity ..." is related to AM recall.

In sum, existing studies on patients with diagnoses of an affective disorder, as well as studies on persons with a suicide attempt suffer from the same weakness: Affective disorders and suicide attempts frequently co-occur, but most of the studies do not make explicit reference to this fact. According to Schmidtke and Löhr (2004) 29% of the female suicide attempters and 21% of the male suicide attempters suffer from an affective disorder. These figures underline why it is important that both conditions need to be unconfounded. We therefore designed a study whose aim it was to clarify the question as to whether impaired AM recall in suicide attempters depends on the presence of an affective disorder, or not.

METHOD

Participants

The study was conducted at the Centre for Suicide Prevention and Research (CSPR) at the Paracelsus Private Medical University Salzburg, Austria, the only specialised institution within the catchment area, comprising about half a million people. The CSPR does not admit patients with addictions or psychoses. Four groups of persons were compared: (1) patients with a current major depression (MD) and with suicide attempt (SA) (MD+/SA+; $n = 17$); (2) patients after SA but without a lifetime affective diagnosis (MD−/SA+; $n = 21$); (3) patients with current MD without SA (MD+/SA−; $n = 23$); and (4) healthy control persons free of both conditions over their lifetime (MD-/SA−; $n = 23$). The diagnosis of a current MD (as an inclusion criterion for group 1 and group 3) and the lifetime diagnosis of any affective disorder (as an exclusion criterion for group 2 and group 4) were formed using the Structured Clinical Interview for DSM-IV Axis I Disorders (SCID-I; First, Spitzer, Gibbon, & Williams, 1994; German version:

Wittchen, Zaudig, & Fydrich, 1997). In the case of a SA, the incidence was the triggering event for the hospital admission. SA has been considered a self-destructive act that required medical attention. Contrary to that, the absence of a SA referred to a lifetime absence. Due to organisational and legal reasons, the range of methods for a SA was assumed to be representative of the population. Not included in the sample were persons after SA who needed continued intensive medical treatment.[1]

Variables and instruments

Autobiographical Memory Test (AMT). Autobiographical memory testing followed the procedure as described by Williams and Broadbent (1986). Individuals were presented six positively and six negatively valenced cue words with the instruction to recall related specific events from their past. The cue words of the German test version were selected according to word norms provided by Schwibbe, Räder, Schwibbe, Borchardt, and Geiken-Pophanken (1981). In a minor deviation from Williams' and Broadbent's procedure, we asked our participants to recall memories from more than 2 years ago. The reason for imposing this time barrier was to circumvent the "reminiscence bump" (Jansari & Parkin, 1996). An experienced independent rater, blind to the hypothesis, conducted the coding of the memories. Reliability of the coding procedure has been reported to be acceptable (e.g., Mackinger, Pachinger, Leibetseder, & Fartacek, 2000; kappa = 0.75–0.86).

Beck Depression Inventory (BDI; Beck et al., 1961; German version: Hautzinger, Bailer, Worall, & Keller, 1995). The 21-item BDI is a self-rating scale for the assessment of depression. Test-retest reliability varies from $r = .60$ to $r = .90$, internal consistency from $\alpha = .79$ to $\alpha = .90$; test validity reached an $r = .72$ (Beck, Steer, & Garbin, 1988).

Beck Hopelessness Scale (HS; Beck, Weissman, Lester, & Trexler, 1974; German version: Krampen, 1994). HS is a self-rating scale consisting of 20 items. Hopelessness means a generalised negative conception about oneself and control of future life. The scale total shows strong association with suicidal ideation even after controlling for actual depression levels. Internal consistency: $\alpha = .86$ (Hautzinger & Meyer, 2002).

---

[1] In the case of an ascertained diagnosis of MD we use the acronym MD+. For convenience of the readers we also use the acronym MD—which, however, refers to the lifetime absence of *any* affective disorder.

Hamilton Rating Scale of Depression (HRSD; Hamilton, 1967; German version: Collegium Internationale Psychiatriae Scalarum, 1996). The HRSD is an interview-based rating scale of the severity of depression. Interrater reliability coefficients are reported of above $r = .83$. The HRSD differentiates between depressed and nondepressed psychiatric patients (Hedlund & Vieweg, 1979).

Zahlen-Verbindungs-Test (ZVT; Oswald & Roth, 1978; Roth, 1964). The ZVT is a measure for general intelligence in the format of a mental speed test. Given a time limit, the participant is required to combine numbers in an ascending order and therefore to make simple decisions as quickly as possible. A retest reliability of $r = .97$ is reported by the authors. Vernon (1993) found significant correlations ($r = .59$) between the ZVT and the Multidimensional Aptitude Battery (MAB; Jackson, 1983).

Procedure

Consecutively admitted patients and control persons were assessed using the SCID-I for DMS-IV, the ZVT, the BDI, the HRSD, the HS, and the AMT. All testing took place during afternoons on the second or third day after admission. Study participants of the control group (MD−/SA−) were recruited from the general population. They came either from the hospital personnel or their acquaintances and were matched by age, gender, and intelligence (ZVT). The latter being necessary, because in their study Dalgleish et al. (2005) found substantial correlations between specific AM and fluid intelligence scores. Williams and Scott (1988) indirectly compared AMs of a hospital control group to control persons of a subject panel and found "strikingly similar" (p.692) results for the two. This justifies the use of nonhospitalised individuals as controls. After being briefed about the study, formal written consent was obtained.

RESULTS

Participant characteristics

In comparing the four groups, all univariate analyses of variances for the BDI, HRSD, and HS were significant (all $ps < .001$). Separate t-tests revealed that the control group was significantly less affected than the other three groups on all three scales (all $ps < .001$). Patients of the MD−/SA+ group differed significantly from the other two clinical groups on the BDI and the HRSD, on the HS they differed from the MD+/SA−. The two groups of patients with MD differed from each other significantly with respect to both of the depression scales (the nonsuicidal group scoring higher on depression), but not on the HS (see Table 1).

With respect to intelligence no significant group differences were found, $F(1, 80) = 0.638, p = .593$.

TABLE 1
Means (and standard deviations) of demographic data, depression scores, and proportions of specific autobiographical memories for four study groups

Groups	MD+/SA+ (n = 17)	MD+/SA− (n = 23)	MD−/SA+ (n = 21)	MD−/SA− (n = 23)
Age	36.7 (12.8)	42.4 (10.5)	35.4 (10.9)	37.8 (11.2)
Gender (M/F)	3/14	5/18	4/17	6/17
BDI	26.2 (7.1)^{b,c,d}	31.7 (9.5)^{a,c,d}	17.6 (8.7)^{a,b,d}	4.8 (3.8)^{a,b,c}
HRSD	19.9 (6.6)^{b,c,d}	26.1 (4.2)^{a,c,d}	15.3 (5.2)^{a,b,d}	5.4 (3.8)^{a,b,c}
HS	30.1 (4.2)^{d}	31.5 (3.7)^{c,d}	28.8 (3.9)^{b,d}	23.9 (2.7)^{a,b,c}
ZVT	91.1 (24.9)	92.2 (30.7)	94.4 (27.3)	100.7 (13.9)
Spec.AM-tot.	4.2 (2.3)	3.7 (2.1)	3.8 (2.7)	8.0 (2.7)
Spec.AM-pos.	1.9 (1.1)	1.8 (1.1)	1.9 (1.6)	3.8 (1.6)
Spec.AM-neg.	2.2 (1.4)	1.9 (1.5)	2.0 (1.5)	4.1 (1.4)

BDI, Beck Depression Inventory; HRSD, Hamilton Rating Scale of Depression; HS, Hopelessness-Scale; ZVT, Zahlenverbindungstest; Spec.AM-tot., specific AMs in response to 12 cue words; Spec. AM-pos., specific AMs in response to 6 positively valenced cue words; Spec.AM-neg., specific AMs in response to 6 negatively valenced cue words. Superscripts indicate significant differences to the respective groups (^{a} MD+/SA+; ^{b} MD+/SA−; ^{c} MD−/SA+; ^{d} MD−/SA−).

Autobiographical memories

The 2 (MD: yes, no) × 2 (SA: yes, no) analysis of variances for specific AMs in response to all 12 cue words,[2] showed a significant main effect for MD, $F(1, 80) = 13.08$, $p = .001$, a significant main effect for SA, $F(1, 80) = 11.59$, $p = .001$, and a significant interaction between MD and SA, $F(1, 80) = 18.47$, $p < .001$. Both groups comprising patients with MD showed reduced specific AM, whether they attempted suicide or not. Similarly, both groups of persons with SA showed reduced specific AM, whether they were affected by MD or not. These results mean that patients of our index group (MD−/SA+) (i.e., individuals after a SA without receiving a lifetime diagnosis of an affective disorder) were just as overgeneral as were patients with the diagnosis MD. Control persons were significantly more specific than each of the three clinical groups (all $ps > .001$). All other group comparisons were without statistical significance (all $ps < .50$).

---

[2] In a 2 (MD: yes, no) × 2 (SA: yes, no) × 2 (Repeated measure: Cue-valence: positive, negative) ANOVA with the number of specific AMs as the dependent variable we found no significant main effect for cue valence, $F(1, 80) = 1.57$, $p = .21$, no significant interactions between cue valence and either MD, $F(1, 80) = 0.001$, $p = .97$, or SA, $F(1, 80) = 0.005$, $p = .95$, nor a significant three-way interaction between these factors, $F(1, 80) = 0.32$, $p = .57$. Therefore, for further statistical analyses we collapsed the specific responses to the positive cues and to the negative cues into one combined measure for specific AMs.

The direct comparison of MD+/SA+ and the MD−/SA+ showed a p of .875, $t(36) = 0.158$.[3]

If we consider the four groups separately, the correlations between specificity of AM and the scores for BDI, HRSD, and HS were only moderate, and none of them approached significance (all $ps > .20$). Also in none of the groups was intelligence (ZVT) significantly correlated with specificity of AM.

DISCUSSION

Prior studies on autobiographical memory confounded patients with having suicide attempt and affective disorders. To our knowledge this is the first study to disentangle the effects of these two factors. The core result of the study was that patients with a recent suicide attempt but without a lifetime diagnosis of an affective disorder show equally reduced specific AM recall as patients with a current major depression—with or without a suicide attempt. From this we can conclude that reduced specific AM is indicative for patients with current major depression and also for patients after a suicide attempt without a lifetime diagnosis of an affective disorder.

As we excluded persons with a history of an affective disorder when composing the index group (MD−/SA+), past depressive episodes can not be considered the cause for reduced specific AM. Although their actual depression scores were significantly below the values of the other two clinical groups, these scores were still significantly above those of the control group. In clinical settings it is highly unlikely that a person after a suicide attempt will be completely unaffected emotionally. Although we know that specificity of AM in patients remains unaltered after remission from major depression (Brittlebank et al., 1993; Mackinger et al., 2000), increasingly more studies (Maccullom, McConkey, Bryant, & Barnier, 2000; Svaldi & Mackinger, 2003; Watkins & Teasdale, 2001; Watkins, Teasdale, & Williams, 2000) demonstrated some degree of state dependency. There was some chance that elevated depression scores have contributed to the results. Therefore, we computed an ANCOVA with measures of depression severity as covariates. Because the results were virtually the same as with the ANOVA, we maintain the validity of our study results. We assume that persons with reduced specific AM have an increased risk to develop an affective disorder, but a considerable number of them may

---

[3] In addition to this ANOVA we computed a 2 (MD: yes, no) × 2 (SA: yes, no) ANCOVA, controlling for BDI, HRSD and HS. Specificity of AM showed significant main effects for MD, $F(1, 77) = 6.82, p = .011$, for SA, $F(1, 77) = 12.35, p = .001$, and a significant interaction between MD and SA, $F(1, 77) = 13.77, p = .000$. Although partialling severity of depression in this case can be seen as problematic (see Miller & Chapman, 2001), these results further support our view that the reported significant main effects and interactions of the ANOVA ought to be attributed to the group constituencies (Diagnoses, SA), and not to depression level.

attempt suicide without suffering from a significant depression or some other pathology.

As a first limitation of the study we have to take into consideration the possibility that our index group (MD−/SA+) differs from the two clinical groups with respect to variables that we did not control for. It is known that individuals with a childhood abuse history are over-represented in groups of individuals with a suicide attempt (e.g., Mann, Waternaux, Haas, & Malone, 1999), who at the same time show reduced recall of specific AMs (Burnside, Startup, Byatt, Rollins, & Hill, 2004). Reduced specific AM as a sequel of successful affect regulation (Raes, Hermans, de Decker, Eelen, & Williams, 2003) further complicates the picture.

Second, two recent studies (Wessel et al., 2001; van Minnen, Wessel, Verhaak, & Smeenk, 2005) found substantial correlations between specificity of AMs and educational level. We did not control for educational level, instead we used an intelligence measure (ZVT; Oswald & Roth, 1978), which did not reveal any differences between the four groups, also all within-group correlations between specificity of AM and ZVT were nonsignificant. We do not know, however, the extent of overlap between intelligence (ZVT) and educational level. One minor limitation is the order of presentation of the assessment instruments. In future studies, it might be preferable to present the AMT before the depression measures.

Several theoretical models exist to explain AM recall deficits. Williams (1996), in his model of the "mnemonic interlock" describes overgeneral memory as resulting from a circular search process on the general level of autobiographical knowledge. Due to inefficient executive functions, individuals are not able to abort this circular search process and remain on a categoric level. Conway and Pleydell-Pearce (2000) conceive their self-memory system as an interplay between the working self and the autobiographical knowledge base. Current goals of a person are represented within the working self. If information from the autobiographical knowledge base is accessed, it is contrasted with the current goals. A difference between the two leads to an iterative process aiming at the reduction of discrepancies which can be accomplished by modification of the search cues, gradual modification of the memories, or by changing goal structures. If congruency cannot be achieved, negative emotions arise. Strong emotions, in turn, can disrupt ongoing cognitive processes (e.g., problem solving). It is easily conceivable that this model provides a sound theoretical basis not only for the development of depression, but also for suicidal behaviour.

From this concept alone one cannot predict why one person with reduced specific AM should develop an affective disorder, whereas another one attempts suicide. The introduction of one or more additional factors is necessary. Such factors can be impulsivity (Corruble, Damy, & Guelfi, 1999; Mann et al., 1999), problem-solving skills (Goddard, Dritschel, & Burton, 1996), affect regulation (Raes et al., 2003), coping skills, etc.

REFERENCES

American Psychiatric Association. (1980). *Diagnostic and statistical manual of mental disorders* (3rd ed.). Washington DC: Author.

Beck, A. T., Steer, R. A., & Garbin, M. G. (1988). Psychometric properties of the Beck Depression Inventory: Twenty-five years of evaluation. *Clinical Psychology Review, 8*, 77–100.

Beck, A. T., Ward, C. H., Mendelson, M., Mock, J. E., & Erbaugh, J. K. (1961). An inventory for measuring depression. *Archives of General Psychiatry, 4*, 561–571.

Beck, A. T., Weissman, A., Lester, D., & Trexler, L. (1974). Measurement of pessimism: The Hopelessness Scale. *Journal of Consulting and Clinical Psychology, 42*, 861–865.

Brittlebank, A. D., Scott, J., Williams, J. M. G., & Ferrier, I. N. (1993). Autobiographical memory in depression: State or trait marker? *British Journal of Psychiatry, 162*, 118–121.

Burnside, E., Startup, M., Byatt, M., Rollinson, L., & Hill, J. (2004). The role of autobiographical memory in the development of adult depression following childhood trauma. *British Journal of Clinical Psychology, 43*, 365–376.

Collegium Internationale Psychiatriae Scalarum (CIPS). (1996). *Internationale Skalen für Psychiatrie* [International Scales for Psychiatry]. Weinheim, Germany: Beltz Test.

Conway, M. A., & Pleydell-Pearce, Ch. W. (2000). The construction of autobiographical memories in the self-memory system. *Psychological Review, 107*, 261–288.

Corruble, E., Damy, C., & Guelfi, J. D. (1999). Impulsivity: A relevant dimension in depression regarding suicide attempts? *Journal of Affective Disorders, 53*, 211–215.

Dalgleish, T., Perkins, N., Williams, J. M. G., Golden, A.-M. J., Barrett, L. F., Barnard, Ph.J., Au-Yeung, C., Murphy, V., Elward, R., Tchanturia, K., Spinks, E. & Watkins, E. (2005). *Reduced specificity of autobiographical memory and depression: The role of executive processes.* Manuscript submitted for publication.

Evans, J., Williams, J. M. G., O'Loughlin, S. O., & Howells, K. (1992). Autobiographical memory and problem-solving strategies of parasuicide patients. *Psychological Medicine, 22*, 399–405.

First, M. B., Spitzer, R. L., Gibbon, M., & Williams, J. B. W. (1994). *Structured clinical interview for DSM-IV Axis I disorders (SCID-I).* New York: Biometrics Research Department, New York State Psychiatric Institute.

Goddard, L., Dritschel, B., & Burton, A. (1996). Role of autobiographical memory in social problem solving and depression. *Journal of Abnormal Psychology, 105*, 609–616.

Hamilton, M. (1967). Development of a rating scale for primary depressive illness. *British Journal of Social and Clinical Psychology, 6*, 278–296.

Hautzinger, M., Bailer, M., Worall, H., & Keller, F. (1995). *Das Beck Depressionsinventar (BDI)* (Neuauflage, 2001) [The Beck Depression Inventory (rev. ed., 2001). Bern: Huber.

Hautzinger, M., & Meyer, T. D. (2002). *Diagnostik affektiver Störungen* [Diagnoses of affective disorders]. Göttingen: Hogrefe.

Hedlund, J., & Vieweg, B. (1979). The Hamilton Rating Scale for Depression: A comprehensive review. *Journal of Operational Psychiatry, 10*, 149–162.

Jackson, D. N. (1983). *Multidimensional Aptitude Battery.* Port Huron, MI : Research Psychologists Press.

Jansari, A., & Parkin, A. J. (1996). Things that go bump in your life: Explaining the reminiscence bump in autobiographical memory. *Psychology and Aging, 11*, 85–91.

Krampen, G. (1994). *Skalen zur Erfassung von Hoffnungslosigkeit (H-Skalen).* [Scales for the measurement of hopelessness; H-scales]. Göttingen: Hogrefe.

Kuyken, W., & Dalgleish, T. (1995). Autobiographical memory and depression. *British Journal of Clinical Psychology, 34*, 89–92.

Maccallum, F., McConkey, K. M., Bryant, R. A., & Barnier, A. J. (2000). Specific autobiographical memory following hypnotically induced mood state. *International Journal of Clinical and Experimental Hypnosis, 48*, 361–373.

Mackinger, H. F., Pachinger, M. M., Leibetseder, M. M., & Fartacek, R. R. (2000). Autobiographical memories in women remitted from major depression. *Journal of Abnormal Psychology, 109*, 331–334.

Mann, J. J., Waternaux, Ch., Haas, G. L., & Malone, K. M. (1999). Toward a clinical model of suicidal behaviour in psychiatric patients. *American Journal of Psychiatry, 156*, 181–189.

Miller, G. A., & Chapman, J. P. (2001). Misunderstanding Analysis of Covariance. *Journal of Abnormal Psychology, 110*, 40–48.

Moore, R. G., Watts, F. N., & Williams, J. M. G. (1988). The specificity of personal memories in depression. *British Journal of Clinical Psychology, 27*, 275–276.

Oswald, W. D., & Roth, E. (1978). *Der Zahlen-Verbindungs-Test (ZVT); Ein sprachfreier Intelligenz-Schnell-Test. Handanweisung* (2. Aufl.) [The tracking figures test (ZVT); A culture-free brief intelligence test, manual (2nd ed.)]. Göttingen: Hogrefe.

Pollock, L. R., & Williams, J. M. G. (2001). Effective problem solving in suicide attempters depends on specific autobiographical recall. *Suicide and Life-Threatening Behavior, 31*, 386–396.

Puffet, A., Jehin-Marchot, D., Timsit-Berthier, M., & Timsit, M. (1991). Autobiographical memory and major depressive states. *European Psychiatry, 6*, 141–145.

Raes, F., Hermans, D., de Decker, A., Eelen, P., & Williams, J. M. G. (2003). Autobiographical memory specificity and affect regulation: An experimental approach. *Emotion, 3*, 201–206.

Roth, E. (1964). Die Geschwindigkeit der Verarbeitung von Informationen und ihr Zusammenhang mit Intelligenz [Speed of information processing and its correlation with intelligence]. *Zeitschrift für experimentelle und angewandte Psychologie, 11*, 616–623.

Schmidtke, A., & Löhr, C. (2004). Socio-demographic variables of suicide attempters. In D. de Leo, U. Bille-Brahe, A. Kerkhof, & A. Schmidtke (Eds.), *Suicidal behaviour: Theories and research findings* (pp.81–91). Göttingen: Hogrefe & Huber.

Schwibbe, M. K., Räder, K., Schwibbe, G., Borchhardt, M., & Geiken-Pophanken, G. (1981). Zum emotionalen Gehalt von Substantiven, Adjektiven und Verben [The emotional valences of nouns, adjectives and verbs]. *Zeitschrift für Experimentelle und Angewandte Psychologie, 28*, 486–501.

Sidley, G. L., Calam, R., Wells, A., Hughes, T., & Whitaker, K. (1999). The prediction of parasuicide repetition in a high-risk group. *British Journal of Clinical Psychology, 38*, 375–386.

Sidley, G. L., Whitaker, K., Calam, R. M., & Wells, A. (1997). The relationship between problem-solving and autobiographical memory in parasuicide patients. *Behavioural and Cognitive Psychotherapy, 25*, 195–202.

Svaldi, J. J., & Mackinger, H. F. (2003). Obstructive sleep apnea syndrome: Autobiographical memory predicts the course of depressive affect after nCPAP therapy. *Scandinavian Journal of Psychology, 44*, 31–37.

van Minnen, A., Wessel, I., Verhaak, Ch., & Smeenk, J. (2005). The relationship between autobiographical memory specificity and depressed mood following a stressful life event: A prospective study. *British Journal of Clinical Psychology, 44*, 405–428.

Vernon, Ph.A. (1993). Der Zahlen-Verbindungs-Test and other trail-making correlates of general intelligence. *Personality and Individual Differences, 14*, 35–40.

Watkins, E., & Teasdale, J. D. (2001). Rumination and overgeneral memory in depression: Effects of self-focus and analytic thinking. *Journal of Abnormal Psychology, 110*, 353–357.

Watkins, E., Teasdale, J. D., & Williams, R. M. (2000). Decentring and distraction reduce overgeneral autobiographical memory in depression. *Psychological Medicine, 30*, 911–920.

Wessel, I., Meeren, M., Peeters, F., Arntz, A., & Merckelbach, H. (2001). Correlates of autobiographical memory specificity: The role of depression, anxiety and childhood trauma. *Behaviour Research and Therapy, 39*, 409–421.

Williams, J. M. G. (1996). Depression and the specificity of autobiographical memory. In D.C. Rubin (Ed.). *Remembering our past* (pp.244–267). Cambridge, UK: Oxford University Press.

Williams, J. M. G., & Broadbent, K. (1986). Autobiographical memory in suicide attempters. *Journal of Abnormal Psychology, 95*, 144–149.

Williams, J. M. G., & Dritschel, B. (1988). Emotional disturbance and the specificity of autobiographical memory. *Cognition and Emotion, 2*, 221–234.

Williams, J. M. G., & Scott, J. (1988). Autobiographical memory in depression. *Psychological Medicine, 18*, 689–695.

Wittchen, H.-U., Zaudig, M., & Fydrich, T. (1997). *Strukturiertes Klinisches Interview für DSM-IV* [Structured clinical interview for DSM-IV]. Göttingen: Hogrefe.

Autobiographical memory specificity in adults reporting repressed, recovered, or continuous memories of childhood sexual abuse

Richard J. McNally, Susan A. Clancy, Heidi M. Barrett, Holly A. Parker, Carel S. Ristuccia, and Carol A. Perlman
Harvard University, Cambridge, MA, USA

> Some psychotherapists believe that adult survivors of childhood sexual abuse (CSA) are characterised by memory deficits for their childhood. Using the Autobiographical Memory Test (AMT), we asked nonabused control participants and participants who reported either continuous, recovered, or repressed memories of CSA to retrieve a specific personal memory in response to either positive or negative cue words from either childhood or adolescence/adulthood. The results indicated that participants who believed they harboured repressed memories of abuse tended to exhibit the greatest difficulty retrieving specific memories from their childhood. Neither posttraumatic stress disorder (PTSD) nor major depression was related to diminished memory specificity.

According to some psychotherapists (e.g., Harvey & Herman, 1994), many adults who experienced childhood sexual abuse (CSA) have difficulty recalling events from their early years. Indeed, some experts on dissociative disorders assert that vague memory for one's childhood is a sign that one may harbour repressed memories of early trauma (e.g., Loewenstein, 1991).

In this study, we tested whether adults reporting either continuous or recovered memories of CSA, or who believe they harbour repressed memories of CSA, experience difficulty retrieving specific memories from their childhood. To accomplish this aim, we used the Autobiographical Memory Test (AMT; Williams & Broadbent, 1986). The AMT requires participants to retrieve a specific personal memory in response to cue words (e.g., *happy*). A specific memory is one referring to an event that lasted no longer than one day (e.g., "I was very happy on the day my daughter was born"), whereas nonspecific

---

Correspondence should be addressed to Richard J. McNally, Department of Psychology, Harvard University, 33 Kirkland Street, Cambridge, MA 02138 USA; e-mail: rjm@wjh.harvard.edu

Preparation of this article was supported by National Institute of Mental Health grant (MH61268) awarded to the first author.

("overgeneral") memories can be either extended in time (e.g., "I was happy during my senior year in high school") or denote a category of event (e.g., "I have always been happy when playing tennis").

METHOD

Participants

To recruit participants, we placed newspaper advertisements that read:

- Were you sexually abused as a child?
- Do you think you might have been sexually abused?
- Do you have no history of childhood sexual abuse?

The notices said that individuals responding "yes" to any of these questions "may be eligible to participate in a research study at Harvard University concerning memory and trauma".

After providing written informed consent, respondents underwent an interview regarding their abuse memories that permitted them to be classified into one of four groups (Clancy & McNally, in press; McNally, Clancy, Barrett, & Parker, 2004). Reported abuse involved sexual contact with the participant (e.g., fondling, rape) by a perpetrator at least 5 years older than the participant. Using the PTSD Symptom Scale-Interview Version (Foa & Tolin, 2000) and the Structured Clinical Interview for DSM-IV (SCID-I; First, Spitzer, Gibbon, & Williams, 1996), the second author also interviewed participants to assess for PTSD, major depression, and several other psychiatric disorders.

The *continuous memory group* consisted of 71 adults (53 female) who reported always having remembered their sexual abuse. We corroborated the abuse reports for 16 participants. The *recovered memory group* consisted of 29 adults (17 female) who reported having recovered long-forgotten memories of CSA, none corroborated. The *repressed memory group* consisted of 39 adults (33 female) who believed that they had been sexually abused as children. They inferred their abuse histories from various "indicators", such as weight gain, sexual dysfunction, "body memories", and depressed mood. The *control group* consisted of 25 adults (16 female) who said they had never been sexually abused.

Questionnaires

Participants completed the Dissociative Experiences Scale (DES; Bernstein & Putnam, 1986); the Absorption Scale (Tellegen & Atkinson, 1974)—a correlate of fantasy proneness; the Beck Depression Inventory (BDI; Beck & Steer, 1987); the short form of the Manifest Anxiety Scale (MAS; Bendig, 1956); the Marlowe-Crowne Social Desirability Scale (MC; Crowne & Marlowe, 1960);

and the Shipley verbal and nonverbal measures of cognitive ability (Zachary, 1991). The means and standard deviations for these variables are shown in Table 1. We submitted these data to analyses of variance (ANOVAs), and conducted post hoc contrasts [Least-Significant Differences method] to explore these further.[1]

Design

The design was a 4 (Group: Continuous Memory, Recovered Memory, Repressed Memory, Control) × 2 (Cue Valence: Positive, Negative) × 2 (Time Period: Childhood, Adulthood) factorial with repeated measurement on the second and third variables.

Materials

Our 10 positive cue words (*happy, brave, strong, love, special, surprised, interested, successful, important, safe*), and 10 negative cue words (*clumsy, angry, sorry, hurt, doubt, strange, fear, tense, stress, lonely*) were from previous research (Kuyken & Brewin, 1995). Our 4 neutral practice words were *persistent, cautious, patient,* and *quick*. Each word appeared in lower case letters on a separate 3 in × 5 in. card, and was read aloud by the experimenter.

Procedure

Participants were instructed that they will be shown a series of words and asked to retrieve a specific personal memory in response to each word. They were told that a specific memory is one that happened to the participant, and that lasted no

---

[1] As these analyses show, the groups differed on several variables (e.g., anxiety). However, because participants were not randomly assigned to groups, we cannot "control for" anxiety, and so forth when testing for differences among the groups in memory performance. As Miller and Chapman (2001) emphasised in their article on the inappropriate use of analysis of covariance in psychopathology research, one cannot achieve "the superficially appealing goal of 'correcting' or 'controlling for' real group differences on a potential covariate" (p. 40). At any event, correlational analyses indicated that questionnaire measures on which some of the groups differed were not significantly related ($ps > .05$) to the key dependent variable: Specificity of childhood memories. The main findings were: specificity of childhood memories correlated with the measures of depression ($r = -.10$), dissociation ($r = .02$), absorption ($r = .13$), and anxiety ($r = -.07$), and percentage of first memories retrieved from childhood that were specific correlated with the measures of depression ($r = -.16$), dissociation ($r = .00$), absorption ($r = .10$), and anxiety ($r = -.08$). Even if a variable (e.g., anxiety) differs across groups, its negligible correlation with the dependent variable (e.g., memory specificity) means that it does not pose interpretive problems as a confound. However, one measure of cognitive ability was significantly related to specificity of memory retrieval from childhood: the greater a participant's nonverbal (but not verbal) ability, the greater the proportion of childhood memories retrieved that were specific ($r = .33, p < .01$). Neither verbal nor nonverbal cognitive ability was significantly related to the percentage of first childhood memories retrieved that were specific.

TABLE 1
Means (and standard deviations) for demographic and psychometric data

Variable	Group				F	p
	Control	Contin.	Recovered	Repress.		
	M	M	M	M		
Age (3, 160)	37.6$_a$ (14.1)	37.8$_a$ (10.6)	41.4$_a$ (14.8)	42.3$_a$ (11.4)	1.61	.20
Education (3, 160)	15.4$_a$ (1.6)	14.8$_a$ (2.3)	14.9$_a$ (2.5)	15.9$_a$ (2.0)	2.15	.10
DES (3, 155)	8.0$_a$ (7.8)	17.5$_b$ (13.7)	16.2$_b$ (10.4)	19.7$_b$ (14.7)	4.74	.003
Absorption (3, 153)	14.4$_a$ (7.5)	18.1$_a$ (7.1)	19.6$_a$ (7.0)	18.0$_a$ (6.7)	2.66	.051
BDI (3, 153)	6.9$_a$ (7.4)	14.5$_{bc}$ (10.4)	11.4$_{ac}$ (7.3)	16.5$_b$ (10.3)	6.00	.001
MAS (3, 151)	5.0$_a$ (4.8)	9.3$_b$ (5.4)	8.5$_b$ (4.6)	12.5$_c$ (4.8)	11.02	.001
MC (3, 133)	16.7$_a$ (7.4)	14.6$_a$ (5.4)	15.1$_a$ (5.1)	14.1$_a$ (5.3)	.94	.43
Shipley-V (3, 159)	34.8$_a$ (4.0)	30.9$_b$ (6.6)	33.1$_a$ (5.4)	33.3$_a$ (6.3)	3.28	.02
Shipley-NV (3, 160)	17.0$_a$ (2.6)	14.0$_b$ (4.0)	14.5$_{bc}$ (4.2)	16.0$_{ac}$ (4.3)	4.74	.003

Note: Because of missing data, degrees of freedom vary. The degrees of freedom for each ANOVA are in parentheses beneath the variable heading. DES, Dissociative Experiences Scale; BDI, Beck Depression Inventory; MAS, short form of the Manifest Anxiety Scale; MC, Marlowe Crowne Social Desirability Scale; Shipley-V, verbal scale; Shipley-NV, nonverbal scale. Means sharing a subscript do not significantly differ ($ps > .05$).

longer than one day. The experimenter provided examples of memories that would and would not qualify. Participants were informed that they had up to 1 minute to recall a specific memory in response to each cue word. The responses of participants were audiotaped. Participants were told that they would be asked to date each memory after recalling it. For half of the word cues, participants were asked to retrieve a specific memory from childhood (i.e., before the age of 13), and for the remaining word cues, they were asked to retrieve a specific memory from postchildhood (i.e., after the age of 13), hereafter denoted as "adulthood".

Participants were given four practice words, one at a time, and were asked to retrieve a specific memory in response to each one. If the participant retrieved a memory that did not qualify, the experimenter asked: "Can you think of a specific memory? A specific event that happened on a particular day?" Participants were given unlimited time and prompts until each demonstrated mastery of the task by retrieving a specific memory in response to each practice word.

The experimental words were presented in random order with the restriction that positive and negative words alternated. For each word, the experimenter first presented it and then immediately told the participant from what time period the memory should be recalled. As with the practice words, the experimenter prompted the participant if the first memory retrieved was not specific. Word cues were counterbalanced across participants (e.g., a specific word cued childhood memories for half of the participants, and for adulthood memories for the remainder).

The experimenter presented each card to the participant and said the word out loud, activating a stopwatch as soon as she showed the participant the word. The experimenter terminated the trial as soon as the participant retrieved a specific memory or until 1 minute elapsed, whichever came first. The experimenter then recorded the latency to retrieve the memory, and then asked the participant to date the memory as accurately as possible.

Data reduction

The first author blindly scored the audiotapes of 10 randomly selected participants, noting whether the response was specific or not. The kappa was .92 for agreement between this rater and the experimenter (either the third or fourth author) who scored each participant's responses. Because analyses failed to reveal any significant effects ($p < .05$) involving the cue valence variable, we collapsed across valence for the analyses reported here.

We randomly selected 10 audiotaped diagnostic interviews, conducted by the second author. Blind to the diagnosis assigned by the second author, the sixth author scored participants responses for PTSD and major depression. These two raters agreed on the presence (or absence) of PTSD and of depression in each case.

For one set of analyses, we coded a response as specific if the participant retrieved a specific memory within the 60 second time limit, regardless of whether the experimenter had to prompt the participant to be specific after he or she initially retrieved a nonspecific ("overgeneral") memory. This dependent variable reflects inability to retrieve a specific memory, at least within the time period permitted.

We also reanalysed our data in terms of the proportion of first memories that were retrieved that were specific. Although this dependent variable does not tap inability to retrieve a specific memory, it is often sensitive to psychopathology.

We were able to rescore the data because we had audiotaped the responses of our participants. Audiotapes were unavailable for several participants, making it impossible for us to code first responses (e.g., the participant's voice was inaudible). Accordingly, the numbers of participants for this second set of analyses were: continuous ($n = 64$), repressed ($n = 35$), recovered ($n = 29$), and control ($n = 23$).

RESULTS

Proportion of specific memories retrieved

A 4 (Group: Control, Continuous, Recovered, Repressed) × 2 (Time Period: Childhood, Adulthood) ANOVA revealed the following effects: Group, $F(3, 160) = 2.72, p = .047$, effect size eta = .22; Time Period, $F(1, 160) = 26.05, p < .0001, r = .37$; Group × Time Period, $F(3, 160) = 2.35, p = .08$, eta = .21.

Post hoc analyses (Least-Significant Differences method) on the effect of group revealed that the control group retrieved proportionately more specific memories ($M = 0.94, SD = 0.07$) than did the repressed memory group ($M = 0.84, SD = 0.19; p < .05$). The data for the recovered and continuous memory groups were ($M = 0.90, SD = 0.14$) and ($M = 0.88, SD = 0.13$), respectively. There were no other significant effects.

The significant effect of time period emerged because all groups found it easier to retrieve specific memories from adulthood than from childhood. Because predictions concerned childhood, we reanalysed the data separately for adulthood and childhood. Whereas an ANOVA revealed no significant differences among the groups for adulthood memories, $F(3, 160) = 1.17, p = .32$, differences did emerge for childhood memories, $F(3, 160) = 3.35, p = .02$, eta = .24. Post hoc Least-Significant Differences tests ($ps < .05$) revealed that the repressed memory group retrieved fewer specific memories than did the recovered memory group ($M = 0.77, SD = 0.25$ vs. $M = 0.89, SD = 0.18$) and the control group ($M = 0.91, SD = 0.09$). The data for the continuous group were ($M = 0.84, SD = 0.18$).

Collapsing across groups and time periods, we found no difference between participants who qualified for PTSD ($n = 35$) vs. those who did not ($n = 114$) in terms of the proportion of memories that were specific (90% vs. 88%). The same held true for those who qualified for major depression ($n = 11$) vs. those who did not ($n = 141$): 87% vs. 89%.

Proportion of first memories retrieved that were specific

A 4 (Group) × 2 (Time Period) ANOVA revealed the following effects: Group, $F(3, 147) = 2.27, p = .083$, eta = .21; Time Period, $F(1, 147) = 16.41, p < .0001, r = .32$; Group × Time Period, $F(3, 147) = 0.92, p = .44$.

Post hoc analyses (Least-Significant Differences) on the near-significant effect of group revealed that the control group provided proportionately more first memories that were specific ($M = 0.84$, $SD = 0.13$) than did the repressed memory group ($M = 0.73$, $SD = 0.21$; $p = .02$) and the continuous memory group ($M = 0.74$, $SD = 0.18$; $p = .03$). The data for the recovered memory group were ($M = 0.78$, $SD = 0.17$).

The significant effect of time period emerged because all groups found it easier to retrieve specific memories from adulthood than from childhood. Because predictions concerned childhood, we reanalysed the data separately for adulthood and childhood. An ANOVA revealed no significant differences among the groups for adulthood memories, $F(3, 147) = 1.01$, $p = .39$, and a near-significant difference for childhood memories, $F(3, 147) = 2.62$, $p = .052$. Post hoc analyses indicated that the control group ($M = 0.82$, $SD = 0.17$) provided proportionately more first memories that were specific compared to the continuous memory ($M = 0.70$, $SD = 0.21$) and repressed memory ($M = 0.67$, $SD = 0.26$) groups. The data for the recovered memory group were ($M = 0.76$, $SD = 0.23$).

Collapsing across groups and time periods, we found no difference between participants who either qualified for PTSD ($n = 32$) or did not ($n = 105$) in the proportion of first memories retrieved that were specific (75% vs. 78%). The same held true for those who qualified for major depression ($n = 8$) vs. those who did not ($n = 132$), 70% vs. 78%.

DISCUSSION

The results did not indicate clear-cut, consistent patterns of deficits for retrieving specific memories, even for childhood, across all three groups reporting a history of CSA. Although the control group was always numerically superior to the other groups, this difference was often not statistically significant. The repressed memory group did, however, tend to experience the greatest difficulty retrieving specific memories from childhood. However, although the repressed memory group performed consistently and significantly worse than the control group in terms of retrieving specific memories from childhood, the repressed memory group was not always *significantly* worse than the other groups in terms of memory specificity.

Previous research on deficits in retrieving specific autobiographical memories among adults reporting CSA has been inconsistent. Some studies have detected this deficit (e.g., Dalgleish et al., 2003; Kuyken & Brewin, 1995), whereas others have not (e.g., Arntz, Meeren, & Wessel, 2002; Hermans et al., 2004; Wessel, Meeren, Peeters, Arntz, & Merckelbach, 2001).

Deficits in retrieving specific memories are more common in trauma-exposed individuals with PTSD than in trauma-exposed individuals without PTSD, at least among war veterans (e.g., McNally, Litz, Prassas, Shin, & Weathers,

1994). Yet in the present study, we found no hint of greater deficits in participants reporting CSA who had PTSD (or depression) vs. those without PTSD (or depression). On the other hand, although sexual abuse and combat trauma are both deemed traumatic stressors, they may have different effects on cognitive functioning.

Finally, although the repressed memory group tended to experience the greatest difficulty retrieving specific memories, it is unclear whether individuals in this group had actually been abused during childhood. Lacking memories of abuse, they inferred a (repressed) trauma history from a diverse range of symptoms they had been experiencing. In an apparent effort to make sense of their difficulties, they hypothesised that they must have been abused but could not remember it. Although popular books for incest survivors emphasise that many kinds of psychological phenomena and psychiatric symptoms, including difficulty remembering one's past, may indicate the presence of inaccessible memories of CSA (e.g., Blume, 1990, pp. xviii–xxi), this is a hazardous and unfounded assumption (McNally, 2003, pp. 100–104).

REFERENCES

Arntz, A., Meeren, M., & Wessel, I. (2002). No evidence for overgeneral memories in borderline personality disorder. *Behaviour Research and Therapy*, *40*, 1063–1068.

Beck, A. T., & Steer, R. A. (1987). *Beck depression inventory manual*. San Antonio, TX: Psychological Corporation.

Bendig, A. W. (1956). The development of a short form of the Manifest Anxiety Scale. *Journal of Consulting Psychology*, *20*, 384.

Bernstein, E. M., & Putnam, F. W. (1986). Development, reliability, and validity of a dissociation scale. *Journal of Nervous and Mental Disease*, *174*, 727–735.

Blume, E. S. (1990). *Secret survivors: Uncovering incest and its aftereffects in women*. New York: Wiley.

Clancy, S. A., & McNally, R. J. (in press). Who needs repression? Normal memory processes can explain "forgetting" of childhood sexual abuse. *Scientific Review of Mental Health Practice*.

Crowne, D. P., & Marlowe, D. A. (1960). A new scale of social desirability independent of psychopathology. *Journal of Consulting Psychology*, *24*, 349–354.

Dalgleish, T., Tchanturia, K., Serpell, L., Hems, S., Yiend, J., de Silva, P., & Treasure, J. (2003). Self-reported parental abuse relates to autobiographical memory style in patients with eating disorders. *Emotion*, *3*, 211–222.

First, M. B., Spitzer, R. L., Gibbon, M., & Williams, J. B. W. (1996). *Structured clinical interview for DSM-IV Axis I disorders (SCID-I)*. New York: Biometrics Research Department, New York State Psychiatric Institute.

Foa, E. B., & Tolin, D. F. (2000). Comparison of the PTSD Symptom Scale-Interview Version and the Clinician-Administered PTSD Scale. *Journal of Traumatic Stress*, *13*, 181–191.

Harvey, M. R., & Herman, J. L. (1994). Amnesia, partial amnesia, and delayed recall among adult survivors of childhood trauma. *Consciousness and Cognition*, *3*, 295–306.

Hermans, D., van den Broeck, K., Belis, G., Raes, F., Pieters, G., & Eelen, P. (2004). Trauma and autobiographical memory specificity in depressed inpatients. *Behaviour Research and Therapy*, *42*, 775–789.

Kuyken, W., & Brewin, C. R. (1995). Autobiographical memory functioning in depression and reports of early abuse. *Journal of Abnormal Psychology, 104*, 585–591.

Loewenstein, R. J. (1991). An office mental status examination for complex chronic dissociative symptoms and multiple personality disorder. *Psychiatric Clinics of North America, 14*, 567–604.

McNally, R. J. (2003). *Remembering trauma*. Cambridge, MA: Belknap Press/Harvard University Press.

McNally, R. J., Clancy, S. A., Barrett, H. M., & Parker, H. A. (2004). Inhibiting retrieval of trauma cues in adults reporting histories of childhood sexual abuse. *Cognition and Emotion, 18*, 479–493.

McNally, R. J., Litz, B. T., Prassas, A., Shin, L. M., & Weathers, F. W. (1994). Emotional priming of autobiographical memory in post-traumatic stress disorder. *Cognition and Emotion, 8*, 351–367.

Miller, G. A., & Chapman, J. P. (2001). Misunderstanding analysis of covariance. *Journal of Abnormal Psychology, 110*, 40–48.

Tellegen, A., & Atkinson, G. (1974). Openness to absorbing and self-altering experiences ("absorption"), a trait related to hypnotic susceptibility. *Journal of Abnormal Psychology, 83*, 268–277.

Wessel, I., Meeren, M., Peeters, F., Arntz, A., & Merckelbach, H. (2001). Correlates of autobiographical memory specificity: The role of depression, anxiety and childhood trauma. *Behaviour Research and Therapy, 39*, 409–421.

Williams, J. M. G., & Broadbent, K. (1986). Autobiographical memory in suicide attempters. *Journal of Abnormal Psychology, 95*, 144–149.

Zachary, R. A. (1991). *Shipley Institute of Living Scale* (Revised). Los Angeles: Western Psychological Services.

Autobiographical memory deficits in schizophrenia

Nikki Wood and Chris R. Brewin
University College London, UK

Hamish J. McLeod
University of Wollongong, Australia

This study investigated autobiographical memory processes in a group of individuals diagnosed with schizophrenia and matched controls. The schizophrenia group displayed an overgeneral style of autobiographical memory retrieval on two widely used measures, and displayed problems retrieving both autobiographical facts and events. They showed a specific impairment in the recall of autobiographical events and facts in early adulthood, around the time of onset of their illness. Retrieval deficits were independent of mood state and premorbid intellectual functioning. The magnitude of the deficits in autobiographical memory retrieval specificity were considerably greater than any general impairments in episodic and working memory.

Autobiographical memory is considered to serve functions related to the continuity of the self (Wilson & Ross, 2003), to the development and maintenance of relationships with others (Cohen, 1998; Nelson, 2003), and to problem solving (Pillemer, 2003). Disturbances of all of these functions have been reported in people with schizophrenia (Falloon, 2000; Garety, Kuipers, Fowler, Freeman, & Bebbington, 2001; Hemsley, 1998; Mills, 2001), but the degree to which autobiographical memory biases and deficits contribute to or interact with the symptoms of schizophrenia is still under investigation. Various authors have suggested that autobiographical memory disturbances contribute to the symptoms of schizophrenia (Baddeley, Thornton, Chua, & McKenna, 1996; Feinstein, Goldberg, Nowlin, & Weinberger, 1998: Riutort, Cuervo, Danion, Peretti, & Salamie, 2003) but have not established whether this is a specific deficit, is attributable to comorbid depression, or is part of the general long-term memory impairment seen in people with schizophrenia (Elvevag & Goldberg, 2000; McKay et al., 1996).

Autobiographical memory (AM) includes personal semantic memory, (knowledge of personal facts, e.g., "where I went to school"), and episodic

---

Correspondence should be addressed to Nikki Wood, Institute of Neurology, University College London, Queen Square, London WC1N 3BG, UK. Email: N.Wood@ion.ucl.ac.uk

memory, (e.g., recall of a specific event, such as one's first day at school). Deficits in episodic memory manifest as overgeneral retrieval, where an individual instructed to recall an event that happened at a specific place and time instead recalls extended events or categories of repeated events. This retrieval style is common in depressed people (van Vreeswijk & de Wilde, 2004; Williams, 1996). Such a deficit in people with schizophrenia might partly explain the maintenance of delusional beliefs because of a failure to reliably recall specific personal episodic information that contradicts the delusion. This type of retrieval failure has been posed to explain the maintenance of bizarre beliefs in other populations, such as confabulating patients who have suffered neurological damage (Burgess & Shallice, 1996; Moscovitch & Melo, 1997).

Tamlyn et al. (1992) used the Autobiographical Memory Interview (AMI; Kopelman, Wilson, & Baddeley, 1990) to study four people with schizophrenia. This structured interview provides standard prompts for eliciting examples of specific personal events and facts from three time periods. Tamlyn et al. reported that participants with schizophrenia displayed overgeneral autobiographical memory for childhood, early adult life, and the recent past. Feinstein et al. (1998) also observed an overgeneral retrieval style in their sample of people with schizophrenia ($n = 19$). In contrast to the Tamlyn et al. study, their sample exhibited a strong U-shaped temporal gradient for personal facts, with the recall being poorest for the early adult period, and childhood memories being the best preserved. Feinstein et al. (1998) concluded that these deficits were noteworthy as they corresponded to the onset period of psychosis and suggest that little memory for this period was retrievable. They attributed this to a disruption of the normal processes of encoding or consolidation in the acute period of illness.

More recently, Riutort et al. (2003) investigated autobiographical memory specificity in a group of 24 patients diagnosed with schizophrenia and a matched healthy control group. The participants with schizophrenia exhibited impairment in the recall of both autobiographical facts and events in comparison with the control group, and produced fewer specific memories. They concluded that the retrieval deficits were most apparent after the onset of illness and suggested that this reflected a deficit of encoding. The authors linked this finding with Conway and Pleydell-Pearce's (2000) model of autobiographical memory and suggested that the time of onset of illness may be a period when the encoding and consolidation of memories and information relating to the self is impaired, thus leading to a breakdown in the development of personal identity. However, a limitation of their study is that the schizophrenia group had a significantly lower full-scale IQ.

The potential link between AM deficits and delusional thinking has been examined in a small number of studies. Baddeley et al. (1996) used the AMI to examine five deluded and five nondeluded participants diagnosed with schizophrenia. They found that both groups were normal in their ability to recall autobiographical facts, but that the nondeluded group showed significantly worse recall of autobiographical events and displayed an overgeneral retrieval style for all time periods. Following this, Kaney, Bowen-Jones, and Bentall (1999) compared AM retrieval specificity in 20 individuals who met criteria for delusional disorder, with 20 depressed and 20 healthy control subjects. The deluded participants recalled more general memories and fewer specific memories than the control subjects.

The understanding of AM retrieval in people with schizophrenia will be advanced by studies with larger samples and attention to potential confounding variables. Previous findings suggest that individuals with schizophrenia do exhibit an overgeneral retrieval style for personal events but data on the temporal gradient of these deficits is inconsistent. Moreover, it is unclear whether AM retrieval deficits are correlates of schizophrenia or are related to comorbid depression or general memory impairments. The current study attempts to address some of these issues. We investigated AM retrieval in people with schizophrenia and determined the temporal gradient of their recall of both personal events and personal facts. A healthy control sample was matched at the group level for age, education level, and premorbid IQ and measures of depression and general memory ability were administered to investigate the influence of potential confounding factors.

METHOD

Participants

Twenty patients (14 men, 6 women) with a chart diagnosis of chronic schizophrenia (American Psychiatric Association, 1994) were recruited from the nine long-term rehabilitation or low secure forensic rehabilitation psychiatric inpatient wards at two North London Hospitals. All were currently symptomatic and experiencing at least one positive psychotic symptom. Exclusion criteria for the study included a history of organic brain disease, epilepsy, head injury, or the use of ECT within the past year. Subjects were also excluded if they had a comorbid diagnosis of a personality disorder or depression, met criteria for substance abuse or dependence, or showed levels of disorganisation or negative symptoms that precluded completion of the tasks. The mean age of onset of symptoms, defined as the first psychiatric consultation or hospitalisation was 20.6 years ($SD = 4.33$, range = 16–33) and the mean duration of illness was 17.3 years ($SD = 7.73$). All participants were medicated.

The control group consisted of 20 healthy participants (14 men, 6 women) who had no known history of mental illness, and were not intoxicated at the time of testing (no consumption of alcohol or drugs in the last 8 hours). None were taking prescribed medication. The groups were matched on age, gender, number of years in education, and estimated premorbid Full Scale IQ measured with the National Adult Reading Test (NART; Nelson & Willison, 1991) (see Table 1).

TABLE 1
Mean performance (and standard deviations) on neuropsychological and depression measures of patients with schizophrenia and controls

Measures	Schizophrenia group	Control group	t(38)
Age	37.9 (9.04)	34.8 (12.53)	<1
Years of Education	14.75 (3.37)	14.1 (3.08)	<1
Forward Digit Span	5.9 (.97)	6.55 (.99)	−2.09*
Backwards Digit Span	4.1 (.85)	4.65 (.93)	−1.95*
Immediate Story Recall	28.65 (10.65)	34.45 (7.43)	−2.00*
Delayed Story Recall	25.96 (10.79)	31.6 (8.64)	−1.83*
BDI	12.65 (11.41)	7.9 (5.29)	1.67
NART	102.6 (11.53)	107.3 (9.95)	−1.38

* $p < .05$ (one-tailed).

Measures

Autobiographical Memory Interview (AMI: Kopelman et al., 1990). This test provides an overall estimate of remote memory function and provides information about the retrieval over time. Participants are asked to recall specific incidents and autobiographical facts from three time bands: childhood, early adulthood, and the very recent past. Specific personal events are scored for descriptive richness of the recollection and its specificity in time and place. The personal semantic schedule assesses the ability to recall facts, such as home address and names of friends or colleagues. Interrater reliability reported in the AMI manual (Kopelman et al., 1990) ranges from 0.83 to 0.86 and previous studies (e.g., Brewin & Stokou, 2002) found interrater reliability to be good (89%, weighted kappa = 0.73).

When it was not clear whether a memory was delusional, the patient's case notes and psychiatric reports were reviewed and staff members who knew the patient were consulted. It was normally clear when a memory was delusional (e.g., "I was a fighter pilot in the US Armed Forces" or "I was kidnapped and forced to pull huskies in Alaska"), and in such circumstances the response was scored as '0'.

Autobiographical Memory Test (AMT: Williams and Broadbent, 1986). Participants generate a specific memory detailing an event which can be located in time and place in response to positive and negative cue words. Participants were given three practice words (enjoy, friendly, and bold). Once they were able to perform the task, six positive words (happy, proud, relieved, pleased, excited, and hopeful) and six negative words (miserable, guilty, angry, insecure, lazy, and uncomfortable) were presented in a randomised order. The cue words were taken from previous studies using this paradigm (Brittlebank,

Scott, Williams, & Ferrier, 1993; Kaney et al., 1999) and the subjects were allowed up to 30 seconds to produce a response. The participants were presented with each word verbally and visually (on a 10 cm × 30 cm card) and were asked "Can you tell me of something that has happened to you that you are reminded of when you see the word...?". When it was not clear whether the initial response referred to a specific event the examiner provided the standard prompt from Williams' (unpublished) procedures: "Can you think of a particular time?".

A response was coded "specific" if it was a single event, located in time and place and lasting no more than a day in duration. Overgeneral responses were coded as either "categoric" (multiple occurrences of the same event) or "extended" (a single event lasting more than one day and having a definite beginning and end). Kaney et al.'s (1999) further category of "uninterpretable" was used for any responses that were clearly delusional in nature or that did not qualify as the recall of a memory. Responses were timed and responses were audiotaped for all but one participant who refused. The responses of 10 participants from each group were randomly selected and independently rated using the protocol described above. There was good agreement between ratings made by the interviewer and the independent rater (88.33% agreement, Cohen's kappa = .82).

National Adult Reading Test (NART; Nelson & Willison, 1991). The NART is a 50-item word pronunciation task that is widely used to provide an estimate of expected premorbid IQ as assessed with the Wechsler Adult Intelligence Scale-Revised (WAIS-R; Wechsler, 1981).

Beck Depression Inventory (BDI-II; Beck, 1996). This is a widely used 21-item self-rated measure of depression with excellent reliability (Beck, 1996).

Digit Span. This subtest of the Wechsler Adult Intelligence Scale (WAIS-III: Wechsler, 1999) is a widely used measure of auditory short-term working memory and attention.

Story Recall. This subtest from the Adult Memory and Information Processing Battery (AMIPB; Coughlan & Hollows, 1985) involves participants being read a short story which they are then asked to recall in as much detail as possible immediately and after a delay of between 27 and 35 minutes.

RESULTS

Demographic, clinical, and memory characteristics of the two samples are presented in Table 1. There were no significant group differences in age, gender, education, depression, or premorbid full-scale IQ. The two groups were found to differ on digit span forward, digit span backward, and immediate and delayed recall, with the schizophrenia group performing worse. A repeated-measures ANOVA on the four memory measures indicated that there was a significant main group effect, $F(1, 38) = 4.28$, $p < .05$, partial eta-squared = .10.

Autobiographical Memory Interview

The scores of the schizophrenia and control groups on the three different time periods for personal facts and events are presented in Table 2.

Personal facts. A 2 (Group) × 3 (Time Period) mixed-model ANOVA on recall of personal facts was conducted. There was a significant main effect for Group, $F(1, 38) = 140.29$, $p < .001$, partial eta-squared = .79, a main effect for time period, $F(2, 76) = 15.08$, $p < .001$, and a significant interaction between Group and Time Period, $F(2, 76) = 8.40$, $p < .001$. Post hoc tests showed that the groups were significantly different in each time period (all $ps < .001$). The schizophrenia group exhibited a U-shaped temporal gradient, with performance being significantly worse in early adulthood than in either of the other time periods (both $ps < .001$). Recall from recent times was significantly better than that from childhood ($p < .001$). The control group recall did not differ between time periods, all $ps > .05$.

Personal events. A 2 (Group) × 3 (Time Period) mixed-model ANOVA on recall of personal events was conducted. There was a significant main effect for group, $F(1, 38) = 97.01$, $p < .001$, partial eta-squared = .72, a significant effect for Time period, $F(2, 76) = 9.58$, $p < .001$, and a significant Group × Time Period interaction, $F(2, 76) = 5.23$, $p < .01$. Significant group differences were found for each time period (all $ps < .001$). The schizophrenia group were found to recall significantly more recent events than events in childhood, $t(19) = -2.97$, $p < .01$, or early adulthood, $t(19) = -3.69$, $p < .01$. No significant

TABLE 2
Mean Autobiographical Memory Interview performance (and standard deviations) in patients with schizophrenia and normal controls

	Childhood	Early adulthood	Recent
Personal facts			
Schizophrenia group	12.55 (3.89)	10.83 (4.74)	15.9 (2.51)
Control group	19.38 (1.21)	20.33 (0.73)	20.87 (0.32)
Personal events			
Schizophrenia group	4.65 (2.37)	4.3 (2.32)	6.35 (1.72)
Control group	8.3 (1.18)	8.9 (3.08)	9 (0)

differences were found between recall of autobiographical events in childhood and those in early adulthood. The control group recall did not differ between time periods, all $ps > .05$. Within the schizophrenia group total scores on autobiographical events and autobiographical facts were not significantly correlated, $r(19) = .33, p > .05$.

Autobiographical Memory Test

Recall data. A 2 (Group) × 2 (Valence) × 4 (Memory Type) ANOVA was conducted on the AMT data presented in Table 3. The analysis showed there was a significant main effect for Memory Type, $F(3, 114) = 54.86, p < .001$, but no significant main effects for Valence, $F(1, 38) < 1$, or Group, $F(1, 38) < 1$. There was a significant Group × Memory Type interaction, $F(3, 114) = 60.43, p < .001$, partial eta-squared = .61, but no other interactions involving Group were significant, largest $F < 1$. Post hoc tests showed that the schizophrenia group produced significantly fewer specific memories than the control group, significantly more categorical memories, and significantly more responses that were considered "uninterpretable" (all $ps < .001$). The groups did not differ on the proportion of extended memories ($p > .05$). Within the schizophrenia group a significant positive correlation was observed between the proportion of specific events recalled on the AMT and the total number of autobiographical events recalled on the AMI, $r(19) = .61, p < .01$, but not with the number of personal facts recalled, $r(19) = .30, p > .05$.

Response latency. The average time to the first response for the schizophrenia group was 7.85 s ($SD = 3.05$), compared to 14.53 s ($SD = 4.53$)

TABLE 3
Mean percentage of responses on the Autobiographical Memory Test (and standard deviations)

Type of memory produced	Schizophrenia group			Control group		
	Positive cue words	Negative cue words	Total	Positive cue words	Negative cue words	Total
Specific	28.33	20.00	22.9	84.17	75.83	80
	(24.24)	(21.38)	(19.5)	(13.75)	(13.76)	(10.3)
Categorical	34.17	45.83	40.1	5.83	7.50	6.7
	(20.57)	(23.49)	(18.46)	(9.78)	(10.08)	(6.4)
Extended	10.83	12.50	11.7	6.67	14.16	10.4
	(11.18)	(15.17)	(9.53)	(9.97)	(12.41)	(8.5)
Uninterpretable	26.67	21.67	25.3	3.33	2.51	2.9
	(24.42)	(24.24)	(20.5)	(6.84)	(6.11)	(5.6)

for the controls. The schizophrenia group responded more quickly than the control group to both positive cue words, $t(38) = 4.18, p < .001$, and negative cue words, $t(38) = 5.61, p < .001$. Within the schizophrenia and control groups there was no significant difference in the response latency to positive and negative cue words, $t(19) = -1.40, p > .10$ and $t(19) = 0.52, p = .62$, respectively.

DISCUSSION

The results presented here are consistent with previous findings that schizophrenia is associated with impaired memory for autobiographical facts and events. By using a carefully matched control group, we were able to show that these deficits are unlikely to be due to differences in premorbid IQ or depression. Although we cannot rule out the possibility that the AM retrieval impairments are due to general memory problems, the magnitude of the differences in AM scores, as reflected by eta-squared, was considerably greater than that of the general memory measures. Also, the finding that the schizophrenia group recalled significantly fewer specific memories than the control group on the AMT is consistent with previous research (Kaney et al., 1999; Riutort et al., 2003). Interestingly, they were significantly faster in producing a first response in comparison to the control subjects. One interpretation is that the memory retrieval process was aborted prematurely, possibly reflecting a general deficit of response inhibition.

Retrieval on the AMI is divided into recall of autobiographical facts and autobiographical events. The schizophrenia group in this study recalled fewer facts and events for childhood, early adulthood and recent time periods with poorest recall in the early adult period. This is consistent with Feinstein et al.'s (1998) description of a U-shaped temporal gradient of recall for autobiographical facts possibly attributable to disruption of encoding and consolidation processes around the onset of illness. Such a deficit in early adulthood was less pronounced for the recall of autobiographical events, with both childhood and early adulthood time periods being significantly impaired, and this was found to be the case in the current study. In contrast, Riutort et al. (2003) did not find a U-shaped temporal gradient of recall of autobiographical facts or events but did find that impairments in recall were most apparent after the onset of illness.

The findings from this study suggest that there are significant disruptions in the process of encoding or retrieval for memories formed around late adolescence and early adulthood. Recent neurodevelopmental models of schizophrenia suggest that cognitive impairments appear before the onset of clinical symptoms (Harrison, 1997; Raedler, Knable, & Weinberger, 1998) and the mean age of illness onset in the current study (20.6 years) is consistent with this proposition. However, this does not explain the global impairment of recall for events from childhood and early adulthood time periods in the current study. This suggests that there are encoding deficits which are present from a very early age that remain stable even around the time of onset of illness. Instead, it may be that disruption of retrieval processes contributes most to AM deficits.

Conway and Pleydell-Pearce (2000) and Riutort et al. (2003) have suggested that late adolescence and early adulthood, in particular, is a time when autobiographical knowledge is being acquired, organised, and consolidated to form a coherent personal identity. Disruptions in AM processes around the time of onset of illness are likely to have a negative impact on the development of self, at a lifetime stage that Erikson (1966) hypothesised to be crucial in the development of identity or identity confusion. Conway and Holmes (2004) have recently argued that the goals of the self play a major role in both the encoding and accessibility of autobiographical memories and that in normal populations, memories from adolescence or early adulthood were generally reflective of themes relating to identity and intimacy.

Disturbances in the concept of the self are believed to contribute to the inner-outer confusion that has been considered to be a major factor in the development of psychotic symptoms (Fowler, 2000; Freeman, Garety, Kuipers, Fowler, & Bebbington, 2002), and leads to the attribution of internal events to an external source (Bentall, 1990; Frith, 1992). Fowler (2000) has suggested that the inner-outer confusion which he believes characterises psychosis, may arise from a catastrophic interaction between basic neurocognitive impairments in the domains of perception, and belief, appraisals, and emotional biases. Hemsley (1993) has suggested that disturbances in the moment-to-moment integration of stored regularities may be associated with disruptions in self-monitoring of intentions and actions. It is suggested here that the concept of the working self, which contains information about current goals and intentions, is a useful framework for understanding how such a process may develop. If anomalies in perceptual processes lead to the destabilisation of the working self, possibly through the mechanism of unexpected experiences that would not be predicted by the working self, then it is plausible to assume that confusion may arise about what intentions and goals should be held and maintained.

The ability to retrieve specific autobiographical memories may also serve social functions as sharing autobiographical memories develops bonds with others and facilitates learning about the intentions and experiences of others (Nelson, 2003; Pillemer, 1998). Corcoran, Mercer, and Frith (1995) have argued that aspects of theory of mind, such as making mental state inferences, involves reference to specific autobiographical memories of ones own mental processes in similar circumstances, from which the individual infers that similar processes operate in others. Problems with retrieval may then contribute to an individual's problems in forming relationships and learning about others. Bentall, Corcoran, Howard, and Blackwood (2001) have also hypothesised that theory of mind deficits in people with psychosis may be linked to a biased retrieval of events from autobiographical memory.

Autobiographical memory retrieval specificity might also serve directive functions (Pillemer, 2003) in that efficient problem solving may be reliant on the satisfactory retrieval of specific memories to provide a database from which to construct solutions to real life problems. This might help to explain the problem-solving deficits often found in psychotic individuals (Addington & Addington, 2000) and may have an impact on an individual's ability to cope with their symptoms (Tarrier et al., 1993).

Although the memory deficits observed here do not seem to be attributable to group differences in premorbid intellectual functioning we cannot exclude the possibility that the effects are mediated by current general intellectual impairment. Future studies could incorporate measures of both premorbid and current intellectual capacities. Our conclusions are also constrained by the absence of structured symptom assessment data. However, the current findings suggest that further investigation of AM retrieval specificity in people with schizophrenia is warranted and will potentially elucidate a number of features of this complex disorder.

REFERENCES

Addington, J., & Addington, D. (2000). Neurocognitive and social functioning in schizophrenia: A 2.5 year follow up study. *Schizophrenia Research, 44,* 47–56.

American Psychiatric Association. (1994). *Diagnostic and statistical manual of mental disorders* (4th ed.). Washington, DC: Author.

Baddeley, A., Thornton, A., Chua, S. E., & McKenna, P. (1996). Schizophrenic delusions and the construction of autobiographical memory. In D. Rubin (Ed.), *Remembering our past: Studies in autobiographical memory* (pp. 384–427). Cambridge, UK: Cambridge University Press.

Beck, A. T. (1996). *The Beck Depression Inventory-II.* San Antonio, TX: Harcourt Brace.

Bentall, R. P. (1990). The syndromes and symptoms of psychosis: Or why you can't play twenty questions with the concept of schizophrenia and hope to win. In R. P. Bentall (Ed.), *Reconstructing schizophrenia* (pp. 23–60). London: Routledge.

Bentall, R. P., Corcoran, R., Howard, R., & Blackwood, N. (2001). Persecutory delusions: A review and theoretical integration. *Clinical Psychology Review, 21,* 1143–1192.

Brewin, C. R., & Stokou, L. (2002). Validating reports of poor childhood memory. *Applied Cognitive Psychology, 16,* 509–514.

Brittlebank, A., Scott, J., Williams, J. M. G., & Ferrier, I. (1993). Autobiographical memory in depression: state or trait marker? *British Journal of Psychiatry, 162,* 118–121.

Burgess, P., & Shallice, T. (1996). Confabulation and the control of recollection. *Memory, 4,* 359–411.

Cohen, G. (1998). The effects of ageing on autobiographical memory. In C. Thomson, D. Herrman, D. Bruce, J. Read, D. Payne, & M. Toglia (Eds.), *Autobiographical memory: Theoretical and applied perspectives* (pp. 105–124). Mahwah, NJ: Erlbaum.

Conway, M., & Holmes, A. (2004). Psychosocial stages and the accessibility of autobiographical memories across the life cycle. *Journal of Personality, 72,* 461–480.

Conway, M., & Pleydell-Pearce, C.W. (2000). The construction of autobiographical memories in the self-memory system. *Psychological Review, 107,* 261–288.

Corcoran, R., Mercer, G., & Frith, C. (1995). Schizophrenia, symptomatology, and social inference: Investigating 'theory of mind' in people with schizophrenia. *Schizophrenia Research, 17,* 5–13.

Coughlan, A., & Hollows, S. (1985). *Adult memory and information processing battery.* Leeds, UK: St James University Hospital.

Elvevag, B., & Goldberg, T. (2000). Cognitive impairment in schizophrenia is the core of the disorder. *Critical Reviews in Neurobiology, 14,* 1–21.

Erikson, E. (1966). The eight ages of man. *International Journal of Psychiatry, 2,* 281–300.

Falloon, I. R. (2000). Problem solving as a core strategy in the prevention of schizophrenia and other mental disorders. *Australian and New Zealand Journal of Psychiatry, 34,* 185–190.

Feinstein, A., Goldberg, T., Nowlin, B., & Weinberger, D. (1998). Types and characteristics of remote memory impairment in schizophrenia. *Schizophrenia Research, 30,* 155–163.

Fowler, D. (2000). Psychological formulation of early episodes of psychosis: A cognitive model. In M. Birchwood, D. Fowler, & C. Jackson (Eds.), *Early intervention in psychosis: A guide to concepts, evidence and interventions* (pp. 101–127). Chichester, UK: Wiley.

Freeman, D., Garety, P., Kuipers, E., Fowler, D., & Bebbington, P. (2002). A cognitive model of persecutory delusions. *British Journal of Clinical Psychology, 41,* 331–347.

Frith, C. D. (1992). *The cognitive neuropsychology of schizophrenia.* Hove, UK: Psychology Press.

Garety, P., Kuipers, E., Fowler, D., Freeman, D., & Bebbington, P. (2001). A cognitive model of the positive symptoms of psychosis. *Psychological Medicine, 31,* 189–196.

Harrison, P. J. (1997). Schizophrenia: A disorder of neurodevelopment? *Current Opinion in Neurobiology, 7,* 285–289.

Hemsley, D. (1993). A simple (or simplistic?) cognitive model of schizophrenia. *Behaviour Research and Therapy, 31,* 633–646.

Hemsley, D. (1998). The disruption of the 'sense of self' in schizophrenia: Potential links with disturbances of information processing. *British Journal of Medical Psychology, 71,* 115–124.

Kaney, S., Bowen-Jones, K., & Bentall, R. P. (1999). Persecutory delusions and autobiographical memory. *British Journal of Clinical Psychology, 38,* 97–102.

Kopelman, M. D., Wilson, B. A., & Baddeley, A. D. (1990). *Autobiographical memory inventory.* Bury St Edmunds, UK: Thames Valley Test Company.

McKay, A. P., McKenna, P. J., Bentham, P., Mortimer, A. M. M, Holbery, A., & Hodges, J.R. (1996). Semantic memory is impaired in schizophrenia. *Biological Psychiatry, 39,* 929–937.

Mills, N. (2001). The experience of fragmentation in psychosis: can mindfulness help? In I. Clarke (Ed.), *Psychosis and spirituality* (pp. 222–235). London: Whurr.

Moscovitch, M., & Melo, B. (1997). Strategic retrieval and the frontal lobes: Evidence from confabulation and amnesia. *Neuropsychologia 35,* 1017–1034.

Nelson, H. E., & Willison, J. (1991). *Restandardisation of the NART against the WAIS-R.* Windsor, UK: NFER-Nelson.

Nelson, K. (2003). Self and social functions: Individual autobiographical memory and collective narrative. *Memory, 11,* 125–136.

Pillemer, D. (1998). What is remembered about early childhood events? Development of flashbulb memories. *Clinical Psychology Review, 18,* 895–913.

Pillemer, D. (2003). Directive functions of autobiographical memory: The guiding power of the specific episode. *Memory, 11,* 193–202.

Raedler, T. J., Knable, M. B., & Weinberger, D. R. (1998). Schizophrenia as a developmental disorder of the cerebral cortex. *Current Opinion in Neurobiology, 8,* 157–161.

Riutort, M., Cuervo, C., Danion, J., Peretti, C., & Salame, P. (2003). Reduced levels of specific autobiographical memories in schizophrenia. *Psychiatry Research, 117,* 35–45.

Tamlyn, D., McKenna, P., Mortimer, A., Lund, C., Hammond, S., & Baddeley, A. (1992). Memory impairment in schizophrenia: Its extent, affiliations and neuropsychological character. *Psychological Medicine, 22,* 101–115.

Tarrier, N., Beckett, R., Harwood, S., Baker, A., Yusopoff, L., & Ugateburu, L. (1993). A trial of two cognitive–behavioural methods of treating drug-resistant residual psychotic symptoms in schizophrenic patients: I. Outcome. *British Journal of Psychiatry, 162,* 524–532.

van Vreeswijk, M. F., & de Wilde, E. J. (2004). Autobiographical memory specificity, psychopathology, depressed mood and the use of the Autobiographical Memory Test: A meta-analysis. *Behaviour Research and Therapy, 42*, 731–743.

Wechsler, D. (1981). *Wechsler Adult Intelligence Scale - Revised.* San Antonio, TX: The Psychological Corporation.

Wechsler, D. (1998). *Wechsler Adult Intelligence Scale (WAIS-III-UK)* (3rd ed.). London: Psychological Corporation.

Williams, J. M. G. (1996). Depression and the specificity of autobiographical memory. In D. Rubin (Ed.), *Remembering our past: Studies in autobiographical memory* (pp. 244–265). Cambridge, UK: Cambridge University Press.

Williams, J. M. G., & Broadbent, K. (1986). Autobiographical memory in suicide attempters. *Journal of Abnormal Psychology, 95*, 144–149.

Wilson, A., & Ross, M. (2003). The identity function of autobiographical memory: Time is on our side. *Memory, 11*, 137–150.

Capture and rumination, functional avoidance, and executive control (CaRFAX): Three processes that underlie overgeneral memory

J. Mark G. Williams
University of Oxford, UK

This article reviews the papers published in this Special Issue of *Cognition and Emotion* on Specificity in Autobiographical Memory. Together, the studies address some critical issues relating to the etiology of and mechanisms underlying the phenomenon of overgeneral memory. In terms of etiology, there is now substantial evidence of links between overgeneral memory and current or past depression, and between overgeneral memory and trauma history, and suicidal ideation and behaviour, independent of depression. In terms of mechanisms, three factors are emerging as the critical mechanisms underlying the phenomenon: *Capture and rumination* (CaR), *functional avoidance* (FA), and *executive control dysfunction* (X). Each of these has separately been found to produce overgenerality in memory; together they are almost certain to do so.

In the centre of Oxford, the main roads come together and cross each other in a busy clash of bus, taxi, and pedestrian. Here, a stone's throw from the peace of college quadrangles, everything seems hectic; everyone seems to be going somewhere fast or waiting expectantly for something to happen. The sense of busyness is heightened by the array of road signs indicating the direction you have come from and your possible destinations. Some signs are meant for cars driving through, and inform them that only one turn is possible for "All Routes". Others are for delivery vehicles and tell them what times they can enter Cornmarket. Then there are the smaller tourist signs that tell you how to get to "The Oxford Story" or the "Westgate Centre", of interest to those on foot, but irrelevant to the long-distance traveller or the van delivering soap to Boots the Chemist. Knowing where to go involves not only seeing the signs but

---

Correspondence should be addressed to Professor Mark Williams, University Department of Psychiatry, Warneford Hospital, Oxford OX3 7JX, UK; e-mail: mark.williams@psych.ox.ac.uk

Professor Williams' research is supported by the Wellcome Trust GR067797. The author wishes to thank Thorsten Barnhofer and Catherine Crane for help with this article.

© 2006 Taylor & Francis
DOI:10.1080/02699930500450465

knowing which ones apply or do not apply. Without understanding which type of sign is which, crossroads are really confusing.

Our memories are like crossroads. Our memory tells us where we have come from, and helps us plan the future. Memory provides us with a map and signposts from which we solve the problems of how to get to our destinations. Without it we would get lost: Lost in the sentence we were speaking, or in the road along which we were travelling. But we need to be skilled in knowing which aspect of memory is useful in which context. Only then will our memory orient us in the world, and help us avoid the same blind alley twice (well, sometimes). If we need a reminder of the importance of memory to who we are, we only need to see how memory loss in severe dementia affects the sufferer, and to witness the tragedy of their family gradually coming to terms with the fact that their loved one has already died in all important respects, despite their body continuing to live.

Since our memories are so critical both to cognition and to our sense of who we are, it is no surprise to find that memory is inextricably involved in emotional disorders and other mental health problems. The series of articles in this Special Issue address one aspect of autobiographical memory and mental health: The fact that when many of our patients (or others who have similar problems with past trauma or current mood), attempt to recollect personally experienced past events, they sometimes fail not because they have forgotten, but because they seem unable to specify the event in sufficient detail for it to guide them. Asking someone who is depressed what event a word such as "*happy*" reminds them of, they will often say something like "having lunch with my father every Tuesday when we both worked in London". Notice that this memory does not single out a specific event. Rather the response summarises a series of similar events, or a *category* of events.

This turns out to be only one of several ways in which people may fail to be specific in their memory. But in each case, it is as if they have come to a crossroads and read the wrong *type* of sign. They are on foot and should have read the small brown signs pointing them in all sorts of different directions, but they only read the large sign saying "All Routes". As a result, they find it difficult to navigate through their problems.

We need to be quite clear that the problem is not the presence of nonspecific memories per se: This response-type needs to be in our repertoire. If someone asks us where they can buy a loaf of bread, we need to recall where the nearest bakery is located by using our general knowledge. Such knowledge is derived from our autobiographical event memory, but abstracted in such a way that we can summarise times in the past when we have had to get to that destination. Our questioner does not want to hear about each specific visit we have made to the baker. He or she wants bread, not conversation.

On the other hand, taking account of a recent specific memory can be important and may modify our advice: One road may be blocked since an accident yesterday; or the nearest baker may have sold us a stale loaf last week. In this case, we will update our general event memory with specific episodic knowledge.

Categoric memories summarise information but lose important detail. Specific memories contain detail, but may lose the larger context. Fluent access to each memory type is required for skilful navigation through the complexities of the world, especially the interpersonal world. How can we understand what is happening when people are not specific in their memory?

Models of autobiographical memory

Conway and Pleydell-Pearce (2000) make a distinction between generative (top-down) and direct (bottom-up) retrieval. *Generative* retrieval involves the intentional, staged search that uses abstract general descriptions to help search through a hierarchy of memory representations in an iterative procedure that *searches*, *evaluates*, and *verifies* candidate (retrieval) output against an original retrieval specification (Burgess & Shallice, 1996; Norman & Bobrow, 1979). In generative retrieval, intermediate "generic" representations are seen as a critical step in searching the "hierarchy" of memory. In terms of neuropsychological mechanisms, strategic search is initiated by the brain's frontal systems that are also responsible for holding a representation of the retrieval goal in working memory, against which candidate retrieval outputs can be compared.

By contrast, *direct* retrieval is "bottom-up", and arises because some cues activate event-specific knowledge directly, and thereby set up stable patterns of activation (experienced as spontaneous and unexpected recall). Event-specific knowledge is represented over several different memory systems, particularly those subserved by posterior networks. Conway and colleagues have reviewed several electroencephalogram (EEG) studies showing a temporal progression from frontal to posterior areas as a participant elaborates the cue, sets up a retrieval plan, searches for, then holds an autobiographical memory in mind (Conway, Pleydell-Pearce, Whitecross, & Sharpe, 2003). The "experience" of recalling a specific event represents a "fusing" of the output from these frontal and posterior systems—a transitory pattern of activated specific knowledge under central control, conjoined with the initial retrieval model that was used to shape that pattern.

Overgeneral memory as truncated search

These and other data have suggested to many that nonspecific responses in autobiographical memory represent the failure of hierarchical search, with the truncation of the search resulting in an *omission*, or output of a *semantic associate* of the cue (the very first stage of iterative search) or output of an *intermediate description* that would normally be used to aid the retrieval process. According to these accounts, depressed, suicidal, or traumatised patients may access some mnemonic material early in the search (such as an "intermediate description") successfully, but stop short of a specific example. They abort the search for a specific event prematurely, a process called by Conway and Pleydell-Pearce (2000) a *dysfacilitation* of the retrieval process. After a number of failed retrieval attempts, a highly elaborated network of intermediate mnemonic information will exist. In future attempts at retrieval, an initial cue is likely to activate an intermediate description that simply activates other self-descriptions: the search moves "sideways" in the hierarchy rather than "downwards" (Barnhofer, Jong-Meyer, Kleinpass, & Nikesch, 2002). The term "mnemonic interlock" was coined to describe this phenomenon (Williams, 1996).

Two types of investigation can be done to research this phenomenon. The first is to look for *causes*. Causal questions ask what *diagnoses*, or *personality types*, or *events* or *moods* are responsible for producing overgenerality. By seeing which of these are or are not associated with the phenomenon, we can begin to narrow down its causal precursors. The second type of question investigates *mechanisms*. These ask what mechanisms in the (cognitive-affective-motivational) information-processing systems of the mind these causes act upon.

The papers in this volume address several key issues relating to *etiology* and *mechanisms*; but also address *treatment* and *methodological* issues. Let us consider each of these in turn.

ETIOLOGY

Diagnoses

Leibetseder, Rohrer, Mackinger, and Fartacek (this issue) aim to clear up an important issue about some of the first diagnostic groups that were found to show overgeneral memory: Suicidal and depressed patients (Williams & Broadbent, 1986; Williams & Scott, 1988). These early studies looked either at people who had attempted suicide, without distinguishing those who had major depression from those who did not have such a diagnosis, or they studied depressed patients without considering fully their previous suicide ideas or attempts. So we do not know whether it is specifically the suicidal aspects or the depression aspects that are responsible for overgeneral memory. In this study, patients who had made a suicide attempt and also had a diagnosis of depression were compared with patients who had made a suicide attempt but did not have a diagnosis of major depression, and also with patients with major depression who had not made a suicide attempt. These three groups were compared with healthy control patients without either a suicide attempt or a diagnosis of affective disorder. The results were clear-cut: Both a suicide attempt and a diagnosis of major depression impaired autobiographical memory specificity equally. This study is the first in this area which separates these two issues.

Another diagnostic issue is addressed by Wood, Brewin, and McLeod (this issue), who examine whether overgeneral memories occur in *schizophrenia*, and if so, whether they are due to general memory deficits or to comorbid depression. Examining memory in schizophrenia is important partly because of the association with problem-solving deficits that have been found many times (and examined in Williams et al., this issue), and also because many of the difficulties faced by such patients in discriminating between internal and external stimuli might be compounded by an inability to be specific about past episodes. Checking delusional beliefs against reality is always going to be difficult for such patients; this difficulty is going to be immense if their access to the database of past events is nonspecific.

The authors used both the Autobiographical Memory Test (AMT) and the Autobiographical Memory Interview (AMI). The latter asks participants to retrieve memories from different periods in their lives. The authors found that retrieval success differed between different lifetime periods. This raises an important issue for future research on autobiographical memory using the AMT, since the lifetime period from which one is retrieving autobiographical memories has never been a major concern within the depression AMT literature. This is because it is mostly assumed that what we are observing is a *retrieval* deficit. If the field turns again to look at possible *encoding* problems in psychopathology it will become important to specify the time periods from which to sample the memories.

Trauma

The paper by McNally and colleagues (this issue) addresses the etiological issue of the extent to which reports of childhood sexual abuse are important in overgenerality. The particular interest in this paper was not merely whether people reported abuse, but whether they had *always* remembered that they were abused, had *recovered* a memory of abuse at some point in their life, or *believed* they might have been abused but could not actually remember the event. Their hypotheses were specifically related to whether memory would be overgeneral for childhood (defined as before the age of 13). Their sampling from this time frame turned out to be significant in that there was very little difference between the groups in levels of overgenerality for *adult* memories, but the childhood memories tended to discriminate those who reported abuse from those who did not, with the most overgeneral group being those who believed that they had been abused but had no memory for it. The authors point out the difficulty of attributing overgeneral memory in this "no memory" group to abuse that must have taken place but cannot be remembered. They remind us that using current psychological phenomena to infer abuse is "a hazardous and unfounded assumption". Their paper helps us to clarify the sort of questions that need to be asked in this domain, extends existing evidence (e.g., Hermans et al., 2004) and again emphasises the value of investigating the time period from which the events are to be recalled.

Developmental perspectives

The paper by Kuyken and Howell (this issue) extends our understanding of autobiographical retrieval by examining a number of aspects of memory in depressed and nondepressed adolescents. Adolescence is, as the authors indicate, a critical time for the development of the self-concept. Particularly striking is the fact that at the outset of adolescence virtually none of the disorders we associate with adulthood are present. By the end of adolescence the prevalence rates for psychiatric disorders are equivalent to those found in adult populations. This alone provides tremendous impetus for us to look at the changes that occur during this critical time. They examined individual differences in autobiographical memories in depressed and nondepressed adolescents. The participants were between 12 and 18 years old, exactly mapping onto the time of greatest change and emergence of adult psychopathology.

They found that the depressed adolescents rated their memories as more personally important than the never-depressed adolescents, with depressed participants rehearsing their negative memories significantly more often than positive memories (with potentially important effects on ability to retrieve other memories—see Wessel and Hauer, below). The depressed adolescents were significantly less likely to report memories from the field perspective (i.e., as seen through their own eyes), a pattern that has been found to be associated with dissonance between current and past self-concept and a high degree of self-focus.

The authors suggest that memories are perhaps rated as more important by depressed adolescents because they are using them more in the service of resolving dissonance. This is an elegant and testable hypothesis. The tendency to try and resolve discrepancies by ruminating about one's problems has been found in both adolescents and adults to be a major factor in the onset and the maintenance of depression. How such rumination relates to the field/observer perspective in memory is intriguing. Of particular interest in Kuyken and Howell's data is the possibility of connecting this research domain with the research on abstract vs. experiential modes of processing (Watkins & Teasdale, 2004). Possible links between experiential modes of processing and field memories on the one hand, and between abstract modes of processing and observer memories on the other hand is ripe for investigation.[1]

---

[1] It may be of note that in the original Williams and Broadbent (1986) study, we had also looked at field/observer perspective but did not report any data in that paper because we found the test-retest reliability to be very poor indeed. That is, asking nondepressed participants to give the perspective judgement ("field" or "observer") of the *same* event 4 weeks apart yielded almost as many changes in perspective as there were stable perspectives, with the same event being rated on one occasion "field" and on the next "observer" and vice versa. We concluded that these ratings were not stable enough to be reliable enough for further investigation.

The paper by Drummond, Dritschel, Astell, O'Carroll, and Dalgleish (this issue) addresses the important issue of the specificity of memory in *children*. They rightly point out there has been much more speculation about the development of specificity in young children than there have been studies. While it seems that studies in adolescents replicate those in adults, with more depressed and dysphoric adolescents being more overgeneral than controls, nondysphoric adolescents, there are also some paradoxical effects. For example Swales, Williams, and Wood (2001) found that within their clinical sample the greater the depression and hopelessness the more specificity of the response. Drummond et al.'s paper pushes the developmental investigation into younger children, contrasting 7- to 8-year-olds with 10- to 11-year-olds. The findings for the older children matched those in adolescents and adults, with a main effect for dysphoria: Dysphoric children between 10 and 11 years old were more overgeneral than nondysphoric children.

In the younger children, however, the pattern was more complex. First, they were generally more overgeneral than the older children, consistent with an overall developmental increase in specificity over this period. But, second, there was an interaction between cue valence and dysphoria in these younger children. Nondysphoric children were more specific for positive than for negative cue words.

They suggest that dysphoria might affect positive and negative recall through different underlying mechanisms. Dysphoria might affect positive recall simply by mood congruence, that is negative mood at retrieval making access to the cues that one needs to construct a memory more difficult. They point out that if this was true, then the mood effect would be relatively autonomous, based on automatic spreading activation, and therefore less dependent on age or cognitive ability than other mechanisms. They contrast this with the impact of dysphoria on retrieval to negative cues which may be more schema-dependent. This would be consistent with the developmental trends found within their paper: The effect of dysphoria on negative recall was not observed until later in childhood, when schemata are more fully developed. Indeed, this account would be consistent, not only with schema development, but also the development of ruminative tendencies (see Barnard, Edward, Watkins, & Ramponi, below), which are more dependent on conceptual processing.

These authors were also able to show that children who were more emotion focusing (as measured by tasks assessing the extent to which children categorised images and themes on the basis of the emotion being expressed in the card) were more *specific* in their autobiographical recall. These data seem contrary to the prediction that would have been made on the basis of Williams (1996), and open the question of what later developmental changes might be brought about by such an association (see discussion of Raes, Hermans, Williams, & Eelen, below).

MECHANISMS

The paper by Barnard et al. (this issue), offers an intriguing and creative experimental investigation of specificity in memory. Previous research has shown that by reducing the degree to which depressed or dysphoric people ruminate (e.g., using distraction) one can reduce categoric recall (Watkins, Teasdale, & R.M. Williams, 2000). Other research by Watkins and Teasdale (2004) has found that it is the analytic aspect of self-focus that is associated with overgeneral retrieval. The Interacting Cognitive Subsystem (ICS) model (Teasdale & Barnard, 1993) characterises rumination as an analytic, evaluative mode of processing involving global, undifferentiated, negative self-representations. In this paper, the authors' aim is to see if increasing a process analogous to rumination will increase categoric memories and/or decrease specificity. In order to analogise rumination, they drew upon a recent analysis by Barnard (2003, 2004) which suggests that the *rate of change* associated with different levels of representation within the interacting cognitive subsystems determines the particular configuration that is in place at any particular time. According to this view, one can analogise rumination in normal people by asking them to repeatedly generate information on the same theme.

The results were fascinating: They showed that when participants were required to do a category generation task by returning to the same theme each time, they produced less specific memories to a standard set of AMT cues (and more categoric and extended memories to such cues) than in a condition in which material to be generated came from different themes from trial to trial. The second study showed that this was not true for nonself-related category generation (to do with "animals foraging", for example). They were also able to show that the results were not due to mood changes, or simply to "cue fatigue".

The authors conclude that the data is consistent with rumination-induced overgeneral memory. More than this, the results indicate *which aspect* of rumination is important. Up until now we have thought of rumination as being analytic processing about self-related material. However, in *both* conditions in (Barnard et al.) Study 1 there was analytic material which was equally self-related. What differed was that, in the critical condition, the participants were induced to *perseverate*: To repeatedly return to the same higher order theme. But not any perseveration will do: It has to be concerned with the self—at least to show its effects in *autobiographical* retrieval. (The effect of perseveration for animal themes may still be shown up on retrieval of memories concerning nonself-related material or performance on neutral tasks that nevertheless demand specific processing and that would be disadvantaged by a tendency to categorise material.)

These results provide an enormously creative perspective from which to view the autobiographical memory deficits that we wish to explain. It adds to these authors' previous data on affect-related schematic models. There is a genuine sense of cumulative science beginning to help us understand in a comprehensive way the processes that underlie specificity in memory.

Raes et al. (this issue) address the issue of affect regulation. They point out that, although the affect regulation hypothesis has been prominent in explaining why some people have overgeneral memories (in brief, the theory states that some people truncate memory search originally because specific memories contain some events that are highly aversive), it had never received direct experimental support until a study by the authors in 2003, in which students who were highly specific on the autobiographical memory test showed more affective disturbance after failure on a puzzle task. This represented the first evidence that a high degree of specificity in memory could exacerbate affect and motivate a switch to alternative mnemonic strategies (cf. Drummond et al.'s emotion focusing results). In the current study they were able to replicate this effect and additionally show that students who were low specific tended to be high repressors. Even when repression scores were covaried, however, specificity of memory still predicted the affective reaction to failure on a puzzle task.

However, this pattern of results contrasts with data from Pierre Philippot's group in Louvain who have found that *overgeneral* retrieval is associated with greater mood disturbance. So Raes et al.'s second study examines the possibility that *naturally* occurring low specificity in a student sample, that occurs mainly because of omissions, may be different from the lack of specificity that occurs in clinical or more severely dysphoric groups due to a high number of overgeneral memories. In the first case (omissions in students) it may simply be a repression effect: a truncation of a search as a functional avoidance strategy. In the second case (overgeneral memories in highly dysphoric groups), such memories (especially categoric errors) may indicate a more serious psychopathological processing style.

Consistent with the hypothesis and with Philippot's work, Raes et al. (Study 2) show that those who had been manipulated to increase retrieval of categoric memories showed more intense negative affect following failure.

This is the first study to suggest that "lack of specificity" can be different from "presence of overgeneral memory". It allows the authors to develop a developmental hypothesis for why this might come about: That initial *adaptive* attempts to regulate affect by truncating the search can lead later, and only in certain subgroups, to the development of the more psychopathological type of overgeneral (categoric) memory.

Roberts, Carlos, and Kashdan's paper (this issue) examines the individual trajectories of specificity of retrieval over 18 cue words using multilevel analysis, looking both at the linear slope and the quadratic term in the rate of change of specificity across trials. Intriguingly, they found that the general shape of the curve suggested that overgeneral memory is likely to occur over the first few trials in all participants (these were nonclinical, student participants) but then mostly fades away towards the end of the trial sequence. However, in those participants who have low self-esteem or a high degree of somatic symptoms on the Beck Depression Inventory, this effect does not apply: They continue to become more and more overgeneral as the task proceeds to the end. The fact that such an effect should occur in those with somatic symptoms is consistent with the cognitive effort hypothesis. These participants may simply be getting tired. However, the low self-esteem effect is less likely to be due to this and may instead be an effect of the mnemonic cues gradually becoming ineffective. Perhaps most nonclinical participants are able to change strategy to alternative higher order themes to renew their search for specific memories. However, those with high somatic distress or low self-esteem may perseverate in using the ineffective mnemonic strategies, producing an increasing trajectory of overgeneral memories. Second, the very return to the same thematic cues may be bringing on the low rate of change at the thematic level that induces "stuckness" at the conceptual level (Barnard et al., this issue), independently of the gradually increasing ineffectiveness of the cues. This method of analysing trial-by-trial overgenerality is highly innovative in this field and no doubt will be taken up by many researchers in the future.

The paper by Williams et al. (this issue) addresses a number of issues about the mechanisms underlying overgenerality and its consequences. A number of previous theories have explained overgenerality in terms of the point at which people exit as they are searching through a memory "hierarchy". Since the mid 1980s, this hierarchical search model of memory has been assumed, but not so often tested. In the current paper, we found that random number generation as a secondary task interfered with memory, making memory less specific, but only when participants were given difficult cues that are assumed to induce generative retrieval. In another study, we observed that whenever people were unable to give us the level of memory specified in the instructions (i.e., "be specific!" or "be general!"), then if the task was difficult they would output a memory which was higher in the hierarchy. If asked to be general and given a difficult cue, then they would tend to produce semantic associates. If asked to be specific and given a difficult cue, then they would generate categoric memories.

Together, these studies suggested that memory search is indeed hierarchical. The next question was how such truncated search would affect other variables. In previous work we and others had found *correlations* between overgeneral memory and problem solving. We wanted to see whether this effect was causal by manipulating the level of overgenerality in memory. In Studies 4 and 5 we found that problem solving was indeed affected by experimental manipulation of the level of specificity in memory, indicating a causal role for overgeneral memory in problem solving.

Wessel and Hauer (this issue) point out that several studies (though not all) have found that there is a correlation between intrusive memories of some traumatic event and the inability to recall specific autobiographical memories in other, nontraumatic, domains. Although the link between the involuntary return of traumatic memories and nonspecificity of memory has been made before, it is usually couched in terms of an affect regulation mechanism. The authors point out that it would be more parsimonious if the very intrusiveness and over-retrieval (or overrehearsal) of certain events from the past could, in itself, induce an inhibition of other related memories.[2] They suggest that the phenomenon of over-retrieval of some memories being associated with the inhibition of other related memories is reminiscent of the retrieval-induced forgetting (RIF) effect. The usual explanation for this phenomenon is that the repeated rehearsal of *some* of the items from a semantic category brings about a corresponding *inhibition* of items that would normally have been related to that semantic category but are not being rehearsed. It is as if elements of our memories suffer "sibling rivalry": One sibling pushes out another at the meal table; over time the sibling who gets less food ends up with a lower bodyweight than the unrelated guest who is not pushed aside by the sibling at all.

In two intriguing experiments, the authors show that the retrieval-induced forgetting effect can be demonstrated for autobiographical memory material. This work is a great example of pushing the boundaries of a field to examine in great detail what mechanisms underlie the phenomena of interest. Of course, they indicate a number of interesting caveats and limitations on the ability to generalise from these results. As they point out, the RIF effect is found with *voluntary* retrieval of memories, whereas the posttraumatic intrusive recall is *involuntary*. In fact, it may well not be posttraumatic intrusive recall that is the most closely analogous to the situation they want to model, but rather ruminative processing. In rumination, people *do* voluntarily bring up events from the past in an attempt to explain why it is they feel so dreadful (see Kuyken & Howell, this issue), so the voluntary/involuntary memory issue is not a huge stumbling block to the RIF explanation of impoverished autobiographical memory in some instances.

It will be intriguing to see where future research goes in this important area. One possible way forward is to examine a group which, by varying in dysphoria

---

[2] The authors mention that retrieval-induced inhibition may be a better explanation for over-generality of memory than an affect regulation explanation: Why would an affect regulation system fail with the very memories that they are intended to deal with? However, the very reason why our patients have problems is because normal mechanisms have failed. Another example would be behavioural avoidance, aimed to reduce anxiety but increases it, or thought suppression, where normal attempts to suppress or avoid thinking about things, which might work very well in most people, fails to work in some. These are the people who come to us for help. Affect regulation does not refer to the phenomena we *see* but the causes or mechanism through which the phenomena we see have developed, especially when, as happens in our patients, things have gone wrong. This is not to argue that the affect regulation mechanism and resulting mnemonic interlock is the only possible explanation for over-general memory (see later), but that we see in the clinic many examples of a mechanism that has evolved to be effective for most people but which, when it breaks down, produces many clinical phenomena.

or in trauma history, demonstrates natural variations in their ability to retrieve memories specifically or categorically. If the overgeneral memory phenomena were due to retrieval-induced forgetting, one might expect that those who were the least specific would show the greatest susceptibility to the RIF effect. Second, the relation between RIF and rumination will likely be a huge and very productive area to examine. This paper is an invitation to investigate the mechanisms underlying overgeneral memory in new and deeper ways than many of us have attempted hitherto.

TREATMENT

Kremers, Spinhoven, van der Does, and van Dyck (this issue) examine the phenomenon of overgeneral memory change during psychotherapy in borderline personality disorder patients who have a diagnosis of depression. To date there have been very few studies of whether memory specificity (as measured with the AMT) is modified by psychotherapy (Serrano, Latorre, Gatz, & Rodriguez, 2004; Williams, Segal, Teasdale, & Soulsby, 2000). Their study, which used both psychoanalytic transference-focused psychotherapy and schema-focused cognitive-behavioural therapy, is therefore of great interest to the field. Although, as they point out, the absence of a no-treatment control limits what one might be able to say of these data, they did find a significant change in specificity levels with the patients becoming more specific over the course of 15 month's treatment. This specificity was seen not just in the increase in the number of memories recalled overall, but attributable to a decrease in the number of categoric memories that were recalled.

There was some evidence that specific recall of negative events at the outset of psychotherapy predicted a better outcome for patients in terms of their severity of borderline symptoms. This result, at trend level, deserves following up. It is entirely plausible that those who have better access to specific negative memories should derive more benefit from psychotherapy.

One of the interesting aspects of the paper was that the changes in autobiographical memory specificity over the course of the treatment was not attributable to, or correlated with, changes in levels of depression, dissociation, or of a tendency to suppress unwanted thoughts. This is consistent with the notion that autobiographical memory specificity is not an epiphenomenon of these other processes or clinical conditions. However, it does not seem consistent with an affect regulation model. There is accumulating data suggesting that people with borderline symptoms have particular problems in the use of cognitive mechanisms to regulate their affect. If overgenerality in memory is a normal affect regulation procedure, then not to be able to have any strategic control over specificity level of memories, either due to temperamental/constitutional factors or to prior learning, will render the person vulnerable to much

METHODOLOGICAL ISSUES

Rekart, Mineka, & Zinbarg (this issue) examine whether type of cue (*words* vs. *events*) makes a difference to the pattern of retrieval in dysphoric and nondysphoric students. Results showed that the dysphoric group made significantly fewer specific responses than nondysphoric for negative *event* cues. The main effect for group was not significant for negative *word* cues however. Interestingly, the effect of type of cue did not apply to the positive cues, where there was the expected main effect, replicating many other studies that find that response to positive word cues more easily distinguish depressed groups from nondepressed groups.

The authors were able to show that the lack of specificity they observed was accounted for mainly by an increase in categoric memories, rather than an increase in extended memories. This pattern is consistent with that shown by earlier studies (e.g., Williams and Dritschel, 1992). Williams & Dritschel (1992) found this pattern by reanalysing their data for a group of suicidal patients. The fact that the same pattern can be shown so clearly with dysphoric students is interesting.[3] I think it is fair to say that, at least in clinical groups, it remains true that we tend to see more categoric memories than extended memories. However the major variance in *non*clinical groups is whether people are specific or not. When they are not specific they may give a range of responses: omissions, extended memories, categoric memories, or semantic associates of the cue word. Of course, semantic associates, extended memories, and categoric memories are all examples of mnemonic material that comes from the "top" of the memory hierarchy. There is no theoretical reason a priori to imagine that any one of these would be preferred if somebody wanted to truncate the search for a memory because of functional avoidance. In this case, we might expect that in *nonclinical* participants one would see any or all of these, as well as omissions, as contributing to nonspecificity. However, it is likely that, given the close links between rumination and overgeneral memory, one might expect that in *clinical* groups, rumination would be more closely linked to categoric memories and semantic associates than to extended memories.

---

[3] Note that this study did not simply take a medium split on a measure of depression, but sampled the highest 20% and the lowest 20% for the depression subscales of the Mood and Anxiety Symptoms Questionnaire. It is quite likely that many of the students in the dysphoric group would have met criteria for major depression or a previous episode of major depression. A recent sample of students from our own collaborative research with Leiden University found 16% met a current diagnosis of major depression.

This completes my overview of the studies in this Special Issue. I turn back now to current theoretical issues, how these results may inform them, and to new directions.

TOWARDS AN INTEGRATIVE MODEL

Current views of autobiographical memory structure and processes have been influenced heavily by Conway's theories (see Conway & Pleydell Pearce, 2000; Conway, Singer, & Tagini, 2004). These assume that voluntary retrieval is hierarchical, in that it starts with elaborating the cue semantically, and moves through generating generic descriptions to more specific mnemonic material. Both verbal/analytic processing code and sensory/perceptual processing code is available during retrieval, but there is an assumption that, early on the retrieval, more semantic processing is involved, and more sensory/perceptual code is used later in the process. This sequence is almost certain if a verbal cue is used for voluntary retrieval.

Most models of retrieval also assume that setting up the retrieval specification at the earliest stage is effortful, and will use central executive capacity. This hypothesis might explain the data on suicidal and depressed individuals (Leibetseder et al., this issue) and on patients with schizophrenia who show a range of memory deficits (Wood et al., this issue). Could we completely explain overgeneral memory, wherever it was found, in terms of reduced executive capacity? This is unlikely: Williams, Barnhofer, Crane, Hermans, Raes, Watkins, and Dalgleish (2006) have suggested that there are three processes, each of which may contribute alone or in combination to reduce the specificity of memory. It is not only reduced executive capacity, but also the way retrieval processes can be hijacked by semantic overlap between current concerns and the cues that are being used to search memory, triggering rumination, and also the tendency of some individuals to avoid certain specific knowledge.

1. Capture and rumination

We have seen that there is accumulating and compelling evidence for the close link between rumination and over-general memory (see Barnard, et al., this issue, and Watkins & Teasdale, 2004). Kuyken and Howell's data show how depressed adolescents rehearse their important memories, and Barnard et al.'s data show the importance of repeated, perseverative return to the same theme as a critical factor in creating the conditions for overgeneral memory.

How are these ruminative processes activated? There may be a hint in the fact that studies in this area find that although nonspecific memory is sometimes seen in response to positive, sometimes to negative or neutral cues; most often it is shown for all cues (van Vreeswijk & de Wilde, 2004; but see Rekart et al., and Drummond et al., this issue). Williams et al. (2006) suggested that overgenerality may result from a particular *mapping* of a cue word onto the concerns of the individual. The divergent results of the effects of positive and negative cues may be due to the fact that there are idiosyncratic matches between a person's concerns and the cues. Depending on the sample and the testing context (hospital or laboratory), these matches will sometimes occur within the positive domain and sometimes in the negative domain. The cue word "happy" might elicit, in some people, the immediate feeling of "I cannot be happy, I've never been happy, I'm just an unhappy person". In other words, although they may strive to get a happy memory because of the constraints of the task, and may indeed eventually do so, what they are faced with (and what they then have to try to inhibit), is a large amount of ruminative thinking activated by a positive cue word but immediately launching them into negative analytical processing (Watkins & Teasdale, 2004). Together with Philip Spinhoven of Leiden University, we have now collected evidence that is consistent with this hypothesis. Where there is overlap between the cue words used in the AMT and a person's long-term attitudes and concerns, the memory is more likely to be overgeneral (Barnhofer et al., 2005; Spinhoven, Bockting, Kremers, Schene, & Williams, 2005).

2. Executive capacity and control

A number of researchers (e.g., Burgess & Shallice, 1996; Conway & Pleydell-Pearce, 2000) suggest that generative retrieval involves supervisory executive processes, so interfering with these processes might result in retrieval that stops short of its target. Consistent with this, studies of young children, and of elderly and brain damaged groups show that the ability to be specific in retrieval of events develops during the third and fourth years of life, and that this ability is impaired by reduced working memory capacity in ageing and in brain damage (Williams, 1996). Goddard, Dritschel, and Burton (1998) used a choice reaction time as a secondary task in normal participants and found that the secondary task increased categoric memories, but only when the task was more difficult.

The papers by Roberts et al. and Williams et al. (this issue) add further evidence and suggests that truncated search in emotionally disturbed groups may similarly be due to reduced executive capacity, consistent with the suggestion of Ellis and Ashbrook (1988), Hertel (2000), and Hertel and Hardin (1990) that depressed subjects show poor memory partly because of limited resources or reduced cognitive initiative.

The impact of reduced executive resources, particularly problems that arise in keeping track of the instructions to "be specific" in autobiographical memory tasks, has been further explored by a series of studied by Dalgleish et al. (2006). The studies mesh well with recent data (see earlier) that show how particular difficulties in the AMT arise due to "capture" by concern-related stimuli. The data by Wessel and Hauer (this issue) are relevant here: Repeated capture and rumination provide the conditions in which retrieval-induced forgetting (RIF) may be important.

3. Functional avoidance

Until recently, there was no independent evidence that suggested that avoidance (some sort of affective gating mechanism; Williams, 1996) might explain overgenerality in memory (Hermans, Defranc, Raes, Williams, & Eelen, 2005). At a minimum, any affect gating theory requires that, at some point, a person who tends to retrieve memory more specifically would risk experiencing greater affective disturbance. Otherwise, there is no motivation for the negative reinforcement of a less specific retrieval style. Raes, Hermans, de Decker, Eeelen, and Williams (2003; and this issue) showed just such evidence. They found that degree of mood disturbance following experimentally induced frustration was greater in those participants with a more specific retrieval style. This would be consistent with Drummond et al.'s findings in children: *Greater* emotion focusing children had *more* specific memories. Both papers suggest a developmental trajectory with an earlier association between greater affective disturbance and greater specificity promoting functional avoidance (truncated retrieval) in turn giving way to categoric memories later in those adolescents who experience serious trauma and/or depression—consistent with McNally et al.'s findings (this issue).

How does executive control interact with such avoidance. If executive control and/or resources are required for the operation of such avoidance, such processes may be independent of the supervisory attentional processes that are required for setting up a retrieval specification (Burgess & Shallice, 1996). This has important implications. Naturally occurring reduction in executive control or resources, or its experimental analogue (giving dual tasks to participants) may affect either or both supervisory processes, but with rather different effects.

Reducing executive capacity from the initial retrieval specification processes is (a) likely to slow down all memory retrieval; and (b) increase the output of categoric memories if top-down, generative retrieval is being used. Williams et al.'s data (this issue) show that a secondary task can make a participant more overgeneral in their recall, but only when given a low imageable cue. For emotionally disturbed groups, positive memories may be most vulnerable to the effects of reduced capacity at the retrieval specification stage, since depressed mood will reduce the availability of mnemonic cues needed for the memory specification (by an automatic mood congruency effect, see Drummond et al., this issue). Such slowing, and greater output of categoric memories (especially, although not confined to, response to positive cues) might be seen as the signature of reduced capacity at this stage of the retrieval process.

What, then, is the signature of reduced capacity affecting the resources that are needed for avoidance. If special purpose resources are reduced at this point, one should see faster output of specific (involuntary) memories. These will be more likely to be negative memories in those individuals who have events that they have been attempting to suppress or keep out of consciousness (Swales et al., 2001). These negative memories are likely to be more specific, since their output is the result of reduced "gating" of material that the top-down processes have been working to keep out of consciousness. If this gating mechanism is slower to develop in children, requiring greater development of schematic or conceptual processing skills, might this explain Drummond and colleague's data on the asymmetry of reaction to positive and negative cues over development? Disruption to the development of such gating mechanisms is also likely to be important in explaining why people with a diagnosis of borderline personality disorder do not show overgeneral memory despite high levels of past reported trauma and adversity (Kremers et al., this issue).

Thus, as shown in Figure 1, we have three categories of explanation for overgeneral memory: the first involves *capture and rumination*, the second involves *functional avoidance*, and the third involves *executive control and initiative*. Each of these has been found to affect overgeneral memory, but it is likely that each of these also affects other cognitive processing. So for example, as illustrated Figure 1, if we take the Means End Problem Solving we would expect that each of these would have an effect on overgeneral memory, through which they would have an effect on problem solving (Williams et al., this issue), but each of them may also have a direct effect on problem solving which is not mediated by overgeneral memory. Also, as represented in this diagram, there will be interactions between the three principal components of capture and rumination, functional avoidance, and executive control, and initiative. Separating them in this way, however, implies that one may occur without the other.

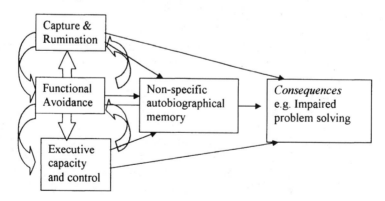

Figure 1. The CaRFAX Model. Three processes contributing to overgeneral memory can each have effects on cognition and behaviour either independently or through their individual or combined effect on autobiographical memory.

This is different from the original affect regulation hypothesis put forward by Williams (1996). In that model, the affect regulation was the initiator of a process which would eventually end up in mnemonic interlock. It was argued that repeated truncation of a search for memory (due to avoidance—the *etiological* aspect of the model) would mean that the person would end up with an overelaborated network of categoric descriptions (the *mechanism* aspect of the model). This overelaborated network would take quite a good deal of effort to inhibit when, in the future, attempting to retrieve a specific memory. Mnemonic interlock arose when one categoric description simply activated other categoric descriptions on the same level of the hierarchy rather than activating, as it was intended to, a specific memory.

We see now that expressing the theory like this has too easily been taken to imply that mnemonic interlock always *results from* affect regulation. However, this need not be the case and, in fact, it was argued in that paper that the difference between mnemonic interlock and Freudian repression was that mnemonic interlock (with its interaction with the amount of cognitive resources available in the central executive of working memory) could explain a larger range of data than repression. For example, it could explain why people who had suffered various forms of brain damage might show overgeneral memory and why older people with reduced working memory capacity would show overgeneral memory.

Over the years, a great deal of research has helped us understand both affect regulation and mnemonic interlock. We can now see that neither is necessary but both may be sufficient. That is, one can see the effects of experiential avoidance in the absence of working memory deficits; and one can see the effects of working memory deficits, or cognitive executive fatigue (e.g., in Roberts et al.'s paper) without it being affected by the affective valence of the cue. Further, overgenerality can be induced without disturbing mood (Barnard et al., this issue).

The fact that Raes et al., as well as Phillipot and colleagues, have been able to show that manipulating overgeneral memory affects emotional intensity following failure and that Williams et al. have been able to show that a similar experimental manipulation of specificity of memory affects problem-solving performance, shows that no matter how overgeneral memory comes about, it has downstream consequences: Overgenerality can cause other deficits in addition to any direct effects of other cognitive processes on these same outcomes.

How do these three principal mechanisms interact with each other? In our current work, we are examining the extent to which overlap between the cues used in autobiographical memory tests and self-guides (as defined by Carver, Lawrence, & Scheier, 1999) interrelate. In one study, our group has found that the greater the overlap between memory cues and self-guides the more overgeneral people were in their responses (Crane, Barnhofer, & Williams, 2005). In another study, we found that overlap between autobiographical memory cues and dysfunctional attitudes produced more overgeneral memories but only, interestingly, when executive control was compromised by giving participants another task to do while they tried to do the memory task (random button pressing, Barnhofer et al., 2005). We are therefore beginning to demonstrate connections between the *capture and ruminate* aspects of overgeneral memory and the *executive control* aspects. The relationship between these two and *functional avoidance* remains a question which Raes, Hermans, and colleagues in Leuven are addressing in their current studies.

CONCLUDING REMARKS

The papers in this collection show enormous promise that the phenomenon of overgeneral memory is being understood more and more clearly, both what causes it and the mechanisms that underlie it. As we said at the outset, memory is like a crossroads. Our ability to learn from experience and to remember what has happened in the immediate and remote past stands at the centre of all information processing, and at the centre of how we understand ourselves and navigate successfully through our world. We have seen that memory can be adversely affected (a) when our retrieval is hijacked by other material that is self-relevant, triggering analytic, conceptually based processing (capture and rumination: CaR); (b) when our retrieval is aborted due to learned passive avoidance strategies (functional avoidance: FA); (c) when retrieval is affected either at the early specification stage or at the affective gating stage by reduced effort, initiative or resources (executive control or capacity: X). We started by comparing memory with the crossroads at the centre of Oxford. You may already know the name of this crossroads, or may have guessed: It is called Carfax.

REFERENCES

Barnard, P. (2003). Asynchrony, implicational meaning and the experience of self in schizophrenia. In T. Kircher & A. David, (Eds.), *The self in neuroscience and psychiatry* (pp. 121–146), Cambridge, UK: Cambridge University Press.

Barnard, P. (2004). Bridging between basic theory and clinical practice. *Behaviour Research and Therapy*, 42, 977–1000.

Barnhofer, T., Crane, C., Spinhoven, P., & Williams, J.M.G. (2005). *Specificity of memories related to dysfunctional attitudes in previously depressed and never depressed individuals.* Manuscript submitted for publication.

Barnhofer, T., Jong-Meyer, R., Kleinpass, A., & Nikesch, S. (2002). Specificity of autobiographical memories in depression: An analysis of retrieval processes in a think-aloud task. *British Journal of Clinical Psychology*, 41, 411–416.

Burgess, P. W., & Shallice, T. (1996). Confabulation and the control of recollection. *Memory*, 4, 359–411.

Carver, C. S., Lawrence, J. W., & Scheier, M. F. (1999). Self-discrepancies and affect: Incorporating the role of feared selves. *Personality and Social Psychology Bulletin*, 25, 783–792.

Conway, M. A., & Pleydell-Pearce, C. W. (2000). The construction of autobiographical memories in the self-memory system. *Psychological Review, 107*, 261–288.

Conway, M. A., Pleydell-Pearce, C. W., Whitecross, S. E., & Sharpe, H. (2003). Neurophysiological correlates of memory for experienced and imagined events. *Neuropsychologia, 41*, 334–340.

Conway, M. A., Singer, J. A., & Tagini, A. (2004). The self and autobiographical memory: Correspondence and coherence. *Social Cognition, 22*, 491–529.

Crane, C., Barnhofer, T., & Williams, J. M. G. (2005). *Cue self-relevance affects autobiographical memory specificity in individuals with a history of major depression.* Manuscript submitted for publication.

Dalgleish, T., Perkins, N., Williams., J. M. G., Golden, A. M. J., Barrett, L. F., Barnard, P. J., et al. (2006). *Reduced specificity of autobiographical memory and depression: The role of executive processes.* Manuscript submitted for publication.

Ellis, H. C., & Ashbrook, P. W. (1988). Resource allocation model of the effects of depressed mood states on memory. In K. Fiedler & J. Forgas (Eds.), *Affect, cognition and social behavior* (pp. 25–43). Toronto: Hogrefe.

Goddard, L., Dritschel, B., & Burton, A. (1998). Gender differences in the dual-task effects on autobiographical memory retrieval during social problem solving. *British Journal of Clinical Psychology, 89*, 611–627.

Hermans, D., Defranc, A., Raes, F., Williams, J. M. G., & Eelen, P. (2005) Reduced autobiographical memory specificity as an avoidant coping style. *British Journal of Clinical Psychology, 44*, 583–589.

Hermans, D., van den Broeck, K., Belis, G., Raes, F., Pieters, G., & Eelen, P. (2004). Trauma and autobiographical memory specificity in depressed inpatients. *Behaviour Research and Therapy, 42*, 775–789.

Hertel, P. T. (2000). The cognitive-initiative account of depression-related impairments in memory. *Psychology of Learning and Motivation: Advances in Research and Theory, 39*, 47–71.

Hertel, P. T., & Hardin, T. S. (1990). Remembering with and without awareness in a depressed mood: Evidence of deficits in initiative. *Journal of Experimental Psychology: General, 119*, 45–59.

Norman, D. A., & Bobrow, D. G. (1979). Descriptions: An intermediate stage in memory retrieval. *Cognitive Psychology, 11*, 107–123.

Raes, F., Hermans, D., de Decker, A., Eelen, P., & Williams, J. M. G. (2003). Autobiographical memory specificity and affect regulation: An experimental approach. *Emotion, 3*, 201–206.

Serrano, J. P., Latorre, J. M., Gatz, M., & Rodriguez, J. M. (2004). Life Review Therapy using autobiographical retrieval practice for older adults with depressive symptomatology. *Psychology and Aging, 19*, 272–277.

Spinhoven, P., Bockting, C. L. H., Kremers, I. P., Schene, A. H., & Williams, J. M. G. (2005). *The endorsement of dysfunctional attitudes is associated with retrieval of overgeneral memories in response to matching cues* Manuscript submitted for publication.

Swales, M., Williams, J. M. G., & Wood, P. (2001). Specificity of autobiographical memory and mood disturbance in adolescents. *Cognition and Emotion, 15*, 321–331.

Teasdale, J. D., & Barnard, P. J. (1993). *Affect, cognition and change: Re-modelling depressive thought.* Hove, UK: Lawrence Erlbaum Associates Ltd.

van Vreeswijk, M. F., & de Wilde, E. J. (2004). Autobiographical memory specificity, psychopathology, depressed mood and the use of the AMT: A meta-analysis. *Behaviour Research and Therapy, 46*, 731–743.

Watkins, E., & Teasdale, J. D. (2004). Adaptive and maladaptive self-focus in depression. *Journal of Affective Disorders, 82*, 1–8.

Watkins, E., Teasdale, J. D., & Williams, R. M. (2000). Decentring and distraction reduce overgeneral autobiographical memory in depression. *Psychological Medicine, 30*, 911–920.

Williams, J. M. G. (1996). Depression and the specificity of autobiographical memory. In D. C. Rubin (Ed.), *Remembering our past: Studies in autobiographical memory* (pp. 244–267). Cambridge, UK: Cambridge University Press.

Williams, J. M. G., Barnhofer, T., Crane, C., Hermans, D., Raes, F., Watkins, E., & Dalgleish, T. (2006). *Autobiographical memory specificity and emotional disorder*. Manuscript submitted for publication.

Williams, J. M. G., & Broadbent, K. (1986). Autobiographical memory in suicide attempters. *Journal of Abnormal Psychology, 95*, 144–149.

Williams, J. M. G., & Dritschel, B. (1992). Categoric and extended autobiographical memories. In M. A. Conway, D. C. Rubin, H. Spinnler, & W. A. Wagenaar (Eds.), *Theoretical perspectives on autobiographical memory* (pp. 391–410). Dordrecht: Kluwer.

Williams, J. M. G., & Scott, J. (1988). Autobiographical memory in depression. *Psychological Medicine, 18*, 689–695.

Williams, J. M. G., Segal, Z. V., Teasdale, J. D., & Soulsby, J. (2000). Mindfulness-based cognitive therapy reduces over-general autobiographical memory in formerly depressed patients. *Journal of Abnormal Psychology, 109*, 150–155.

SUBJECT INDEX

Absorption Scale, 528
Abstract processing, 553
Acute stress disorder, 383, 384, 517
Adolescents, 466–487
  depression, 467, 468, 476–480,
    481–484, 489, 506–507, 553
  mood disorders, 466
  personal identity, 544
  sense of self, 466, 468, 484
Adult Memory and Information Processing
  Battery (AMIPB), 540
Affect gating, 563, 564
Affect regulation hypothesis, 403, 405,
  413, 415, 416–417, 422, 423, 445,
  490, 556, 565
Ageing, 562, 565
Analytical processing, 330, 340, 344, 345,
  386, 398
Analytical rumination, 331, 332, 347
Anxiety, 347, 384, 405, 406
Attention, 385
Autobiographical memory
  accuracy, 469
  children, 489, 500, 503
  educational level, 523
  functions, 321, 536
  intelligence, 520
  models, 550
  specific, 322
  see also Overgeneral autobiographical
    memory
Autobiographical Memory Interview
  (AMI), 537, 539, 541–452, 552
Autobiographical Memory Test (AMT),
  335, 359, 384, 387–388, 403, 406,
  407, 451, 453, 461, 509, 519, 527,
  539–540, 542–543, 552
  adolescents, 471–472
  children, 493–494, 503
  computerised, 507–508, 510, 513–514

dual-task paradigm, 363–366

Beck Depression Inventory (BDI), 336,
  386, 453, 470, 471, 519, 528, 540
Beck Hopelessness Scale, 519
Bipolar disorder, 449
Borderline personality disorder, 383, 517,
  559–560
  depression, 449, 459, 461–462
  mood instability, 459
  psychotherapy, 451, 458
  somatic distress, 397
  stability of autobiographical memory,
    451, 458–459
Borderline Personality Disorder Severity
  Index (BPDSI), 453–454
Bottom-up retrieval, 363, 550
Brain damage, 562, 565

Capture, 561–563, 564, 566
Card Sorting task, 494–495
CaRFAX, 564
Categoric memory, 346, 368, 416–417,
  421, 423, 424, 425, 507, 512, 513,
  549, 550
Category fluency, 341
Central executive, *see* Executive capacity
Child Depression Inventory, 493, 495–496
Children, 488–505, 554
  abuse, 322, 523
  autobiographical memory, 489, 500, 503
  dysphoria, 490, 496–498, 500, 501–502,
    554
  physical abuse, 347
  sexual abuse, 347, 424, 527–535, 552
  trauma, 397, 403, 449, 489, 491
Children's Attributional Style
  Questionnaire, 490
Children's Impact of Event Scale (CIES),
  471

Cognition and emotion, 325, 341
Cognitive behaviour therapy, 451, 458, 559
Cognitive interventions, 450
Cognitive resources, 406, 415
Cognitive style, 352, 450, 488, 490, 491
Concentration, 385
Conditional self-esteem, 405
Confabulation, 537
Conscientiousness, 405
Contingent self-esteem, 405
Contingent Self-Esteem Scale (CSES), 408–409
Coping style, 406, 412–413, 414–415, 425, 556
Cue words
  contexts and events, 507, 508, 509, 512, 560
  mapping, 561–562
  self-guides, 565–566
  valence, 460, 490, 496–498, 500

Decentring, 450
Delusions, 537–538
Depression
  adolescents, 467, 468, 476–480, 481–484, 489, 506–507, 553
  cognitive performance, 384–385
  dysphoria and, 503
  effortful processing, 384
  life events, 482
  neuroticism, 384
  overgenerality, 322, 329, 347, 383, 384, 385, 449, 488, 506, 507, 537, 551
  prediction, 450, 490
  prognosis, 329, 384
  resource limitation, 352
  self-focus, 345–346, 385–386, 398
  somatic symptoms, 384
  source monitoring, 469
  subclinical, 512–513
  trauma, 347, 483
  vulnerability marker, 326, 424, 503
Depressive interlock, 331, 332
Depressive paradox, 481–482
Descriptions framework, 353
Diagnostic Statistical Manual for Mental Disorders (DSM-IV), 470

Digit span, 540
Direct retrieval, 363–367, 550
Discovery research, 324
Dispositional attributions, 482
Dissociation, 451–452, 460
Dissociative Experiences Scale (DES), 454, 528
Distraction, 450
Dual task paradigm, 363–366
Dysfacilitation of retrieval, 551
Dysphoria, 490, 496–498, 500, 501–502, 503, 507, 512–513, 554

Educational level, 523
Effortful processing, 384
Elaboration, 330
Elderly, 562, 565
Electroencephalogram, 550
Emotion focusing, 490–492, 494–495, 498–500, 502–503, 554
Emotionality, 469
Emotions, cognition and, 325, 341
Encoding, 492, 537, 543–544, 552
Evans RNG, 355
Executive capacity, 378–379, 406, 523, 561, 562, 563, 564, 565, 566
  measurement, 354, 358
Experiential processing, 553
Experiential self-focus, 330, 386
Extended memories, 507, 512, 513
Eysenck Personality Questionnaire, 387

Facial emotion, 490
Factor analysis, 388
Field memories, 468, 478–479, 553
Flashbulb memories, 469, 483
Fluid intelligence, 520
Frontal system, 550
Functional avoidance, 563–566

Generalised anxiety disorder, 347
Generative retrieval, 363–367, 550
Generic mechanisms, 347–348
Goal neglect, 378–379, 385
Group Administrable Adaptation of the Operation Span Test (GOSPAN), 409

Hamilton Rating Scale for Depression, 460, 520
Hierarchical model, 353, 358, 362, 364, 367, 376–377, 449, 557, 561
Hopelessness Scale, 519

Identity, 544
Image Description Task, 495
Imageability, 358, 360–361, 362, 364
Imagery, 468–469
Impact of Event Scale (IES), 404, 432
  children's version, 471
Impact of Puzzle task Scale (IPS), 404, 408, 419
Implicational meanings, 331
Index of Self-regulation of Emotion (ISE), 413
Information-processing, 325
Initiative, 564
Inner-outer confusion, 544
Intelligence, 520
Interacting Cognitive Subsystems (ICS), 331, 555
Internalising disorders, 384
Intimacy, 544
Intrusive memory, 430–431, 432, 445

Kindling theory, 501

Language acquisition, 489
Level of Emotional Awareness Scale (LEAS), 330, 334, 336–337, 346, 347
Life events, 482
Life stressors, 384

Manifest Anxiety Scale (MAS), 528
Marlowe-Crowne Social Desirability Scale (MC), 409, 528
Means Ends Problem Solving (MEPS), 352, 370, 371, 372–375, 377
Mindful experiencing, 482
Mindfulness-based cognitive therapy, 450, 451
Mnemonic interlock, 421, 423, 523, 551, 565
Mood
  adolescents, 466

congruency, 490, 501, 554
cue valence, 460
overgenerality, 451
regulation, 397
visual analogue scale, 336
Mood and Anxiety Symptom Questionnaire (MASQ), 508–509
Motivation, 385, 405

National Adult Reading Test (NART), 334, 538, 540
NEO-Five Factor Inventory (NEO-FFI), 409
Neuroticism, 384, 386, 392, 406

Objectified self, 482
Observer memories, 468, 478–480, 481–482, 553
Obsessive-compulsive disorder, 383, 397, 449, 459
Output interference, 437, 442–443, 444–445
Overgeneral autobiographical memory, 322, 324, 328–329, 403, 430
  adaptive role, 459
  capacity limitations, 352
  categoric memories, 416–417, 421, 423, 424, 425, 507, 512, 513
  clinical intervention input, 326
  consequences, 352
  content, 326
  discovery, 325, 351–352
  encoding, 492, 543–544
  extended memories, 507, 512, 513
  fewer specific memories, 416, 425
  functional strategy, 423
  intrusive memories, 431, 432
  mood regulation, 397
  process, 326
  prognostic indicator, 329, 384
  scope-enlargement, 325–326
  storage, 492
  top-down retrieval, 363
  trait-like feature, 326, 352, 379, 416, 449–450
  trajectories, 386, 388–394, 395, 396, 397–399, 538, 543, 556–557

two types, 416–417, 425–426, 507, 556
vulnerability marker, 326, 424, 426, 503

Personal salience, 467, 469, 477, 480, 483
Personality, 405
Physical abuse, 347, 379
Planning, 377
Positive and Negative Affect Schedule Scales (PANAS), 408, 419
Posttraumatic stress disorder
 depression, 483
 intrusive memory, 445
 overgenerality, 329, 383, 517, 532, 533–534
 somatic distress, 397
Practice effect, 461
Prediction, 384, 450–451, 452, 458, 460–461, 462, 490
Problem solving,
 overgenerality, 329, 352, 367–368, 371, 374–375, 377, 397, 557, 564
 psychosis, 545
 rumination, 368
Processing mode, 330, 340–341, 344
Prognosis, 329, 384
Programmatic research, 325
Propositional representations, 331
Psychoanalytic transference focused psychotherapy, 451, 458, 559
Psychosis, 544–545
Psychotherapy, 450, 451, 458, 559

Random generation task, 354–358, 361–362, 376, 377, 557
Rate-of-change methodology, 333
Raven's Advanced Progressive Matrices, 434
Rebound effect, 423
Recency effect, 467, 468, 476–477, 480, 482–483
Recovered memories, 527, 528, 532, 533
Rehearsal, 467, 468, 477, 483
Reminiscence bump, 519
Repeated memory phenomenon, 489
Repressed memories, 527, 528, 532, 533, 534

Repressive coping, 406, 412–413, 414–415, 425, 556
Resilience, 466–467
Resource limitation, 352, 415
Response inhibition, 543
Response Style Questionnaire, 334, 336
Retrieval
 competition, 431
 direct/generative, 363–367, 550
 dysfacilitation, 551
 schizophrenia, 537–538, 543–544, 552
 staged, 353, 358, 367, 376
Retrieval-induced forgetting (RIF), 431–432, 437–438, 443–445, 558–559
Retrieval practice paradigm, 431, 432, 433, 434–435, 439, 445
Rosenberg Self-Esteem Scale, 387
Rumination
 analytical, 331, 332, 347
 capture and, 561–562, 564, 566
 categoric retrieval, 368
 defined, 329
 field/observer perspective, 553
 induction, 332–333
 overgenerality, 329–330, 340, 344–345, 368, 421–422, 423, 555
 problem solving, 368
 processing modes, 330
 thought suppression, 424

Schema activation, 490, 501, 554
Schema focused cognitive behaviour therapy, 451, 458, 559
Schematic models, 331, 340–341, 344
Schizophrenia, 536–547, 551–552
 autobiographical memory, 536, 537–538
 cognitive impairments, 543
 delusions, 537–538
 encoding, 537, 543–544, 552
 general memory problems, 541, 543
 onset, 537, 543, 544
 overgenerality, 537, 538, 543
 response inhibition, 543
 retrieval, 537–538, 543–544, 552
Seasonal affective disorder, 329
Secondary goal neglect, 385

SUBJECT INDEX

Self, objectified, 482
Self-concept, 489, 544
  adolescence, 466, 468, 484
Self-defining memories, 469, 477, 480, 483
Self-defining Memory Task, 472–473
Self-esteem
  contingent (conditional), 405
  internalising disorders, 384
  overgenerality, 386, 391, 392, 393, 395, 396–397, 557
  scale, 387
Self-focus, 330, 345–346, 385–386, 398, 468, 482, 555
Self-guides, 565–566
Self-related category generation task, 334–335
Self-representations, 330–331
Sensitisation theory, 501
Sentence Completion Task, 418
Sexual abuse, 347, 379, 424, 527–535, 552
Shipley measures of cognitive ability, 529
"Sibling rivalry", 558
Somatic distress, 384, 391, 392, 395, 396–397
Source memory, 469
Source monitoring, 469, 481, 484
Staged retrieval, 353, 358, 367, 376
State-Trait Anxiety Inventory, Trait version (STAI-T), 408
Storage, 492
Story recall, 540
Strategic inhibition hypothesis, 404–405, 415–416, 421
Structured Clinical Interview (SCID), 452, 473
Suicidal patients, 322, 324, 383, 449, 517–518, 521, 522–523, 551
Sustained attention, 385

Tangram puzzles, 404, 407–408, 418
Theory of mind, 544
Thought suppression, 423–424, 452, 460
Top-down retrieval, 363, 550
Trade-off, 363, 377
Trait anxiety, 405, 406
Trait hypothesis, 326, 352, 379, 416, 449–450
Transdiagnostic approach, 348
Transference focused psychotherapy, 451, 458, 559
Trauma, 347, 352, 379, 397, 403, 424, 449, 467, 469, 480–481, 483, 489, 491, 552, 557–558
Trauma History Questionnaire (THQ), 470, 471
Truncated search, 363, 367, 368, 375–376, 550–551, 562, 565

Valence, 467
  cue words, 460, 490, 496–498, 500
Verbal Fluency Task (VFT), 473
Visual Analogue Impact Scales (VAIS), 408, 419
Vividness, 467, 469, 477, 480, 481, 483
Vulnerability marker, 326, 424, 426, 503

Wechsler Adult Intelligence Scale (WAIS), 540
White Bear Suppression Inventory, 454
Working memory, 405, 406
  brain damage, 562, 565
  elderly, 562, 565
  frontal systems, 550
  intrusive memories, 431
  overgenerality, 352, 378
Working self, 341, 353, 482, 483, 523, 544

Zahlen-Verbindungs-Test, 520